Adorno's Aesthetic Theory

Adorno's Aesthetic Theory

The Redemption of Illusion

Lambert Zuidervaart

The MIT Press, Cambridge, Massachusetts, and London, England

Third printing, 1994

This book was set in Baskerville by DEKR Corporation and printed and bound in the United States of America.

Library of Congress Cataloging-in-Publication Data

Zuidervaart, Lambert.
  Adorno's Aesthetic theory : the redemption of illusion / Lambert Zuidervaart.
  p.   cm. — (Studies in contemporary German social thought)
  Includes bibliographical references.
  ISBN 0-262-24032-7 (HB), 0-262-74016-8 (PB)
  1. Adorno, Theodor W., 1903–1969. Ästhetische Theorie.
2. Aesthetics, Modern—20th century. I. Title. II. Series.
B3199.A33A438   1991
111'.85'092—dc20
                                                                90-23862
                                                                    CIP

For my mother and in memory of my father

Contents

Contents

Acknowledgments

Work on this book has spanned many years and four different countries. It is, in a sense, the work of a migrant, and it has given me a deeper appreciation of people who, like Adorno, have immigrated to the United States. My parents, Tena Beuving and Martin Zuidervaart, left the Netherlands in their youth to make their homes in California. They came from what the Dutch call *de kleine Luyden*, the little people, hardworking but not obsessed, lacking many possessions yet generous toward others. My father died shortly before I completed the first draft of this book. I had hoped to thank him here for his gentle nurture and his unassuming pursuit of justice and peace. I dedicate this book to his memory, and to my mother, whom I admire for her courage, her persistence, and her loyalty to the people and institutions she loves. I shall ever be thankful for having these two remarkable people as my parents.

There have been times when I thought seriously about abandoning this project. At such dark times, and all the times between, I could count on the encouragement of my wife, Joyce Alene Recker. I am deeply grateful to her. She is a lovely companion, a faithful source of joy and strength.

I have received help from many colleagues at various stages of my writing, more than I can mention by name. I have enjoyed stimulating discussions and correspondence with Susan Buck-Morss, Martin Jay, Douglas Kellner, Christian Lenhardt, Margaret Rose, and the late Carl Dahlhaus, all of whom have made distinguished contributions to scholarship on Adorno and his tradition. Hendrik Hart, Johan van der Hoeven, and Nicholas Wolterstorff have inspired me by their encouragement and their own writings. I am honored to count them among my mentors in philosophy. My greatest debt is to Calvin Seerveld, who first introduced me to the German tradition in aesthetics, and who has been my closest discussion partner on the issues treated in this book. To all these colleagues, and to others not named, I say thank you. I hope they enjoy the results of their help and do not take offense at any failures to follow their advice or example.

Calvin College has provided invaluable support through its library and computer center and through research fellowships awarded by the College and by the Calvin Alumni Association. My colleagues in the Philosophy Department have applied their impressive analytical tools to parts of the manuscript and weeded out many a wild formulation. If the book is not a proper garden, the responsibility lies with the author or the subject matter and not with them. I thank Donna Kruithof, Philosophy Department secretary, for typing a rough draft of the manuscript and for doing the many little things that make an author's lot less tedious. I also thank my former research assistants, Lisa De Boer and Christopher Eberle, students in art history and philosophy, respectively. I have happy memories of our work together.

An earlier version of chapter 10 appeared as "Realism, Modernism, and the Empty Chair," in *Postmodernism/Jameson/Critique*, edited by D. Kellner (Maisonneuve Press, 1989). Other parts of this book have appeared in earlier versions under the following titles: "Methodological Shadowboxing in Marxist Aesthetics: Lukács and Adorno," *The Journal of Comparative Literature and Aesthetics* 10 (1988–89); "The Social Significance of Autonomous Art: Adorno and Bürger," *The Journal of Aesthetics and Art Criticism* 48 (Winter 1990); and "Contra-Diction: Adorno's Philosophy of Discourse," in *Philosophy of Discourse*, edited by G. Jensen and C. Sills (Heinemann Educational Books). I am grateful to the editors and publishers for permission to incorporate materials, sometimes verbatim, from these earlier publications.

A Note on References

References to Adorno's translated writings give first the page of the German edition and then the page of the English translation, thus: DA 31/15. The bibliography lists the translations and abbreviations used in such citations. Where published translations of Adorno are unsatisfactory, they are replaced or revised without indication. I cite from his *Gesammelte Schriften* whenever possible. Otherwise the editions used are those indicated in section 1 of the bibliography.

The main text is Theodor W. Adorno, *Ästhetische Theorie*, ed. Gretel Adorno and Rolf Tiedemann, *Gesammelte Schriften* vol. 7 (Frankfurt am Main: Suhrkamp, 1970; 2d ed., 1972). Pages 47–68 differ in the first and second editions; a passage first printed on p. 47 appears on pp. 67–68 in the second edition. All references are to the second edition. The translation used is T. W. Adorno, *Aesthetic Theory*, trans. C. Lenhardt (London: Routledge & Kegan Paul, 1984). My modifications of this translation appear in brackets within the passages cited. In-text citations of *Aesthetic Theory* give the pagination in the second German edition, followed by the pagination in Lenhardt's translation, thus: (317/304). Citations in the notes use the abbreviation AT.

The dates listed are dates of publication, unless the sign (–) is given to mark the date of writing. When the same article has appeared in significantly different versions, a date is given for each year in which a version was published, thus: "Fragment über Musik und Sprache," 1953/1956.

Introduction

Theodor W. Adorno's *Aesthetic Theory* is a labyrinth filled with stylistic, conceptual, and methodological puzzles. Entire books could be written deciphering Adorno's language, reconstructing his dialectical arguments, or examining his phenomenological methods, only to have readers find no path to the meaning of this complex work. Even the most obvious sources of illumination seem insufficient. Adorno's other writings provide clues to obscure passages in *Aesthetic Theory*, but his most important books present their own mazes. A look at Adorno's philosophical precursors is also enlightening, yet his ties to these are tangled, and the most important ones resist paraphrase. Additional guidance comes from recent debates on Adorno's legacy. Heavy reliance on these, however, would divert attention from his aesthetics to the contemporary discussions for which it holds promise. Although it would be foolish to ignore any of these guides, they all too easily lead outside one labyrinth into another.

None of this renders it impossible to identify crucial areas in which *Aesthetic Theory* makes significant contributions to philosophical aesthetics. In an attempt to do this, I have constructed a configuration of topics in the context of Adorno's other writings. The configuration is guided by his idea of artistic truth. Adorno's critical attitude toward abstract methodologies encourages flexibility in interpretative strategies. Accordingly, I make selective references to historical sources and contemporary debates, while ignoring numerous passages in *Aesthetic Theory*.

As many commentators have noted, the idea of artistic truth is a central theme in Adorno's aesthetics.[1] This idea pervades Adorno's writings, from his earliest literary review on "Expressionism and Artistic Truthfulness" (1920) to the philosophical essays published in the last year of his life (1969). It also weds the disparate philosophical sources of his aesthetics: Kant's notion of beauty as a symbol of morality and Hegel's view of art as a semblance of truth; Marx's critique of ideology and Nietzsche's suspicion of the ideology of critique; Lukács's emphasis on social totality and Benjamin's stress on artistic fragments. The same idea of artistic truth places *Aesthetic Theory* in opposition to Heideggerian mystifications of art and Wittgensteinian attacks on traditional aesthetics, and it marks a point of departure for Adorno's most loyal critics. At several levels, then, the idea functions as a "problematic," an interlocking set of issues whose controversial theme provokes ongoing debate among participants who are aware of the history of their debate.[2]

In pursuing this theme, I do not intend to give a detailed textual commentary or an expansive intellectual history, important and legitimate though such approaches would be. Detailed commentaries can clarify the contours of a difficult philosophical text, but they presuppose a familiarity that cannot be assumed of *Aesthetic Theory* in the English-speaking world. Broad intellectual histories can help readers construct the narrative within which various writings operate, as the best studies on Adorno in English demonstrate. Because some excellent historical studies are available, as is an English translation of *Aesthetic Theory*,[3] I have decided upon a different approach, one that I call a philosophical critique.

My primary aims are to uncover significant issues and evaluate Adorno's contributions. I do not ignore the need to clarify Adorno's text or refuse to construct a historical narrative, but clarification and narration are not the overriding goals. Instead, my commentary identifies interrelated issues, and the elements of historical narration define a problematic animating the text itself. The idea of artistic truth provides an intersection for several significant issues in *Aesthetic Theory*. I plan to identify these issues in order to evaluate Adorno's contributions to philosophical aesthetics.

Philosophers differ on the nature and sources of criteria for evaluating a philosophical position. The history of philosophy provides three different models: transcendent, immanent, and transcendental critique.[4] Transcendent critiques locate their criteria in the critic's own position; immanent critiques locate them in the position being criticized; transcendental critiques locate them in preconditions making possible both the criticism and the position criticized. A review of some historical examples will indicate the type of critique this book attempts.

Modern philosophers who follow the first model tend to employ a foundational epistemology, although nonfoundationalist approaches are also possible. Foundationalists seek to secure for our knowledge foundations that are indubitable and evident or self-evident. René Descartes's "Cogito ergo sum" is just such a foundation for what some would call a rationalist epistemology. Sensory impressions fulfill a similar role for so-called empiricists such as John Locke. With a foundation in place, foundationalist philosophers test knowledge claims to see which are well-founded and which are specious. A foundationalist assumes that proper argumentation will establish the necessary link between claims and foundation or show the absence of such a link. Because there is no thought of going behind or beyond the foundation, the foundationalist's criticisms of another philosopher often take the form of a transcendent critique. Such a critique tries to demonstrate that the opponent's claims fail to comport with the evident or self-evident truths of which the foundationalist is certain.

Just as the name of René Descartes can stand for the model of transcendent critique, so Immanuel Kant's name can indicate the model of transcendental critique. Kant argues that both rationalism and empiricism beg the most important question. How is it possible for us to acquire any knowledge, no matter what status it has on the scale of indubitable truth and well-founded claims? Kant finds his answer in the fundamental capacities and ordering principles by which we make sense of the world. Kant's own term for his enterprise is transcendental critique. When directed toward another philosopher's position, a transcendental critique does not simply ask whether that position comports well with various indubitable or well-founded truths. Rather, a transcendental critique asks what preconditions make it possible to adopt the position being criticized. If consistent, a transcendental critic will also examine the preconditions that make it possible to engage in this critique. Most transcendental critics assume that ultimate preconditions are the same on both sides of the debate.

Reason itself is the ultimate precondition and final court of appeal in Kant's *Critique of Pure Reason*. This disturbed some of Kant's contemporaries; two of them, Herder and Hamann, wrote "metacritiques" of Kant's critique.[5] But it was left to Hegel to undertake a thorough reexamination of Kant's transcendental critique and of all foundational epistemologies. According to Hegel, the problem with Kant's critique, and with all foundational epistemologies, is the failure to be sufficiently critical. That is to say, Kant fails to scrutinize the conception of knowledge with which he begins.

This objection does not lead Hegel to say that every philosopher has ungrounded epistemological presuppositions and to adopt a general skepticism. Hegel's *Phenomenology of Spirit* follows the path of immanent critique, conducting a movement through various epistemological positions. Each position puts forward not only claims about what is known or can be known but also views about what counts as knowledge. Hegel's immanent critique tests each position to see whether its claims about the known are consistent with its own criterion of knowledge. When fundamental inconsistencies emerge, the position has proved itself inadequate according to its own criterion. There is no need for the phenomenologist to measure these positions according to some transcendent or transcendental standard. The inadequacy of each position can be corrected by a more adequate position whose own internal inconsistencies will subsequently surface. Only by going through this laborious process does Hegel think we can come to know the truth.

Hegel's *Phenomenology of Spirit* provides the model for many subsequent challenges to Cartesian and Kantian projects, challenges coming from Kierkegaard and Nietzsche in the nineteenth century and from Dewey and Heidegger in the twentieth.[6] Immanent critique is central to Marx's critique of ideology, despite his disagreements with Hegel. The same approach continues in the critical theory of Adorno and his colleagues, where it provides "a means of detecting the societal contradictions which offer the most determinate possibilities of emancipatory social change."[7]

Immanent critique is also the model for the ensuing discussion. This book does not set out to measure Adorno's claims according to truths of which the author is convinced. Undoubtedly there are indubitable truths, both for Adorno and for his critics. But simply relying on these would be inappropriate for the task at hand. A transcendent critique would obstruct the elements of exegesis that Adorno's text requires, leaving the idea of artistic truth insufficiently explored.

A transcendental critique seems more appropriate: it would be instructive to examine the preconditions making possible Adorno's position on the truth of modern art. One way to conduct such an examination would involve a nonhistoricist search for permanent structures of the sort Kant locates in the fundamental capacities of knowledge. A second, more historicist way would be to look for pervasive historical tendencies of the sort Adorno identifies in twentieth-century culture and society. Each of these approaches would have significant disadvantages, however. A nonhistoricist approach would block the elements of narrative that are needed to uncover the historical subtext of Adorno's aesthetics. A historicist approach would fail to indicate why the historical narrative is philosophically important. Indeed, given Adorno's criticisms of recourses to permanent structures, a nonhistoricist transcendental critique of *Aesthetic Theory* would soon turn into a transcendent critique, as would a historicist critique, given Adorno's insistence on the distinction between the genesis and the validity of philosophical insights.

The project at hand, then, is an immanent critique involving issues whose intersection is the idea of artistic truth in *Aesthetic Theory*. The book reconstructs these issues in the text and its historical subtext, indicates their contemporary significance, and assesses Adorno's contributions to their formulation and resolution. The critique is immanent in the sense that the issues discussed are those of the text, the expectations voiced are Adorno's expectations, and criteria for inadequacies and contributions come from his own position.

Just as Adorno's own immanent criticisms try to move beyond their object, however, so the proposed immanent critique of *Aesthetic Theory* has a metacritical intent. Where the text shows itself inadequate according to its own criteria, these criteria become problematic, as do the ways in which the text's problems have been posed. At such points it becomes clear that immanent critique is not locked into its object, though it openly depends on the position being criticized. As a method employed with metacritical intent, immanent criticism moves beyond deadlock. Immanent critique becomes metacritique—a combination, often precarious, of dependence upon, and transcendence of, the object of criticism. Because of such dependence, the process of transcending the object takes on the character of self-criticism. Indeed, that is how the present study should be read, for it arises from solidarity with the concerns driving Adorno's text, with its opposition to philosophical foundationalism, its engagement with modern art, and its desire for social liberation. Yet none of these concerns is beyond question, and each merits further scrutiny in the critical community.

One can approximate the issues linked in our central theme by asking a question that Adorno would recognize as his own: If modern society is a "false" totality, then how can modern art, a part of that totality, disclose sociohistorical truth? This question is central not only to *Aesthetic Theory* but also to debates surrounding Adorno's work. It is difficult to understand the question apart from a tradition of German philosophy stretching from Kant and Hegel through Marx, Nietzsche, and Freud to Lukács, Benjamin, Heidegger, and Gadamer. This does not mean that Adorno's question is irrelevant for scholars in English-speaking countries.[8] Nevertheless it must be connected first with its primary historical context.

Accordingly, chapter 1 summarizes Adorno's biography, intellectual tradition, and research program. I argue that Adorno shares Western Marxism's reservations about the appropriateness of classical Marxist social theories and political strategies under the conditions of advanced capitalism. In response, Adorno and other members of the Frankfurt School develop a critical theory keyed to the connections between culture and capitalism, the relation of theory to praxis, and the sociohistorical role of rationality.

Such emphases provide a context for Adorno's debates with other Western Marxists about the issues of artistic autonomy, political art, and aesthetic modernism. As is shown in chapter 2, Adorno's debates with Benjamin, Brecht, and Lukács have a direct bearing on his idea of artistic truth and the prominence this has in his aesthetics. His idea is also informed by the philosophical agenda summarized in chapter 3, where I argue that the difficulties in interpreting Adorno's *Aesthetic Theory* arise from its philosophical motivations. Only a new way of reading can provide passageways through a book that mediates art's implicit truth content with philosophy's explicit truth claims in order to expose the antagonisms of contemporary society.

The results of my own reading, reported in the next five chapters, constitute a selective interpretation of Adorno's aesthetics. These chapters examine how Adorno situates art in society, production, politics, and history, and they uncover the social, political, and historical dimensions of his idea of artistic truth.

Chapters 4 and 5 construe Adorno's account of art's place in society as a complex transformation of Hegel and Marx, both of whom see art as a vehicle of truth. Exactly how this vehicle operates, and exactly which works of art best carry social truth, are central concerns in Western Marxist aesthetics. Chapter 4 claims that Adorno has an internalist and expressivist model of art's social mediation. This model turns autonomy into a flawed but necessary precondition for art's social truth. Moreover, Adorno's account of advanced capitalism as a functional system of exchange and domination leads him to attribute great social significance to autonomous art. Chapter 5 demonstrates that a polarity of subject and object provides the philosophy unity to Adorno's model of social mediation. This polarity allows Adorno to view art as social labor involving a

continual dialectic between artistic materials and artistic practices. Indeed, art is a type of production that participates in
society's general mode of production and lets social truth
materialize.

Adorno's autonomism has important ramifications in the
area of cultural politics. According to chapter 6, Adorno's cultural politics reworks the aesthetics of Immanuel Kant, who
regarded aesthetic judgments as noncognitive links between
scientific knowledge and moral practice. For Adorno, the best
modern art is a form of nondiscursive knowledge and impractical praxis in a society where rational praxis has become irrational. Such knowledge and praxis hinge on the import (*Gehalt*)
of authentic works of art. Being nondiscursive, artistic import
can provide a formal liberation from oppressive social structures. Being impractical, artistic import can have an indirect
but transformative political impact. This cognitivist approach
to questions of art and politics makes urgent an adequate reception of authentic art. Because Adorno thinks philosophy
mediates nondiscursive and discursive rationality, the philosophical interpretation of artistic import acquires an unusual
political status. All of this results, I argue, in a cultural politics
that threatens to make art's political truth politically irrelevant.

The political limitations of Adorno's autonomism and cognitivism are tied to what chapter 7 describes as paradoxical
modernism. Adorno's preference for certain modern works
brings into play a "dialectic of enlightenment" reflecting the
impact of Nietzsche on Adorno's philosophy of history. Using
Adorno's interpretation of Samuel Beckett's *Endgame* as a
touchstone, I show that Adorno's qualified defense of modern
art is part of an attempt to retain a historical telos without
making inflated claims about human progress. A central paradox in Beckett's *Endgame,* as interpreted by Adorno, is a central paradox in *Aesthetic Theory* as well. There seems to be an
irresolvable conflict between the claims of human autonomy
and the need for historical meaning.

"Truth content" (*Wahrheitsgehalt*) indicates the crux of artistic
knowledge and of philosophical interpretation in *Aesthetic Theory.* Chapter 8 characterizes Adorno's aesthetics as an attempt
to redeem artistic phenomena from their illusory character by

disclosing their truth content. Artistic "truth content" has the social, political, and historical dimensions discussed in previous chapters. Adorno's critical appropriation of Hegelian aesthetics is crucial to understanding this concept, for in rejecting Hegel's claim to an absolute knowledge of the truth, Adorno seems to retain some of his deepest metaphysical impulses. Adorno portrays modern art and negative dialectic as reciprocal vehicles of truth. In this way, I suggest, he runs the risk of rendering art philosophical and installing philosophy as art's redeemer, contrary to his own criticisms of Hegel.

The commentary in chapters 4 through 8 raises several questions about the worth of Adorno's contributions to philosophical aesthetics. The last three chapters pursue such questions by presenting the objections of three sympathetic critics. Their objections are used to evaluate Adorno's contributions and to propose ways of reclaiming his aesthetics under current conditions. While questioning aspects of Adorno's autonomism, cognitivism, and modernism, I show the importance of related insights that his critics abandon.

Chapter 9 uses Peter Bürger's criticisms of autonomism to explore the strengths and weaknesses of Adorno's model of social mediation. I argue that neither Adorno nor Bürger gives a satisfactory account of art's social significance. Whereas autonomism leads Adorno to neglect popular art, historicism leads Bürger to abandon normative aesthetics. The chapter suggests ways in which philosophical aesthetics can do justice to popular art without surrendering Adorno's critique of the culture industry. I also propose a model of complex normativity that does not lose Adorno's insight into the historical character of aesthetic norms.

The next chapter uses the criticisms of Fredric Jameson to reexamine Adorno's cultural politics. After presenting Jameson's criticisms of Adorno's paradoxical modernism, I argue that Jameson's own ambivalent postmodernism is hindered by the notion of reification. Whereas Adorno makes exaggerated claims about the political impact of authentic modern art, Jameson has difficulty locating the political relevance of any specific artistic phenomena. I claim that the notion of reification must be relativized without abandoning Adorno's insight into the necessity of giving political evaluations of specific cultural phenomena. At the same time, Adorno's intellectualizing of cultural politics must be rejected without losing Jameson's engagement with the culture of postmodernism.

The final chapter evaluates Adorno's view of the relationships among history, art, and truth. The chapter begins with a summary of Albrecht Wellmer's "stereoscopic" critique of Adorno's aesthetics. Countering Adorno's tendency to make artistic truth esoteric, Wellmer replaces the notion of artistic truth content with the notion of artistic truth potential. While I acknowledge the limitations of Adorno's cognitivism, I make a case for the legitimacy of philosophical claims about artistic truth content. Such claims are the most comprehensive historiographic judgments one can make about artistic phenomena, and they are important to make precisely because current conditions militate against them.

The book's extended argument is that Adorno's idea of artistic truth content is vitiated by his assumptions of autonomism, cognitivism, and modernism. Yet critics of Adorno who ignore or reject his idea of artistic truth content risk losing insights that are important for contemporary philosophical aesthetics. These include the following claims: that the historical character of aesthetic norms does not eliminate their validity; that politically committed philosophy must evaluate the political merits of specific cultural phenomena; and that philosophical truth claims about artistic truth content have legitimacy as comprehensive historiographic judgments. Moreover, as the concluding pages indicate, Adorno presents all these claims in a way that presses upon us the need for social liberation. My hope is that this book provides compelling reasons to reconsider the tasks of philosophical aesthetics in contemporary society. Nothing less would do justice to the intentions of Adorno's *Aesthetic Theory*.

I
Context

1

Historical Positions

1.1 Theodor W. Adorno (1903–1969)

The ironical motto of *Aesthetic Theory* provides an indirect epitaph for its author: "What is called philosophy of art usually lacks one of two things: either the philosophy or the art" (544/498). In his life, as in the *summa aesthetica* he did not live to complete, neither philosophy nor art was lacking.

He was born Theodor Ludwig Wiesengrund on September 11, 1903, in Frankfurt am Main.[1] Frankfurt was to be his home for the first three and last two decades of his life. In the intervening years, from 1934 to 1949, he resided in Oxford, New York, and southern California. During this exile from Nazi Germany he adopted the name by which he is best known: Theodor W. Adorno. The middle initial stands for the surname of his father, Oskar Wiesengrund, a wealthy assimilated Jewish wine merchant. Adorno is the surname of his mother, Maria Calvelli-Adorno, a Catholic of Corsican and Genoese descent. The other member of the family was Maria's sister Agathe. Accomplished performers in their own right, Maria and Agathe gave young "Teddie" the love for music that would motivate much of his scholarly work.

Philosophy fed a voracious intellectual appetite during Adorno's formative years in the Weimar Republic. Weekly sessions on Kant's *Critique of Pure Reason* began with Siegfried Kracauer, a friend of the family, when Adorno was fifteen. Close readings of philosophical texts became a lifelong passion. Three years at Frankfurt's Johann Wolfgang Goethe University sufficed to earn the twenty-one-year-old Adorno a doctorate in philosophy in 1924. His dissertation analyzed the phenomenology of Edmund Husserl. By this time he had already made the acquaintance of two older men who were to be his closest intellectual collaborators—Max Horkheimer, whom he met in a seminar on Husserl in 1922, and Walter Benjamin, to whom Kracauer introduced Adorno in 1923.

The same year marked the founding of the Institute of Social Research in Frankfurt and the publication of Georg Lukács's *History and Class Consciousness*.[2] Although Adorno read Lukács's book soon after it appeared, and although he would later become director of the Institute, the impact of these two formative influences on his philosophy emerged slowly. During his university years Adorno was reading such unorthodox works on the arts as Lukács's *The Theory of the Novel* and Ernst Bloch's *Geist der Utopie*. These were to inspire his own radical approach to philosophical aesthetics.[3] Two other crucial sources of inspiration, both of them mentioned in the "Draft Introduction" to *Aesthetic Theory* (494/457), were Benjamin's treatise on "Goethe's *Elective Affinities*"[4] and his book on *The Origin of German Tragic Drama*.[5]

Just as important for the development of Adorno's philosophy was his intense involvement with "new music." Most of his published writings in the 1920s reviewed contemporary works by Paul Hindemith, Béla Bartók, Igor Stravinsky, Arnold Schönberg, Alban Berg, and Anton Webern. Two of these years, 1925–1926, Adorno spent in Vienna as the composition student of Alban Berg and the piano student of Eduard Steuermann. From the 1920s come not only the beginning of Adorno's discussions with Ernst Krenek and Hanns Eisler, two composers then living in Berlin,[6] but also Schönbergian impulses that would become conceptual tone rows, as it were, in Adorno's writings on the arts. These motifs include an emphasis on the historical character of musical materials, a demand that music be up-to-date and compositionally consistent, the claim that authentic compositions express something objectively true, and the assumption that authentic modern art rejects bourgeois cultural norms. Commenting on a manuscript

Adorno began at Oxford and eventually published as *Against Epistemology*, Susan Buck-Morss writes, "Schönberg's revolution in music provided the inspiration for Adorno's own efforts in philosophy, the model for his major work on Husserl during the thirties. For just as Schönberg had overthrown tonality, the decaying form of bourgeois music, so Adorno's Husserl study attempted to overthrow idealism, the decaying form of bourgeois philosophy."[7] Adorno took from his Vienna days the model for an "atonal philosophy"[8] whose style and concerns prefigure the antifoundational and deconstructive themes of more recent philosophies.

It would be a mistake, however, to read Adorno's aesthetics as no more than a peculiar fusion of anti-idealist philosophy and expressionist art. The catalyst for this fusion is a social critique mainly derived from Lukács and gradually elaborated in dialogue with Benjamin, Horkheimer, and other members of the Institute of Social Research. Its earliest stirrings appear in Adorno's first *Habilitationsschrift*.[9] Although neo-Kantian in method, the study defends Freudian psychoanalysis as a rational theory of the unconscious, and it attacks irrationalist accounts of the unconscious as ideological supports for the status quo. Already here Adorno's philosophical analysis implies a critique of society. Additional incentives for Adorno's social critique came from frequent trips to Berlin in the late 1920s to visit his future wife, Gretel Karplus, and a circle of politically leftist writers and artists including Bloch, Benjamin, Eisler, Moholy-Nagy, Bertolt Brecht, Lotte Lenya, and Kurt Weill. The role of art in transforming social consciousness was uppermost in their discussions.

Even more decisive, according to Buck-Morss, was a methodology Adorno derived from the introductory chapter of Walter Benjamin's *The Origin of German Tragic Drama*.[10] Adorno's methodology emphasizes a close, imaginative reading that exposes social conflicts by uncovering problems inherent in works of art, philosophical texts, or the phenomena of daily life. The critic elicits a sociohistorical truth that might not have been intended by the artist, philosopher, or social agent. Such critical interpretations have political relevance, even when they are not directly useful for political purposes.

Although Adorno's actual methods differ from Benjamin's, a Benjaminian inspiration surfaces in his writings in the early 1930s. These include two lectures given during Adorno's first, brief career on the Frankfurt philosophy faculty,[11] a programmatic essay on music sociology,[12] and *Kierkegaard: Construction of the Aesthetic*, Adorno's first book.[13] The latter was published on the day Hitler came to power in 1933. Soon afterward Adorno, Horkheimer, and many other Jewish professors were dismissed from German universities. The Institute of Social Research, under Horkheimer's direction since 1930, moved to New York, where it became loosely affiliated with Columbia University. Adorno enrolled as an "advanced student" at Oxford University but frequently returned to Germany to visit Gretel Karplus, whom he married in 1937. Benjamin had already moved to Paris, where he lived until 1940, when he committed suicide at the Spanish border while fleeing the Nazis.

The social-critical program forged in the early 1930s would remain central to Adorno's work until his death in 1969. So would his passionate interest in philosophy and modern art, especially music. One can trace gradual shifts in the topics and tone of his writings, however, shifts connected to his social circumstances and his collaboration on various projects. For convenience we may speak of three phases in his mature writings.

The first phase (approximately 1933–1949) is marked by interdisciplinary critiques of popular culture. In this phase Adorno published several pathbreaking essays on the music industry, most notably "On the Fetish-Character in Music and the Regression of Listening."[14] He also worked with Paul Lazarsfeld on Princeton University's Radio Research Project, collaborated with Hanns Eisler on the manuscript of *Composing for the Films*, and coauthored *Dialectic of Enlightenment* and its crucial chapter on "The Culture Industry: Enlightenment as Mass Deception."[15] These writings display an increasingly Hegelian style, a self-conscious importing of Freudian categories, and a complex appropriation of Nietzsche and of conservative culture critics such as Oswald Spengler. Closely connected with these writings is Adorno's collaboration on *The Authoritarian*

Personality.[16] During his years in the United States, Adorno was exploring popular culture in search of the economic, political, psychological, and deeply historical sources of fascism, anti-Semitism, and the loss of a critical public consciousness.

Whereas the first phase is characterized by interdisciplinary cultural critique, the second phase (approximately 1949–1958) is marked by essayistic interventions in high culture. The second phase begins with Adorno's and Horkheimer's return to Frankfurt in 1949 and the reopening of the Institute of Social Research in 1951. It ends around the time Adorno replaced Horkheimer as director of the Institute in 1958. Although written earlier, Adorno's first major publications in this phase can be read as attempts to provoke the superintendents of German high culture during postwar reconstruction. *Philosophy of Modern Music* challenges the official music scene; *Minima Moralia* meditates upon the bitter experiences of German exiles; *In Search of Wagner* decodes the ambiguous work of the Nazis' favorite composer.[17]

The clue to such a reading comes from "Cultural Criticism and Society," an article written in 1949 and published in 1951. Republished in 1955 as the lead essay in *Prisms,*[18] it claims that "cultural criticism must become social physiognomy" because cultural phenomena have become increasingly integrated into the structure of capitalist society. Such integration does not spare the cultural critic: "The more total society becomes, the greater the reification of the mind and the more paradoxical its effort to escape reification on its own. Even the most extreme consciousness of doom threatens to degenerate into idle chatter. Cultural criticism finds itself faced with the final stage of the dialectic of culture and barbarism. To write poetry after Auschwitz is barbaric. And this corrodes even the knowledge of why it has become impossible to write poetry today."[19] Many of Adorno's writings on the arts in the 1950s share this provocative combination of polemical exaggeration and agonizing self-criticism. The combination seems intended to interrupt "business as usual" and to recall the horrors that consumers of high culture would like to forget.

Two programmatic essays announce the concerns occupying the last decade of Adorno's life. The first is the introduction to *Against Epistemology* (1956), in which Adorno insists on the need to historicize ontology and epistemology.[20] The second is "The Essay as Form," a self-conscious reflection on philosophical style that opens Adorno's first volume of literary criticism.[21] Together the two essays announce a turn toward philosophical consolidation. Although by this time Adorno was becoming a well-known radio guest and public lecturer, the focus of his scholarly work shifted toward sustained treatments of topics that had been central to his earlier writings. Besides numerous volumes of essays on music[22] and literature,[23] Adorno published monographs on Mahler and Berg,[24] a book on Hegel,[25] and collections of essays in sociology and aesthetics.[26]

He also entered numerous academic debates about education, university politics, and sociological methods, the most famous of which was the "positivism dispute" with Karl Popper.[27] Whereas Popper continued to cling to a modified version of the ideal of value-neutrality, Adorno insisted that no social theory is politically neutral. His central claim is that "the idea of scientific truth cannot be split off from that of a true society. Only such a society would be free from contradiction and lack of contradiction. In a resigned manner, scientism commits such an idea to the mere forms of knowledge alone. By stressing its societal neutrality, scientism defends itself against the critique of the object and replaces it with the critique merely of logical inconsistences."[28] Despite miscommunication on both sides, the debate led to a better understanding of an issue that has since come to dominate university politics in English-speaking countries. It also provided considerable impetus for followers of Adorno such as Karl-Otto Apel, Jürgen Habermas, and Albrecht Wellmer, all of whom have worked to diminish miscommunication while continuing Adorno's quest for a politically committed social theory.

Adorno's major works of this decade were *Negative Dialectics* and *Aesthetic Theory*.[29] *Negative Dialectics* is a work of metaphilosophy: it presents philosophical reflections on philosophy, and it elaborates the categories and procedures employed in Adorno's previous writings about other philosophers. In a similar fashion *Aesthetic Theory* is a work of meta-aesthetics. It presents philosophical reflections on philosophical aesthetics, and it elaborates the categories and procedures employed in Adorno's previous writings on the arts. Each book provides a summation, not only of Adorno's own writings, but also of the philosophy of the Frankfurt School.

In light of Adorno's life and work, in view of his passion for art and philosophy and his uncompromising criticisms of contemporary society, it is nearly impossible to read *Aesthetic Theory* without a sense of tragedy. A *summa aesthetica*, it is also a fragment, in the words of its editors, "a work that has been tampered with by death" (537/493). Caught up in the endless wranglings of university politics, and under attack from his own militant students, Adorno died of a heart attack in August 1969, one month short of his sixty-sixth birthday. His wife Gretel and his student Rolf Tiedemann prepared the incomplete manuscript for publication. It appeared in 1970, the first of twenty-three volumes in Adorno's *Gesammelte Schriften*. Translations in French (1974), Italian (1975), and English (1984) indicate a perception of the book's significance among scholars outside Germany. Conferences and anthologies on Adorno attest to his continuing importance for intellectuals inside Germany.[30]

Aesthetic Theory has become the last testament, as it were, of a truly remarkable man: a Hegelian Marxist who distanced himself from both Hegel and Marx; an assimilated German Jew who wrote several seminal works in American exile; a polished modern musician who subjected music to a critique of ideology; an imaginative and rigorous philosopher who was better known for his work in the social sciences. After many readings, the indirect epitaph for Adorno's life will stand as a motto for his last major work. In this book, neither philosophy nor art is lacking.

According to Martin Jay, Adorno's writings occupy a historical "force field" that includes "Western Marxism, aesthetic modernism, mandarin cultural despair, and Jewish self-identification, as well as the more anticipatory pull of deconstructionism."[31] No one force dominates Adorno's work; disparate forces converge within it. In *Aesthetic Theory* the mix becomes explosive. It is this incendiary combination of historical forces, together with the substance of Adorno's thought, that gives his fragmentary *summa* its larger significance, as well as its resistance to historical classifications.

Indeed, an initial survey of the secondary literature brings to mind Habermas's remark that "Adorno has left philosophy with a chaotic landscape."[32] Like other of Adorno's writings, *Aesthetic Theory* lends itself to divergent appropriations. Such divergence was especially pronounced in the politically charged atmosphere of Germany immediately after Adorno's death. More than twenty years later, it is still not clear where his life and work should be located in recent intellectual history.

A first step toward mapping this chaotic landscape is to uncover the historical subtext to Adorno's aesthetics. The rest of this chapter argues that *Aesthetic Theory* embodies the central concerns of Western Marxism and critical theory. Like others in the tradition of Western Marxism, Adorno had deep reservations about the appropriateness of classical Marxist theories and strategies under the conditions of advanced capitalism. Along with other critical theorists, he developed an innovative research program keyed to the connections between culture and capitalism, the relation of theory to praxis, and the sociohistorical role of rationality. No reading of *Aesthetic Theory* can afford to ignore either the reasons for his reservations or the emphases of his scholarly agenda.

1.2 Western Marxism

Terms intended to designate historical movements are often vague. "Western Marxism" is a case in point. Even if there were agreement on criteria for defining "Marxism," there would be no obvious reason for using a geopolitical qualifier. In its most common usage, "Western Marxism" indicates a political and intellectual tradition animated by shared concerns and arising in central Europe during the 1920s. Motivated in part by loyal opposition to the Leninist model of party politics, and in part by the apparent failure of proletarian revolution and the rise of fascism, Western Marxists such as Georg Lukács, Karl Korsch, and Antonio Gramsci reformulated Marx's intellectual legacy in order to understand dramatically new conditions in Europe.

As a historiographic term, "Western Marxism" is embedded in the very history it designates.[33] It began as a derogatory label used in polemical attacks on the supposed deviations from orthodox Marxism in Lukács's *History and Class Consciousness* and Karl Korsch's *Marxism and Philosophy,* both published in 1923. The attack came from two sides, from German Social Democrats and from leading spokespersons for the Communist International, who labeled Lukács and Korsch "Western Communists."[34] The intellectual issues at stake were the authors' emphasis on philosophy and ideological struggle, their critique of dogmatism, and their attention to changing relationships between theory and practice in the history of Marxism. Politically, the attack involved the authors' sympathy for workers' councils rather than either the parliamentary trade unionism of the Social Democrats or the centralized vanguard party of the Russian Bolsheviks. This polemical exchange foreshadowed a major split within international Marxism between an increasingly Stalinist Communist Party and its increasingly fragmented opposition in Germany, Italy, France, and the Netherlands.

A significant reuse of "Western Marxism" occurred in 1956, the year Krushchev denounced Stalin at the Twentieth Party Congress. Maurice Merleau-Ponty used the term to indicate an important "subterranean tradition of humanist, subjectivist and undogmatic Marxism" spawned by Lukács's *History and Class Consciousness.*[35] Without simply endorsing Lukács's work, Merleau-Ponty portrayed it as an important alternative to the evolutionary reformist economism of Karl Kautsky and the revolutionary voluntarist vanguardism of Lenin and Trotsky.[36] For the next twenty years commentators tended to equate Western Marxism with a Hegelian revision opposed to both economist and vanguardist versions of Marxism.

A new stage of usage begins with Perry Anderson's *Considerations on Western Marxism* in 1976. Anderson expands the term to include anti-Hegelian Marxists such as Louis Althusser and Lucio Colletti who came to prominence after World War II. This expanded usage continues in Anderson's *In the Tracks of Historical Materialism* and in Martin Jay's *Marxism and Totality.* According to Anderson's Anglo-Trotskyist interpretation,

Western Marxism was "born from the failure of proletarian revolutions in the advanced zones of European capitalism after the First World War,"[37] and it flourished in the gap between a Stalinist version of Marxism in the East and the strongholds of capitalism in the West. In this narrow zone the labor movement was still strong enough to stir up intellectual life—not a politically active life, but an academic life. After the first generation of Western Marxists was forcibly depoliticized—Lukács was forced to recant, Korsch expelled from the Communist Party, and Gramsci imprisoned—subsequent thinkers took their activities from the political into the theoretical realm. Whereas Marx had progressed from philosophy to politics and economics, Western Marxists moved in exactly the opposite direction, leading to extreme separations between theory and practice.

Martin Jay adopts Anderson's terminology to tell a somewhat different story. Not the inability to find effective political strategies but the search for an adequate concept of totality unifies Jay's account. This search begins with Lukács's attempt to fashion the concept of totality as "the critical category that would restore Marxism's theoretical vigor, enabling it to match the practical achievements of Lenin and the Bolshevik Revolution."[38] Jay concludes that the search has failed and, in fact, has come into strong disrepute among Anglo-American commentators who follow the poststructuralism of Jacques Derrida and Michel Foucault. Yet Jay hopes that amidst the debris of Western Marxism "there lurks, silent but still potent, the germ of a truly defensible concept of totality—and even more important, the potential for a liberating totalization that will not turn into its opposite."[39]

The accounts of Jay and Anderson have been criticized for various reasons. Ferenc Fehér, for example, claims that " 'Western Marxism' . . . has no meaning in [Jay's] book other than a more or less geographically based catalogue of 'eminent thinkers,' a principle of selection based on less than scientific rigor."[40] Russell Jacoby's *Dialectic of Defeat* criticizes Anderson for ignoring the political activists and economists in Western Marxism, and it challenges the inclusion of Althusser and Colletti, who have little connection with the historical sources of Western Marxism.[41] Alvin Gouldner, by contrast, questions the fruitfulness of even tracing a Western Marxist tradition. Commenting on Gouldner's *The Two Marxisms,* Douglas Kellner says that Gouldner challenges "the muddled theory of 'Western Marxism.' " Kellner considers it "historically and analytically absurd" to oppose a Western Marxism to a non-Western Leninism à la Merleau-Ponty or Perry Anderson.[42] It would be better to distinguish along Gouldner's lines between "critical" and "scientific" Marxism, the one emphasizing philosophy, critique, and social transformation, the other stressing science, empirical research, and economic development, and neither one laying legitimate claim to being the "true" Marxism.

Despite such criticisms, I do not think the notion of Western Marxism should be abandoned. In the first place, the conflict between Western Marxists and Marxist-Leninists is a real conflict, one that animates the accounts of Merleau-Ponty, Anderson, and Jacoby. In the second place, this conflict cannot simply be summarized as one between critical and scientific Marxism. Not only do the critical and scientific subsystems predate the rise of Marxist-Leninism, but also both subsystems show up on each side of the conflict.[43] To absorb "Western Marxism" into "critical Marxism" would be to collapse an historiographic category into a sociological typology. If the theory of Western Marxism is muddled, then perhaps this is due in part to the tangled history from which it arises.

It is premature, then, to give up the term "Western Marxism." The term recalls struggles that have shaped much of twentieth-century Marxism, and it has become a useful shorthand for a complex historical movement and for a continuing effective tradition. To expand the usage of "Western Marxism" in the manner of Anderson and Jay can be misleading, however, for it smooths over fundamental tensions that have generated crucial discussions concerning the shape of Marxism in the English-speaking world. The differences between Habermas and Althusser, for example, are too important to cover with a neutralized label. It is preferable to use the term more or less in the way it has been used throughout most of its history, despite the vague and polemical connotations of the adjective "Western."

More specifically, in the usage being proposed, "Western Marxism" indicates a political and intellectual movement that emerged from European socialism and communism soon after the First World War. One can distinguish two main schools within the movement: the Frankfurt School, and the existentialist Marxism of Henri Lefebvre, Jean-Paul Sartre, and Merleau-Ponty. Initially inspired by the Russian Revolution, the founders of Western Marxism came into conflict with the Bolsheviks over questions of political strategy and organization in Europe. Often the intellectual dimensions of this conflict approximated the opposition between scientific and critical Marxism discussed by Gouldner. Writings from this time by Lukács, Korsch, and Gramsci became the seminal sources of Western Marxism as an intellectual movement.

Toward the end of the 1960s the movement of Western Marxism shades into a tradition as its contributions come under intense scrutiny and gain a wide reception in conjunction with other schools of Marxism. These other schools include two of importance in the Anglo-American world: the Della Volpe School, including Lucio Colletti, and structuralist Marxism, including Louis Althusser.[44] Neither school shares the intellectual sources and leading concerns of the Frankfurt School or existentialist Marxism. For this reason it is misleading to include figures such as Colletti and Althusser under the rubric of Western Marxism without considerable qualification. Their writings approximate the paradigm of scientific Marxism without necessarily endorsing Marxist-Leninism.

The point of these terminological clarifications is not to argue for a specious orthodoxy. Rather, it is to locate Adorno and his colleagues with relative accuracy within the history of twentieth-century Marxism. The proposed usage of "Western Marxism" indicates a set of shared experiences and concerns that animate an entire generation or two on the European continent. In addition, the classification says something about the sorts of contributions that have contemporary significance. Such experiences and contributions cohere in a tradition characterized by a relatively cohesive set of issues. These can be thought of as the generative challenges of Western Marxism. They were there to be recognized, even though for many reasons, including psychological and sociological ones, Western Marxists were unusually predisposed to spell them out.

The generative challenges of Western Marxism have politico-economic and philosophical-historical dimensions. At the politico-economic level, the failure of proletarian revolutions needed to be understood, and the political role of Marxist intellectuals had to be reconsidered. A key factor, which gradually became thematic, was a structural shift in capitalism that forestalled its expected collapse and rendered Marx's theory partially obsolete. At the philosophical-historical level, the scientism and economic determinism of prominent theorists after Marx had to be confronted, and the importance of philosophy and other cultural regions had to be reexamined. For Western Marxists the "failure of the socialist revolution to spread outside Russia" was not simply what Anderson describes as the "cause and consequence of its corruption inside Russia."[45] The failure was also an indication of theoretical deficiencies in the classical tradition of Marxism.[46]

Both dimensions permeate Adorno's aesthetics. His account of the social and political significance of modern art provides a response to the self-perpetuating character of advanced capitalism. So, too, his account of the critical and utopian thrust of artistic truth provides an alternative to classical Marxism's confidence in scientific and economic progress. The specific shape of Adorno's alternative owes a great deal to his participation in the Frankfurt School and its project, critical theory.

1.3 Critical Theory

Like "Western Marxism," "critical theory" is a disputed label. Perhaps it is best to think of critical theory as a "research program," to use Helmut Dubiel's term.[47] The program was first developed by scholars whose primary institutional affiliation was the Institute of Social Research[48] and whose main institutional expression was the *Zeitschrift für Sozialforschung*.[49] As a group these scholars make up the Frankfurt School, whose members include Adorno, Walter Benjamin (1892–1940), Max Horkheimer (1895–1973), and Herbert Marcuse (1898–1980), to mention only the most prominent philosophers among them.[50]

What distinguishes critical theory from other research programs is its combination of an interdisciplinary methodology, a dialectical mode of presentation, and an orientation to Marx's critique of capitalism. Although Dubiel claims that this research program collapsed in the early 1940s, lively discussions in recent years suggest that critical theory has undergone further development—first under the guidance of "Adorno's less totalizing vision of the relation between theory and research,"[51] and then under the impact of Jürgen Habermas's systematic reformulation. There are critical theorists at work today who were never members of the Frankfurt School, an entity that has faded into history. The following account attempts to situate *Aesthetic Theory* in ongoing debates about critical theory.

Critical theory can be said to have drawn fire from three types of critics: dogmatic, constructive, and hermeneutical.[52] There are two distinct camps of dogmatic critics, though both prefer the method of transcendent critique as a way to uphold doctrines at odds with critical theory. In one camp are the scientific Marxists, whose ranks include Marxist-Leninists such as Phil Slater and Tom Bottomore, structuralist Marxists such as Göran Therborn, and Lucio Colletti during his Della Volpean phase. In the other camp are strident anti-Marxists, such as Leszek Kolakowski and George Friedman, who tend toward political neoconservatism.

Unlike these two camps, "constructive critics" adopt critical theory as their own research program and try to improve it in various ways. Much of the secondary literature on critical theory has this intention. Two sorts of construction stand out, both of them employing the method of immanent critique. On one side, particularly in Germany, is the refashioning of central categories for the sake of systematic studies. Here scholars such as Helmut Dubiel, Jürgen Habermas, Alfred Schmidt, Alfons Söllner, and Albrecht Wellmer come to mind. On the other side, particularly among American scholars, is the recovery of critical theory's history for the sake of political and intellectual orientation.[53] This group includes Andrew Arato, Seyla Benhabib, Susan Buck-Morss, David Held, Russell Jacoby, Martin Jay, and Douglas Kellner, to name some prominent authors.[54]

"Hermeneutical critics," by contrast, tend to engage in transcendental critique. Despite differing orientations, they share a desire to uncover the preconditions of critical theory without either simply rejecting or endorsing it. Representative of this approach are the writings of Rüdiger Bubner, Paul Connerton, Raymond Geuss, and Michael Theunissen.

The critics of critical theory raise three sets of issues that are relevant for understanding Adorno's aesthetics. The first concerns critical theory's attempt to grasp contemporary society and culture as a totality. A second set pertains to a postulated unity of theory and praxis. A third group clusters around the sociohistorical role of rationality. Each set overlaps debates in Western Marxist aesthetics concerning, respectively, artistic autonomy, political art, and aesthetic modernism, debates that directly inform Adorno's idea of artistic truth. By reviewing the ways in which critical theory has been criticized, I shall set up a framework for interpreting and evaluating *Aesthetic Theory*.

Culture and Capitalism

Considered as a global account of contemporary culture and society, critical theory is daunting in its complexity. The account goes through several phases, has differing foci for various critical theorists, and raises many difficult questions. For present purposes it will suffice to summarize some reactions to critical theory's peculiar conjunction of culture, polity, and economy. This conjunction gives a more prominent place to aesthetics and cultural studies than was common in classical Marxism. According to Perry Anderson, Western Marxism as a whole has a markedly "cultural and ideological focus," and its "most permanent collective gain" lies in the fields of aesthetics and cultural studies.[55] Anderson's comment is particularly apt with regard to critical theory. Detailed attention to contemporary art and culture is one of critical theory's most striking characteristics. It is also controversial, eliciting dramatically different responses.

The two camps of dogmatic critics dislike this emphasis, but for conflicting reasons. According to scientific Marxists, critical theory's emphasis on art and culture betrays the negative influence of German idealism, and comes at the expense of economic analysis and political strategy. The Althusserian Göran Therborn, for example, blames critical theory for reducing both economics and politics to philosophy, with the result that "the specificity of Marxism as a theory of social formations and its autonomy as a guide to political action are thereby simultaneously abolished."[56] Neoconservative critics, by contrast, interpret critical theory's emphasis on contemporary art and culture as a nihilistic perversion of authentic idealism. They also see its global account as a failure, demonstrating the inevitable bankruptcy of Marxism. In the words of the Straussian political philosopher George Friedman, "The Frankfurt School played Marxism out to its end and gave it its *coup de grâce*. . . . The Frankfurt School marks the close of [Marx's] system."[57]

According to constructive critics, both camps of dogmatic critics blame critical theory for the symptoms it diagnoses, ignore the actual diagnosis, and simply assume that their own paradigms are correct. Constructive critics consider it "sheer nonsense to assert that critical theorists focused their contributions on 'superstructural' considerations to the complete exclusion of political economy."[58] They also find it absurd to see critical theory as the nemesis of Marxism. The crucial problems lie not in critical theory's emphasis on culture, nor in its supposed failure to resolve the crisis of Marxism, but in its model for drawing mutual implications among economic, political, and cultural studies.[59]

Andrew Arato traces such problems to a "political sociology" generated around 1937–1941. During these years, Horkheimer, Adorno, and Friedrich Pollock decided that monopoly capitalism had consolidated in a new social formation they called "state capitalism," of which Nazi Germany, Soviet Russia, and New Deal America exemplified three types. This political-sociological model implied that politics and culture were rapidly becoming cement in an already rigid and potentially to-

talitarian system. Arato argues that Horkheimer and Adorno
were misled by an overemphasis on fascism and an outdated
longing for proletarian revolution. Consequently their analyses
of political administration and the culture industry overlooked
significant crisis tendencies and subjective resistance within
state capitalism.[60] As David Held also claims, the critical theorists overestimate the "internal homogeneity" of advanced capitalist society.[61] For many constructive critics, Jürgen Habermas
has advanced critical theory by recovering a diagnosis of crisis
tendencies without dropping the critique of politics and
culture.

That Habermas has advanced critical theory is not obvious
to hermeneutical critics. Paul Connerton, for example, insists
that Habermas shares the fatal flaw of all critical theory. Connerton argues that critical theory's "critique of domination"
repeatedly founders for two historical reasons. First, critical
theory compromises Marx's paradigmatic critique of capitalism
through admixtures with universalistic *Geschichtsphilosophie* and
pessimistic social theory.[62] Second, critical theory suffers from
Germany's lack of a heritage of "political humanism" and
"bourgeois revolution." Hence the critique of domination must
"appeal to a critical public which is never securely localised."[63]
In Connerton's opinion, this combination of unavoidable appeal and hidden addressee is the fatal flaw of critical theory.

The criticisms we have reviewed indicate problems in critical
theory's conjunction of culture, polity, and economy. Yet the
conjunction itself seems highly significant. Critical theory has
avoided both the economic reductionism and the political voluntarism toward which many other Marxists have inclined, but
it has not fallen into the reactionary culturalism shared by
many opponents of Marxism.

It is in the context of critical theory's global account that
Adorno insists on the social significance of autonomous art.
Aesthetic Theory makes a definite departure from traditional
Marxist approaches to the place of art in society. The reasons
for this departure are the very ones that inform critical theory's
controversial conjunction of culture, polity, and economy. Although this conjunction will not be discussed at length, chap-

ters 4, 5, and 9 examine its specific shape in Adorno's aesthetics.

Theory and Praxis

A closely related topic is the nexus of theory and praxis in critical theory. It is not surprising that this theme preoccupies some critics, for, as George Lichtheim states, the relation of theory to political practice is "the central theme of political thought."[64] Ever since Lukács developed his "philosophy of practice," Western Marxists have postulated that there must be a unity of theory and praxis, and that this unity must directly involve philosophy.[65]

Critical theory's attempts to build upon this postulate have proved profoundly dissatisfying, especially for scientific Marxists. The Marxist-Leninist Phil Slater says critical theory fails "to achieve the relation to praxis which is central to the Marxist project." It neglects the theories of class struggle and proletarian revolution, refuses to view itself as an "agitational weapon," and proposes no theory of political organization and political action. So too, Adorno's aesthetics fails to redirect modern art for oppositional purposes: "The aesthetic praxis of class-struggle loses all significance for Adorno's theory." What we have here is an "ideological degeneration."[66]

Similar charges come from the opposite end of the political spectrum. According to neoconservative critics such as Günter Rohrmoser and Arnold Künzli, critical theory failed to achieve the unity of theory and praxis it demands. Instead, the critical theorists, especially Adorno, pursued a sterile, unrealistic theory. This theory encourages irrational and irresponsible political practices, whose disastrous consequences became clear in the student uprisings and urban terrorism of the 1960s and 1970s. Indeed, Rohrmoser finds parallels between Adorno's thought and fascism,[67] while Künzli views Adorno's "fear of praxis" as literally neurotic.[68] In a similar vein, George Friedman suggests that Adorno flirts with a "fascist" aestheticizing of politics.[69]

Although it is not hard for constructive critics to expose the factual inaccuracies, logical fallacies, and rhetorical bombast in such charges,[70] they cannot ignore the issues these charges raise. It is no accident that Habermas devoted a book in the early 1960s to the theme of theory and praxis,[71] nor is it mere coincidence that Adorno's own activist students turned on him—contributing, some have said, to his untimely death. Critical theory expects to be "mediated" with system-transformative praxis, but seems unable to meet this expectation. The constructive critic David Held argues that the critical theorists "offer a theory of the importance of fundamental social transformation which has little basis in social struggle." By exaggerating the cohesion and co-optive power of advanced capitalism, they underestimate the "complexity of political events," the "significance of certain types of political struggle," and the "importance of their own work for these struggles."[72]

Whereas dogmatic critics condemn critical theory for its political consequences, and constructive critics find critical theory short-sighted about its own political basis, hermeneutical critics trace such difficulties to problematic historical sources. Rüdiger Bubner, for example, argues that critical theory has difficulty with praxis because it reverts to a Young Hegelian position. Young Hegelians such as Ludwig Feuerbach and Bruno Bauer, who faulted Hegel's philosophy for its conformist isolation, tried to put this philosophy into practice through their own critical reflections on society. As Marx and Engels demonstrate in *The German Ideology*, however, the results are no more practical and considerably less insightful than Hegel's philosophy. They are the politically impotent musings of "critical critics." Like the Young Hegelians, says Bubner, the critical theorists absolutize a dialectical method, thereby reducing Hegel's and Marx's systematic theories to a mere critique of ideology. Lacking systematic comprehensiveness, their social criticisms are divorced from questions of actual practice.[73] Not even Habermas escapes the Young Hegelian tendency to engage in "critical reflection for reflection's sake."[74]

Clearly the relation of theory to praxis is a central issue for critical theory and its critics. This is not to suggest, however, that the various criticisms cited are equally well-founded. Slater, for example, seems unwilling to entertain the critical theorists' reasons for rejecting Marxist-Leninist voluntarism;

Rohrmoser's diatribe is hardly a good example of the political "responsibility" that Adorno is said to lack; and Held does not show that the political forces underestimated by critical theory can actually transform the system of advanced capitalism.

At the same time, I am not inclined to call the critics misguided or to settle for a diplomatic approach along the lines of Martin Jay's *The Dialectical Imagination*. Jay claims that the "relative autonomy" of critical theorists from political organizations and institutions, "although entailing certain disadvantages, was one of the primary reasons for the theoretical achievements produced by their collaboration."[75] Although this is a defensible assessment, one must still ask whether such "theoretical achievements" measure up to critical theory's own postulate of a unity between theory and praxis.[76]

At the very least, one should recognize the complexity of this postulate and of critical theory's attempts to build upon it. One should distinguish, as Dubiel does, among the historical events and political experiences informing critical theory, its theoretical position toward these sources, and its theory of the relation between theory and praxis.[77] In addition there are questions, ignored by Dubiel and exaggerated by dogmatic critics, concerning the political involvements and effects of critical theory.[78]

A similar complexity characterizes Adorno's claims concerning art and politics. These claims will be easily misunderstood and inadequately criticized if one does not distinguish between the political import and the political impact of art, and of Adorno's aesthetics. Otherwise, to say, for example, that Adorno "aestheticizes politics" will be just as uninformative as to argue that he should have supported "political art." Adorno's claims about art and politics have definite political sources, as does the sociological model in his aesthetics. *Aesthetic Theory* takes a theoretical position toward these sources, and it develops a theory about the relation between taking a theoretical position in aesthetics and carrying out transformative praxis. Critical theory's much-criticized nexus of theory and praxis provides a context for Adorno's cognitivism with respect to art and politics, which is discussed in chapters 6 and 10.

Critique of Rationality

Most critics agree that *Dialectic of Enlightenment* marks a watershed in critical theory, but they disagree about the significance of Horkheimer and Adorno's "critique of instrumental reason." By persistently questioning the historical accomplishments of the Enlightenment and the social functions of modern science and technology, this book has generated wide-ranging debates about the role of rationality in modern societies. While the debates are far too complex to be done justice here, some representative criticisms will be summarized, and their relevance for Adorno's aesthetics indicated.

Scientific Marxists are nearly unanimous in blaming critical theory for a disastrous rejection of rationality. This is hardly surprising, given their tendency to identify reason with science and technology in precisely the manner that critical theorists reject. Lucio Colletti, for example, attacks the "horror of the scientific mind" in *Dialectic of Enlightenment*. He calls Horkheimer and Adorno "beautiful souls" who mistake the "romantic critique of intellect and science for a socio-historical critique of capitalism."[79] Tom Bottomore also connects the book with a "hostility to science and technology" said to be prominent in twentieth-century German social thought.[80] By fusing a critique of scientism with a critique of science and technology, Horkheimer and Adorno strip "domination" of any class character.[81] Because scientific Marxists consider (social) science a "guide to political action," they regard critical theory's apparent attack on science as a recipe for political disaster.[82]

Like the scientific Marxists, the neoconservative camp associates critical theory with "the romantic tradition" and "existential philosophy," which are assumed to be bad company. Some neoconservatives such as Leszek Kolakowski share the scientific Marxist view that critical theory rejects empirical science and is mistaken to do so.[83] Other neoconservatives claim that critical theory, although right to criticize empirical science, criticizes it for the wrong reasons and with the wrong results. According to George Friedman, the critical theorists see correctly that reason, science, and technology have not redeemed the hopes of the Enlightenment. Yet they mistakenly cling to an Enlightenment faith in rationality and, like other modern philosophers, fail to find the meaning of life.[84]

The most interesting criticisms of critical theory's view of rationality have not come from scientific Marxists and neoconservatives, however, but from constructive critics such as Jürgen Habermas and Albrecht Wellmer.[85] Wellmer finds two limitations in Horkheimer and Adorno's account of rationality. The first is a reduction in conceptual categories. The second is a chasm between utopia and reality. Together, they make for a highly paradoxical critique of reason's role in human history. Like Habermas, Wellmer traces both limitations back to Marx.

Concerning the first limitation, Wellmer suggests that there is a tension between Marx's concrete analyses and his formal categories. Whereas Marx's concrete analyses of social history treat forces and relations of production as mutually irreducible factors in the historical process, his formal categories reduce the relations of production to forces of production. Marx regards instrumental action upon the environment as the paradigm for all human action, including the social interaction that goes into class struggle and social critique.[86] In a similar way, *Dialectic of Enlightenment* uses "instrumental reason" to conceive both the technological "transformation of external nature (technology, industry, domination of nature)" and the institutional "transformation of internal nature (individuation, repression, forms of social domination)."[87] Although directed at the ideologies of scientism and technicism, Adorno's critique of instrumental reason threatens to reject reason in general, making it difficult to produce an immanent critique of contemporary society and to locate a historical basis for society's transformation.

These difficulties point to the second limitation, namely, an unbridgeable gap between utopia and historical society. Again, Wellmer traces the problem back to Marx, whose critique of "alienation" improperly lumps together two distinct phenomena: exploitation and societal differentiation.[88] As a result, Marx thinks the abolition of capitalist property will eliminate not only exploitation but also societal differentiation, a feature that Wellmer considers desirable and unavoidable. Hence a theoretical chasm opens between bourgeois society and the utopian future, even though Marx believes that communism must emerge from the society of his day.

The chasm becomes even deeper in *Dialectic of Enlightenment.* On the one hand, Horkheimer and Adorno retain Marx's Enlightenment idea of a rational organization of society. A truly rational society would accord with an emphatic conception of reason that comprises the ideas of freedom, justice, and happiness. On the other hand, they take over Max Weber's picture of the modern rationalization process as ineluctably leading to a closed system of instrumental and administrative rationality where substantive ideas of freedom, justice, and happiness play no role. The result is a "radical negativism" toward capitalist society and an "abstract utopianism" with respect to post-capitalist society: "The idea of reason must under such conditions appear as the idea of a future state of society *beyond* human history—a human history, i.e., which as a whole appears hopelessly godforsaken."[89]

Together these two limitations generate what Habermas calls a "totalizing" critique of reason—an ideology critique that questions the basis of all ideology critique. According to Habermas, ideology critique normally tries to show that the theory being criticized conceals an inadmissible mixture of power and validity. In *Dialectic of Enlightenment,* however, "reason itself is suspected of the baneful confusion of power and validity claims, but still with the intent of enlightening." Horkheimer and Adorno try to show that the pervasive instrumentalizing of reason assimilates reason to power and destroys its critical force. This demonstration is paradoxical, however, because it must employ the same critical rationality it has declared dead—a "performative contradiction" that is central to Adorno's *Negative Dialectics* and *Aesthetic Theory.*[90] On Wellmer's analysis, the fundamental constraint in Adorno's aesthetics is that it embodies a highly paradoxical and totalizing critique of reason.

At issue for both dogmatic and constructive critics is the meaning and viability of a critique of rationality in modern society. The dogmatic critics cited earlier make one wonder how insightful a critique of modern society can be if it does not consider the systemic roles of science and technology in contemporary capitalism. Given the power of science and technology as productive forces, and the effectiveness of scientism and technicism as ideologies, it may be necessary to reconstruct traditional theories of class conflict and revise traditional strategies of party politics. Although Horkheimer and Adorno may not have gone far enough along these lines, their critique of instrumental rationality brings such issues to the fore.

The constructive criticisms of Wellmer and Habermas raise important questions about the critique of instrumental rationality. Yet one wonders whether their criticisms do not necessitate a reversion behind Marx and Hegel to the Kantian critique of reason, with all the attendant problems of transcendentalism. Raymond Geuss, for example, suggests that Habermas's purported advance over Horkheimer and Adorno carries new "transcendental baggage" that critical theory would be "better off without."[91] Robert Hullot-Kentor attacks Habermas in even stronger terms, saying that Habermas wrongly attributes to Adorno a division between reason and the aesthetic and misses the idea of a possible reversal of domination into liberation that pervades Adorno's aesthetics.[92]

These brief comments indicate a way to approach Adorno's "aesthetic modernism." Adorno's strong preferences for modern art will not be read as the longing of a latter-day romantic who cannot feel at home with modern science and technology, nor will his *Aesthetic Theory* be considered the last refuge for a critique of rationality that cannot avoid its own performative contradiction. Adorno's embrace of modern art helps situate his critique of rationality squarely in the modern world, and his aesthetic theory contains an implicit critique of his own critique of rationality. These topics are treated in chapters 7, 8, and 11.

My brief survey of Western Marxism and critical theory helps set the stage for an interpretation that spotlights Adorno's idea of artistic truth. Critical theory provides a response to the generative challenges of Western Marxism, and, as we shall see in more detail, the autonomism, cognitivism, and modernism of *Aesthetic Theory* reflect critical theory's accounts of advanced capitalism, the theory-praxis nexus, and instrumental rationality. At this point it is well to consider three thinkers whose debates with Adorno echo across the pages of *Aesthetic Theory:* Walter Benjamin, Bertolt Brecht, and Georg Lukács. All three are prominent figures in Western Marxist aesthetics, and the issues they address directly inform Adorno's idea of artistic truth.

2

Aesthetic Debates

Adorno's aesthetics is closer to Marx's critique of capitalism than the casual reader might think. Although Marx never wrote a treatise on aesthetics, his scattered remarks on literature and the arts are the seeds of a Marxist aesthetics. The main aesthetic problems considered by Marx include the origins of aesthetic sensibility, the alienation of art, the class conditioning of artistic values, the merits of literary realism, and the relation of basic human values to the values of art.[1] Such themes are Marx's legacy in aesthetics, a legacy given new life by Western Marxists, especially by critical theorists.[2] The comprehensive character of *Aesthetic Theory* gives it great significance for Marxist aesthetics. Indeed, Adorno's idea of artistic truth is a benchmark for the aesthetic issues contained in Marx's project and revitalized by Western Marxism.

This chapter reconstructs three aesthetic issues from Adorno's debates with Benjamin, Brecht, and Lukács. "Debate" is used loosely here, since Adorno's disagreements do not always occur in formal exchanges. My account is guided in part by themes in Marx's legacy, in part by recent discussions of Adorno's aesthetics. The treatment is selective; I do not plan to provide a history of Western Marxist aesthetics or to summarize the state of more recent scholarship. Instead, my aim is to uncover key issues in Western Marxist aesthetics and to see how they intersect the Adornian problematic of truth.

2.1 Artistic Autonomy

No other debate in Western Marxist aesthetics has received more commentary than that between Adorno and Benjamin in the 1930s. Apart from the inherent fascination of this debate, there are quasi-political reasons for such attention. Although Adorno did much to preserve Benjamin's contributions, some of his activist students thought Benjamin provided a "more Marxist" alternative to Adorno's aesthetics. When Habermas declared in 1972 that Adorno "was certainly the better Marxist," the lines of battle were clearly drawn.[3] Since then numerous studies have tried to reconstruct the debate and assess its contemporary significance.[4]

It would not be difficult to find in this debate all the issues already mentioned. The one most clearly formulated, however, and the one whose formulation is genuinely new in Marxist aesthetics, concerns the relation between autonomous art and the culture industry. The debate consists mainly of Adorno's letters about essays that Benjamin had submitted for the *Zeitschrift für Sozialforschung*.[5] The theoretical differences emerge most clearly from a comparison of Benjamin's "The Work of Art in the Age of Mechanical Reproduction," written in 1935,[6] and Adorno's "On the Fetish-Character in Music and the Regression of Listening," published in 1938.[7] These differences concern the impact of mass media, the social significance of art in the 1930s, and the political-economic basis for this significance.[8]

According the Benjamin, the "mechanical reproducibility" of photography and film has a progressive effect. It undermines the aura in art. By aura he means the authenticity, unique presence, and traditional authority of the work of art. In film production, for example, the positioning of camera and editor between actor and audience means that the aura enveloping the actor vanishes, and with it the aura of the character the actor portrays.[9] Similarly, in the viewing of films, a focused but playful public appropriation replaces disinterested private contemplation by privileged art spectators: "Mechanical reproduction of art changes the reaction of the masses toward art. The reactionary attitude toward a Picasso painting changes into the progressive reaction toward a Chaplin movie. The progressive reaction is characterized by the direct, intimate fusion of visual and emotional enjoyment with the orientation of the expert. Such fusion is of great social significance."[10]

According to Adorno, however, mass mediated music strengthens rather than weakens the aura of art. He has in mind not only commercial jazz recorded for the mainstream market but also classical music programmed for "easy listening." In such music the performers don the pseudo-genius of stardom, and audiences become addicted to the baby food of the latest hit tunes: "However it may be with films, today's mass music shows little . . . progress in disenchantment. Nothing survives in it more steadfastly than the illusion. . . . It is illusory to promote the technical-rational moments of contemporary mass music—or the special capacities of the regressive listeners which may correspond to these moments—at the expense of a decayed magic. . . . The technical innovations of mass music really don't exist."[11]

The target of this passage is the "great social significance" Benjamin assigns to the decline of auratic art. Benjamin's essay tends to treat new cultural technologies as inherently progressive. Their social significance lies in their replacing the ritual function of traditional works—the "cult value" of traditional works as objects of religious or aesthetic contemplation—with the predominantly political function of photography and film.[12] The cinema has the potential to be an instrument of emancipating the masses. Although Benjamin recognizes that "the movie-makers' capital" thwarts this potential,[13] and that fascists misuse the new medium for reactionary purposes,[14] he believes this new "force of production" challenges the prevailing "relations of production."

In Adorno's opinion, Benjamin's assessment is naive. Radio and film have become a new social cement for the capitalist system rather than agents for collective self-emancipation. Adorno points to a new fetishism of commercial success in the production of recorded music. Recorded music is produced primarily as a commodity, even though the marketing of this product makes it seem to serve consumers' needs.[15] To this "fetishism" corresponds a regression of listening among consumers, whose needs are manipulated. Many listeners are easily impressed with the stellar performances of a Toscanini. Such listeners go in for impressionistic color effects; they content themselves with a standardized repertoire; they love memorable moments ripped out of context. Contemporary listening "is arrested at the infantile stage."[16] Nevertheless, some art, although part of the system, does transcend it. This is the modern music of Schönberg, Webern, and others. Through truly progressive musical technique, such music consistently liquidates the aura of traditional art without succumbing to the aura of the music industry.[17] It offends aesthetic contemplation without promoting the regression of listening, and it voices the radical needs that mass mediated music suppresses.

To summarize: both authors find something progressive in the decline of traditional auratic art. Whereas Benjamin attributes this decline to the impact of mass media, Adorno associates it with the technical advances of modern art, which has maintained its autonomy but dispensed with ritual functions. Adorno criticizes Benjamin for ignoring both the progressive side of autonomous art and the regressive side of mass mediated art. The point of his criticism is not to promote autonomous art and demote mass mediated art, but to see the dialectic within and between them as parts of the total system: "Both bear the stigmata of capitalism, both contain elements of change. . . . Both are torn halves of an integral freedom, to which however they do not add up."[18] That, at least, is what Adorno's letter to Benjamin says. As a matter of fact, however, many readers find Adorno's treatment of the culture industry much harsher than his discussions of autonomous art, and his claims on behalf of autonomous art much loftier than those on behalf of popular art. Charges of "elitism" and "left mandarinism" have been leveled against Adorno by some of his more populist critics.[19]

Such perceptions bring us to the issue of artistic autonomy with which *Aesthetic Theory* begins and ends. Adorno's initial formulation recalls his debate with Benjamin:

Absolute freedom in art . . . contradicts the abiding unfreedom of the social whole. That is why the place and function of art in society have become uncertain. To put it another way, the autonomy art gained after having freed itself from its earlier cult function . . . depended on the idea of humanity. As society grew less humane, [this idea was shattered]. . . . There is no point in trying to allay the self-doubts of art . . . by restoring to her a social role. Such attempts are in vain. Today, however, autonomous art shows signs of being blind (9/1–2).

As this passage suggests, Adorno finds the autonomy of art significant, unavoidable, and disturbing.

Although the concept of autonomy needs further elaboration, it can be equated for now with the freedom of art from religious, political, and other social roles. Within an unfree society, such freedom has come to afflict art itself. In fact, Adorno says, artistic freedom performs an ideological function: "The principle of artistic autonomy willy-nilly creates the false impression that the world outside is . . . a rounded whole. . . . By rejecting reality . . . art vindicates reality" (10/2). Yet he retains the thesis advanced against Benjamin, namely, that certain works of art transcend an unfree system and crack the cement of the culture industry. Autonomy, the very principle that renders art ideological, also provides a precondition for art's emancipatory role. Truth content (*Wahrheitsgehalt*) is the driving force of emancipatory works.

The issue of artistic autonomy can be posed as follows: What are the social preconditions of artistic autonomy? What is the significance of autonomous art in an advanced capitalist society? And what does autonomy contribute in this regard? For Adorno, the issue concerns the mediation of autonomous art and advanced capitalism, a mediation from which socio-artistic truth can emerge.

2.2 Political Art

The Adorno-Benjamin debate carries political overtones from a famous controversy over literary realism in the 1930s. As recounted in recent years, the main figures in that controversy were Georg Lukács and Bertolt Brecht.[20] Still audible in the 1930s controversy is a lively debate held in Russia one decade earlier and recorded in Trotsky's *Literature and Revolution*

(1923). Trotsky argues that "it is fundamentally incorrect to contrast bourgeois culture and bourgeois art with proletarian culture and proletarian art. The latter will never exist."[21] Trotsky's argument is directed against the Proletcult movement and against a left-wing formation of futurists, constructivists, and formalists whose members included the film director Sergei Eisenstein and the theater director Vsevolod Yemilyevich Meyerhold.[22] In agreement with Lenin, who saw attaining mass literacy and preserving a cultural legacy as the most pressing needs, Trotsky argues that the primary question is not about class origins or class orientation. The primary question concerns the fruitfulness of various artistic schools and tendencies for the ongoing revolution. We need a revolutionary culture, he says, not a proletarian culture, whatever that might be.

It is in this context that Trotsky comments on realism. The importance of realism does not lie in any specific forms or techniques but in a preoccupation with life under revolutionary conditions: "This means a realistic monism, in the sense of a philosophy of life, and not a 'realism' in the sense of the traditional arsenal of literary schools. On the contrary, the new artist will need all the methods and processes evolved in the past, as well as a few supplementary ones, in order to grasp the new life. And this is not going to be artistic eclecticism, because the unity of art is created by an active world-attitude and active life-attitude."[23] If such realism does not seem proletarian, so be it, says Trotsky; a complete revolution will not usher in proletarian art but rather the socialist art of a classless society.

Trotsky's sweeping cultural strategy and the leftists' provocative experiments seemed equally inappropriate in the increasingly nonrevolutionary conditions of 1930s Germany. Nevertheless the questions raised about proletarian culture echo in the realism controversy. At bottom, both the Russian debate and the German controversy concern the appropriateness of specific artistic practices for definite political conditions, the political effectiveness of these practices, and the position of artists and art critics in current political struggles.

Answers to such questions depend in part on one's position in political struggles and one's assessment of current political conditions. For example, Lukács's prescription of realism and his proscription of expressionism comport well with his prominence in the Stalinist Party and his support for a "popular front" uniting workers and the liberal bourgeoisie against the Nazis. Similarly, Brecht's emphasis on artistic innovation and confrontational theater coincides with a more "leftist" politics of class conflict that wants to knock the stuffing out of bourgeois morality and galvanize the lower classes for clear-headed activism.[24] Insofar as Adorno's critique of Brechtian theater also addresses questions of political appropriateness and effectiveness, as it surely does, his answers can also be related to his own political position and political assessments. By itself, however, such a sociological analysis would not provide a philosophical evaluation of his answers, unless one already had a dogmatic position on the correct political line to take. This point needs to be made in view of various attacks on Adorno's alleged apolitical "idealism."[25]

"Commitment" (1962), Adorno's provocative essay on Sartre and Brecht,[26] is a belated response to Benjamin's rather Brechtian essay "The Author as Producer" (1934).[27] Both essays address the tension between artistic freedom and political commitment, and both essays use Brecht's theater to elaborate their theses. Comparing the two essays serves to clarify the issue of art and politics in Adorno's aesthetics.

Benjamin wishes to go beyond an unfruitful debate between those who ask artists to toe the correct political line and those who defend artists' freedom to pursue aesthetic quality. He holds that aesthetic quality and political correctness are necessary conditions of each other: "The tendency of a literary work can only be politically correct if it is also literarily correct. . . . The politically correct tendency includes a literary tendency. . . . This literary tendency . . . alone constitutes the quality of the work. The correct political tendency of a work includes its literary quality *because* it includes its literary *tendency*."[28] For Benjamin the correctness of a literary tendency depends on the progressiveness of a work's literary technique in the context of "the literary relations of production of its time."[29]

Whereas Benjamin finds many examples of such progressiveness in the Soviet press, he says the situation in Western Europe is different. Here there is a fundamental conflict between the forces and the relations of production, in literature as in every other region of society. Many writers have acquired revolutionary attitudes, but their writing continues to serve a bourgeois apparatus of publication. What is needed is neither simply revolutionary attitudes nor merely innovative writing, but a revolution in literary techniques that transforms the productive apparatus: "For the transformation of the forms and instruments of production in the way desired . . . Brecht coined the term *Umfunktionierung*. He was the first to make of intellectuals the far-reaching demand: not to supply the apparatus of production without, to the utmost extent possible, changing it in accordance with socialism."[30]

Not surprisingly, Benjamin's best example of such refunctioning is the epic theater of Bertolt Brecht. Brecht's strategies for interrupting the plot incorporate the procedure of montage, developed in film and radio, to counteract the illusion of reality in bourgeois drama. The result is the famous *Verfremdungseffekt*. The spectator recognizes the situation enacted on stage as the real situation, not with satisfaction, but with astonishment and insight: "Epic theatre, therefore, does not reproduce situations, rather it discovers them. . . . It is less concerned with filling the public with feelings, even seditious ones, than with alienating it in an enduring manner, through thinking, from the conditions in which it lives."[31] The clear implication is that Brechtian theater is both technically progressive and politically correct. In contrast to Brecht, however, who had attempted direct collaboration with the workers, Benjamin concludes that intellectuals can best demonstrate solidarity by attempting to transform the media and institutions of their own professions.[32]

Writing nearly thirty years later, Adorno spells out his stance on art and politics in response to the German translation of Sartre's *What Is Literature?* The essay "Commitment" hinges on the antinomy of committed art versus autonomous art, although Adorno begins with both political and aesthetic reasons for questioning this antinomy. By "committed art" he does not mean tendentious art, which aims at immediate objectives such as the change of labor laws, nor does he mean propaganda, which serves the official goals of a government or political party. In the course of the essay, "committed art" comes to mean art that is intended to change fundamental political attitudes, but often fails. "Autonomous art" comes to mean art that is not intended to change political attitudes, yet often does. Adorno's thesis drops like a bombshell at the essay's end: "This is not a time for political works of art, but politics has migrated into autonomous works, and nowhere more so than where these seem politically dead."[33] The essay adduces three reasons in support of this thesis, namely, the ineffectiveness of committed art, the political situation in Germany after World War II, and the effectiveness of certain autonomous works under advanced capitalist conditions.

Adorno uses Brechtian theater to illustrate the first reason. Brecht's plays try to catalyze the audience toward political consciousness and action, he writes, and to achieve this Brecht transforms traditional theater through a process of aesthetic reduction. Adorno says this is a promising way to strip capitalism's abstract essence of its camouflage in the sphere of consumption. Unfortunately, the same process of aesthetic reduction trivializes the political content of a play like *The Resistible Rise of Arturo Ui* (1941): "Instead of a conspiracy of the wealthy and powerful, we are given a trivial gangster organization, the cabbage trust. The true horror of fascism is conjured away; it is no longer a slow end-product of the concentration of social power, but mere hazard, like an accident or crime. . . . The consequence is bad politics, both in literature as in practice before 1933."[34] The result of such a trivialization is to reduce the intended political effect. At the same time Brecht's distortions of political reality weaken his plays as art. Plays such as *Mother Courage* (1939) are dramatically implausible, and the peasant-like diction of *The Caucasian Chalk Circle* (1949/1954) is highly artificial. "Bad politics becomes bad art and vice versa," Adorno concludes.[35]

This is not Adorno's final word on Brecht, neither in "Commitment" nor in subsequent writings. The comments on "bad politics" and "bad art" should be read as challenges to the rising Brecht-Industrie in West Germany, and they must be con-

nected with Adorno's assessment of current political conditions. In Germany, he says, two peculiar conditions render
committed works less appropriate. One is the national repression of guilt and suffering after World War II.[36] The second
peculiarity is a strong German tendency toward moralism and
asceticism that renders committed art susceptible to manipu-
lation and easy consumption: "In Germany, commitment often
means bleating what everyone is already saying or at least
secretly wants to hear."[37]

The conclusion Adorno draws from this assessment relies on
his theory that advanced capitalism vitiates traditional strategies in politics and undermines the intended effect of committed art:

Nevertheless, an emphasis on autonomous works is itself sociopolitical
in nature. The feigning of a true politics here and now, the freezing
of historical relations which nowhere seem ready to melt, oblige the
mind to go where it need not degrade itself. Today, every phenomenon of culture . . . is liable to be suffocated in the cultivation of
kitsch. Yet paradoxically in the same epoch it is to works of art that
has fallen the burden of wordlessly asserting what is barred to
politics. . . . This is not a time for political works of art, but politics
has migrated into autonomous works, and nowhere more so than
where these seem politically dead.[38]

Adorno's controversial claim, then, is that committed works
have become politically inappropriate in West Germany because of the peculiarities of post-war culture and the system of
advanced capitalism. Under current conditions, fully autonomous works, which lack directly political intentions, have the
political effect that committed works rarely achieve: "Kafka's
prose and Beckett's plays . . . have an effect by comparison
with which officially committed works look like pantomime. . . . The inescapability of their works compels the change
of attitude which committed works merely demand."[39]

Whereas Benjamin points French Communists to Brecht in
the early 1930s, Adorno points West German *Bürger* to Beckett
in the early 1960s. Whereas Benjamin sees epic theater as a
model of committed art that is effective for turning art toward
socialism, Adorno sees epic theater as a type of committed art
that has become ineffective for transforming attitudes about

advanced capitalism. Decisive for Benjamin is Brecht's progressive position within the current mode of literary production. Decisive for Adorno is Beckett's uncompromising work in the context of literary consumption. Beckett offers stronger resistance than Brecht to the easy consumption that lubricates the engines of economic expansion. Certain autonomous works expose the hidden contradictions of advanced capitalism, and they do so more inescapably than committed works can.

In the post-Reagan era the positions of Benjamin and Adorno may seem equally inappropriate. Benjamin's techno-political optimism may seem naive, and Adorno's autonomist modernism may seem outdated.[40] Nevertheless, a central issue arises from their conflicting approaches to Brecht in two different situations. The issue concerns the connections between artistic import and political impact.

It would be a mistake to assume that *Aesthetic Theory* ignores these connections. On the contrary, they occasion some of Adorno's more provocative and obscure claims, such as that "art works are less and more than praxis" (358/342), or that their impact "operates at the level of remembrance" (359/343), or that "praxis is not the impact works have; it is the hidden potential of their truth content" (367/350). For now the issue may be put like this: Is there any sense in which the import (*Gehalt*) of artworks is genuinely political? Does either the import or the impact of artworks provide a precondition for the other? And are the criteria for an artwork's truth (*Wahrheitsgehalt*) artistic, political, or both? While seemingly distant from Trotsky's concerns about political appropriateness, effectiveness, and positioning, such questions are philosophical expressions of similar concerns in a significantly different context.

2.3 Aesthetic Modernism

To find artistic truth, Adorno turns to modern art. Picasso, Schönberg, and Beckett provide some of the clues for his search. Thus it is not surprising that astute commentators such as Richard Wolin and Thomas Huhn have interpreted *Aesthetic Theory* as a "defense of modern art."[41] The debate with Benjamin suggests, however, that Adorno would not simply defend modern art but subject it to a thorough critique. This expectation is confirmed in the chapter titled "Situation" (31–74/23–67), which the editors describe as "a philosophy of history of *modernité*" (543/498). There Adorno portrays modern art as providing a partial corrective to the ideological functions of mass mediated art. Because modern art also has ideological functions, however, he says "it becomes impossible to criticize the culture industry without criticizing art at the same time" (34/26). Moreover, he distinguishes within modern art between authentic and inauthentic works.

If there is a sense in which Adorno defends modern art, this must be understood as a response to various attacks. The main provocation comes from Georg Lukács, whose *Theory of the Novel* and *History and Class Consciousness* inspired Adorno's own writings on the arts. In a well-known review published in 1958, Adorno accused Lukács of reenacting Hegel's "reconciliation under duress."[42] Lukács replied that Adorno had moved into the "Grand Hotel Abyss" where "the daily contemplation of the abyss . . . can only heighten the enjoyment of the subtle comforts offered."[43] Beneath the sophisticated rhetoric, Adorno was calling the Hungarian Lukács a repressed political dupe, and Lukács was labeling the West German Adorno a self-serving nihilist. The occasion for these Cold War pleasantries was Lukács's *Realism in Our Time*,[44] published twelve years before Adorno's *Aesthetic Theory*. Adorno's polemical review illuminates his apparent defense of modern art and gives shape to the issue of aesthetic modernism.

In dispute, it would seem, are the relative merits of modernist and realist literature. Yet the conceptual and historical complications of "modernism" and "realism" obscure the nature and extent of this dispute. A terminological synopsis will help. Lukács distinguishes three main streams in twentieth-century literature: modernism, critical realism, and socialist realism, represented by Franz Kafka, Thomas Mann, and Maxim Gorki, respectively. Modernist literature is bourgeois literature that is characterized by ahistorical angst in the face of advanced capitalism. Critical realism, although ideologically bourgeois, displays sober optimism and does not reject socialism. Socialist realism is similarly historical and optimistic. Unlike critical realism, however, it employs a socialist perspective "to describe the forces working towards socialism *from the inside*."[45] Whereas critical and socialist realism can form a common front against the Cold War, modernism inadvertently supports the forces of destruction.

Adorno rejects this system of classification and tries to subvert it case by case. He touts "modernist" works as genuinely realistic, in the sense that they provide "negative knowledge" of sociohistorical reality. The supposed "worldlessness" of modern art, for example, is the dialectical truth about socially induced alienation.[46] Works classified as "critical realist" Adorno claims to be less "realist" and more "modernist" than Lukács thinks.[47] Adorno's tactic toward "socialist realism" is more direct. He says socialist realist works are historically out of date and technically regressive. Their regressiveness originates in backward social forces of production and serves to hide oppressive features of Soviet bloc countries.[48] In effect Adorno declares socialist realist works to be both less modern and less realistic than the "modernist" works Lukács condemns.

Clearly this dispute concerns both the political merits and the sociohistorical meaning of twentieth-century literature. The dispute becomes rather messy, however, because the descriptions and evaluations of such meaning employ contrasting methodologies.[49] For Lukács, the key to literary meaning is a literary worldview, which will always have profound formal ramifications. When he attacks modernism, he does so primarily because of its despairing worldview and secondarily because of the formal distortions stemming from this worldview. Neither the worldview nor the formal distortions are appropriate under modern conditions. For Adorno, by contrast, the key to literary meaning is the technique of individual works. When he rejects socialist realism, for example, he does so primarily because of its technical backwardness, and secondarily because of the ideological functions that such backwardness supports. Technically inferior and outdated works cannot be appropriate under modern conditions. Such methodological differences inform Adorno's frequent charges that Lukács has ignored form or technique, overemphasized the message or subject matter, imposed meaning on literary works, and failed to detect their true import (*Wahrheitsgehalt*). Contrasting emphases on world-view and technique serve contrasting approaches to literary meaning.

Permeating such methodological differences are substantial agreements as well as an even deeper conflict. Both authors believe that certain works and literary tendencies are more appropriate than others under modern conditions, and both consider such works to be authentic works of art. Both authors also assume that authentic works of art give us true knowledge of the contemporary sociohistorical totality; that artistic autonomy is a precondition for such knowledge; and that there is a sociohistorical totality, however fragmentary its surface may seem. What seems to unite them in all these ways, however, also generates their deepest conflict. This is a dialectic of reification and reconciliation, which generates two different stories of aesthetic modernism. A Lukácsian reply to Adorno's "Reconciliation under Duress" could be titled "Reification in Comfort." The point here is not that Adorno emphasizes reification while Lukács emphasizes reconciliation. Rather, the two authors have incompatible constructions of a historical dialectic between reification and reconciliation and of the place of modern art within it.

This is not the place to detail such constructions.[50] Suffice it to say, as Burkhardt Lindner has argued, that both Lukács and Adorno see advanced capitalism as a historical formation where the commodity form has permeated culture. "Reification" indicates the process and structure of this all-pervasive commodification. Because reification constitutes the central mechanism of all forms of alienation, disalienation requires the transcending of reification. Neither Lukács nor Adorno expects the working class in capitalist countries to propel this transcendence. Both of them treat certain autonomous works of art as privileged opponents of reification. Such works are "media of transparency" allowing recognition of the global structure and transformable character of alienation.[51]

For Lukács, realism provides the necessary art. Because of their worldview and form, realist works give access to the sociohistorical totality and penetrate reified social life under advanced capitalist conditions. Modernist literature must be rejected because of its reified worldview and reifying forms. Kafka and Beckett simply reinforce our ahistorical angst; they offer no perspective toward a socialist future. For Adorno, by contrast, modernism provides the requisite works. Certain modernist works have sufficient experiential depth and technical progressiveness to resist the commodification of consciousness and to expose the hidden contradictions of advanced capitalism. Modern literature must be endorsed, with suitable qualifications, because of its critical experience and technique. Works such as Beckett's *Endgame* provide a "precise, wordless polemic" against "a nonsensical world."[52] In this polemic resides the possibility of a fundamentally transformed society.

Adorno's own polemic against Lukács expresses both methodological and substantive concerns about aesthetic modernism. These become thematic in *Aesthetic Theory.* When Adorno calls the truth content of artworks "unconscious historigraphy" (286/274), he summarizes his own historiography of art. When he calls artistic truth content the "crystallization" of history (200/193), a philosophy of history crystallizes in his own aesthetics. His historiography of art rejects classifications à la Lukács in order to resist a specific sociohistorical formation. His philosophy of history oscillates between reification and reconciliation in order to undermine reification without supporting a premature reconciliation. The model in each case is the unconscious historiography and historical crystallization that Adorno finds in authentic works of modern art. At the same time Adorno's interpretation of such works follows a conscious history whose touchstone is the *Dialectic of Enlightenment.*

Adorno's approach to aesthetic modernism gives rise to methodological questions about the hermeneutic circle between modern art and his own philosophy of history. It also raises two substantive considerations. The first pertains to the dialectic of reification and reconciliation: What is the character and the extent of this dialectic in modern art? A second concerns historico-philosophical interpretations of the meaning of modern art: How are the concepts employed in such interpetations related to the sociohistorical process within which modern art has meaning? Here too the idea of truth is crucial. In some sense yet to be explored, Adorno locates the historical meaning of modern artworks in their carrying a truth that is itself historical. Their truth content is a "crystallization of history," and this crystallization constitutes their historical meaning.

The issues of artistic autonomy, political art, and aesthetic modernism intersect in Adorno's idea of truth. For Adorno, autonomy is an ambiguous precondition for truth in art. The political impact of artworks is the "hidden potential" of their truth content. And modern art has historical meaning as a damaged vehicle of historical truth. The intersection of these three issues gives rise to a fourth—the status of *Aesthetic Theory*. The title is obviously and deliberately ambiguous, provoking puzzles about the character of Adorno's project. The book's motto points ironically to Adorno's intention: in this work neither art nor philosophy should be lacking. Does this intention mean, as some have said, that Adorno wants to render philosophy artistic? Or does it mean, as others contend, that art is to be rendered philosophical? The solution one finds can shape an entire interpretation and critique of Adorno's text. A good way to look for clues is to consider why the text, like the title, resists interpretation. Such a consideration, to be undertaken next, exposes the philosophical motivations of Adorno's aesthetics.

3

Philosophical Motivations

Commentators often describe the difficulties of Adorno's writings. Martin Jay begins one discussion by frankly admitting that Adorno "would have been appalled" at an attempt "to render his thought painlessly accessible to a wide audience."[1] In a similar vein, Fredric Jameson asks:

What serious justification can be made for an attempt to summarize, simplify, make more accessible a work which insists relentlessly on the need for modern art and thought to be difficult, to guard their truth and freshness by the austere demands they make on the powers of concentration of their participants, by their refusal of all habitual response in their attempt to reawaken numb thinking and deadened perception to a raw, wholly unfamiliar real world?[2]

Gillian Rose prefaces her introduction to Adorno as follows:

Adorno's work, the most ambitious and important to have emerged from the Institute for Social Research before 1969, is the most abstruse, and . . . still the most misunderstood. This is partly a result of its deliberately paradoxical, polemical and fractured nature which has made it eminently quotable but egregiously misconstruable.[3]

Such descriptions help introduce readers to the intractable density of Adorno's thought.

Some problems in interpreting *Aesthetic Theory* can be attributed to the fact that it is a torso. Had Adorno lived to complete the book, the "Draft Introduction" would have been replaced; numerous passages now relegated to appendices would have been incorporated into the main text; and various infelicitous formulations and incomplete thoughts would have been revised.[4] Nevertheless significant obstacles would have remained, ones that match Adorno's intention and resemble difficulties in his other writings. There is no way around the paratactical presentation, dialectical logic, and phenomenological method of *Aesthetic Theory;* the author was writing a paratactical and dialectical phenomenology of (modern) art. Unless Adorno's readers understand the philosophical motivations of such features, his book will be susceptible to drastic misinterpretations.

3.1 Parataxis

The most obvious obstacles for readers in English are matters of translation. Such obstacles are reported in the first of Adorno's German books to appear in English. The title of the translator's preface tells the story: "Translating the Untranslatable." Samuel Weber says the concreteness of Adorno's style has little in common with the immediacy expected of contemporary English. Instead Adorno's concreteness has to do with "the density with which thought and articulation permeate each other." This density derives from the use of such resonant terms as *Geist, Sache, Erkenntnis, Begriff,* and *Aufhebung* for which English lacks fully meaningful equivalents. Also, in contrast to the dynamic potential of German sentence structure, contemporary English grammar "taboos long sentences as clumsy" and seeks "brevity and simplicity at all costs."[5] It seems, then, that the problems of interpreting Adorno's writing resemble those facing any English-language student of German philosophy.

Yet there may be a special reason why only two translators have tackled more than one book by Adorno. Apart from frequent allusions to various authors and events, the main reason for hesitation probably lies in Adorno's unusual stylistic strategies. Adorno himself discusses these strategies and his reasons for employing them. Indeed, Gillian Rose asserts that "Adorno discussed his method and style in everything he wrote, often at the expense of discussing the ostensible subject of the piece."[6] Among the devices Rose describes are impersonal and passive constructions, parallactic formulations, chiasmatic structures, and ironic inversion. She suggests that all of these strategies reflect a concern "to achieve a style which will best intervene in society."[7] This concern arises from Adorno's conviction that we live in an "administered world" in which conflicts are papered over and unmet needs repressed.

According to a frequently quoted passage from *Negative Dialectics,* true philosophy resists paraphrasing.[8] By itself, this statement is less striking than some commentators have thought. Its point is borne out whenever someone summarizes Kant's *Critique of Pure Reason* or Heidegger's *Being and Time.* Adorno's next claim is more controversial. He says the fact that most philosophy can be paraphrased speaks against it. Whether most philosophy can be paraphrased is a moot point, but the claim does say something about Adorno's own work. His writing deliberately resists easy consumption; the need for powerful expression weighs heavier than the desire for direct communication. Martin Jay is probably right; Adorno would have been appalled at attempts to render his thought painlessly accessible.

No less important than resisting easy consumption, however, is Adorno's desire to achieve a fit between the form and content of his philosophy. This desire helps explain why his unusual strategies culminate in *Aesthetic Theory*'s thoroughly paratactical presentation. The editors quote Adorno as follows: "My theorem that there is no philosophical 'first thing' is coming back to haunt me. . . . I cannot now proceed to construct a universe of reasoning in the usual orderly fashion. Instead I have to put together a whole from a series of partial complexes which are concentrically arranged and have the same weight and relevance. It is the constellation . . . of these partial complexes which has to make sense" (541/496). The resulting text is neither a systematic treatise nor a collection of essays, yet it is neither haphazard nor disjointed. *Aesthetic Theory* employs parataxis throughout: sentences, paragraphs, and entire chapters lie side by side without explicit coordination or subordination, and the topics of one part intersect those of others. In a way that resists easy explanation, the movement from one passage to another makes sense, despite Adorno's rejection of traditional patterns of philosophical writing. The text resembles a continually shifting constellation.

Adorno had explicit reasons for developing such a style. These are closely tied to his logic and methods, which will be discussed later. The main reason has to do with the philosophical theorem mentioned above. This theorem states that there is no first principle, no origin, no *arche* or Archimedean point from which philosophy may proceed. Although the theorem operates in all Adorno's writings on philosophy, it is fully elaborated for the first time in his book on Husserl (1956). Thereafter it undergoes frequent reformulation, whether in programmatic articles such as "The Essay as Form" (1958), "Ohne Leitbild" (1960), "Why Philosophy?" (1962), and "Parataxis" (1964), or in his book on Hegel (1963) and *Negative Dialectics* (1966).[9] Besides providing a clue for understanding Adorno's own writing, his rejection of first principles announces an opposition to logocentrism and foundationalism that links him with many pragmatist, poststructuralist, and feminist philosophers.

Adorno's book on Husserl makes clear that his theorem serves a metacritique of "idealist" epistemology whose ultimate target is Heideggerian ontology. By "idealism" Adorno means the affirmation of an identity between subject and object. This affirmation assigns constitutive priority to the epistemic subject. In Adorno's judgment, idealism has dominated Western philosophy since Descartes. It continues in Husserl's struggle against idealism and in Heidegger's attempt to return to a Being prior to the split between subject and object. Idealism is the modern form of "first philosophy," of philosophy that assigns primacy to one original principle, whether this be the epistemic subject or primordial Being.

Adorno makes two claims against first philosophy. The first, derived from Kant and Hegel, is that anything taken as first or original is already second or derivative simply by virtue of its being taken that way in a humanly constructed philosophy. We cannot jump out of our epistemological skin. Perhaps this is the force of the epigraph from Epicharmus in *Against Epistemology*: "A mortal must think mortal and not immortal thoughts."[10] The second claim, derived from Marx and

Nietzsche, is that every principle or structure elevated above the flux of appearances is inescapably historical. It is inescapably historical both because the principle comes to be elevated amid the push and pull of ongoing philosophical debate and because the act of elevating occurs within unavoidable social conflicts. Both claims can be summarized as follows: "The first and immediate is always, as a concept, mediated and thus not the first."[11]

Because no first principle is first, and because every supposedly first principle is inescapably historical, Adorno refuses to proceed from any first principle. Because he insists that a philosophy's presentation must match its claims, Adorno continually seeks a style that does not suggest a hierarchical derivation from first principles. The paratactical presentation of *Aesthetic Theory* stands at the end of this search. The consistent employment of parataxis represents not only a deliberate attempt to jar the reader but also a stylistic strategy to oppose "first philosophy." Just as Schönberg undermined the tonal center without embracing chance as an organizational principle, so Adorno has found a way to defy traditional philosophical styles without becoming merely rhapsodic. Just as Schönberg's compositions call for new ways of listening, *Aesthetic Theory* demands a new way of reading, one that continually circles back upon itself. The text requires what Adorno attributes to a proper reading of Hegel: both submersion in details and distance from them; following the flow while introducing ritardandos.[12] Readers of *Aesthetic Theory* soon discover the meaning of Adorno's favorite description of philosophy. It is, he says, "the labor of Sisyphus."[13]

3.2 Negative Dialectic

Adorno's opposition to first philosophy also affects the logic of his aesthetics. "Logic" refers not simply to the patterns, principles, or categories of Adorno's arguments but rather to all of these matters together with the substantive considerations behind them. "Negative dialectic," Adorno's own term, best indicates what I have in mind. Adorno's arguments are dialectical in the sense that they highlight unavoidable tensions between polar opposites whose opposition constitutes their unity and generates historical change. The dialectic is negative in the sense that it refuses to affirm any underlying identity or final synthesis of polar opposites, even though Adorno continually points to the possibility of reconciliation. The main oppositions occur between the particular and the universal and between culture in a narrow sense and society as a whole.

The tension between universal and particular occurs both in philosophy and in the phenomena philosophers interpret.[14] In philosophical aesthetics there is a tension between the need to employ universal concepts on the one hand, and the desire to honor particular facts on the other. The traditional ways to ease this tension have been through deduction or induction. Adorno thinks that neither approach does justice to conflicts among concepts, and that each overlooks important details: "If aesthetics is to avoid the extremes of positing prescription alien to art, on the one hand, and inconsequential classification of empirical data on the other, it must be dialectical. Speaking generally, one could define dialectical method as an endeavour to overcome the rift between deduction and induction so prevalent in reified thought" (510/471). Deductive aesthetics places art in a theoretical straitjacket, and inductive aesthetics turns "art" into a meaningless abstraction. What is needed is a dialectical aesthetics.

Adorno's description of the essay as a genre also summarizes the intentions of his dialectical aesthetics: "It is not unlogical; rather it obeys logical criteria in so far as the totality of its sentences must fit together coherently . . . The essay neither makes deductions from a principle nor does it draw conclusions from coherent individual observations. It co-ordinates elements, rather than subordinating them; and only the essence of its content, not the manner of its presentation, is commensurable with logical criteria."[15] *Aesthetic Theory* tries to maintain a circular movement between universal concepts and particular facts without turning concepts into mere generalities, without treating facts as mere examples, and without covering up tensions between concepts and facts.

Substantive justification for a dialectical approach comes from the "unconscious interaction" between universality and particularity within modern art. According to Adorno, modern art has taken a "radically nominalistic position" (521/480) in rejecting traditional forms and genres. This position even affects fundamental categories such as "art" and "the work of art." At the same time, however, modern art retains elements of universality. Anton Webern's compositions transform traditional sonata form into miniature "nodal progressions" (270/259–60). Indeed, "wherever art on its way to concreteness tries to eliminate the universal . . . this negation preserves what it ostensibly eliminates" (522/481). Artists and art critics cannot avoid using universal concepts such as "form" and "material," even though their contemporary meaning is far from clear (507/468).

Thus modern art calls for a philosophy that respects the particularity of artistic phenomena but illuminates the universal elements within art itself. Dialectical aesthetics tries to raise art's "unconscious interaction" between universality and particularity "to the level of consciousness" (270/259). It "deals with reciprocal relations between universal and particular where the universal is not imposed on the particular . . . but emerges from the dynamic of particularities themselves" (521/481). If the refusal to impose prescriptive universals places Adorno in opposition to deduction, the emphasis on reciprocal relations places him in opposition to inductive approaches. Dialectical logic is his alternative.

Adorno's justification for a dialectical approach calls into play the opposition between culture and society mentioned earlier. According to Adorno, quantitative exchange is the dominant principle in contemporary society. Deductivist and inductivist approaches tend to ratify this principle, whether by subsuming qualitatively different phenomena under a universal concept or by treating them as unrelated atoms. Like modern art, Adorno's aesthetics pursues a "utopia of the particular" (521/480) that places both art and aesthetics in conflict with traditional logic and an "exchange society." Yet Adorno also insists that modern art and his own philosophy belong to the social totality against which they struggle. It would be utopian in a bad sense to act as if the utopia of the particular has already arrived. A major task for Adorno's aesthetics is to show exactly how modern art and his own philosophy participate in the very society they oppose.

A key to this demonstration is the claim that the dialectic is not simply a cultural matter. The ongoing opposition between the universal and the particular is not simply a matter of philosophical argument, nor is it simply a tension within art: it permeates all of advanced capitalist society. In the words of *Negative Dialectics*, the dialectic is neither a purely conceptual method nor simply a real process nor a mere mishmash of argument and subject matter: "To proceed dialectically means to think in contradictions, for the sake of the contradiction once experienced in the thing [*Sache*], and against that contradiction. A contradiction in reality, [the dialectic] is a contradiction against reality."[16] When *Aesthetic Theory* speaks of "contradictions," it is not simply referring to logical incongruities that could be cleared up by more careful thought. Instead the reference is to unavoidable conflicts in a historical society that are brought to consciousness by philosophy and art. The latter oppose the society to which they belong. Indeed, within culture itself an unavoidable conflict occurs between Adorno's own philosophy and modern art. This conflict is intended to make us conscious of sociohistorical contradictions.

There are two obvious objections to such a construal of the dialectic. One is that by applying the same category of "contradiction" to so many distinct matters, Adorno has emptied it of any precise meaning. The other objection is that he has subsumed qualitatively different phenomena under a universal concept, contrary to his own intent. After all, is not dialectical philosophy supposed to be "the consistent consciousness of nonidentity"?[17]

Such objections, which Adorno addresses,[18] take us one step further into his understanding of negative dialectic. He does not deny that "contradiction" postulates an underlying identity between philosophical concepts and sociohistorical reality. These "are of the same contradictory essence."[19] He insists, however, that such identity must not be considered complete and irrevocable. Instead all "contradictions" are to be thought of with a view to their *possible* resolution. Philosophical concepts, sociohistorical reality, and their common "essence" are all open to transformation. Dialectical logic is not the final word: "In view of the concrete possibility of utopia, dialectics is the ontology of the wrong state of things. A right state of things would be free of dialectics: neither a system nor a contradiction."[20]

The emphasis on possible resolution sometimes prompts Adorno to suspend dialectical logic. His temporary suspensions are philosophical attempts to acknowledge the presence and possibility of what escapes the net of logic. Adorno attributes such attempts to the impact of Walter Benjamin, who bequeathed "the obligation to think dialectically and undialectically at the same time."[21] Dialectical logic must sometimes be suspended on behalf of the "nonidentical." There is a need to unite spontaneous experience and critical argumentation, even when experience threatens the consistency of an argument.[22]

Adorno's models for such thinking come from certain works of art. Their unification of spontaneity and formal rigor seems to refract the light of possible reconciliation upon a contradictory world.[23] When Adorno says "the paradoxes of aesthetics are those of its subject matter" (113/107), however, he is telling only half the story. The other half is Adorno's own "utopia of knowledge." His philosophy seeks to give thoughtful expression to the nonidentical without subsuming it under rigid categories. Unlike Wittgenstein, Adorno wants to say what cannot be said.[24] Unlike Heidegger, Adorno does not want this attempt to slide into nonphilosophical sayings. Despite artistic models, Adorno's thought does not purport to be artistic. It aims for the conceptual rigor of dialectical logic even while it suspends dialectical logic in order better to express what things would be like if freed of dialectic.

To think both dialectically and undialectically is a highly paradoxical endeavor. As a result, Adorno's "contradictions" come across as ones that may or may not turn out to be contradictory. The central paradox of *Aesthetic Theory*'s logic is that its argumentation seems to be both fundamentally contradictory and fundamentally paradoxical. The text tries to give shape to an overriding tension between real contradictions and possible reconciliation.

Adorno's book puts critical interpreters in an awkward position. Normally a dialectical argument leaves one with two options. Either one can reject the formal and substantive premises of dialectical logic and determine which insights are worthwhile despite the rejected premises. Or one can accept the premises of dialectical logic and determine whether the argument is consistent with these premises and correct in its substance. Adorno pulls the rug from under either stance. To the hostile critic, Adorno can always say that his book does not fully accept the premises of dialectical logic. To the sympathetic critic, Adorno can say that the book need not always be consistent with such premises. There is no graceful way to enter or leave Adorno's negative dialectic. Perhaps the best one can do is to grasp its substantive concerns, ask whether Adorno develops these concerns in a convincing manner, and consider what the central paradox of *Aesthetic Theory*'s logic does to the construal of its subject matter.

3.3 Critical Phenomenology

The methods of this construal can be described as those of a "critical phenomenology" inspired by Hegel and Marx. "Methods" refers to the characteristic procedures of Adorno's research and of its presentation. In this sense Adorno's methods must be distinguished from his "methodology," his own reflections on proper procedures. Some of these reflections suggest the absence of characteristic procedures in his philosophy. The essay on essays, for example, hints that Adorno's own work proceeds "methodically unmethodically."[25] Similarly, the "Draft Introduction" to *Aesthetic Theory* questions the legitimacy of stating a general methodology for work in aesthetics: "A methodology in the ordinary sense of the term . . . would fail to do justice to the relation between the aesthetic object and aesthetic thought. The only sound methodological imperative seems to be Goethe's: enter into works of art as you would into a chapel. . . . Method is . . . legitimated in its actual use, which is why it cannot be presupposed" (530/489). Yet such passages must not be taken at face value. Not only might some procedures characterize "methodically unmethodical" work, but, in Adorno's own words, to refuse to outline a general methodology "is to state some kind of methodology of one's own" (530/ 489). Besides, to claim that methods are legitimated in their actual use is philosophically insufficient. The "legitimate" use of a method does not in itself provide a philosophical rationale for that method. Philosophers still must determine what makes for legitimacy or illegitimacy in the use of methods.

The basis for Adorno's qualified "anti-methodism" is also the primary reason for describing his methods as phenomenological, namely, his devotion to particular phenomena as objects of investigation. The "Draft Introduction" rejects abstract methodologies because they emphasize methods at the expense of the subject matter for which methods are devised. Adorno's own methodological reflections usually occur within specific investigations of particular phenomena. Whereas Husserl called philosophy "back to the things themselves" only to write general studies on how to get there, Adorno takes the call so seriously that his methods seem embedded in the things themselves.

This embeddedness renders problematic an attempt such as Susan Buck-Morss's to isolate negative dialectic as a "method" and then present it "in action." Negative dialectic was never a mere method for Adorno, nor were his methods ones that could simply be "applied" as if they were indifferent to the subject matter at hand. He would have objected to the claim that his originality "lay not in the . . . substance of his theoretical arguments, but in the way he put them together." He would have found puzzling a critique that depicts his philosophy as primarily a method and then objects to it because his "method . . . became total."[26]

Nevertheless there are good reasons for trying, as Buck-Morss does, to abstract Adorno's methods from the text at hand. Otherwise Adorno's own "methodological imperative" could force his readers to suppress methodological questions until a specific investigation has proved unconvincing. It would be hard to raise general questions about his methods. This difficulty is compounded in Aesthetic Theory, as it is in Negative Dialectics. Neither book is simply about specific objects of investigation. Each book also addresses pertinent categories and criteria for philosophical inquiry, especially ones that are prominent in Adorno's own previous writings. At the same time Adorno engages in substantive analyses, whether of Heidegger, Kant, and Hegel in *Negative Dialectics,* or of selected philosophical positions and artistic phenomena in *Aesthetic Theory.* The text continually shifts across various levels of inquiry. Without some general understanding of Adorno's methods, readers quickly lose their way.

Some clues for orientation come from Adorno's own methodological comments. These help one reconstruct the intentions of his phenomenology. Whether the text fulfills his intentions is another question. Adorno envisions an aesthetics that combines "production-oriented experience and philosophical reflection" (498/460). Contemporary aesthetics must be as close to the phenomena as the practicing artist is, but it must have the conceptual energy to go beyond them without relying on a preconceived system. How can such an aesthetics be achieved? Adorno points to three methodological principles: to interpret art from a contemporary perspective, to historicize aesthetic norms, and to construct conceptual constellations. All three principles provide guidelines for a program of "determinate negation" in aesthetics.

Determinate Negation

Adorno's program of determinate negation is derived from the introduction to Hegel's *Phenomenology of Spirit.* Adorno wants to carry out this program more consistently than Hegel;[27] whether he does is debatable. It is clear, however, that he thinks the "phenomenology of anti-spirit"[28]—Marx's critique of capitalism—corrects Hegel's program. Moreover, Adorno thinks ideology has become all-pervasive and systematic in advanced capitalist society. Hence the context for Hegelian phenomenology has shifted. For Hegel, the true is the whole. Philosophy comprehends truth through determinate negation of partial truths. For Adorno, the current sociohistorical totality is the untrue.[29] Philosophy criticizes society through determinate negation of cultural phenomena as partial untruths. Every part of contemporary society, even philosophy, becomes an untrue part of the whole.

Determinate negation à la Adorno uncovers the untruth of various cultural phenomena, shows this untruth to be that of society as a whole, and helps phenomena refer beyond themselves to their possible truth in a transformed society. As part of an untrue totality, philosophy should not presume to have an absolute knowledge of the truth. Because all parts can refer to their possible truth, however, neither philosophy nor any other part is wholly untrue. Determinate negation is not simply negative criticism. Determinate negation remains what it was for Hegel—a process of disclosing truth. Truth itself is seen as a historical process rather than as a fixed criterion for the correctness of propositions.

Besides the shift in context, Adorno's program evinces another departure from Hegel. Whereas various epistemological positions undergo immanent criticism in Hegel's *Phenomenology*, Adorno suggests that art history proceeds in a similar fashion. The history of art is a process of determinate negation, with one work "criticizing" another and thereby suggesting larger issues of truth and falsity (59–60/52). This view of art history gives rise to Adorno's first methodological principle, the only one explicitly labeled in this way: "One methodological principle . . . is to try to shed light on all art from the perspective of the most recent artistic phenomena. . . . Just as, according to Valéry, the best features of the new correspond to an old need, so authentic modern works are criticisms of past ones. Aesthetics becomes normative by articulating these criticisms. . . . This kind of aesthetics would be able to deliver what aesthetics so far has only promised" (533/492). Such a principle of contemporaneity suggests both a retrospective and a prospective aesthetics.

On the one hand, Adorno's aesthetics has a retrospective character. The best way to understand artistic phenomena, whether recent or not, is from the needs articulated when the best modern works establish themselves in an objective "context of problems" (532/491). Thus, for example, *Aesthetic Theory* begins with the tendency in modern art to question its own legitimacy. From this tendency Adorno constructs a larger picture of modern art as the "social antithesis" of advanced capitalist society, and he develops the general thesis that the arts derive from a larger social process, oppose it, and point beyond it, all the while remaining within that process: "It is through its dynamic laws, not through some invariable principle, that art can be understood. It is defined by its relation to what is different from art. This other makes it possible for us to arrive at a substantive understanding of the specifically artistic in art. . . . [Art] evolves by segregating itself from its own matrix. Its law of motion and its law of form are one and the same" (12/4).[30]

On the other hand, Adorno's aesthetics has a prospective edge. Because the old needs remain, aesthetics must go beyond recent phenomena to consider what art could become in a society where those needs would be met: "Art and art works are what they may become. Aesthetic theory cannot rest content with an interpretation of existing works and their concepts. . . . In approaching the truth content of works, philosophical aesthetics goes beyond them" (533/491). Though aesthetics becomes normative by articulating the process of determinate negation from a contemporary perspective, authentic modern works are not completely normative for Adorno's aesthetics. They fall under a prospective light when he asks what the future holds for art, for society, and for currently definitive relationships between art and society. It is as if recent social history is a disclosure of untruth awaiting the disclosure of truth. Modern art serves to disclose sociohistorical truth through its own internal process of determinate negation. An aesthetic theory that wishes to articulate such truth would do well to concentrate on modern art.[31]

Historicism

Modern art throws into question the norms of traditional aesthetics. From this comes Adorno's second principle, namely to historicize aesthetic norms. Adorno asserts that traditional norms have become outdated and irrelevant. More appropriate norms cannot be invented de novo, however: previous philosophies make possible the very project of writing a contemporary philosophical aesthetics. Instead we need to recapitulate

in philosophy the sort of determinate negation that characterizes the history of art:

> In an age of conflict between contemporary art and traditional aes-
> thetics, a pertinent philosophical theory of art is compelled to con-
> ceptualize categories of perdition as categories of transition in
> determinate negation—to paraphrase a remark by Nietzsche. Modern
> aesthetics can take only one form, which is to foster the rational
> [*motivierte*] and concentrate dissolution of conventional aesthetic cat-
> egories. In so doing it releases a new truth content in these categories
> (507/468).[32]

Much of *Aesthetic Theory* can be read as an attempt to release
new and relevant meanings from traditional norms such as
"beauty," "expression," and "meaning."

Adorno's historicizing does not assume that traditional
norms never had genuine validity. Nor does it imply that their
validity is limited to the historical situations in which they arose.
In both these ways Adorno differs from many historical rela-
tivists. He assumes that the norms of traditional aesthetics had
genuine validity in their own day and can receive a new validity
today. The principle of historicizing requires that traditional
norms be tested and reformulated with an eye to an historical
process culminating in the current situation.

Adorno has three procedures, all closely related, for historicizing aesthetic norms: giving evidence of their historical
character, reconstructing philosophical debates, and confronting traditional concepts with the current sociohistorical situation. The first procedure is to demonstrate the transcience and
variability of traditional norms, especially ones like "beauty"
that philosophers since Plato have often regarded as timeless
universals. The key here is to show how the meaning of these
norms is deeply entangled with the art and society of a particular time: "In aesthetics there have emerged so-called eternal
norms, which in effect are without exception transitory products of becoming. They are dated precisely because they raise
such a claim to immutability in the first place" (529/488). The
concept of taste, for example, once the crux of Kant's aesthetics, quickly fell from philosophical favor after Hegel's tren-
chant criticisms, and it has met with increasing suspicion and

hostility among artists (509–510/470). Yet it continues to function in the consumption and criticism of art and cannot simply
be written off as an outmoded concept. In order to determine
its contemporary meaning and function, however, we need to
show that it is not a timeless concept for an invariant human
capacity. Instead, the tendency to think of taste in this way is
itself a product of the eighteenth century.[33]

Adorno's second historicizing procedure is to pit various
philosophical positions against each other in such a way that
they exercise mutual correction. From such reconstructed debates emerges a new understanding of central notions, which
Adorno then employs in their newly emergent meanings. Indeed, "there is only one way in which aesthetics can hope to
understand art today, and that is through critical self-reflection" (505/467). The main sources for Adorno's "self-reflection" are Kant and Hegel, mediated by Marx, Nietzsche, and
Freud, and brought closer still by Lukács and Benjamin. *Aesthetic Theory*'s critical appropriation of traditional German aesthetics is most clearly evident in chapters 6, 7, and 9, where
Adorno tries to move beyond Hegel and Kant by using each
to correct the other. He combines a Hegelian notion of art as
truth's semblance with a Kantian emphasis on the indeterminacy of specific works, but he criticizes both authors for misreading the collective subjectivity expressed in authentic works
of art.

The third procedure, implicit in the first two, is to confront
traditional norms with a "historico-philosophical analysis" (*ge-
schichtsphilosophischen Analyse*) of the situation of contemporary
art. The analysis finds its primary subject matter in the mani-
festos, programs, and slogans put forward by contemporary
artists:

History is intrinsic to the truth content of aesthetics. This is why it is
up to a historico-philosophical analysis of the historical situation to
bring to light what used to be regarded as an aesthetic *a priori*. The
watchwords . . . distilled from an analysis of the situation have greater
objectivity than the general norms to which they are said to be
accountable. . . . In confronting [traditional aesthetic categories with
an historical-situational analysis], one relates the dynamics of art and
[of] conceptualization to each other (530/489).

Although chapter 2 is Adorno's most direct commentary on
the situation of contemporary art, the confrontation between
traditional notions and his historico-philosophical analysis occurs throughout *Aesthetic Theory.*

Given Adorno's contemporary perspective, the historicizing
of aesthetic norms suggests that his aesthetics represents a
"construction of the modern."[34] This phrase captures his aims,
so long as two points are kept in mind. First, Adorno is not
providing a naive apology for modern art, but seeking to uncover its conflict and unity with advanced capitalism. His transformation of traditional aesthetics serves a social-critical
modernism. Second, Adorno's "construction of the modern" is
definitely a construction, and intentionally so. *Aesthetic Theory*
does not simply interpret modern art from within, even though
closeness to the phenomena is a programmatic concern. The
book also builds a conceptual environment with materials taken
from various disciplines and prepared for by Adorno's previous writings in philosophy and the social sciences. Indeed, the
third methodological principle at work in *Aesthetic Theory* is to
construct conceptual constellations.

Constellations

As Buck-Morss shows, Adorno's inspiration for constructing
constellations came from Walter Benjamin.[35] Yet Adorno's
principle is also a deliberate rewriting of a "central teaching"
in Hegel's *Phenomenology of Spirit.*[36] According to Adorno, Hegel saw that the phenomena to be interpreted are mobile and
internally mediated. When providing an interpretation, philosophers must keep their own concepts flexible. Adorno does
not want to attribute the mobility and mediation of the phenomena to the conceptual work carried out by the philosopher,
however. There is more to the phenomena than even the most
flexible concepts can grasp. Against Hegel's glorification of the
concept, Adorno sympathizes with the Husserlian aim to "in-
tuit" the essence within particular phenomena.[37]

Unlike Husserl, however, Adorno thinks of essences as intrinsically social and historical. They characterize a particular
society at a particular time, and they undergo development

within society. The meaning of "essence" in Adorno's philosophy is closer to Marx's concept of "objective tendencies" than either Hegel's or Husserl's concept of "essence." Adorno thinks of the essence within specific phenomena as a sedimented social prehistory and a possible social posthistory. Social history dwells both inside and outside a particular object. The object has become what it is within a larger sociohistorical process and in relationship to other objects, but this process and these relationships are intrinsic to the object's own identity.

The problem for such a conception is that historical phenomena resist conceptual definition, and the concepts of specialized disciplines suppress what is unique about particular objects. The constructing of conceptual constellations is a way of solving this problem. Adorno describes conceptual constellations as attempts to unlock the sociohistorical essence of particular objects without simply subsuming these under static universal concepts. Conceptual constellations are also attempts to disclose what the phenomena could still become if the current direction of society were transformed, a disclosure exceeding the scope of current concepts.[38] Only in relation to other concepts can a concept begin to approximate particular phenomena and their implicit social history. Constellations let concepts interrelate in such a way that both the sociohistorical essence of phenomena and their unique identities can emerge. A philosophical constellation provides conceptual mediations for mediations within the phenomena, but it refuses to equate conceptual and phenomenal mediations.

The conceptual constellations in *Aesthetic Theory* reflect Adorno's ambivalent attitudes toward Hegelian and Husserlian phenomenology. Hegel is praised for the "programmatic idea" that "knowing is giving oneself over to a phenomenon rather than thinking about it from above" (494/475), but his *Lectures on Fine Art* are criticized for imposing a "deductive system" on artistic phenomena (524/484). Husserl is credited with proposing a fruitful method that is neither inductive nor deductive, but phenomenological aesthetics is criticized for coming up with an "essence of art" that "has little interpretive power" (522/482). Instead of setting out on a wild goose chase for the original essence of art, Adorno proposes to think of artistic phenomena in "historical constellations": "No single isolated category captures the idea of art. Art is a syndrome in motion. Highly mediated in itself, art calls for intellectual mediation terminating in a concrete concept" (523/482).

In keeping with this proposal, Adorno refuses to define the concept of art with which he works. Instead he explains why the search for a straightforward definition is misguided: "The concept of art balks at being defined, for it is a historically changing constellation of moments" (11/3). We cannot derive the nature of art from its historical origins because the historical facts are indecisive. We cannot subsume the disparate historical facts under some ontological essence because no universal concept of art can accommodate the phenomenal plurality of "the arts." Nor can we distinguish neatly between the questions of historical origin and of ontological essence. The attempt to define art must simultaneously aim at both: "The definition of art does indeed depend on what art once was, but it must also take into account what has become of art and what might possibly become of it in the future" (11–12/3).

Adorno has reached an anti-essentialist conclusion like that of ordinary language philosophers, but for different reasons and with different implications.[39] Whereas Morris Weitz rejects traditional attempts at defining art because "art" is an "open concept" for which necessary and sufficient conditions cannot be specified, Adorno says such attempts are misguided because of the sociohistorical dynamic within both the phenomena and the concept of art. Whereas Weitz claims that at best we can generalize to a set of "family resemblances" among the things labeled "art," Adorno holds we must construct a constellation of concepts to illuminate the shifting contours of a continually unfolding phenomenon. Traditional attempts at defining art must be transformed into a dialectical phenomenology.

In *Aesthetic Theory* concepts once used to define art, such as imitation, semblance, and form, become a complex net for catching art's dynamic structure without killing it. The sociohistorical content of these concepts becomes evident, and each concept takes on new meaning in the context of the others. Similar observations could be made about Adorno's approach to what analytic aestheticians might call "metacriticism": the discussion of concepts of art criticism such as intention and meaning in chapter 8, the "thoughts on a theory of the art work" in chapter 9, and the examination of art historiographical terms such as genre and style in chapter 11.

Just as Adorno's paratactical presentation demands a circular reading of *Aesthetic Theory*, and just as negative dialectical logic requires a grasp of Adorno's substantive concerns, so his phenomenological methods force readers to consult their own experience of modern art and society. There is hardly any other way to check the results of his modernist, historicizing, and constructive approach. Given the methodological intentions of *Aesthetic Theory*, it will not do simply to attack Adorno's apparent blindness toward non-Western art or toward Western art from before the eighteenth century. Nor will it suffice to object that Adorno's own norms are not timeless universals or that his concepts are not clearly defined. One must test the fruitfulness of Adorno's methods for interpreting the phenomena in question.

The need to consult experience does not excuse arbitrary judgments, however. To function as a proving ground, experience must be informed by philosophical reflections on modern art and society, as Adorno himself recognizes (513–20/473–79). At stake in reading *Aesthetic Theory* is neither simply the acceptability of Adorno's approach nor merely the correctness of specific assertions. At stake is what Adorno would call the "truth content" of the entire text and, by implication, the truth content of our own reading.

There are no guarantees that *Aesthetic Theory* will be read aright. It should be apparent, however, that Adorno's ambiguous title points to neither a straightforward aestheticizing of theory nor a direct intellectualizing of art. His text does not try to turn philosophical aesthetics into an elaborate work of art, and it does not aim to reduce art to Adorno's own philosophical claims. At the same time, however, the book intends to mediate between the implicit truth content of art and the explicit truth claims of philosophy, and to do so in a way that confronts readers with both the perils and the promise of contemporary society. It is appropriate, then, for the next four chapters to examine how Adorno's aesthetics situates art in society, production, politics, and history. This will provide multiple entries to his account of artistic truth and prepare the way for an evaluation of his contributions to philosophical aesthetics.

II
Commentary

4

Society's Social Antithesis

Adorno's *Aesthetic Theory* provides a sustained meditation on the social significance of autonomous art under advanced capitalist conditions. Hence the issue of artistic autonomy is fundamental to his aesthetics. As is clear from the debate with Walter Benjamin, Adorno's position on this issue is both complex and controversial. It involves a theory of the social preconditions of artistic autonomy, an argument for the social significance of autonomous art, and an explanation of how autonomy contributes to art's social significance. To sort out Adorno's position, I shall begin by locating his model of art's social mediation in the Marxist tradition.

Two preliminary points need to be made. First, some twentieth-century philosophers of art ignore the social mediation of art or question the legitimacy of emphasizing social mediation. For this reason alone *Aesthetic Theory* cannot avoid being controversial, as are other versions of what Marcia Eaton calls "contextualism."[1] Second, controversies about contextualism occur within a common framework forged in the eighteenth century—what Peter Bürger calls the institution of autonomous art. Both aesthetics and the sociology of art have developed within the institution of autonomous art, and both have contributed to it. Conflicts between romanticism and realism, between aestheticism and moralism, and between formalism and contextualism take place within this institution. To reject *Aesthetic Theory* because it insists on social mediation would be to misunderstand the historical context of recent philosophies of art. A sociological aesthetic à la Adorno is no more a historical aberration than is a formalist aesthetic à la Clive Bell, although this says little about the validity of either approach.

4.1 Marxist Models

Among philosophies that emphasize the social mediation of art, two types of theories have become dominant. In the first type, tendencies within art provide the main locus for social mediation. Theories of this type try to show how such internal tendencies intersect nonartistic tendencies. This is the *internalist* paradigm. In the second type of theory, the *externalist* paradigm, agencies outside art are the dominant locus for social mediation. Externalist theories try to demonstrate how such agencies make for a distinctive interaction between art and other regions of culture and society. While both paradigms are compatible with Marxism, Adorno's model of social mediation can best be located on the internalist side of the Marxist tradition in aesthetics.

Internalism

The Marxian model of art's social mediation relies heavily on a general theory of social formations. It is problematic to speak of "the Marxian model," since Marx and Engels never propounded a comprehensive philosophy of art. To the extent that their scattered comments on art imply a model, however, this incorporates a distinction between base and superstructure from a general theory of social formations. Equally important is the concept of ideology. Although explaining these matters in detail would entangle us in endless debates among the interpreters of Marx, a brief summary will help define Adorno's model.

The preface to *A Contribution to the Critique of Political Economy* summarizes Marx's historical materialist theory for understanding social revolutions.[2] A social revolution transforms an entire social formation, he says. This transformation takes its dynamic from a growing conflict between forces of production and relations of production within the prevailing mode of production. At the same time, the dynamic pervades the society's "legal and political superstructure" as well as its "forms of social consciousness." Marx's thesis is that the critical historian of social revolutions must distinguish conflicts between productive forces and relations from ideological battles in which people become conscious of these conflicts and fight them out.

Here Marx distinguishes a society's technological and economic mode of production from social institutions, such as governments, and cultural regions of conflict, such as philosophy, religion, and art. Translated into the familiar terms of base and superstructure, Marx's distinction locates the forces and relations of production in the base. Other institutions and cultural regions make up the superstructure of a society. It is debatable whether this gives an accurate picture of Marx's actual studies. Commentators agree, however, that in opposition to Hegelian idealism, including that of his own youth, Marx wishes to proceed from the economic ground up, so to speak, and not from the cultural sky down. Marx's historical materialism implies that conflicts within art must be examined in terms of conflicts within the technological and economic base.

Although Marx posits a connection between art and ideology, his writings leave the character of this connection as open-ended as his concept of ideology. Three construals of the connection are plausible. The first equates ideology with forms of social consciousness. These are a "necessary illusion" allowing battles to be fought whose deep structure remains somewhat hidden to the combatants. On this construal, all art is ideological.[3] A second version regards ideology as the expression and defense of the interests of the dominant class. During revolutionary times such ideology is "false consciousness," not because it is simply wrong-headed, but because it suppresses the class's vulnerability in the struggle over the means of production. In this version, art is ideological only to the extent that it expresses and defends dominant class interests.[4] On a third reading, "ideology" designates those dimensions within social consciousness which obscure the underlying tendencies and conflicts in a social formation. Ideology critique lets social consciousness disclose the underlying struggle and its likely outcome. On this reading, all art can have both ideological and nonideological dimensions, regardless of its class interests and origins. This third construal is closest to Adorno's conception of art and ideology.

All three interpretations are compatible with an internalist paradigm of art's social mediation. Any one of them can encourage an examination of the ways in which tendencies within art intersect tendencies within other forms of social consciousness and within a society's mode of production. Yet the categories and methods of this examination are topics for debate. There are several different ways to analyze tendencies within art and to demonstrate how these intersect nonartistic tendencies. Marxists who share an internalist paradigm have developed various accounts, all of them plausible readings of Marx.

Three versions of the internalist paradigm stand out in the history of Marxism. Jameson's discussion of Althusser suggests labeling these as mechanical, expressive, and structural.[5] Mechanical accounts try to show that artistic phenomena are decisively linked to economic factors, even though these phenomena must also be understood on their own terms. The writings of Plekhanov provide clear examples of this approach. Expressive and structural accounts take distance from the economism that easily accompanies a mechanical approach. Expressive accounts attempt to show that artistic phenomena express or reflect not simply the economic base as such, but the inner principle or dynamic of an entire social formation. Such demonstrations characterize the writings of Georg Lukács. Structural accounts, which the Althusserians best exemplify, insist that the structure of the whole consists in the specific combination of its various elements. This structure affects all its elements, not in the sense in influencing them or coming to expression in them, but in the sense of existing and operating within them in their specific combination. To give a structural account of artistic phenomena is to find their unique and necessary location within what Jameson calls "the synchronic system of social relations as a whole."[6]

Adorno's model of social mediation is an internalist theory that encourages expressive accounts of artistic phenomena. His debate with Benjamin in the 1930s occurs within the shared framework of expressive causality, even when he accuses Benjamin of paying insufficient attention to mediation. The main theoretical difference is not the absence or presence of mediation but the manner in which the artistic part expresses the societal whole.

Benjamin's "The Author as Producer" and his "Work of Art" essay posit a parallelism between an artistic mode of production and reception, on the one hand, and a more narrowly economic mode of production and consumption, on the other. What happens in the artistic mode has analogues in the economic mode; artistic transformations will have counterparts in the economic base. Such parallelism, a Leibnizian strain, helps explain Benjamin's technological optimism toward mass media and his political enthusiasm for Brechtian theater. Benjamin expects a transformation in "literary relations of production" to be accompanied by transformation in economic relations of production. For authors who follow Benjamin's lead, a central problem will be to give a systematic description of the relationship "between art as production and art as ideological."[7]

The reference to Leibniz is not accidental. The concept of a "monad" is central to Benjamin's model of social mediation. Adorno inherits this Leibnizian concept from Benjamin but replaces its parallelist connotations with an emphasis on contradictions. Whereas Benjamin traces an homology between artistic and economic modes of production and consumption, Adorno pursues tensions within the work of art that give expression to tensions in society as a whole. The work of art is a monad whose internal tensions express the larger sociohistorical process (14–19/6–11, 349–53/335–37).

Adorno's model of social mediation owes no less to a general social theory than does the base/superstructure distinction. Critical theory's peculiar conjunction of culture, polity, and economy has already been noted, as has the prominence critical theorists give to cultural studies. Critics find these matters problematic, whether because critical theory loses the specificity of Marx's theory of social formations (Therborn), overestimates the internal homogeneity of advanced capitalist societies (Held), or appeals to a critical public for whose existence critical theorists cannot account (Connerton). To understand Adorno's model of social mediation one must consider why the critical theorists developed their much-criticized conjunction of culture, polity, and economy. Their reasons have to do with a structural shift in capitalism. More specifically, Adorno's social theory revises Marx's critique of commodity fetishism and Lukács's theory of reification in order to understand a pervasive commodification of culture under advanced capitalist conditions.

Commodity Fetishism

Marx directs his critique of commodity fetishism against bourgeois economists who accept the capitalist system as given and simply describe its surface operations. The economists relate how money and capital function without really understanding why. Marx says bourgeois economists are not simply mistaken about capitalism. In fact, their theories provide a somewhat accurate description of the capitalist system. Yet such theories are superficial, and their superficiality is itself a function of capitalism's commodity fetishism.

"The Fetishism of Commodities and the Secret Thereof"[8] marks a transition in *Capital* from Marx's dialectical phenomenology of the commodity to a critical analysis of money and its transformation into capital. Whereas bourgeois economists cannot explain how money begets additional money, Marx discovers that transforming money into capital is less magical than pulling a rabbit out of an empty hat. The trick occurs as soon as labor power is purchased at a price that matches its exchange value for the wage laborer but falls short of the exchange value it generates for the capitalist.[9] The law for exchanging commodities is followed on both sides of the labor contract, yet the law operates to the advantage of the buyer, who owns the means of production. Neither seller nor buyer is cheated, yet the buyer comes out on top. Capital is extracted as surplus value from the labor of the working class. There is an inequity in equity; there is domination in free exchange.

To expose this antinomy in exchange is Marx's main goal when he begins his dialectical phenomenology of commodities. People in all societies must produce things to sustain human life. How this occurs varies with a society's mode of production. In a capitalist society, the production of life-sustaining goods occurs by way of exchange among independent owners of the means of production. According to Marx, the commodity is the form products take when production is organized in this manner. When a capitalist mode of production arises, products begin to be produced primarily as commodities, and producers start relating to one another primarily by way of commodities and thus by way of exchange. As Marx writes in his preface, "the commodity-form of the product of labour . . . is the economic cell-form" in bourgeois society.[10]

The commodity form is a Janus-faced creature. On the one hand, the commodity has the power to satisfy human wants. It is a useful thing, a "use value." On the other hand, the commodity has the power to command other use values in exchange. It is an exchangeable thing, an "exchange value." To be exchangeable one for the other, however, commodities must all have something in common. This common substance is what Marx calls their "value," which manifests itself in the exchange values commodities have when they are exchanged. Any product can be a use value by satisfying human needs; nothing can be a value without being useful; but commodities are use values by way of exchange. Commodity A becomes an exchange value for its owner in relation to commodity B, which is a use value that the owner of commodity A wants to acquire. Only by serving to procure commodity B does commodity A gain a use value for its owner. A similar relation holds in reverse for commodity B and its owner. The two owners relate through exchange. In this exchange each commodity can be thought to contain a certain amount of value.

Next Marx asks what underlies this common value, for which exchange value is the only form of expression. According to his labor theory of value, value is created by the expenditure of labor power. The measure of value in a commodity-producing economy is the average amount of labor time that is socially necessary to produce exchangeable commodities. The ideological effect of such an economy, however, is to make it hard to see labor as the common source of all value. In a society where exchange has become predominant, human labor and its features come to be seen as relations and features of the commodities people produce. Products become enigmatic fetishes, not simply for bourgeois economists, but for everyone who lives and works in a capitalist society.

According to Marx, the fetish character of commodities is inextricable from the commodity form itself. Although the labor expended in producing commodities is social labor, it appears to producers themselves as a private effort to satisfy their individual wants and needs. This appearance is unavoidable, since commodities are produced not in order to be directly consumed but in order to be exchanged, whether for wages or for profit. In the same way, although complex social relations actually bind various producers together in one society, these relations appear to the producers themselves as the impersonal and uncontrollable forces of the market where their commodities are exchanged. This appearance of impersonality is also unavoidable, since few can survive in such a society without producing commodities to be exchanged.

As a result of such necessary appearances, commodities come to seem like things that have a life of their own, quite apart from the social labor that produced them, and exchange relations among commodities come to seem like social relations in their own right, quite apart from the human interactions that sustain them. Commodities are like the gods of the religious world: "In that world the productions of the human brain appear as independent beings endowed with life, and entering into relation both with one another and the human race. So it is in the world of commodities with the products of [human] hands. This I call the Fetishism which attaches itself to the products of labour, so soon as they are produced as commodities, and which is therefore inseparable from the production of commodities."[11] Commodity production makes relations between people become confused with relations to things, and it makes the life of human laborers become confused with the power of human products.

Marx exposes this "fetishism of commodities." He shows that commodities would not be values of a definite size if the same abstract labor power were not expended for definite lengths of time by private producers who interrelate by exchanging their products. For Marx, commodities are constituents of a social formation in which the process of production masters human beings while human beings have not mastered the process of production.[12] The fetishism of commodities will not disappear, either in economics or in daily life, until society changes into "a community of free individuals, carrying on their work with the means of production in common, in which the labour-power of all the different individuals is consciously applied as the combined labour-power of the community."[13] Socialism will eliminate the fetishism of commodities by replacing capitalist commodity production with a new mode of production. In the early twentieth century, however, Marxists faced hard questions about the possibilities of this new mode of production once industrialization and mechanization had accelerated and entrepreneurial capitalism had given way to monopoly capitalism.

Reification

Such questions emerge with particular clarity and force in "Reification and the Consciousness of the Proletariat," the central chapter of Lukács's *History and Class Consciousness*. Lukács weds Marx's critique of capitalism with Max Weber's theory of rationalization, thereby extending Marx's analysis of commodity fetishism into a theory of reification. Lukács says that the riddle of the commodity form is "the central structural problem" not merely of the capitalist economy but "of capitalist society in all its aspects." The commodity form is the "universal structuring principle" for all forms of objectivity and subjectivity in capitalist society.[14]

Lukács's emphasis on the social centrality of the commodity form prompts the leading question of his discussion: "How far is commodity exchange together with its structural consequences able to influence the *total* outer and inner life of society?"[15] His answer begins with Marx's description of commodity fetishism. Then Lukács shows that commodity fetishism manifests itself not only in production but also in social institutions such as law, administration, and journalism as well as in academic disciplines such as economics, jurisprudence, and philosophy. The influence of commodity exchange comes to seem very widespread, leaving hardly any area of life untouched.

"Reification" is Lukács's term for phenomena evidencing this pervasive influence. "Reification" also refers to the structural process whereby the commodity form permeates life in capitalist society. The process has both objective and subjective sides. The objective side is an extension of the necessary illusion that commodities have lives and relations of their own: human properties and relations come to seem like the properties and relations of things that, though made by human beings, appear as independent determinants of human life. The subjective side to reification is an extension of the fact that commodity production forces human labor power to operate as a commodity over which the laborer has no control: human beings come to seem like mere things obeying the inexorable laws of the marketplace.

It is with the subjective side that Lukács is most concerned, not only because the structure of reification has been sinking ever "more deeply, more fatefully and more definitively" into human consciousness,[16] but also because the key to unmasking reification lies in the consciousness of the proletariat. Lukács describes proletarian class consciousness as the revolutionary "self-consciousness of the commodity."[17] Unlike other classes, the proletariat has an aspiration toward totality and an orientation toward transformative praxis. Through this aspiration, the phenomena of reification are unmasked for what they really are; through the proletariat's practical orientation, the grip of the commodity form can be broken.

With the rise of fascism in the 1930s, followers of Marx and Lukács faced a new worry about the transformation of capitalist commodity production. This concerns the potential for transformative praxis once wage laborers become "integrated" into capitalist society, and monopoly capitalism turns into a "state capitalism" that fuses political and economic power even more tightly. It is in this context that critical theorists undertake a significant revision of Marx and Lukács and that Adorno develops his own approach to the social mediation of art.

4.2 Art and Ideology

Like Marx, Adorno treats the commodity form as fundamental to a capitalistic mode of production, but without providing a detailed analysis of the commodity form as such. Like Lukács, Adorno extends Marx's critique of political economy into a critique of contemporary culture and social institutions, but without emphasizing the subjective side of reification. Although Adorno does not underestimate the extent to which the commodity form permeates contemporary culture, neither does he overemphasize the need to criticize reified consciousness as such. Instead he looks for the relations of production that govern society and dictate reification.[18]

Cultural Commodification

Adorno's emphasis on relations of production surfaces in his analysis of how musical listening has regressed.[19] His seminal essay on contemporary musical life ties this sphere of distribution and consumption to a dominant characteristic of capitalist production. The regression of listening is derived from the fetish character of music itself, and the fetish character of music is treated as one manifestation of a pervasive commodity form. What manifests itself is not simply the pervasiveness of the cultural commodification, however, but a shift in the commodity form. The shift shows up what Thorstein Veblen called "conspicuous consumption."[20] Adorno revises Lukács's theory of reification to account for this shift.

As Gillian Rose points out, Adorno's theoretical innovation is to anchor his critique of cultural commodification in Marx's theory of value, especially in the distinction between use value and exchange value.[21] Adorno argues in 1938 that the commodity character of music has changed. During earlier stages of capitalism, the musical commodity had both use value and exchange value, and these were somewhat distinct. Music was produced to be purchased, and it was purchased to be enjoyed. It became a use value by way of exchange. Now, however, the musical commodity no longer simply becomes a use value by way of exchange. When the culture industry takes control of musical life, pure exchange value first *replaces* the use value of the musical commodity and then itself seems to be immediately enjoyable. Cultural industrial production destroys use values and then presents exchange value as an enjoyable use value. The concert-goer no longer buys a ticket in order to enjoy the music: "The consumer is really worshipping the money that he himself has paid for the ticket to the Toscanini concert. He has literally 'made' the success which he reifies and accepts as an objective criterion, without recognizing himself in it. But he has not 'made' it by liking the concert, but rather by buying the ticket."[22] The abstractions of an "enjoyable" exchange value underlie the listener's absent-minded pseudo-pleasure. A shift in musical production underlies the regression of listening. This shift manifests a large-scale realignment in capitalist commodity production.

It is because Adorno connects musical phenomena with a realignment in commodity production that he has a harsher view of the mass media than Walter Benjamin. Benjamin's optimism toward new cultural technologies is based on the democratic tendencies of mass perception.[23] Driven by mass perception and reinforcing it, the new technologies have emancipatory potential, unlike auratic works for bourgeois contemplation. Adorno's criticisms of technological optimism are based on a structural shift in the capitalist mode of production and a concommitant change in art's social role.[24]

Adorno sees a twofold significance in musical fetishism and regression. First, they help advanced capitalism consolidate as a total system whose effects burrow ever more deeply into our psychic structure. Second, the solidified system and its psychic effects severely restrict the emancipatory potential of new cultural technologies as well as of oppositional groups within the system. Mass mediated art is now subject to the same economic processes as any other commodities. Moreover, because these processes let exchange values appear as use values, art loses much of its ability to challenge the dominance of exchange value. Art has become a social glue made by the same companies producing other commodities. Hence the traditional Marxist concept of art as ideology no longer directly applies, the distinction between base and superstructure loses its clarity, and optimism about productive forces becomes unwarranted.

Shifts in Ideology

According to the theory of advanced capitalism developed by critical theorists in subsequent years, the base, the superstructure, and their interrelation have changed in ways that make the base its own ideology, as it were.[25] Though most obvious in a fascist state such as Nazi Germany, these changes take place wherever monopolies supersede the "free" market and governments drastically intervene in the economy, as occurred in New Deal America.[26] Advanced capitalism brings a tighter fusion of economic and political power, and this fusion disguises itself through the substitution of exchange value for use value in commodity production. As a result, cultural phenomena no longer have the same status as ideological components in the superstructure of bourgeois society. Ideology's position and function shift in relation to realignments in capitalist production.

During Marx's lifetime, says Adorno, cultural phenomena became independent from the social process to which they belonged. In their independence they could correctly make their own claims to truth, even though they wrongly denied their own socioeconomic moorings. Ideology was both true and false, the objectively necessary justification of a problematic social situation. Since Marx's day, however, ideology has changed. Because exchange and domination have become more closely entwined, doubts can scarcely arise about the discrepancy between formal political equality and actual economic exploitation. Rather than justify indirect domination, ideology now lets people be directly dominated in their conscious and unconscious experience.

This shift in the position and function of ideology affects both popular and autonomous art, as Adorno insisted in his criticisms of Walter Benjamin's technological optimism.[27] Popular music and Hollywood movies simply confirm the status quo. "Ideas" and "norms" are manufactured and imposed. Mass cultural commodities duplicate rather than challenge social reality, for they lack the illusory but substantial autonomy that lets truth claims be made.[28] Not even autonomous art, which continues classical ideology, has escaped shifts in the position and function of ideology: "Compared to the catastrophic processes in the depth structures of society, culture has assumed an ephemeral, attenuated, impotent quality. . . . Together with the crisis of civil society, the traditional concept of ideology seems itself to be losing its objective referent. Culture is being split up into critical truth, which divests itself of illusion but is esoteric and alienated from the immediate interplay of social forces, and managerial administration of what once was ideology."[29] The products of the culture industry are purely immanent parts of social reality. They obscure reality and do not become substantially true. In protest, autonomous artworks are increasingly alienated monads. They express and criticize reality, but often their truth goes unheard, partly because the culture industry plugs our ears. Furthermore, both the culture industry and autonomous art tend to ignore the social changes that are needed to achieve genuine freedom.[30]

Yet the two extremes of ideology do not become identical. "Good" and "bad" reification can still be distinguished.[31] The culture industry promotes effortless diversion, hypostacizing the immediate and prefabricating schemata for experience. Autonomous art elicits extreme concentration, providing a mediated experience and thereby anticipating the social subject (*Gesamtsubjekt*) whose development would spell liberation. Adorno tries to expose not only "the ways in which the conditions and constraints of the capitalist process of production became *introjected* by those who are subject to its power"[32] but also the ways in which autonomous art criticizes such constraints and their introjection.

Social Physiognomy

Shifts in ideology necessitate revisions in ideology critique. Just as the role of ideology changes with the arrival of advanced capitalism, so too Adorno's critique of ideology envisions three additional goals for social transformation: true use value must be achieved, experience must be liberated from the internalized constraints of capitalism, and, somehow, the truth in authentic art must be actualized in society. Yet the underpinnings of Marx's critique of ideology remain intact. Ideology critique continues to presuppose a division between manual and intellectual labor and the formation of classes needing to justify the status quo. Ideology is still criticized in relation to a dialectic between productive forces and relations of production, even though material production itself turns into ideology, and even though consciousness becomes a mere cog in the socioeconomic machinery.

There is a peculiarity, however, in Adorno's essay on the fetish character of music and in *Dialectic of Enlightenment*'s chapter on the culture industry.[33] Adorno's critique of cultural commodification does not engender a thorough examination of the process of production in advanced capitalism. He seems content to uncover the dominant relations of production within cultural commodities and individual experience. He analyzes cultural commodities in order to criticize the political economy, and he uses Marx's critique of capitalism in order to evaluate cultural commodities.

According to some critics, the absence of an exact analysis of the economic mode of production means that Adorno's critique of ideology loses its point. Christel Beier, for example, charges that, by making exchange a sociocultural paradigm, Adorno neglects the unequal exchange that constitutes "the specific presupposition of capitalistic sociation."[34] This charge is not really warranted. Just as Adorno unmasks identity because it masks nonidentity, so he opposes the principle of exchange precisely because it allows the covert appropriation of surplus value. Just as he aims for an identity beyond identity, so he wants the principle he opposes to be actualized in a nonexploitative exchange that would be beyond exchange.[35] Not even Adorno's concentrating on philosophy and art rather than on political economy can be written off as an elitist misinterpretation of Marx. Marx himself continued to interpret the world once he had established that the point was to change it. Though Adorno often interprets the world within philosophy and art, his interest, like Marx's, lies in moving beyond the antinomy of exchange. Adorno retains Marx's hope for a transformation of capitalist commodity production.

This hope has become unsettled, however. The revolutionary working class, Marx's real agent for demythologizing the commodity, has lost its potential, to be succeeded, it seems, by autonomous cultural commodities. Abstract exchange has extended so far that the theorization of society requires a critical phenomenology of cultural products. Indeed, the converging of reality and ideology seems to prompt a concomitant fusing of political economics, social theory, and cultural critique. Adorno criticizes cultural criticism. To avoid absolutizing economics, however, his social theory assimilates a critique of culture. Since the base has become its own ideology, this critique of culture turns into a physiognomy of society.[36] Adorno thinks that the essence (*Wesen*) of society can be disclosed in a more telling way from somewhat isolated regions of culture such as art, philosophy, and individual experience than from the economic mode of production.

The essence to be disclosed is a consolidated version of the politico-economic *Unwesen* discovered by Marx. For Adorno, advanced capitalist society amounts to a process of domination in exchange, a process whose structure abstractly dominates all members of society. His critique of cultural commodification appeals to a theory of domination. To understand that theory is to understand the significance of autonomous art for Adorno's social critique and utopian vision.

4.3 Advanced Capitalism and Autonomous Art

Adorno sees society as a diachronic and synchronic process.[37] Like Marx, he emphasizes the laws of movement that unify society and govern the functions of individuals, institutions, and situations within society.[38] Though historical mobility makes the concept of society hard to define, society displays a definite structure in each historical phase. The static and dynamic dimensions of society are Hegelian poles of being and becoming, with each implying the other.[39] New tendencies flow from the consolidated historical constituents of the entire social system, and these constituents become visible in the light of new social tendencies.[40] Tendencies crisscross the categories of history to date, the perennial but alterable "existential categories" of "prehistory": "domination, bondage, suffering, and ever-present catastrophe."[41] Such crisscrossing poses a double task for Adorno's social physiognomy. He must read contemporary trends from particular phenomena, and he must discover how the categories of a negative ontology surface in society's latest phase.

Domination in Exchange

One category is especially prominent: the concept of domination (*Herrschaft*). For Adorno, new social tendencies necessitate a greater emphasis on domination than is found in Marx. If society is a unitary process, then a dynamic theory of society must change its emphasis when political institutions marry economic institutions and society adopts meta-economic forms of domination. A social theory that pays close attention to economic power, as Marxism does, cannot emphasize purely economic processes once economic power is not merely mediated through economic exchange. Greater stress must fall on the concept of domination.[42] By taking seriously totalitarian tendencies in contemporary society, Adorno seems to be radicalizing rather than abandoning Marx's critique of political economy.

At the same time, Adorno's concept of domination seems ambiguous. The ambiguity shows up in conflicting interpretations of his social theory. Whereas some read Adorno's "domination" as referring to social oppression, others think it refers primarily to technological mastery of nature.[43] Simply charging him with ambiguity will not do, however, nor will it suffice to argue against Adorno that power to influence or control (*Macht*), power to force or enforce (*Gewalt*), power to govern or rule (*Herrschaft*), and power the master (*Beherrschung*) are not the same, or that formative power over things (*Sachkultur*) differs from formative power toward people (*Personenkultur*). The crux of his critique is the thesis that all these kinds of power have become tightly concentrated in advanced capitalist society.

Adorno's thesis leads him to connect recent tendencies with historical categories. In view of advanced capitalism's wedding of monopolistic production with authoritarian states, Adorno identifies several phases in the dialectic of domination.[44] In the control of nature (*Naturbeherrschung*), he says, control by nature over its human members gives way to control over nature by human beings, first through magic and myth, then through rational labor; the control of nature unfolds into domination by some human beings over others, into suppression of nature within human beings, and into the domination of all human beings by what they have made; and domination either will culminate in a catastrophe—the complete destruction of life— or will lead to a reconciliation that transcends control and domination via control and domination. Much of the outcome depends on whether radical changes occur in the structure of modern Western society, where the "impenetrable unity of society and domination"[45] has become an antagonistic totality.

Like entrepreneurial and monopoly capitalism, advanced capitalist society is governed by a principle of exchange and operates by way of exploitation and class conflict. So long as this principle lets some people exploit others, society will not be rationally organized, nor will it actualize humanity, the original goal of society.[46] For Adorno, as for Marx, "humanity" means "a community of free individuals."[47] For Adorno, as for Kant, the removal of antagonisms between the dominating and the dominated would be the beginning of "perpetual peace."[48] Ending domination in exchange would not usher in a quiescent romanticism of nature, nor would organizing society in a rational manner turn the entire world into a "giant workhouse."[49] Achieving "perpetual peace" would mean restoring damaged life in a society where people no longer ignore the needs that resist the agenda of those who wield the greatest power.

To be restructured for humanity and life, however, society needs a self-conscious subject (*Gesamtsubjekt*) to perceive the needs and perform the task. Otherwise society will remain a class society that dominates its own members. Meanwhile, the circle closes. "Living human beings" are needed in order to change hardened social conditions, yet sophisticated ideology has so saturated us that we seem to lack the requisite spontaneity and critical consciousness. Hence a theory interested in social transformation must understand how society itself has become an overpowering fetish, how it blinds the human beings who, having made society, could change it.[50]

All this implies that class relations have shifted since *Capital* was written. For Adorno, as for Marx, a class is constituted by a common objective position in relation to the means of commodity production.[51] Although the advanced capitalist mode of production conserves and intensifies the class conflict analyzed by Marx, it also obscures "common objective positions" and weakens subjective class consciousness. Advanced capitalist production increases the concentration of capital and widens the gap between power and impotence, but it makes these tendencies less obvious.[52]

In this situation the antagonism within the capitalist mode of production turns into an antagonism between this mode and human producers, who have become objects of society. Class distinctions, though still operative, have been sublated into a wider conflict between the apparatus of production and human beings in general, regardless of their positions as wage laborers, capitalists, or landowners.[53] A ruling class still dominates through the economic process; controlling the apparatus of production remains decisive. But what now characterizes society as society is the preponderance of relations over human beings.[54]

In a sense, society has turned into a huge commodity whose fetishism must be exposed so that society can become "rational and genuinely free."[55] Overpowering institutions must be seen as the human labor that certain people have objectified within an economic relation that, though temporarily frozen, can be altered.[56] This relation is one of exchange. It is also a relation of domination, a relation dominating both master and slave. Given humanity's temporary impotence and the exchange society's present power, an impasse seems unavoidable both in society and in Adorno's social theory.

Antinomous Abstraction

This impasse updates the antinomy noted in Marx's *Capital*. Once the antinomy in exchange becomes the antinomy of society as a whole, Marx's critique of political economy loses its ring of confidence.[57] Adorno conceives of contemporary society as a functional totality whose abstract structure governs a process of dominative exchange. This conception poses a theoretical difficulty. The concept of a "functional totality" seems like an antinomous abstraction according to which all functions in society have become one function that functions. For Adorno, this antinomous abstraction is the essence of contemporary society. All social functions are being reduced to one dominant function. This function governs the social totality, each member of society depends on the totality, the totality depends on its own continued functioning, and this functioning can continue only because of the unity of the functions the members of society perform.[58] The unity of advanced capitalist society is functional and abstract.

According to Adorno, such a society displays "total coherence" in the sense that all members must submit to the law of exchange in order to survive. They receive their unity from exchange, exchange relations, and exchange value, all of which seem like the objective properties of independent things. Since the predominant processes in society are quantitative and quantifiable, they require and assume objective abstraction from the diverse qualities of human beings and their needs. Not everyone pursues surplus value, but no one can escape the pursuit. Measurable private profit is primary, not only in the economy but also in society as a whole. The primacy of profit, while abstract, is not neutral, for it reduces human beings to mere vehicles for profitably exchanging commodities.[59] So long as society and its members are ruled by a reductive exchange that serves domination, society must be conceived as the antinomous abstraction that society has become.

This does not mean "society" is an unintelligible concept. Adorno argues against positivist sociology that the totality is what is really real. It appears in every social fact, and it finds forceful expression in individuals' impotence toward the whole.[60] Society is both intelligible and unintelligible: intelligible, because the abstraction carried out in exchange is a subjective act modeled after instrumental reason; unintelligible, because exchange becomes increasingly irrational when profit turns into an antihuman end in itself. What remains intelligible is the social law of irrational rationality, the law of a fair exchange that exploits, the law Marx exposed by analyzing wage labor as the source of surplus value. Society has obeyed this law as it turned into an independent totality controlling its various members.[61]

As a critical category, "totality" aims to resist totality. Adorno tries to trace totality back to its members, and he calls for a social theory that sees how particulars are mediated by a universal derived from the particulars. Though totality and the universal have precedence today, Adorno's dialectical critique shows this precedence to be objectively necessary but false. The transcendental subject of a transformed society would be human beings themselves rather than their economized interactions and relations.[62]

Adorno's critique of antinomous abstraction occupies a puzzling position. Does it confuse his own theoretical abstraction with the abstraction in exchange? If so, then does the antinomy lie in the relation between theory and society rather than in society as a whole? If not, then how can Adorno's own theory extricate itself sufficiently to criticize society from the perspective of a transformed society? In either case, since abstraction can only be identified through theoretical abstraction, and since the antinomy in abstraction seems to escape the consciousness of most people, how can the critique of abstraction retain a hope for structural transformation? Without this hope Adorno's social theory would lose its critical point.

It will become plain that autonomous artworks are among the phenomena giving Adorno reasons to hope. Indeed, his account of advanced capitalism as a functional system of exchange and domination leads him to attribute unusual social significance to autonomous art, a significance tied to the position and operation of autonomous works under advanced capitalist conditions. Where cultural commodity fetishism and domination in exchange prevail, autonomy enables art to mount crucial resistance. Autonomous art is one part of the totality that challenges the totality from within. In the words of *Aesthetic Theory*, autonomous art is "the social antithesis of society" (19/11).

Defetishizing Fetishes

Adorno's argument for the social significance of autonomous art relies on a complex account of the autonomy of particular works of art. The structure of his account contains several crisscrossing polarities: autonomy and social character, artifact and phenomenon, and import and function. These polarities are highly dialectical, with each pole containing and turning into its opposite. Without purporting to capture the full dynamic of Adorno's account, the summary to follow shows how such polarities explain the position, operation, and social significance of autonomous artworks under advanced capitalist conditions. Their position is that of defetishizing fetishes. Their operation is that of social monads. And their significance lies in the dysfunctional function of their truth content.

The polarity of autonomy and social character marks the position of artworks within advanced capitalist societies. Adorno holds that a work of art is both independent of and dependent on society. It is internally consistent as well as inconsistent. It both has and lacks its own identity. Furthermore, what makes for independence, consistency, and singularity is an artwork's social dependence, inconsistency, and universality, and what makes for the latter resides in the former. Thus the tension between autonomy and social character is such that a work's autonomy has a social character, and a work's social character is itself autonomous.

This polarity comes together in the claim that autonomous works are fetishes (337–38/323–24). In the present context, Adorno's claim has three implications, each of them equally important for his model of social mediation. The first stems from Adorno's reception of Marx's critique of commodity fetishism. The implication is that autonomous works of art do indeed belong to a society where exchange has become the dominant principle of social relationships. Autonomous works are produced and consumed in accordance with this principle. Like other products under capitalist conditions, they hide the labor that has gone into them and appear to have a life of their own. In the second place, the fetish character of autonomous works implies that they appear to be superior cultural entities somehow detached from the conditions of economic production. In this way they cover up the problematic division of labor that makes them possible. Autonomous works are also fetishes, in the third place, insofar as they seem to serve no use beyond their own existence. Products without uses seem irrational, and respect for such products seems superstitious.

At the same time, however, Adorno qualifies each of these implications. By appearing to have a life of their own, works of art call into question a society where nothing is allowed to be itself and everything is subject to the principle of exchange. By appearing to be detached from the conditions of economic production, works of art acquire the ability to suggest changed conditions. And by appearing to be useless, works of art recall the human purposes of production that instrumental rationality forgets. Hence their fetish character is not mere delusion; it is "a condition of their truth, including their social truth" (337/323). Their independence, internal consistency, and singularity have social origins and social implications. Works of art follow their own path in their own way, but the path itself and the impetus for traveling come from the surrounding society. Unlike most mass mediated art, autonomous works occupy the position of defetishizing fetishes. Their unique position lets them express the surrounding social process in such a way that a structural transformation seems possible and necessary.

If the dialectic of autonomy and social character marks the social position of works of art, then the polarity of artifact and phenomenon captures the way artworks operate within advanced capitalism. The work is a monad whose internal process brings forth the surrounding social process. One characteristic of the internal process is a continual conflict between the work as a produced artifact and the work as an experienced phenomenon.

By calling attention to this conflict, Adorno summarizes the uneasy relationship in post-Kantian aesthetics between treating the work as a genial creation and treating it as an aesthetic object.[63] The concepts of artifact and phenomenon recast this relationship for a situation where neither inspired self-expression nor contemplative self-satisfaction characterizes how modern works are produced and received. The two concepts recall that artistic entities, despite their independent identities, occur within processes of production and reception that are socially conditioned. It is through such processes that the work incorporates and maintains its own internal process.

The interpretative key to social mediation is neither the production nor the reception of the work, however, but the process within the work between its artifactual and its phenomenal tendencies. Against empirical sociologies of art, Adorno insists on the primacy of production over reception for understanding the social character of art (338–39/324). Against Benjamin's technological optimism, Adorno argues for the primacy of the work itself rather than the production from which a work arises. Although directed against reception aesthetics, Adorno's central claim in the section titled "Reception and Production" attacks production aesthetics as well: "Art and society converge in substance [*Gehalt*], not in something that is extraneous to [the work of art]" (339/324). The tension between artifactual and phenomenal tendencies gives the artwork an internal process through which it can express the surrounding social process.

Just as the polarity of artifact and phenomenon captures the internal operations of the socio-artistic monad, so the poles of import and function indicate the social significance of the work of art. It should be noted here that sociologists of art talk about social significance in two different ways. In an interpretative approach, social significance has the connotations of meaning, whether as intended by the artist, perceived by the public, or embodied in the work. In an explanatory approach, social significance has the connotations of effect, whether intended and perceived or not. Adorno's approach is neither strictly interpretative nor strictly explanatory. Here too it displays a dialectical structure. The main poles are those of import (*Gehalt*) and function.

Yet his emphasis lies on the concept of import. Adorno's sociology of art claims that the import of an artwork must be decoded if the work's functions are to be accurately analyzed.[64] His philosophy of art claims that "if any social function can be ascribed to [art works] at all, it is . . . to have no function" (336–37/322). The two claims are linked by an understanding of social functions as cognitive functions. To say that art's social function is to be socially dysfunctional is to suggest that, through its autonomy, modern art makes its own contributions to society (335–37/321–23). These are primarily contributions to the formation of social consciousness (360–61/344–45). The cognitive character of art's social functions comes through clearly in Adorno's descriptions of modern art's contributions: expression of suffering, broken promise of happiness, inexplicit knowledge of society, negative embodiment of utopia. Because adequate relations to autonomous works become ever more difficult in advanced capitalist societies, Adorno sometimes seems to regard the best modern works as bottles for messages that few of the shipwrecked can read.[65] Adorno does not speak of messages, however. He strongly prefers the concept of import.

To summarize: in Adorno's model of social mediation, autonomy and social character mark the position of the work of art within advanced capitalist societies. Artworks are defetishizing fetishes. Their operation within society involves an internal polarity of artifact and phenomenon. This polarity is crucial for Adorno's notions of autonomy and truth. The artifactual character of the work is a necessary condition for its autonomy, and the autonomy of the work, though conditioned by society as a whole, is itself a precondition for truth in art. The notions of autonomy and truth, in turn, provide the impetus for Adorno's claims about social significance. Although Adorno locates the social significance of the artwork in both its import and its social functions, he understands these social functions as primarily cognitive functions, and he regards their significance as directly dependent on the import of the work. Truth provides the ultimate criterion for the social significance of the work's import and, by extension, for the social significance of the work's social functions. Thus autonomy is a precondition for that which ultimately determines the social significance of the work of art.

A summary of Adorno's model of social mediation would be incomplete, however, without a discussion of his understanding of art as labor. Just as Marx demystifies the commodity by tracing it back to its origins in human labor, so Adorno lifts the veil of romanticism by tracing autonomous art back to its origins in the process of social production. As will become apparent in the next chapter, Adorno's model of social mediation has the polarity of subject and object as its unifying philosophical structure. In this way, Adorno's aesthetics remains close to a Lukácsian theory of reification, even though Adorno does not share Lukács's emphasis on subjective consciousness.

5

Art as Social Labor

A view of art as social labor pervades Adorno's model of social mediation. On this view, artworks arise from society through a dialectic of subject and object. The polarities within autonomous works are thought to stem from a struggle between artists and the materials of art, and to carry the imprint of a general societal conflict between forces and relations of production. Hence Adorno's constant challenge is to show how three dialectical levels interrelate: a dialectic in society between forces and relations of production, a dialectic within artistic production between artists and materials, and a dialectic within artworks between their content and form. Each subsequent dialectic is a microcosmos of the previous one, and all three are supposed to be fully interconnected. Yet these levels must show up differently in interpretations of various works of art. Otherwise Adorno's monadology would generate mere repetitions of an abstract analogy, contrary to his own intention.[1]

5.1 Artistic Material

In "The Decline of the Modern Age," a paper read at the Frankfurt Adorno Conference in 1983, Peter Bürger calls Adorno's aesthetics inadequate for understanding "postmodern" trends. Underlying this inadequacy is an insistence on "historically advanced material." Adorno recognizes only one historically advanced material for a given epoch, and he holds that this artistic material "reflects the state of total social development."[2] Hence he has trouble seeing how neoclassicism and surrealism are integral parts of modern art. Moreover, he does not change his concept of artistic material to accommodate the plurality of media and methods in progressive art after World War II. Bürger's own solution is to maintain that "all relevant art today defines itself in relation to modernism." On the one hand, aesthetic modernism must "recognize as its own much that it has until now rejected," such as musical tonality, visual representation, and traditional literary forms. On the other hand, "the recourse to past stocks of material must be recognized as a modern procedure, albeit an extremely precarious one."[3] Modern art is more variegated than Adorno's concept of artistic material suggests.

Sociohistorical Tendency

The issues raised by Bürger indicate that Adorno thinks artistic material has a sociohistorical tendency. It was mentioned earlier that many of Adorno's philosophical impulses derive from his musical training. These impulses include an emphasis on the historical character of musical materials and a demand that compositions be up-to-date and internally consistent. It is in this context that Adorno's concept of musical material and the wider concept of artistic material must be understood. They express the modernist impulses of the Schönberg school. Just as atonal and dodecaphonic music lost their authoritative status with the rise of serialism and chance in the 1950s, however, so Adorno's concept of artistic material has elicited criticism from his postmodernist followers. Adorno was not unaware of such criticism, having debated with postwar composers over his objections to the "aging" of modern music.[4] Nevertheless his contested concept continues to figure prominently in *Aesthetic Theory*.

A main target for Bürger's criticisms is the harsh treatment of Igor Stravinsky in *Philosophy of Modern Music* (1949). This book contains Adorno's most forceful articulation of the concept of musical material, connecting it with the philosophy of history in *Dialectic of Enlightenment* and using it to make historico-philosophical evaluations of modern music. His later concept of artistic material simply expands the concept of musical material.

In the main passage to be considered, Adorno revises a traditional category and alters the map of musicology.[5] Adorno's crucial innovation is to define musical material as something sociohistorical rather than as a permanent physical substratum. According to Carl Dahlhaus, Adorno conceives musical material to be the historical characteristics of tones and tonal relations as generated by the activity of composing and modified by subsequent composers.[6] Adorno uses this concept to argue that in the early twentieth century the sociohistorical movement of musical material began to run contrary to musical works of art. By attacking the notion of a well-rounded composition, Schönberg's atonal pieces honored the movement of the musical material, thereby acquiring sociohistorical implications and tending toward a critical knowledge of modern society.

Adorno claims that tones and their relations have sociohistorical tendencies, and these make unavoidable demands when compositional decisions are being made. Historical laws of movement (*Bewegungsgesetze*) govern what composers may do with the musical material. At the same time, composers need independence and spontaneity to follow these laws. The "dialectical movement" of musical material is not a free-for-all between an anarchic subject and a determining object, however. Compositional decisions assume certain standards. The requisite standards are implied by Adorno's explanation of why Schönberg prohibited the use of various chords and outlawed tonality as a whole. Adorno says that modern composers properly avoid certain chords such as the diminished seventh because these are out of date, out of place, and unable to fulfill the tasks set by the most advanced level of technique. Such reasons imply that the tonal relations used must be up-to-date, compositionally justified, and technically advanced. According to Adorno, compositional possibilities are so thoroughly governed by the sociohistorical tendencies of musical material that traditional tonality became illegitimate in the early twentieth century.

All of this assumes that one can determine what these tendencies are and where they are headed. It seems obvious to
Adorno that Jean Sibelius's reliance on tonality is illegitimate,
while Arnold Schönberg's development of atonality is not. Unfortunately, some sympathetic critics are not convinced. It
could be, for example, that the most advanced musical material
presented different tasks for Sibelius than for Schönberg. Or
perhaps several different types of advanced material existed
simultaneously then as, according to Bürger, they exist today.[7]
Does not Adorno turn Schönberg's decisions into norms for
all other composers and then declare their work illegitimate
because they do not follow Schönberg's path?

An interesting criticism along these lines comes from Dahlhaus. He points out that tonality continues to operate in the
later works of Béla Bartók and Paul Hindemith, which cannot
be written off as mere failures. Adorno's general claim about
tonality needs to be augmented by an aesthetic judgment to
the effect that compositions retaining tonality are bound to
become internally inconsistent. This judgment would have to
appeal to specific analyses of technical inconsistencies. Even
this would not suffice, however, since Adorno also regards
many of Schönberg's dodecaphonic compositions as technically
inconsistent. Adorno would have to contrast fruitful with unfruitful inconsistencies. Clearly he considers Schönberg's technical inconsistencies more fruitful because they have entered
the musical material to become compositionally decisive. But
this conclusion already assumes Adorno's initial thesis that the
sociohistorical tendencies of musical material govern compositional possibilities.[8] In exasperation, another critic calls Adorno's reasoning circular and self-serving: Adorno considers
technical inconsistencies fruitful to the extent that they support
the interpretation in which their fruitfulness is being
determined.[9]

As such criticisms indicate, the close proximity between
Adorno's Schönbergian impulses and the subject matter he
addresses makes the concept of musical material seem like a
basis for arbitrary and inflexible evaluations. Criteria for evaluation seem to fuse with the decisions made by certain composers and with Adorno's own judgments about how well

certain standards are met. Supporting these judgments, however, are additional claims and postulates that make Adorno's
evaluations more weighty than the charges of arbitrariness and
inflexibility would suggest. Central to these claims, and to
Adorno's concept of musical material, is the notion of "objectified consciousness" (*sedimentierter Geist*).

Objectified Consciousness

The historico-philosophical evaluations in *Philosophy of Modern
Music* rely upon a twofold claim about musical material.
Adorno claims that just one irreversible movement of the musical material sets composers' tasks, and that this movement
proceeds in the same direction as just one social process.[10] To
be plausible, this double claim requires four postulates, either
explicit or implicit. (1) Musical material is "objectified consciousness" or "objective spirit," in the sense that it is socially
preformed by human consciousness. (2) Both the movement
of musical material and the movement of society as a whole
arise from the objectification of human consciousness, which
Adorno describes as a process of subjectivity becoming forgetful of itself. (3) These two historical movements and their laws
do not differ significantly for various locations, for competing
schools of composition, or for composers who have different
qualifications and audiences. (4) By struggling with musical
material, composers struggle with society.
    Each of the postulates can be questioned. First, it is not
immediately apparent why the "objective spirit" of musical material should be thought to originate in human consciousness
rather than in musical instruments and corporeal skills. The
means of producing tones and tonal relations would seem no
less important than consciousness for generating musical material. Second, it is doubtful that the postulate of a common
origin in objectification does much to explain the relationship
between musical material and the social process. By the same
token, everything else in society would have the same origin
and unfold in the same direction as the social process as a
whole. The second postulate says too little about musical material because it says too much.[11] In the third place, one won-

ders how "historical" the musical material is if the force of its laws does not differ significantly for varying responses in a specific epoch. Finally, it seems doubtful that composers can have a genuine altercation (*Auseinandersetzung*) with musical material and with society as a whole. Genuine disputes concern specific issues, not a vague totality called "the musical material" or "the social process."

Adorno himself expresses reservations about the fourth postulate. *Philosophy of Modern Music* depicts the composer's struggle as one in which the musical material issues directives to the composer, and the composer transforms the material by following these directives. In a note to later editions, Adorno expresses a desire to pay more attention to how "the concrete work" mediates the movement of musical material.[12] A hint of this reservation occurs already in the first edition, when Adorno says that society and history restrict the composer through the musical composition's demand for correctness. Yet he does not show how actual compositions leave traces in the musical material and constitute traditions that various composers assume, carry forward, or oppose. Although Adorno says that an epoch's total level of musical technique will be evident only "in the specific constellations of compositional tasks," "technique as a whole" remains the composer's antagonist and society's surrogate. "With every measure," he writes, technique itself demands that the composer "do it justice and give the only correct answer permitted by technique at any given moment."[13]

The more troublesome postulates, however, are those that identify the objectification of consciousness as the common origin of the musical material and the social process. On a first reading, these postulates seem to revive the historical idealism that Marx attempted to invert and that Adorno himself finds problematic in Lukács's theory of reification. The postulates do not tie "objective spirit" to the concept of labor, nor do they characterize modern consciousness by an ability to objectify itself through labor. Consequently Adorno's account of musical material sounds idealistic, despite the fact that his book on modern music is an "extended appendix" to *Dialectic of Enlightenment*.[14] Fundamental to both books, however, is an updating of Marx's assessment of Hegel's *Phenomenology of Spirit*.[15] This provides a background for Adorno's later description of art as a "product of the social labour of spirit" (335/321).

Sociocultural Labor

In 1957 Adorno endorses the following Marxian statement of 1844: "The outstanding achievement of Hegel's *Phänomenologie* and of its outcome, the dialectic of negativity as the moving and generating principle, is . . . that he thus grasps the essence of *labour* and comprehends objective [humanity]—true, because real [humanity]—as the outcome of [humanity's] *own labour*."[16] Like Marx, Adorno understands Hegel's "spirit" (*Geist*) to be "social labor." Hegel's realms of objective and absolute spirit must be derived from modes of labor in society. At the same time, Adorno criticizes Hegel for reducing labor itself to a mere moment within a spirit that claims in the end to be an absolute identity of subject and object. On the contrary, says Adorno, culture (*Geist*) is a mere moment within social labor, one that gradually attains apparent independence from both nature and material labor.

Adorno's updating of Marx seems ambiguous, however, since "social" means "universally synthetic" in this context. It becomes hard to tell whether culture remains a mere moment of social labor, or whether Adorno inadvertently intellectualizes labor. This apparent ambiguity returns in *Aesthetic Theory*'s description of art as a product of the social labor of spirit. Is culture a derivative moment within social labor, or does culture itself do the work? The apparent ambiguity stems from the fact that Adorno's reading of *Phenomenology* is both prospective and retrospective. Hegel's spirit turns into Marx's social labor, but Marx's social labor becomes Kant's synthetic unity of apperception: social labor constitutes the unity of society. At the same time, a fully capitalized society becomes the laboriously objectified, transcendental subject uniting disparate members and their activities and products.

According to Adorno, this society was acquiring its definitive shape during the time of Kant, Hegel, and Marx. Since then, modern society has become first and foremost an "exchange society" (*Tauschgesellschaft*). It universally synthesizes according to the principle of the equivalence of social labor. In material production, the principle is one of abstract mastery. In thought, the same principle prevails as the principle of systematic unity. Social labor is the process whereby society has turned into a total system of exchange relations, a system that itself makes possible all moments of social labor. The more the principle of exchange prevails, the more society itself seems to become the absolute product and subject of social labor.

This process of social labor encompasses the entire dialectic of subject and object in capitalist society. As the "radical mediation" connecting human beings, nature, and culture, all social labor, whether manual or mental, has three characteristics. It is "for others"—for the preservation of society, humankind, and individual subjects. It is inseparable from nature, control of nature, and human suffering. And, as commodity production, labor occurs within an exchange relation through which laborers are exploited by those who control production.[17]

Aesthetic Theory's description of art postulates the same unity of origin ascribed to musical material and the social process in *Philosophy of Modern Music*. Both books treat art as a region of sociocultural labor within a general dialectic of subject and object. What becomes clear from Adorno's updating of Marx on Hegel is that the structure of this dialectic is tied to an all-pervasive exchange principle. To describe art as a product of sociocultural labor is to recall the centrality of commodity production throughout capitalist society, including those regions of culture that Hegel mistakenly described as absolute spirit. At the same time, to recall the centrality of commodity production is to indicate that art and philosophy can intervene in the prevailing mode of production and contribute to a structural transformation of society. Postulating a unity of origin does not explain it, however. For an explanation, one may examine the employment of Marxist categories in Adorno's sociology of music. The crucial category is that of a mode of production.

5.2 Modes of Production

Adorno's view of art as social labor embodies a worry about the structural transformation of advanced capitalist society. In one sense, the problem of structural transformation is also the problem of overcoming the division of labor between intellectual culture and material production. This division supports the capitalist system. In another sense, however, the division of labor has already broken down, and in a manner that need not subvert the system. This can be seen by comparing Adorno's analysis with that of Marx.

Division of Labor

Marx writes that the capitalist mode of production changes labor into a social process potentially engulfing various spheres of society.[18] For this change to occur, the traditional social division of labor must give way to capitalized cooperation. The social division of labor refers to the differentiation of distinct branches of social production, such as agriculture and industry. Cooperation, which occurs in manufacture, is a singular case of the division of labor within just one branch of social production. Although there is a difference in degree and in kind between cooperation in manufacture and the general social division of labor, Marx thinks this difference might disappear if the division of labor within manufacture takes over other branches of production and other spheres of society.

Adorno concludes that, as a matter of fact, the difference between the industrial division of labor and the general social division of labor has faded in advanced capitalism. This conclusion helps explain why he says society and music share "labor processes" and all human beings carry out "social labor."[19] To the extent that the capitalized division of labor within manufacture has spread into all productive branches and social spheres, it makes sense to treat all organized activity, whether manual or mental, as social labor. Adorno's theoretical difficulty is to distinguish and interrelate various types of production that have become amalgamated.

In fact, this amalgamation is so dominant in advanced capitalism that Adorno says the sociology of music must emphasize production over distribution and consumption.[20] In contrast to empiricistic positivism, Adorno's sociology takes its orientation not from individual actions and perceptions but from "the objectified, institutional powers on which the social processes and thus the individuals depend. . . . In a thoroughly formed and highly rationalized commodity society . . . objectivity is the concentrated social power, the machinery of production, and the machinery of distribution which it controls. . . . Social relations are relations of social power; hence the precedence of production over the other domains."[21] Production takes precedence in Adorno's aesthetics as well. He locates art's primary relation to society in the sphere of production (artistry and artworks) rather than in the sphere of consumption (reception), even though his emphasis on philosophical interpretation does not allow art's reception to be ignored.

In keeping with Adorno's views on the division of labor and the precedence of production, *Aesthetic Theory* postulates a unity in opposition between material production and artistic production. This unity provides a two-way path along which historical society enters artworks, disappears in them, and returns, to be elicited by appropriate interpretations (338–40/324–26). Thus, claims Adorno, the struggle between artist and materials is a process of social labor, and the results of that struggle are monads of society.[22] Artworks blindly "represent" society. The process within them is "the same as the social process surrounding them." Their immanent laws "are akin" to the laws of society outside. Because artistic products are always social products and artistic labor is always social labor, forces and relations of social production "crop up" in art, although "shorn of their facticity." Like any other products in advanced capitalist society, artworks are permeated by the commodity form and by the antagonisms in material production (350–53/334–38).

Such antagonisms occur between the forces and the relations of production. According to Marx, the mode of production in a revolutionary social formation displays a conflict between productive forces (*Produktivkräfte*) and relations of production (*Produktionsverhältnisse*). Productive forces consist of a dialectical unity between objectified means of production and acquired capacities to use these means; specialized tools and skilled labor power necessarily depend on each other. Relations of production include all the social relations governing how products are produced and consumed. When relations of production fetter the forces of production, the latter will prompt an upheaval in the former.

While challenging Marx's optimism about the historical primacy of productive forces, Adorno's 1968 article on advanced capitalism restates Marx's theory. According to Adorno, the forces and relations of production continue to mediate each other in contemporary society. Although this is an "industrial society" according to its level of productive forces and an "advanced capitalist society" according to its relations of production, advanced capitalism is highly industrialized, and the latest technology is thoroughly capitalized. Under economic pressure, industrial procedures have extended to most spheres of production, administration, and culture. At the same time, human labor and needs are thoroughly controlled for the sake of maximizing profit.[23] During their gestation, productive forces have developed the material conditions for quieting the conflict in capitalism's productive womb. In self-protection, however, the relations of production have released abortive hormones.

Today's antagonism in production would seem to imply an age of revolution for someone who follows Marx's historiographic principles. Adorno follows Marx's principles but finds no social revolution. Instead, he treats certain forms of consciousness as types of production. The contemporary "division of labor" allows categories traditionally applied to the economic base to be applied to cultural elements of the superstructure. Indeed, as Gillian Rose points out, "the central thesis of [Adorno's] sociology of art is that there is a contradiction between the forces and the relations of production in the realm of culture."[24] This thesis is closely connected with two others. In the first place, contemporary society contains a continual antagonism between material production and areas of intellectual culture such as art and philosophy. In the second place, this antagonism allows the dialectic between forces and relations within material production to be carried out in the dialectic between forces and relations within cultural production. Together the three theses point to a unity of production such that music and other arts can be spoken of as types of production rather than as mere forms of social consciousness.

Unity of Production

Rose finds it "odd" to view music as a type of production. "In standard Marxist terms" music would belong to the superstructure; besides, composing is not "a relational term" in the way work and labor power are for Marx.[25] But if human beings fight out basal conflicts in the forms of social consciousness, as Marx maintains, then Adorno's view of music as a microcosmic type of "production" is less odd than innovative. *Introduction to the Sociology of Music* displays a twofold innovation in Adorno's reception of Marx's categories.[26] Not only does Adorno speak of music in basal terms ("productive forces," "relations of production"), but also he holds that some of musical production is defined by its opposition to the culture industry. The first innovation helps Adorno account for the historical unity of music and society without reverting to a mere history of ideas. The second innovation lets him distinguish ideology and superstructure "far more vigorously" than Marxists had distinguished them before.[27] These innovations postulate a close connection between material and cultural relations of production as well as a fundamental unity to all productive forces. Just as the commodity form is common to all production in advanced capitalism, so productive forces are, in the final analysis, "human forces" and "identical in all areas." During any particular social epoch, "the subjects on whose faculties the material form of production always depends . . . are not absolutely other subjects than the makers of works of art."[28]

Adorno's writings about the arts specify the unity of production by using the concepts of spirit, spontaneity, and technique. Mention has already been made of Adorno's idea of objective spirit (*Geist*) as human labor power that becomes independent from nature and material production but follows the same principle of rationality prevailing outside cultural regions such as art. The subsequent discussion will also point to a fundamental unity at a psychosomatic level of spontaneity. Spontaneity and spirit are bound together by technique, which is also common to all production. Indeed, Adorno's sociology of music sees the development of technique as "the *tertium comparationis*" between superstructure and base.[29] Technique contains his primary code for deciphering links among musical production, the economic base, and the social formation.

Hence, rather than abandon the concept of musical material, Adorno refines his terminology. *Philosophy of Modern Music* uses terms such as material, procedures (*Verfahrungsweisen*), means (*Mittel*), and technique (*Technik*) rather loosely to stress that all these matters are inherently social and historical. Later writings give artistic "technique" two interlocking meanings: artistic procedures for forming material (316/303), and the totality of both the procedures and the material at any given time, with the material always including previous procedures (222/213). Given these terminological refinements, "material" refers to all the means, including procedures, that undergo artistic formation, "procedures" refer to all the ways in which such formation is carried out, and, as a whole, "technique" refers to all the procedures and materials that have come to be objectively available.

Adorno's refinements point up two gaps in his innovative reception of Marx. Without these gaps, Adorno would have greater difficulty positing a unity of production. In the first place, if music shares productive forces with material production, then Adorno should specify exactly which instruments mediate musical and other forces. This he seldom does. In the second place, if music shares relations of production with the material mode, then Adorno should examine exactly how the production of autonomous music participates in the production of commodities. This he fails to do, preferring instead to define autonomous music in opposition to the commodities of the culture industry, and sometimes writing as if autonomous music merely becomes a commodity in the spheres of distribution and consumption. Although Adorno recognizes that research into the economic basis of music is essential to the sociology of music, he tends to limit this task to questions about musical life, which is not the same as musical production.[30]

Both gaps play a role in Adorno's account of the dialectic of forces and relations within music as a type of production.

For Adorno, the musical "relations of production" are "the economic and ideological conditions to which each tone and the reaction to each tone are tied." These relations include "the musical mentality and the taste of audiences." Musical "forces of production" include compositional activities and methods, performance activities and abilities, and the means of mechanical reproduction.[31] Using these definitions, Adorno develops a variable dialectic of forces and relations within music production.[32] Productive forces can change relations of production: Wagner's contributions transformed public taste. Relations of production are able to shackle productive forces, as has become the rule in modern times: the music market has rejected progressive music, and composers have either adjusted so much or become so marginalized that the "autonomous substance" of their music has diminished. Sometimes the relations of production enhance productive forces: without the marketplace, great music would not have acquired its autonomy.

Adorno does not ask whether forces ever inhibit relations. Have some twentieth-century composers helped close down the music market by composing only music that cannot be played or enjoyed by amateurs? He shows greater interest in conflicts between the isolated forces of autonomous art and the commercialized forces of the cultural industry. He is even more interested in a dialectic within autonomous music between musical spontaneity, which contains social forces still to be realized, and musical forms and genres, which internalize and represent social relations of production. Since musical forms help make up musical material, this special interest brings back the dialectic of composer and musical material found in *Philosophy of Modern Music*.

Musical Spontaneity

Indeed, the conflict between spontaneity and form is Adorno's key to the conflict between musical forces and relations and, by extension, to the antagonism between musical and material production:

Strictly speaking, spontaneity, which is inseparable from [social] mediations, is the only part of [musical production] that is a productive force. From the social point of view, spontaneity would be the force that exceeds mere repetition of the relations of production as represented by types and genres. . . . The question to be raised is this: *How is musical spontaneity socially possible at all?* For it always contains social productive forces whose real forms society has not yet absorbed.[33]

For Adorno, spontaneity is the central socialized force of musical production; musical forms are the central socialized relation of musical production; and the dialectic of spontaneity and forms is the center of social conflict within musical production. But what are forms, if not congealed abilities and coagulated procedures? And what are abilities and procedures in isolation from instruments?

In the light of these questions, one of the gaps mentioned earlier becomes all the more visible in Adorno's conception of musical production. Marx's "productive forces" comprise a dialectical unity between objectified means of production such as tools and machines and the acquired capacities to use them. Adorno's discussion of musical productive forces is restricted to activities, capacities, and procedures. Hence his concept of musical "production" seems to leave out instrumental means of production, even though composing, performing, and recording depend upon specific musical instruments, just as musical instruments depend on these activities. Because Adorno overlooks this interdependency, he slips into a metaphorical use of Marx's categories, as Peter Bürger observes.[34] Not that Adorno's metaphorical usage is arbitrary. The metaphor of musical "forces of production" is central to Adorno's conception of musical production, especially to the concept of spontaneity.

Adorno's emphasis on musical spontaneity complements his overlooking musical instruments. Indeed, the social possibility of artistic spontaneity is almost as significant for Adorno's aesthetics as the theoretical possibility of aesthetic judgments was for Kant's.[35] The general question of spontaneity is this: If society is untrue and dominates its own members, then how are spontaneity and critical consciousness still possible? Both are required, says Adorno, in order for human beings to transform the society they have made, but no historical subject seems to retain both spontaneity and an awareness of the need for radical social change. In the apparent absence of a revolutionary proletariat and of a critical public, Adorno's philosophy is driven to discover how spontaneity in authentic modern art can encourage transformative praxis.

Adorno's concept of artistic spontaneity implies a "materialistic" epistemology. Adorno claims that epistemology becomes materialistic by giving precedence to the object.[36] The object's precedence means that conscious cognition can not do without sensation, a preconscious and spontaneous corporeal feeling. In sensation the corporeal emerges as the ontic core of subjective cognition. This is particularly so of sensate suffering, which registers the real antagonism that calls for negative dialectic. Philosophy can label the real antagonism ("subject and object"), and art can lend it a voice, but neither philosophy nor art can remove it. It could only be removed by the socially transformative praxis of the entire human race. "By now, this negation in the interest of all can be realized only through a solidarity that is transparent to itself and to every living being."[37] So long as current relations of production blind human beings to their own interest, however, the real antagonism must be brought to consciousness by art and philosophy, under the impetus of psychosomatic and spontaneous sensation.

Hegel and Marx meet Freud. Adorno regards "spontaneity" as mediated immediacy—the immediacy of primary reactions, broken during the ego's formation.[38] To be an awareness of freedom, consciousness must remember the untamed impulses that preceded the ego, even though the idea of freedom dawns with the ego's formation. Neither the consciousness of freedom nor true praxis would exist, were there no modified impulses to motivate conscious acts and active thought.[39] Artistic spontaneity has transformative potential because art is uniquely tied to "impulse or immediate experience" (384/367). Even more directly than does philosophy's dialectic, artistic practices depend on sensation and spontaneity. To coin a phrase, the making of artworks involves "material artistry," whose dialectical counterpart is artistic material. Material artistry has the potential to be a transformative praxis (384–85/367), one in which socialized artistic spontaneity can induce artistic transformations having social implications. It remains to be determined, however, what artists contribute to this process and how their contribution can have transformative potential.

5.3 The Artist as Worker[40]

Despite the view of art as social labor, *Aesthetic Theory* contains no sustained discussion of the artist's role in the making of art. Perhaps this fact can be explained by Adorno's emphasis on the objectivity of art and society. One passage goes so far as to describe the artist as "the extension of a tool," as the mediator between a problem in artistic materials and its potential solution (249/239). Nevertheless, the absence of a theory of artistic practice is merely apparent. Adorno regularly employs, without defining, Hegelian, Marxian, and Freudian concepts of externalization (*Entäusserung*), alienation (*Entfremdung*), and sublimation (*Sublimierung*). All three concepts refer to the objectively mediated but subjective process of objectification (*Vergegenständlichung* or *Objektivierung*) that characterizes social labor. The process takes on special features in the making of art.

Just as Adorno describes art as a product of the social labor of spirit, so he regards artistry as the shaping of inherently sociohistorical materials and experiences into inherently sociohistorical monads. The process of artistic objectification allows a universal particular to be produced by way of a socialized individual whose subjective experience enters the artwork's objective and universal import. This means that the artist's experience is not strictly individual nor merely subjective. It is preformed by society, and it undergoes configuration along with the artistic material at hand. Indeed, as the transforming of the artist's experience into authentic artworks, artistic objectification amounts to an alienation of the alienation of subject and object. To see why this is so, we should consider how artistic objectification figures in the dialectic of enlightenment.

Objectification and Expression

Adorno once wrote to Walter Benjamin that "the goal of the revolution is the abolition of fear."[41] This sentence became central to *Dialectic of Enlightenment*. Horkheimer and Adorno portray fear as a dread of nature by nature's own members. At the dawn of history, human beings worship everything alien and unknown as primary, undifferentiated *Mana*—in the terms of *Negative Dialectics,* a primeval expression for the material nonidentical. Primitive people fear nature's superior power, the "jungliness of the natural over against the individual member."[42] Their cry of fear becomes a name for the unknown object they dread. In an original act of fetishism, as it were, *Mana* comes to be worshipped by those who named it. Unknown nature is made transcendent, horror enshrined as the holy. Culture (*Geist*) arises from nature through the natural fear of human members, who gradually repress their original anxiety. Prompting the duplication of nature into culture and nature, into subject and object, fear spawns attempts at explaining and controlling what is feared: "Enlightenment is mythic anxiety turned radical."[43]

If enlightenment has always aimed at eliminating fear and establishing human dominion, however,[44] then enlightenment seems bound to fail so long as it arises from fear. If repressed dread of the unknown drives the cultural elimination of fear, how can fear be removed without abolishing culture itself? The question itself suggests an alternative. Instead of dreading the unknown, culture must understand its own fetish character, recognizing itself as alienated nature afraid of itself, and remembering nature as the origin of culture.[45] Horkheimer and Adorno have attempted this in their prehistory of enlightenment. *Aesthetic Theory* enlists art in the same attempt.

Adorno's aesthetics depicts artworks as afterimages of *Mana* in an age of objectification. The historical antagonism of subject and object constantly reproduces the old object of fear, allowing it to become as alien to human experience as *Mana* once was (130/124). Objectification of the artist's dissonant experience can make the sociohistorical antagonism accessible to human experience. By giving objectified expression to objectivity

that psychosomatically weighs upon the subject, artworks rescue what the anxious search for truth has wrongly condemmed
as untrue (124/118). The products of artistic objectification
confront us with the alienated object, providing an enclave of
anamnesis amid enlightenment. They remember and anticipate what would be beyond fear, beyond the alien unknown,
and beyond the alienation of subject and object (124–25/118–
19). The absence of alienation has its pre- and posthistory
written in the artistic language of historical alienation.

The core of this language is what Adorno describes as mimetic expression. Art's ability to preserve mimesis is what most
clearly distinguishes it from other types of labor. In its simplest
meaning, "mimesis" refers to the attempt to make oneself like
something else. It is not the same as mimicry, however, as W.
Martin Lüdke points out. Mimicry becomes mimesis when the
subject's imitation of the object occurs in a conscious and intentional way, leading to a "doubling" of nature. Adorno sees
mimesis as the original form of rationality.[46]

Adorno's notion of mimetic expression, which recalls
Nietzsche's "Dionysian" and Freud's "libido" and "id," implies
an ontogenetic hypothesis about mimesis as a mode of human
conduct.[47] He conjectures that mimesis originally involved no
objectification. Later, it became tied to two different modes of
objectifying conduct, the first magical, the second aesthetic.
Aesthetic behaviour is characterized by the attempt to make
oneself like something else using something that is neither
oneself nor that which one wants to be like. The aesthetic mode
of conduct arises when human beings begin to master nature
through rational labor rather than through magical influence.
Although aesthetic behavior has become increasingly rudimen-
tal compared to the rational domination of nature, such mediate mimesis remains indispensable to art. Art, in turn,
preserves mimesis, although not in its original, preobjectifying
form. Artistic objectification gives a simultaneous voice to objectivity, which impresses itself upon the subject, and to mimetic
impulses, through which this impression occurs.

Expression is the objective pole of the modified mimesis that
makes up aesthetic behavior. Here Adorno includes both human and nonhuman expression. Human expression is an ob-

jectified miming of pain and suffering (168–69/161–62) and is permeated by moments of collectivity (485/451). The behavior captured in human expression continually crosses a threshold from psychosomatic drives to consciousness and from collectivity to individuality (172/165). Expression is not merely human, however. Adorno also attributes expression to things or situations as the utterances of their sedimented historical processes and functions (111/104–5, 170/163). Hence the artistic objectification of objectified mimetic impulses can be approached from the side of either nonhuman or human expression.[48] On the one hand, the expression or "beauty" of things is a model for understanding artistic expression (170/163). On the other hand, the voice of sedimented history in these things can not be heard without human mimesis. Indeed, the "language of nature" (121/115) remains mute unless artistically objectified, a process that proceeds through "the primal history of subjectivity."

The artistic objectification of human expression transforms aesthetic behavior into productive labor. Art does not copy mimetic impulses, but converts them into an artistic expression that speaks from the artwork itself. In every human being there survive mimetic impulses that antedate the dawn of objectification. These art uses and preserves. In a world of rational domination, art needs expression to keep from withering inside; mimetic functioning needs art to stay alive. If human expression is a sublimation of mimetic functioning, artistic expression is a sublation of this sublimation. Artistic expression preserves mimesis, cancels it by bringing it into an artwork, and supercedes both preserved and canceled mimesis by negating the objectification of mimesis within human expression.

Alienation and Creativity

Adorno's theory of artistic objectification recalls the four forms of alienation discussed in Marx's *Economic and Philosophic Manuscripts of 1844:* the alienation of human beings from the object and product of their labor, from their productive activity, from their "species-being," and from other human beings. *Aesthetic Theory* does not spell out the character and interrelationships of these forms of alienation, constructing instead a fluctuating dialectic between Marx's "economic fact" of alienated labor and Adorno's own notion of mimesis. For Adorno, alienated labor lies at the heart of material production in capitalist societies. Being modeled along the lines of material production, artistic production also has alienated labor at its heart.

The making of art is alienated labor. But when the artist objectifies mimetic impulses—spirit's "physiological pre-form"[49]—nature is rendered cultural in a peaceful manner. The making of art absorbs nature into human products where modified impulses can be plenipotentiaries of nature (172/165). Artistic objectification provides a model of how, in a liberated society, the ego could integrate libidinous impulses without repression, and human laborers could find solidarity without domination. Art is also alienated nature. Like all culture, art differs from that which exists in material objectivity, even though culture derives from nature and wishes to know it. In art, however, culture comes close to self-knowledge. It comes close to knowing the nature from which culture derives.

All objectification requires an alienation between subject and object, but artistic objectification alienates this alienation. The making of art objectifies mimetic impulses without placing them under explicit control. In this way artistry provides a corrective to the alienation involved in all social labor, especially in discursive rationality: "Art amends conceptual knowledge in that [art] attains, on its own and in complete isolation, what conceptual knowledge vainly expects to learn from its focus on the . . . subject-object relation, which is that an objective quality discloses itself through subjective effort" (173/166). Indeed, artistic expression provides knowledge of a sort that once pre-ceded and that now aims to surpass the polarity of subject and object. Artistic expression turns nonartistic expression into an expressive self-miming carried out by works of art. Artistic illusion is carried by a mimesis that becomes doubly expressive in artifacts; artistic expression is made articulate by an illusion that has become self-mimetic (169/162, 172/165). Transformed into the artwork's self-imitation, mimesis becomes a screen on which society and history can project a reconciled subject-ob-ject. This projected subject-object expresses itself as sadness and yearning so long as society is torn by the historical antagonism that makes artistic objectification possible.

If Adorno simply took mimesis to be art's strength, his theory of artistry would revert to naive romanticism. Against romanticism, he insists that art could not correct conceptual knowledge if artistic practices were not both rationally mimetic and mimetically rational. This is the context for his references to qualitative differences between artistic and other modes of knowledge. He does not mean that art is irrational or merely subjective, but that the objectivity of artistic knowledge is more specifically mediated by the subject. Artworks objectify the primary experience of artistic subjects and call for a receptive subject (245–48/235–38). Yet the making of art must be directed by objective artworks, problems, and materials—the various superegos, as it were, of an artist's mimetic id and rational ego. Adorno's theory of artistry is essentially one of objective creativity.

Accordingly, Adorno refuses to use traditional categories of artistry such as "genius" and "fantasy" to glorify the supposed freedom of individual artists. He sees the making of art as rational labor, not irrational innovation. Against the Romantic myth of the artist as irrational genius, Adorno treats "genius" as a quality of artworks themselves, the paradoxical quality of obligatory newness. "Fantasy," its organ, is not an ability of absolute discovery but an imaginative ability to transfigure given elements into another world and to discover genuine solutions for artistic problems (256–59/246–49). As an unrestricted disposal over possibilities for solving artistic problems, fantasy is mediated with reflection. The paradox of artistry is that "blind expression" must be produced through formative reflection, and that neither expression nor reflection can enter artworks without its counterpart (174–75/166–68).

The notion of reflective expression points to a crucial connection between art and social history. It points to the artist's sociohistorical experiences, unconscious and unintentional, that enter artworks and become objective. Adorno's version of aesthetic realism calls for unswerving faithfulness to such experiences. If these go deep enough, they touch the essential "historical constellations" beneath "the facade of psychological givens" and "the facade of objective reality" (422/397). An artist's unconscious experience is not merely artistic. It absorbs a highly industrialized and capitalized society, and it connects an artist with artistic problems that reflect the current level of society's productive forces (39/31–32, 56–58/48–51, 287–88/ 275–76, 324–25/310–12). Such experience would not become objective, however, if it were not carried into artworks. And for this to occur, artists must exercise self-reflection: spontaneity must be corrected by critical consciousness. In this way artistic objectification can correct prevailing patterns of alienated labor, and social truth can be materialized in art.

Materialization of Truth

The term "materialization" summarizes the dialectical process through which art partially disalienates the alienation of subject and object. Adorno thinks that the dialectic of artistic material and material artistry lets truth be materialized in particular works of art. The phrase "in particular works of art" reflects an attempt to correct his earlier construal of musical material. *Aesthetic Theory* explicitly ties the dialectic of material and artist to particular artworks, thereby returning to artists some of the initiative that "the tendency of musical material" seemed to absorb. The claim that truth can be materialized lets Adorno argue that some art transcends the capitalist system.

Adorno's notion of materialization is closely tied to his view of progress in history. Refusing either to affirm or to deny progress,[50] he wants to test the truth of every purported progress, whether artistic or societal (310/297). He says, for example, that genuine technical progress in art is an advance in the spirit's consciousness of its freedom (316/303). Here he relies heavily on Hegel's understanding of history and truth. At the same time, however, Adorno sees through the advance of consciousness to a motivating and unconscious experience. In other words, *Aesthetic Theory* wears Hegel's glasses without sharing his view of world history. The reciprocation of consciousness and the unconscious is essential to genuine technical progress in art.

The same reciprocation is a necessary condition for the materialization of truth in art. According to Adorno, artworks pose objective problems that usually defy complete solutions. Significant artworks contain traces of failure, and qualitatively new works negate those that leave behind such traces (58–62/ 50–55). But an artwork cannot be qualitatively new unless unconscious experience connects the artist's consciousness with current technical level. Unconscious experience becomes productive when it spontaneously registers whatever is stale, provincial, outdated, unsuccessful, or problematic. Such spontaneity, a sediment of collective reactions, contains and changes the objective development of productive forces (60/ 52–53, 287–88/275–76). In this context Adorno endorses Rimbaud's postulate that art must be "the most advanced consciousness where sophisticated technical procedures and equally sophisticated subjective experiences interpenetrate" (57/49, 286/274). Only in such art can truth materialize.

The reciprocation of consciousness and spontaneity does not suffice for materializing truth, however. The most advanced consciousness must also be correct, in the sense of recognizing sociohistorical contradictions within the horizon of possible reconciliation (285/274). Hence Adorno has two criteria for genuine progress in art, both of them conditions for the materialization of truth. The progressiveness of an artwork depends both on the level of productive forces it displays and on the social position the artwork takes. Artistic truth cannot be equated with technical modernity.

To meet these criteria requires a unitary process. The social contradictions to be criticized are registered by the same spontaneity that detects what is technically outdated and unsuccessful. Advanced consciousness goes beyond both the artistic and the social status quo by criticizing what has been spontaneously registered (285/274). In this way material artistry lets correct consciousness be artistically materialized. Artistic truth content, says Adorno, is the materialization in artworks of the most advanced consciousness of contradictions within the horizon of their possible reconciliation (285–86/274).

Looked at from the side of the artist, the materialization of truth can occur as follows.[51] If an artist is devoted to the artistic material, which carries residues of society and history; if, while using this material to make an artwork, the artist consciously objectifies an antagonistic, largely unconscious, and inherently sociohistorical experience; if the artist attempts an imaginative solution to the problem that the emerging artwork poses; if the artist senses and surpasses the technical level of contemporary art and society; and if the artist ignores neither the broader antagonisms of society nor their possible resolution, then correct consciousness will be materialized as an artwork's truth content.

Thus "materialization" has at least five interdependent meanings. (1) Consciousness objectifies itself in an artwork through productive labor on artistic materials. (2) By objectifying itself in an artwork, consciousness becomes part of the artistic material, which confronts subsequent artistic endeavors. (3) Consciousness enters an artwork and becomes part of the artistic material only by working with the problematic material left behind by previous works. (4) Through such labor, artistic consciousness takes part in the general dialectic between material forces and relations of production. (5) Artistic consciousness itself becomes a productive force only by depending on the material unconscious—on sensation, mimetic impulses, spontaneity.

The fifth meaning lies behind Adorno's defining artistic truth content as "unconscious historiography." Dependence on the material unconscious ties the materialization of advanced consciousness to the material nonidentical continually suppressed during the course of civilization (286–87/274–76). As suppression increases, achieving reflective expression becomes more difficult, and artistic expression becomes more reflective. More and more dissonance is needed in order to express the suppressed, but increased dissonance requires ever more sophisticated reflection on how to achieve dissonance. Paradoxical though it may seem, the history of artistic materialization is a history of advancing spiritualization. If art is to continue its reflective rescue of the alien unknown, artworks must become more and more spiritualized (180–82/173–75). Freud has met Hegel and Marx. *Aesthetic Theory* connects an anticipatory remembrance of the material nonidentical with a reflective advance in the spirit's consciousness of its own freedom. This freedom is not unconnected with the possibility of a liberated society.

Subject and Object

The notion of materialization makes clear that Adorno's view of art as social labor assumes a version of the subject-object paradigm common to much of modern philosophy. A dialectic of subject and object pervades Adorno's descriptions of such polarities as artist and material, culture and nature, forces of production and relations of production, objectification and expression, and consciousness and spontaneity. In this sense, *Aesthetic Theory* remains close to the Lukácsian theory of reification. Unlike Lukács, however, Adorno gives strategic precedence to the particular object and to the individual subject rather than to proletarian class consciousness.

This is the context for Adorno's view of the artist as an exemplary worker. He takes it as a given that the most advanced consciousness is in conflict with social consciousness as a whole, and that at present the most advanced consciousness "is the consciousness of individuals and not of groups" (69/63). His account of how advanced consciousness is possible in art is the same as his account of the possibility of spontaneity and critique in philosophy. In both cases a false society grants the possibility as a privilege of experience.[52] Society retains the upper hand. Yet, in dialectical interdependence with previously materialized impulses, socialized artistic spontaneity can induce artistic transformations having social implications. The making of art can transcend the advanced capitalist mode of production.

Yet *Aesthetic Theory* insists that individual artists and interpreters are not "the subject of art." The subject in the *artwork* is the spirit of that artistic entity (248/238). The subject in *art* is a collective voice (249/239), an artistically mediated expression of something transsubjective (170–73/162–66). When an individual artist works with historical materials, collective sociohistorical experience enters specific works of art (249–51/239–41, 459–60/428–29). By virtue of artistic configuration (*Gestaltung*) there emerges the universal and objective content that was latent in the artist's experience (288/276, 528/487). Just as philosophical universality—Kant's transcendental subject—refers to the collective universality of a not yet rational society, so artistic universality points to a collective historical subject that has not fully awakened to its task.[53] The collective subject's real universality can come only after the development of individual self-consciousness, which itself is fundamentally social.

This collective subject can enter artworks only by way of each artist's idiosyncratic impulses, which are mainly unconscious and collective, and by way of critical reflection, which only individual artists can carry out. Art must give shape to individuals' experiences of society (385/367). Adorno argues that this does not necessitate a solipsistic view of art, however: artistic objectification enables art to express a latent social content and thereby to supersede merely individual subjects (386/368). When art is discordant but synthesizes the conflicts of art and society, art speaks the truth (251/241). The collective subject of art speaks of an antagonistic society in the horizon of a possible reconciliation. By performing a synthesis that tends toward reconciliation, art anticipates a society that does not yet exist. The collective subject of this society would transcend an individualistic society that systematically suppresses individuality (452–53/422–23).

For Adorno, the centrality of commodity production means that social transformation requires a reversal in the antagonistic relation between subject (human beings) and object ("nature"). In this reversal social labor would transcend its alienated form. Instead of aiming at quantitative control for private profit, labor would embody qualitative respect for the object of labor. Such a change cannot take place unless the alienation between subject and object is experienced by all human laborers. But the experience of alienation has been increasingly banked by a full-fledged consumer society. In this situation art can fan the flames of liberation.

Adorno sees authentic modern art as a mode of social labor transcending alienated labor and expressing the alienation of subject and object. On the one hand, artistic and nonartistic labor participate in the same polar mediation of subject and object and in the same capitalist mode of production. On the other hand, having become separate from nonartistic labor and isolated within capitalist society, modern art can retain the original goal of labor and expose the tendency to ignore this goal. Material artistry on artistic material can produce artworks that defy the exchange value and the manipulated use value dictated by the principle of exchange. Although Adorno does not wish to ignore the exchange value of even the most esoteric artifacts, he thinks the maker of authentic artworks provides models of reconciled labor.

As a product of sociocultural labor, art occurs within the subject-object dialectic. This location lets art contribute to the requisite shift in the subject-object dialectic and thereby to social transformation. The same can be said about philosophy, which Adorno also regards as a product of sociocultural labor. Adorno's negative dialectic tries repeatedly to show that subject and object are reciprocally mediated and that their mediation is carried out by both subject and object.[54] His theoretical approach is also his social goal: critical spontaneity on the side of the subject, and flexible order on the side of the object. A new pattern of social labor is prepared within art and philosophy by the momentary and mediated transcendence of the current antagonism between subject and object. Such transcendence serves as a reminder that if labor were rid of blind domination in exchange, the predominance of society over its members would turn into the precedence of the qualitative object for all laborers and for the society arising from their labor. Genuine needs would be satisfied, and exploitation would end. This "qualitative leap"[55] is suggested by anti-systematic cultural critiques of the dominant system. In this way, constituents of society's "superstructure" can intervene in the prevailing mode of production, despite the apparent impotence of the social class through which philosophy was supposed to help change the world.

Hence the objections mentioned along the way about Adorno's concepts of artistic material and artistic production have significant political and philosophical ramifications. Those who object to his concept of artistic material must face the political implications of an emphasis on the artistic materialization of social truth. Those who object to Adorno's conception of art as a type of production should explore the philosophical implications of an emphasis on the dialectic of subject and object in the production of art.

6

Political Migration

The previous two chapters indicate the centrality of "truth" to Adorno's model of social mediation. Looked at from the perspective of the artwork as finished product, truth provides the ultimate criterion for the social significance of a work's import and functions. Looked at from the side of the process of production, truth materializes in the work of art by way of a dialectic between artistic material and material artistry. The autonomy of the artwork and the division of social labor between cultural and industrial production are necessary conditions for art's social truth.

Adorno's emphasis on artistic truth and its necessary conditions provides a setting for examining his account of art and politics. According to Adorno's essay on "Commitment," politics has migrated into autonomous works of art. This claim, along with Adorno's forthright criticisms of politically engaged art, raises questions about artistic import—its political character, its connection with political impact, and the criteria of its truth.

6.1 Artistic Import

Adorno's idea of artistic import implies a concept of nonconceptual or nondiscursive knowledge.[1] Two processes intersect in this concept. One is a dialectic between discursive and nondiscursive knowledge. The other is a dialectic between mimesis and rationality within art as a mode of nondiscursive knowledge. According to *Aesthetic Theory*, recent artworks display the second process as a tension between mimetic expression and rational construction or, in traditional terms, between content (*Inhalt*) and form (*Form*). This tension constitutes the import (*Gehalt*) of autonomous works of art.

Content and Form

Sometimes Adorno seems to regard technique and form as more important than material and content for the production and interpretation of import. He claims, for example, that the artwork's import is mediated by technique and extrapolated from it, and that technique and import generate each other in significant works of art.[2] Elsewhere he describes form as the locus of import (342/327). Technique and form seem to make the difference between an entity that has import and one that does not: artistic technique is the medium through which art materializes from prosaic praxis (321–22/308); artistic form shows up where a product becomes an artistic entity (214/205); and import marks an artwork as something that is more than a product.

This impression runs contrary to what one expects if import is truly dialectical. In a dialectical relation, neither pole is less important than the other. This turns out to be so of Adorno's conception of import as the tension between form and content. Form is important for Adorno because it is a way in which artworks both oppose society and communicate with it. Unresolved social antagonisms return in artworks as the immanent problems of artistic form (15–16/7–8). Because form itself is a "a sedimentation of content" (210/202), however, content is equally important for the artwork's import. Unless one traces the contours of content, form, and their dialectic, one misses the way in which social tensions "shape" the artwork itself (479/446).

Adorno postulates that content arises from society and gives rise to form, but he prefers to develop this postulate from particular works of art and specific phases of history. This makes it difficult to reach general conclusions about what is nonetheless a general theory, and it prompts the criticism that

Adorno's notion of content is limited by its historical ties to the atonal expressionism of the Schönberg school. That there are such ties is undeniable. *Philosophy of Modern Music* argues that Schönberg's entire world of form and all his technical innovations derive from how his "musical language" became polarized during his atonal phase. The polarization arises from Schönberg's attempt to register unconscious *Triebkonflikte* directly, without rationalization, in the manner of a psychoanalytic case study. Adorno's Freudian interpretation moves directly from this account of Schönberg's music to a general "insight into the interdependency of form and content in all music. . . . All forms of music, not just those of Expressionism, are precipitated contents."[3] Such contents are human impulses registering the tensions and tendencies of historical society.

Aesthetic Theory retains the pattern to Adorno's account of Schönbergian content and form: unconscious impulses registering social tendencies get translated into artistic content, from which artistic forms arise. As the translations of nonartistic expression having their own tendencies, the artwork's mimetic impulses are its "expression" and "content" (172–76/165–66, 211–19/202–211). At the same time, *Aesthetic Theory* expands the concept of content beyond the notion of transformed human impulses, for example when artistic expression is said to take its cue from historical processes in things and situations, or when Adorno uses terms such as "elements" and "moments" to talk about artistic content. Hence content can be approached from two interdependent sides, as either an artistic sublimation of objectified human impulses or an artistic transmutation of objectified elements and relations in their nonidentity. Inside artworks, impulses and elements become afterimages of reality in its material nonidentity. "Content" comes to stand for mimetic nonidentity within works of art.

Aesthetic Theory fails to discuss exactly how musical content might differ from poetic content or from other sorts of artistic content. In this respect Adorno's account of content lacks the sort of precision that he says is needed to make mimetic nonidentity articulate in works of art. Despite its imprecision, however, Adorno's account has two merits. First, it retains Hegel's doubling of content without confusing artistic content with its nonartistic sources. Second, Adorno retains Kant's emphasis on the formal qualification of artworks without turning subjective taste into their law (244–48/234–38, 526–29/485–88).

The first merit shows up in Adorno's definition of musical content as "happenings, partial events, motifs, themes, developmental sequences: generally speaking, situations in a state of flux. Content is not beyond musical time but essential to it [and musical time is essential to content]: content is all that happens in the dimension of time" (222/213). Even though musicality is crucial to all musical content, this content is never purely musical: "events" and "situations" are more than musical.

The second merit becomes evident in Adorno's claim that artistic forms are a sedimentation of content. The point of this claim is that artistic form can emerge from content rather than being imposed upon it. Form emerges from content by following the artwork's qualitatively different impulses and elements to wherever they want to go. The more mimetic a musical form is, the more it arises as the destination of the occurrences in a composition, and the more substantial the composition will be. There is more to a piece in which sonata form seems an inevitable outcome of the motives and themes than to a piece in which sonata form is forced upon the motives and themes. Yet the import of such a piece is not just musical. It is also social. Together with the doubling within content, the notion of form as a sedimentation of content gives rise to what Adorno calls the linguistic character (*Sprachähnlichkeit*) of music and, by extension, of all autonomous art.

Musical Language

The reference to language provides additional insights into the origins and meaning of Adorno's notion of artistic import. When Adorno compares music with language, he reworks nineteenth-century ideas of aesthetic autonomy and absolute music. His concept of nondiscursive knowledge allows him to go beyond Kierkegaard and Hanslick, both of whom compare music to language when they argue against Romantic and Hegelian aesthetics.[4] "Author A" in Kierkegaard's *Either/Or* says music is sufficiently "abstract" to express sensuous immediacy in its immediacy. Like language, he claims, music is a spiritually determined medium of expression, but music begins "wherever language ceases." On the one hand, music is the medium for expressing the immediate in its immediacy. On the other hand, the immediate in its immediacy is inferior to reflected immediacy, and music is poorer than language.[5] For author A, music is a language "only as a negation of language."[6]

Adorno also considers music to be a negation of language. He does not ignore the reflection that music requires, however, nor does he deem the absence of words and concepts a defect of instrumental music. Instead, Adorno calls on Benjamin's theology in order to echo the Romantic thesis that Kierkegaard tries to destroy out of secretly theological motives.[7] To Adorno, "absolute music" is a definite cipher of the absolute. Music is merely a cipher, however. Although the determinate immediacy of musical language is more than merely immediate, a revised social praxis is needed for the absolute to be fully attained.

Adorno's emphasis on social praxis places him in opposition to Eduard Hanslick's apology for absolute music, even though both authors emphasize the nondiscursive character of music. As Hanslick's paradoxical formulation has it, "The content of music is tonally moving forms."[8] The polemical point of this famous paradox is aimed at Hegel's followers, including renegades such as Schopenhauer and Wagner. Hanslick argues against Wagner for a fundamental distinction between language and music.[9] According to Hanslick, musical content takes form by giving shape to musical material—to musical tones and their inherent possibilities.[10] By distinguishing between essential content and phenomenal material, he can emphasize music's *geistigen Gehalt* without turning this *Gehalt* into the nonmusical feelings and ideas that Wagner wanted music to present.[11] Hanslick claims that only musical thoughts with a musical meaning and a musically logical sequence are relevant for musical beauty. The "language" of music cannot be translated.

Adorno takes both Wagner and Hanslick to task. Whereas Wagner confuses the composer's ambiguous intentions with a composition's unintentional import, Hanslick divorces a work's configuration from "expressive elements" that differ from the configuration and let it become a configuration in the first place. Adorno's "musical content" refers to these elements rather than to Hanslick's tonally moving forms. Adorno defines "musical content" in this context as "the profusion of everything that is subject to musical grammar and syntax" and through which a piece refers beyond itself. Without expressive elements that are more than musical, musical form would lack "specific necessity" or "immanent logic."[12] Adorno's definition goes beyond Hanslick because it implies a doubling within both content and form. Such doubling makes possible a dialectic not only between content and form but also between musical import and historical society. Nonmusical feelings and thoughts have intramusical significance, and the import of musical works has a social meaning.

Yet Adorno insists that music remains distinct from "intentional language" and from discursive forms of rationality. While resembling language (sprachähnlich), music is not a language. The similarity arises because music is a temporal sequence of articulated sounds that say something. Tonal concert music contains statements, phrases, and even grammalogues such as standard cadences. Even modern music, which does away with such conventions, does not eliminate music's Sprachähnlichkeit.[13] The fundamental difference between music and language is that what music says cannot be separated from the music itself. In the terminology of Susanne K. Langer, musical compositions are nondiscursive symbols,[14] and this gives music a different telos from that of language. According to Adorno, intentional language (meinende Sprache) tries to approximate the absolute but fails: the absolute slips away from every finite intention. Music meets the absolute directly, but fails to communicate it.[15] Thus both music and language must undertake endless mediations.

Because music and language are both similar and different, Adorno neither rejects nor affirms the concept of musical meaning (Sinn, Sinnzusammenhang). At the same time, he stipulates a condition music must fulfill in order to be meaningful (sinnvoll). To be meaningful, music must have a form that is the destination (*Bestimmung*) of musical content. Just as unconscious human impulses are the preform of spirit, so, conversely, musical form must arise as the destiny of content that is inherently spiritual.[16] Music is meaningful insofar as it reverses the relation of domination that has prevailed ever since subject and object separated into a meaning-bestowing subject and a meaningless object.[17]

For this reversal to occur, and for music to provide nondiscursive knowledge, music must partake of the same mediation of subject and object that characterizes discursive rationality.[18] This mediation allows a recurring reversal of domination in the history of music, even when composers do not intend a reversal. For example, after serialist composers had tried unsuccessfully in the 1950s to eliminate music's similarity to language, Adorno saw two ways to get past the gap between rationally disqualified material and the musicolinguistic structures Schönberg had generated from this material. Either composers could elicit principles of paratactical organization from the tonal material, principles like those that later govern *Aesthetic Theory*. Or they could drive the inherited structures further until new lingual characters materialize. Both attempts would result in a free disposition over the means of composition, allowing composers to pursue the means wherever these want to go. Subject and object would be mediated and the relation of domination reversed. The social subject concealed in the material would be perceived, and the human objectivity in the inherited structures would be honored.[19]

Formal Liberation

Such a reversal of domination is a process of formal liberation. It can be viewed from two perspectives. On the one hand, artistic form, when properly constituted, serves to liberate content from its chaotic and inarticulate state. To do this, artistic forms must be saturated with content. This lets them display a social prehistory and a potential posthistory. Their social historicity derives from a process of sedimentation, which can be summarized as follows: Through the tonal material, real mimetic affinities and real rational coherences enter a composition's musical content, and through subjective artistry that is open to the material, these affinities and coherences are solidified into a form that synthesizes musical content.

On the other hand, artistic form liberates society from the prevailing social order. As a nondiscursive ordering or logic of content, artistic form sublates the discursive order of society and daily experience (14/16). When empirical social content enters an artwork, empirical social categories come along. Such categories govern social domination and the mastery of nature. Once inside a work of art, they begin to follow artistic laws, even though they continue to obey directions retained from society (420/395). When these categories turn into artistic forms of space, time, or causality, their lawfulness is shown to be alterable, and the liberation of society from subjectively dictated lawfulness becomes a concrete possibility (205–8/197–200). For Adorno, artistic form provides a liberating transformation of socially formative forms.

Artistic liberation comes not only through the critique of discursive order, however, but also through the rescue of qualitative similarities or affinities among disparate impulses and elements. Whereas the concepts and judgments of discursive rationality usually conceal and suppress these similarities, art's nondiscursive "logic" permits illogical connections. An authentic artwork elicits unidentified relations similarly to the way this happens in dreams, which have a "dream-logic," according to Freudian theory. These elicited relations are not simply haphazard, nor is artistic knowledge of them irrational. Art achieves artistic form through goal-oriented artistry, and artistically preserved affinities echo discursively identified coherences. In an exchange society, artistic preservation of unidentified similarities is required by the needs and potentials of existence, which scientific and technological rationality tends to ignore (14–18/6–10, 208/200).

Content and form do not have the identity attributed to them by Hanslick. Nor do they interrelate in the manner prescribed by Hegel, Kierkegaard, and Marx, whose dialectical concerns Adorno shares. For Adorno, artistic form can arise only as a sedimentation of contents, and artistic content can appear only in the crystallization of forms.[20] Moreover, the artistic dialectic

of content and form is a liberating agent of revelatory contradiction and illusory reconciliation. As a nondiscursive mode
of knowing social reality, art is in this world but not completely
of it. On the one hand, form enables artworks to oppose current society in a way that makes us aware of the implicit mediation of immediate and chaotic contradictions (218/209). On
the other hand, form enables artworks to arrange society's
scattered elements into a world that would differ from one
where blind domination and exchange prevail (461–62/430–
31). To the extent that artworks oppose society and its exchange principle, a structural change might occur if society
imitated works of art (199–200/192).

As products of social labor, artworks are not exempt from
relations of production that prevent the reconciliation of subject and object, of culture and nature, of identity and the
nonidentical. As autonomous entities, however, artworks can
come close to reconciling these poles without masking their
tension. Artistic form places transformed elements and impulses into a new constellation that in reality would mean new
relations of production and a restoration of damaged life. By
alienating the empirical and bringing out its real essence, artistic form indirectly refers existences to a different essence
that unmasks their *Wesen* as an *Unwesen*. Artworks are reconstellations rather than copies of social reality. The nondiscursive knowledge they provide is a determinate negation of
contemporary society.[21]

By themselves, artworks cannot actually transform society.
Their dialectic of form and content remains an expression of
suffering and an appearance of society's essential antagonisms.
Nevertheless, the dialectic within artworks can play a political
role. It can disclose society's dialectic and point beyond this
dialectic. In art, social conflict is embodied as something that
can be resolved. What would transcend dialectic is envisaged
dialectically: a changed society in which individuals could be
themselves and enjoy true solidarity.

Hence Adorno attributes a political impact to artistic import.
Although he insists that artistic knowledge is nondiscursive, he
also thinks that art's political relevance depends on the knowl-

edge it provides: he can be said to have a cognitivist approach to questions of art and politics.

6.2 Political Impact

According to *Aesthetic Theory,* art has a political impact, but this impact is indirect. The indirectness has to do with two relationships: art's relationship to knowledge, and art's relationship to praxis. The first relationship involves a dialectic of knowledge. The second involves a paradox of praxis. Each relationship must be examined in order to make sense of the claim that art's political impact is indirect.

Dialectic of Knowledge

Just as Adorno's notion of artistic import points to a dialectic of form and content within a mode of nondiscursive knowledge, so the view of art as a mode of cognitive praxis points to a dialectic between discursive and nondiscursive knowledge within modern societies. Science and art can stand for the two poles of knowledge. Adorno's most forceful statement of this dialectic occurs in *Dialectic of Enlightenment.* An important source for his statement lies in the philosophy of Immanuel Kant, particularly *Critique of Judgment.*[22] Kant's formulation of the problem of nondiscursive knowledge has proved decisive for modern aesthetics in general, and for Adorno's aesthetics in particular.[23]

Adorno accepts the Kantian claim that objectifying categories determine and regulate reality, but he regards these as intrinsically sociohistorical: the categories of thought are themselves determined by society and history. In contrast to Kant, Adorno opposes the categories of current reality, and he stresses the precedence of the object over the subject, which has become increasingly impotent. In this context Kant's aesthetic paradox turns into Adorno's idea of art as a mode of cognitive praxis. Kant's *Critique of Judgment* fails to resolve the paradox that an *aesthetic* judgment of taste cannot be cognitive, and an aesthetic *judgment* of taste cannot be noncognitive. Kant's "Dialectic of the Aesthetical Judgment" simply extends this paradox into an apparently noncognitive concept that is supposed to mediate nature and freedom.[24] Adorno shows greater interest in a nondiscursive cognition than in a noncognitive concept, and he thinks of art as a nondiscursive way to mediate an actually alienated praxis with a praxis that could disalienate.[25]

Adorno refashions Kant's distinction between reflective and determinant judgment into a distinction between artistic and discursive knowledge. Kant describes aesthetic judgments as a type of reflective judgment, and he defines the reflective faculty of judgment as one which seeks a universal for the particular. Determinant judgments, by contrast, subsume the particular under a given universal.[26] Adorno claims that "ordinary" knowledge has become increasingly "determinant" in contemporary society. The social system is such that science, technology, and the culture industry schematize experience, imposing identity on the nonidentical, and forcing universal categories and rules on particulars and individuals. Authentic art opposes such imposing of identity. It is a reflective faculty of judgment, as it were, one which finds a nondiscursive form for particular content.

Yet Adorno follows Kant in insisting upon the unity of reason despite the apparent discrepancy between artistic and discursive rationality (208/200). Just as Kant says that reflection and determination are carried out by one faculty of judgment, so Adorno claims that art and discourse are dialectical poles of knowledge. Although the principle of identity in art opposes the principle of identity that discursive rationality has been forced to impose on the world (19/10–11), they are the same principle of identity. In contemporary society, the principle of identity represses anything neither useful for exchange nor identical with the human subject. In modern art, the principle of identity turns into the ideal of an autonomous artwork. Such a work tries to achieve identity with itself by eliciting its self-identity from disparate content. Identity arises "reflectively" and respectfully from qualitative affinities rather than being "determinately" and arbitrarily posited as quantitative equivalence.

The dialectical unity of knowledge becomes apparent through discursive self-reflection, when reason reflects on its own prehistory.[27] According to *Dialectic of Enlightenment*, the development of reason took a decisive turn when art and science bifurcated out of magic. Each pole of knowledge retains and changes elements of a more original magic.[28] Horkheimer and Adorno argue that magic tries to influence nature through imitation. Instead of presupposing identity or unity in nature, the magician imitates the varying spirits to be influenced in specific ways. Affinity binds the magic image to the object. Magical influence respects the multiple qualities and affinities of nature, even when it establishes a sacred space where mimetic influence can occur.

Unlike magic, science aims at controlling nature through reduction and abstraction. Scientists reduce things to their subjection to human control. Being controllable comes to constitute the identity and unity of everything in nature, which enters a correlation with the identity and unity of the controlling subject. The scientific symbol is merely an abstract sign for the object. Scientific distance is designed to make things universally fungible and controllable.

Art, by contrast, aims at a mimesis that lacks influence on nature. Unlike magic, art does not make itself similar to specific things. Unlike science, art does not reduce things to their being controllable. Instead, art imitates itself, and it contrasts its pure image to reality, whose elements this image has absorbed. At a distance from reality, artworks seek the appearance of the whole in the particular. Hence, as Schelling noted, art might even have precedence over science and technology.

The possible precedence of art does not mean science can be discounted. The task of Adorno's philosophy is to help science and art interpenetrate by letting discursive rigor and experiential flexibility correct each other within philosophy itself.[29] As attempts at discursive self-reflection, *Dialectic of Enlightenment* and *Negative Dialectics* suggest that a dialectic of mimesis and rationality has accompanied the historical separation of subject and object, a dialectic reproduced within both discursive and nondiscursive knowledge. By alienating rationality from what seems to be its inalienable material, art becomes a nondiscursive ally of discursive self-reflection (209/201). Although mimetic, art's nondiscursive knowledge is not naively irrational. On the one hand, mimesis is rationally objectified within art. On the other hand, mimesis is preserved in discursive self-reflection.

Adorno counts on mimetic rationality and rational mimesis within both critical theory and progressive art to mark paths past the modern impasse of rationality, which is also a social deadlock. Mimetic self-reflection and critical mimesis move in the same direction according to two sorts of laws (*Bewegungsgesetze*)—one artistic, the other discursive, but both of them having a certain "logic."[30] As in Adorno's negative dialectic, so in authentic modern art two processes converge whose horizon is a possible reconciliation: the critical rescue of material nonidentity as implicit spiritual identity, and the rescuing critique of spiritual identity as alienated material nonidentity.

Paradox of Praxis

Just as art as knowledge is characteristically nondiscursive, so art as praxis is primarily impractical. This does not mean Adorno thinks art is politically irrelevant. Rather, the impractical character of art as praxis is what makes for its strategic importance under current conditions. To make sense of what seems to be an utter paradox, one must note the peculiarities in Adorno's use of the term "praxis." He uses the term in at least three different ways without trying to keep these usages distinct. Sometimes praxis simply means human conduct in general. At other times it has the more precise meaning of human labor. At still other times it refers to specifically political activity. What is common to all three usages, and what provides the point to describing art as a primarily impractical praxis, is the fact that conduct, labor, and politics are all three properly oriented to accomplishing human purposes. The political relevance of art lies in the way art challenges activity that has lost touch with human purposes, despite a veneer of rationality. Art becomes practical by challenging an irrational praxis. This is the gist of the polemical claim quoted earlier: "If any social function can be ascribed to [artworks] at all, it is . . . to have no function" (336–37/322).

According to Adorno, art's social isolation allows it to challenge the dominant social praxis by recalling the forgotten purpose for which rationality is deployed (180–81/174, 428/402). In an exchange society, the dominant rationality becomes irrational. Reason forgets its *raison d'etre*—to eliminate suffering, to establish human well-being, to let qualitative individuality thrive. Art's impracticality allows it to remember the forgotten purpose of rationality and uncover the absurdity of the dominant rationality. Yet art cannot become merely irrational. Only by becoming increasingly technical can art both remember reason's *telos* and challenge reason's irrationality. Authentic art employs sophisticated technique to express suffering, make a negative promise of sensuous happiness, and honor unique qualities. The rational irrationality of modern art is a determinate negation of the irrational rationality in advanced capitalist society (86–90/79–83).

Adorno's view of art as an impractical praxis reformulates Kant's description of (natural) beauty as "an object's form of *purposiveness* insofar as it is perceived in the object *without the presentation of a purpose.*"[31] Kant's notion of purposeless purposiveness allows him to portray natural beauty as a link between moral freedom and scientifically conceived nature. As the ability to judge beauty, taste is a nontheoretical and nonpractical faculty whose indeterminate functioning indicates that morally good actions are not theoretically impossible. If they are not theoretically impossible, then they are not technically impractical, although natural science is practically amoral so long as it remains insufficient for moral praxis. Kant's concept of purposeless purposiveness amounts to an a priori recognition that it is possible to actualize moral goodness.[32] Natural beauty is a symbol of morality.

In Adorno's theory, philosophic reflection upon art replaces Kantian taste, and art itself replaces the natural symbol of morality. Yet Adorno's critique of reason continues Kant's. *Dialectic of Enlightenment* considers its own theoretical self-reflection a rescuing critique of mythical science as well as a key to transformative praxis.[33] Social morality would amount to ending the purposive purposelessness that pervades thought and action under advanced capitalist conditions.[34] Because this morality has become nearly impossible to carry out under current conditions, art's purposeless purposiveness makes it a temporary trustee for truly transformative praxis.

The assignment of trusteeship to art is prefigured by Schelling's *System of Transcendental Idealism* (1800). According to Schelling, the purposeless purposiveness of artistic products lets them serve the ego's conscious reflection on the identity in the ego of the conscious and the unconscious.[35] For this reason art becomes the highest purpose of human life, science becomes a means to serve art, and art turns into the only true organon and document of philosophy. Art recalls for philosophy what philosophy itself cannot present, namely, the unconscious aspect in human activity and the original identity between consciousness and the unconscious. Art reveals the unknown identity of subject and object before their alienation.[36]

Although Adorno does not share Schelling's aestheticism, there are traces of Schelling's "purposeless purposiveness" in *Aesthetic Theory*.[37] Adorno ties the enigma of art's purpose to a "configuration of mimesis and rationality" (182/175), and his notion of mimesis includes unconscious human impulses, which are comparable to Schelling's *natura naturans*. Adorno's "metacritique of practical reason"[38] claims that there would be neither theory nor praxis without such mimetic impulses. Though repressed during the irrational rationalization of modern society, mimesis is rationally preserved by art. Hence art acquires a new practical relevance, despite its enigmatic lack of purpose in contemporary society. Art is not merely a symbolic link between science and morality à la Kant. Artistic purposiveness does not simply reveal the identity between subjective consciousness and the objective unconscious à la Schelling. Rather, art consciously sublates unconscious motives for conscious theory and praxis in a society where rationality has forgotten its own purpose.

Yet art cannot avoid the social dilemmas confronting any form of rationality that remembers the unconscious purpose of praxis. There is a critical awareness in modern art that artworks show greater concern for their own autonomy than for whatever social contributions they could make. Modern art cannot advocate its lack of social functions, yet it cannot exist in any other way (338/324). At the same time, there is little difference between surrendering artistic autonomy or clinging to it. Either way society can integrate art and make it harmless (352–53/337). The paradox of praxis in general is also a paradox of artistic praxis in particular. Just as the irrationality of labor and politics under current conditions make them forget their transformative purpose, so the rationality of art relative to labor and politics makes it unable to carry out the transformation needed. What is required also seems unavailable, namely an effective mediation of art and social praxis.

Adorno does not suggest precise ways in which both art and social praxis could actually be changed. Instead, he provides a dialectical rationale for artistic autonomy and for purposeless purposiveness. The same rationality that turns artworks into socially irrational fetishes also enables them to expose the irrationality of social praxis. To see beyond art's social aporia we need philosophical insight into the rationality of artistic irrationality (338/324, 506/467). The need for such insight returns us to the import (*Gehalt*) for which autonomous works have shed their social functions and acquired the function of being socially dysfunctional.

Import and Impact

Adorno's emphasis on the import of the work of art implies that modern art has political relevance primarily because of its contributions to the formation of social consciousness (360–61/344–45). This is clear from his discussion of Picasso:

Expression reveals works to be lacerations inflicted by society; expression is the social ferment that is added to their autonomous shape. A telling example of this is Picasso's *Guernica:* it is wholly incompatible with criteria of realism, gaining expression through inhuman construction; eventually this expression takes on the . . . sharp contours of social protest. The socially critical dimensions of art works are those that hurt, those that bring to light . . . what is wrong with present social conditions [*die unwahrheit des gesellschaf-*

tlichen Zustands]. The public outcry evoked by works like *Guernica* is a response to that (353/337).

What is particularly instructive here is not so much what Adorno says as what he does not say. He does not ask who paid attention to Picasso's social protest when *Guernica* was first displayed at the Spanish Pavilion of the Paris World's Fair. He does not consider what impact this protest had on those who did pay attention. Nor does he discuss the potential for having some such impact once the work enters the museums and canons of twentieth-century art.[39] Adorno might not discount such questions, but the crucial point for him is that artworks have something important to present. The political relevance of their functions depends on the social significance of their import. Indeed, their political relevance lies in the functions of their artistic import: expression of suffering, broken promise of happiness, and the like.

A similar tendency shows up when one examines more closely the claim that artistic import has social significance. Adorno's concept of artistic import contains an inherent polarity between "social content" (*gesellschaftlicher Gehalt*) and "truth content" (*Wahrheitsgehalt*). Against student activists who desired the political actualization of artistic import, Adorno argues that they should not "rashly equate" truth content with social content (373/356). Similarly, against the theory of socialist realism Adorno argues that truth content transcends the social content with which it is mediated:

Granted, art implies reality because it is a form of knowledge. Knowledge necessarily points to reality, which in turn necessarily points to society, there being no reality that is not social. Truth content and social content are therefore mediated, although the cognitive quality of art, i.e. its truth content, transcends knowledge of reality *qua* empirical existent. Art turns into [social] knowledge as it grasps the essence of reality, forcing it to reveal itself in appearance and at the same time putting itself in opposition to appearance. Art must not talk about reality's essence directly, nor must it depict or in any way imitate it (383–84/366).

Just as the import of an artwork consists of the poles of truth content and social content, so art as social knowledge (*sociale Erkenntnis*) consists of both a cognitive quality (*Erkenntnischa-*

rakter) and a knowledge of empirical social reality (*Erkenntnis der Realität*).

Such polarities have two implications. First, the only relevant political functions are ones that stem from the import of a work. Second, a proper assessment of their relevance will be governed by an interpretation of the work's truth content. These implications become obvious in the section on "Commitment" (365–68/349–52). Here a contrast between committed and hermetic art replaces the contrast between committed and autonomous art in Adorno's article by the same title. Adorno says committed art and hermetic art share an opposition to the status quo. They disturb both cultural purists, who want art to have nothing to do with politics, and political activists, who want art to be easily accessible. Against both these positions Adorno writes:

No work of art can be true in social and political terms unless it is true in its own terms as well. By the same token, aesthetic authenticity is incompatible with a false political consciousness. The political and the immanent dimension are not congruent, but they are not radically divergent, either. . . . Truth content always points beyond the immanent aesthetic makeup of art works towards some political significance. This duality of immanence and sociality is stamped on every single work of art (368/351).

In other words, political and aesthetic truth provide conditions for each other. Adorno's language suggests, however, that aesthetic truth is the actual truth content of a work, and that this is "immanent" to the work, whereas political truth is not.

Perhaps the best way to interpret such language is to think of political truth as a social function stemming from the import the work contains, not from the political impact it has. An Adornian assessment of a work's political relevance would be governed by an interpretation of its truth content, not by an explanation of its political effectiveness. This hypothesis is borne out by the discussion of Brecht on these pages. Adorno focuses not on the political effectiveness of Brecht's plays but on how Brecht's political commitment motivates dramaturgical innovations and thereby supports the aesthetic quality of his plays. This seems to imply that if Brecht's plays do have political relevance, they have it not because of their political effectiveness but because of their intrinsic quality, which for Adorno hinges on their truth content.

Adorno's approach to political impact assumes that modern art has the task of helping to change social consciousness. Social consciousness must be changed if human beings are going to reshape the society that distorts their consciousness. Through artistic import art can encourage the transformed praxis that is needed in order to change the structure of a false society. Such praxis is the hidden potential of artistic truth content (367/350). According to Adorno, artworks are "less and more than praxis." Less, because, in their opposition to ordinary praxis, they avoid or prevent what must be done for the sake of a changed humanity. More, because they denounce the misguidance of praxis in a deformed world and anticipate the enlightened humanity that would constitute itself while it changes the world (358–59/342–43). Art is a praxis beyond praxis, as it were. Art has become a model for a possible praxis, one that would be rid of violence.

Since models are pointless unless they can be followed, somehow artistic praxis must become practical, in the sense that artworks must have a political impact. Adorno says this impact is highly indirect. It depends both on artistic import and on the entire state of society. Since empiricistic sociology ignores both of these conditions, its concern for effects leads it to misinterpret works of art. To a critical analysis, however, the impact of artworks can say much about their inherent import.

In a sense, the global impact of artistic praxis is an alienation effect, one that should be accomplished subtly rather than in a didactic manner: "[Brecht's] demand for a reflective attitude . . . converges with the valid idea that art works need to be known objectively. . . . Subjectively, art calls for externalization. . . . Art is practical in the sense that it defines the person who experiences art as a *zoon politikón*. . . . In addition art is objectively practical because it forms and educates consciousness, provided it stays away from outright propaganda" (360–61/344–45). By intervening in consciousness, authentic artworks bring back into society their corrective alienation of alienation. In order for artworks to intervene, however, there must be a consciousness that is sufficiently alienated from society to receive their intervention. Hence art's political impact depends on a circular process: autonomous art becomes politically effectual by calling for a consciousness that can let art have a political effect. This circle lies at the heart of Adorno's cultural politics.

6.3 Cultural Politics

As we have seen, Adorno views art as a form of nondiscursive knowledge and impractical praxis in a society where rational praxis has become irrational. Being nondiscursive, art can provide a formal liberation from oppressive social structures. Being impractical, art can have an indirect but transformative political impact. The key to both formal liberation and indirect impact lies in artistic import. This means, however, that for artworks to intervene in social consciousness, certain types of experience and interpretation must disclose artistic import. As a mode of cognitive praxis, art depends on the availability of appropriate knowledge toward art.

The circle of appropriate knowledge and artistic praxis in Adorno's cultural politics resembles the indeterminate relation between the cognitive subject and the natural object in Kant's account of beauty. Now, however, a full dialectic occurs between aesthetic subject and object, and the artwork has priority over subjective taste. Adorno's inversion of Kant presupposes Hegel's attempt to turn the static *adequatio rei et intellectus* into a dynamic process of truth. Like Hegel, Adorno claims that no finite judgment can be completely adequate.[40] The monolithic character of advanced capitalism gives added urgency to the question of adequate knowledge, however, and hence to questions concerning an adequate reception of art.[41]

Adequate Reception

Adorno thinks the criteria of adequate art reception are established by the artwork's dialectical structure. An adequate reception will release a work's congealed dialectic between content and form, doing for each artwork what Marx did for commodities in general. To release the artwork's dialectic, art

reception itself must be a dialectical process between spontaneous reactions and discursive judgments, a process involving
both immanence and distance toward the artwork.

Although Adorno emphasizes psychosomatic spontaneity as
a necessary condition for adequate aesthetic experience, he
opposes the notion that spectators simply react to the artist's
feelings. It is so, he says, that a significant work can prompt a
spontaneous instant of self-forgetting when the recipient disappears, as it were, in the work of art (362–63/346–47). For
this to happen, however, recipients must take distance from
their empirical selves and adopt a reflective attitude toward the
work of art. Only if the recipient's most intense subjective
reaction belongs to a penetrating and comprehensive experience can the possibility of truth be materialized. In this way,
says Adorno, adequate aesthetic experience can be a moment
of objective artistic truth. When Beethoven's music suddenly
overpowers the attentive listener, the ego realizes its own fini-
tude and prepares to surrender its harsh self-interest (364/
347–48). The ego wakes up to the fact that it is not the center
of the universe but a historical product of social forces, derivative from the unconscious id, whose potentials have yet to be
fulfilled. In such a moment, recipients find themselves by losing
themselves in the dawning realization of truth (401/379–80).

Truth is not irrational, however, nor is the knowledge of
truth merely the outcome of a mimetic reaction. The beginning
of the reprise in Beethoven's Ninth Symphony overwhelmingly
affirms "That's the way it is and not otherwise," but this moment of affirmation is mediated by the entire piece. The recipient's task, says Adorno, is to decide whether the music's
affirmation is true, and such a decision must be reached in a
discursive manner (363–64/347). Genuine aesthetic experience
mediates discursive and nondiscursive logic in order to let the
truth content of a piece emerge.[42]

Such a mediation can only occur if, like art itself, the performance and the reception of an artwork is mimetic. According to Adorno, to understand an artwork is to enter it and
follow it along. Artworks are riddles so long as they are perceived as static products. Only when a performer reproduces
an artwork in its own "objective constitution" will the riddle be

mitigated (190/183), and only when recipients reproduce the artwork from within an experience immersed in the artwork will the artwork be understood (183–84/176–78). The proper path into an artwork is by way of imitation: qualified interpreters mime the work itself.

When performers stop to think about the artwork, however, or when untrained recipients hesitate to enter it, questions arise about its point and art's purpose. Something similar occurs when an artwork becomes completely transparent to experience. An enigma returns to compel reflection: What is the sense of it all? What is the artwork for? (183–84/176–78) Adorno argues that artworks pose insoluble riddles because their non-discursive logic is illogical according to criteria of instrumental rationality. The aim of artistic form—to follow disparate impulses wherever they want to go—seems pointless in an exchange society where fixed identity is simply imposed (180–82/173–76). Artworks achieve definite syntheses whose purpose lies inside the works themselves: an entire artwork and all its moments are to become inescapably expressive (211/202–3, 323/309–310).

At the same time, the artwork has extra-artistic implications, and these depend in part on various forms of discourse. To make its political point felt, nondiscursive art needs discursive institutions. Adorno mentions three forms of discourse, interpretation, commentary, and criticism, and his philosophical aesthetics draws on all three.[43] Such discourses can help the work undergo historical unfolding, disclosing a truth content that transcends the work of art. Unless philosophically "honed," however, interpretation, commentary, and criticism will miss inherent artistic truth (289/277–78, 507/468). Aided by philosophy, such forms of discourse can contribute to the practicality of art's cognitive praxis.

All of this indicates the need for a certain kind of philosophy, as is suggested by the title of Adorno's book. What is needed is an aesthetic theory, a critical phenomenology in which neither philosophy nor art is lacking: "Those who have only an inside view of art do not understand it, whereas those who see art only from the outside tend to falsify it for lack of affinity with [works of art]. Rather than fluctuate randomly between these two standpoints, aesthetics must unfold their necessary interconnection in reference to specific works [*an der Sache*]" (520/479). Given Adorno's view of art as a mode of cognitive praxis and his insistence on appropriate knowledge, the notion of an aesthetic theory raises two sorts of questions. The first, which was briefly discussed in an earlier context, pertains to the cognitive status of an aesthetic theory. Is it possible for an *aesthetic* theory to be theoretical and for an aesthetic *theory* to be aesthetic? If so, then how? The second group of questions pertains to the political status of such a theory. Is it possible for an aesthetic theory to disclose the political implications of art? If so, which political implications can be disclosed? If not, then what is the purpose of an aesthetic theory? The two sorts of questions point to the nexus of theory and praxis in Adorno's cultural politics.

Aesthetic Theory

According to Adorno, general philosophical arguments will not solve the enigma of art in the absence of adequate aesthetic experience. There must be an adequate experience of particular artworks, and such experience must undergo theoretical reflection (185/179). A solution requires all the mediations of artistic structure and of a discourse that respects the structure of particular works of art (189/182). Through the interpenetration of aesthetic experience and philosophic reflection, art's enigma can be grasped without being explained away, and a solution can be found without simply being left inside the artworks where it resides. Artistic import and spirit are Adorno's most significant ways of moving outside the work of art. Artistic technique and form are his most significant ways of staying inside. The mediation of technique and import provides the "necessary interconnection in reference to specific works" (520/479), and it joins the enigma with its solution.

The ultimate solution to the enigma of art lies in the truth content of particular works of art. Although guided by an Hegelian notion of truth, Adorno envisions an aesthetics that goes beyond Hegel in honoring individual experience and particular works of art. Yet aesthetics must be discursive and theoretical. It must be discursive because the knowledge of truth is tied to the making of discursive claims.[44] Aesthetics must be theoretical because only a theory can attain sufficient universality for comprehending the false universality of an exchange society. At the same time, the theory must be aesthetic, in the sense that it interacts with adequate experience of particular works of art: to form a proper conception of artistic truth, the theory must honor the nondiscursive logic of artworks themselves. Since these are social monads, however, artistic logic can be fully honored only if the theorist probes its social ramifications.

The title of *Aesthetic Theory* captures various sides to Adorno's innovative reception of Kant and Hegel by way of Marx and Freud. Adorno converts Kant's critique of aesthetic judgments into a theory that tries to grasp art's unintelligibility by basing itself on nondiscursive logic and aesthetic experience. Hegel's glorifying art as absolute spirit turns into Adorno's insisting on the truth of particular works. Marx's critique of political economy gives rise to an aesthetics for which artworks have political relevance but their political truth is inherently aesthetic (519–20/478–79). Freud's theory of sublimation becomes a way to understand the production and reception of art rather than to trace the artwork back to its maker's psyche. And, perhaps most important for an approach that wishes to be both aesthetic and theoretical, Hegel's notion of truth is modified by Kant's insight into the way discursive categories keep discourse from completely knowing the *Ding an sich*.

For Adorno, truth resembles the Kantian thing-in-itself, which he connects with the idea of the nonidentical. Ordinary and scientific discourse cannot fully know the nonidentical, because such discourse imposes identity without respecting nonidentical qualities. In virtue of their mimetic character, artworks honor the nonidentical, but only by flaunting discursive categories. Truth is available for discourse but not attained. Truth is attained by art, but not communicated. Bridging this gap requires a mode of knowledge that mediates art and discourse.

Hence the necessity of an aesthetic theory becomes clear. Questions about the purpose of art or the meaning of an artwork are discursive questions about nondiscursive modes of knowledge. Because art is not discursive, its attempted answer does not suffice. Because most discourse remains merely discursive, it cannot really answer (191–93/183–86). Despite the obvious discrepancy between art and discourse, philosophy seeks an answer in each artwork the philosopher interprets. Such interpretation of specific artworks belongs to what Adorno conceives as the general task of contemporary aesthetics: to understand the apparent unintelligibility of modern works of art (179/173). In the absence of appropriate philosophical interpretation, the enigma of art will not be solved, and the truth deep inside artworks will not be communicated. Then their purposeless purposiveness might be pointless in a world that is already untrue.

To mediate art and discourse in order to disclose internal artistic truth, knowledge must honor nondiscursive artworks when it makes discursive claims. According to Adorno, such mediating knowledge must be philosophical. Only philosophy is fully capable of grasping artistic truth content. Such truth content is a solution demanded by every authentic artwork, and it is the *raison d'etre* of art. While thus establishing the legitimacy of autonomous art in a false society, philosophy justifies itself as aesthetic theory (193/186). This is not to say that philosophy is only possible as aesthetics. Nor does this entail that philosophy must culminate in aesthetics. Instead the point is that an aesthetic theory is needed to disclose artistic truth for the sake of social praxis.

Intellectual Praxis

To see the political implications of Adorno's approach, it will help to recall from chapter 2 that the issue of art and politics has to do with the appropriateness of specific artistic practices for definite political conditions, the political effectiveness of these practices, and the position of artists and art critics in current political struggles. Adorno couches his approach to such matters in a contrast between committed and autonomous art with respect to transforming fundamental political attitudes. If the name of Bertolt Brecht can stand for the one type of art, the name of Samuel Beckett can stand for the other.

When framing his approach this way, Adorno relies on his theory of advanced capitalism, his model of art's social mediation, and his account of the relationship between art and labor. It is because the system of advanced capitalism has become so pervasive in life and culture that Adorno thinks fundamental political attitudes must be transformed. It is because he regards artworks as social monads that he says autonomous art has the greater potential in this regard. It is because he views art as a mode of social labor that Adorno depicts committed and autonomous art as alternative political strategies. All of this provides a global context for the claim quoted earlier: "Praxis is not the impact [*Wirkung*] works have; it is the hidden potential of their truth content [*Wahrheitsgehalt*]" (367/350). This claim and its context raise the question whether the import (*Gehalt*) of artworks is political in any genuine sense of the term.

Given the apparent circle between artistic praxis and appropriate knowledge, one's initial response to this question will be negative. There are two reasons for this response. The first is that Adorno's notion of import cuts truth content off from actual political struggles and wraps it in the mantle of autonomous intellectual culture. The second reason is that autonomous intellectual culture has slight potential for contributing to actual political struggles. For both reasons, the cultural politics of *Aesthetic Theory* is little more than a cultural politics.

On the one hand, Adorno places art and philosophy in a relationship of mutual dependency with respect to the disclosure of political truth. "Philosophy and art overlap in the idea of truth content. The progressively unfolding truth of a work of art is none other than the truth of the philosophic concept" (197/189). Like Hegel, Adorno sees philosophy and art as forms of spirit that are dynamically interrelated. Disclosing artworks and their truth is a sociohistorical process in which both art and philosophy participate. This means, however, that truth content has more to do with the movement of intellectual culture than with the life of ordinary participants in struggles for political liberation.

On the other hand, Adorno himself recognizes the political precariousness of those artworks and philosophical texts that best carry truth in contemporary society. It seems that art and philosophy are caught in the same political dilemma. It does not really matter whether philosophy and art surrender or maintain their autonomy. Either way they can be rendered ineffective and ignored. The circle between art and philosophy offers no exit. The philosophy that tries to help autonomous art become politically effective is itself a social anomaly. In a false society, art needs philosophy just as much as philosophy needs art, but this society rejects both art and philosophy. Such a society puts committed art and autonomous art in the same boat.

Furthermore, Adorno's description of art as a mode of cognitive praxis employs a questionable notion of praxis. This notion is the reverse side of his insistence on autonomy. *Aesthetic Theory* gives to art and philosophy a position similar to that which Aristotle assigned to *theoria,* but for different reasons. Aristotle argues that theory does not serve any alien use because it does not refer beyond itself into the future. Adorno suggests that philosophy and art do not serve any alien use because they refer to a future praxis whose goal they themselves define.[45] Although Adorno rightly indicates that philosophy and art need not be directly "useful" to be worthwhile, and that philosophy and art must challenge the standards implied by the demand for "usefulness," his view of philosophy and art assumes that genuine praxis is primarily contemplative, and that noncontemplative praxis is not genuine.

According to an essay on praxis published in the last year of Adorno's life, most praxis is disfigured by its origins in the subjective need to survive. The goal of genuine praxis is to respect the needs of the object. By showing respect for the object, art criticizes the enslavement of most praxis to subjective needs; by transcending subjective needs, theory becomes a trustee for freedom. "The goal of correct praxis would be the abolition of praxis."[46] Here genuine praxis is defined by freedom from the necessity of self-preservation.

Unfortunately this view of praxis cannot be divorced from the real slavery that first made it possible in classical Greece. Adorno's critical theory is insufficiently critical, not because it

directly encourages political "resignation,"[47] but because it per-
petuates a problematic legacy of Greek philosophy. It perpet-
uates the idea that contemplation unencumbered by manual
labor is both the arbiter and goal of human conduct. Because
most human activities, including those of political struggle, are
not contemplative, they are disqualified from the start, while
more contemplative activities such as art and philosophy occupy a privileged position. It is in authentic art and socially
critical philosophy that Adorno thinks the possibility of genuine praxis can still be envisioned.

Even if one agrees that the envisioning of genuine praxis is
a crucial task, one can question Adorno's tendency to view
genuine praxis as an actualization of art and philosophy. Although he ties this actualization to a self-reflection of nature,
Adorno does not break with an overemphasis on contemplative
modes of praxis. Unfortunately, contemplative actualities need
not become more than mere possibilities. Nothing prevents a
strong emphasis on autonomous art and philosophy as modes
of praxis from leaving the entire nonintellectual world as it is,
while letting art and philosophy appear as the only true voices
for social transformation. As a consequence, actual struggles
for political liberation are devalued, seeming less than genuine
as modes of human praxis.

Adorno's philosophical extrapolation of artistic truth tries to
help art as social labor point to a true praxis in a true society.
Autonomous intellectual culture still seems meaningful, despite
its past failures to help transform the world. In modern art
there darkly shines a ray of hope. Adorno's aesthetics represents a prism for this ray. Hope refracts into the exchange
society from the reconciled life that this society makes possible
and prevents. Without art, Adorno's philosophy would be less
prismatic. Without both philosophy and art, there might be
fewer glimpses of hope. Unless their truth can be politically
actualized, however, it runs the risk of becoming an abstract
utopia, one that inadvertently endorses the status quo. This
would be the undesirable potential of a merely cultural politics.

7

Paradoxical Modernism

Adorno's cultural politics raises the issue of aesthetic modernism. His political preference for Beckett over Brecht is inseparable from his defense of modern art against hostile critics such as Lukács. For Adorno, art's political relevance cannot be divorced from its historical meaning. His concept of historical meaning is not readily transparent, however. Whereas traditional German philosophy ties meaning to a view of history as a continuous process having a telos toward which human endeavors contribute, Adorno has strong reservations about the notion of progress such a view implies. This chapter argues that Adorno's defense of modern art is a part of a paradoxical attempt to retain a historical telos without making inflated claims about what human beings have achieved.

7.1 Culture after Auschwitz

Adorno ties the difficulty of determining the historical meaning of modern art to the precarious position of Western intellectual culture after two world wars. Not only does intellectual culture occupy a precarious position, but also the very concept of historical meaning has come under attack. Enlightenment figures such as Kant and Hegel anchor historical meaning in the autonomy of human beings as rational agents of morality or rational participants in intellectual culture. Post-Enlightenment philosophies such as logical positivism and existentialism, by contrast, place the notions of both meaning and autonomy in question. This turn of events is related to intellectual culture's failure to bring about the more humane existence for which the Enlightenment hoped.

According to *Negative Dialectics,* contemporary reflections on historical meaning must recognize that they occur after Auschwitz.

A child, fond of an innkeeper named Adam, watched him club to death the rats pouring out of holes in the courtyard; it was in his image that the child pictured the first human being. That this has been forgotten . . . is both the triumph of culture and its failure. Culture cannot tolerate the memory of that zone, because culture keeps imitating the old Adam. . . . It abhors the stench because culture stinks; because, as Brecht's magnificent line has it, the palace of culture is built out of dogshit. Years after that line was written, Auschwitz demonstrated irrefutably the failure of culture. . . . All culture after Auschwitz, including its urgent critique, is garbage. . . . Anyone who enters a plea for maintaining this radically guilty and shabby culture becomes an accomplice, while anyone who rejects culture is directly furthering the barbarism that culture showed itself to be.[1]

Adorno questions the idealist claim that autonomous art and philosophy can give meaning to life, since the separation of mental from manual labor is what helped impoverish life in the first place. Yet the separation cannot be overcome in a merely intellectual way, and Adorno cannot avoid contributing to the culture he criticizes. Critical reflections on intellectual culture are necessary, but they must become self-critical. Adorno's cultural critique expresses the ambiguities that arise when art and philosophy recognize their own impotence and complicity but keep hoping for the more humane existence once sought as an outcome of human autonomy in morality and culture.

The traditional attempt to anchor historical meaning in human autonomy places a heavy emphasis on the subject's ability to shape the world to serve human purposes. This is clear in the moral philosophy of Kant, where individuals are obligated to act in accordance with the dictates of reason and not in accordance with natural inclinations or desires. It is also clear in the political philosophy of Lukács, where the motor for social transformation is located in proletarian class consciousness. To a philosopher who challenges the myth of subjective agency, the traditional emphasis on human autonomy becomes problematic. Adorno does not abandon this emphasis, but he makes us wonder what both autonomy and historical meaning come to.

Organon

Adorno's essay "Trying to Understand *Endgame*" is particularly instructive in this regard.[2] Adorno reads Samuel Beckett's play as a "history of the subject's end" (*Endgeschichte des Subjekts*)[3] illuminating the process of self-formation and suggesting a new stage amid the ruins of subjectivity. This reading pits Beckett against Sartre and argues against two other trends in literary criticism.[4] Lukács had charged Beckett with falling into decadent formalism and deriving metaphysical nonsense from Heideggerian "ontologism." More sympathetic interpreters had been trying to find metaphysical meaning in Beckett's plays. Adorno's simple but subtle argument undercuts both Lukács and the sympathizers: *Endgame* translates metaphysical absurdity into aesthetic meaning without making the play a Sartrean pretext for philosophical pronouncements. Rather than denounce decadent formalism, the interpreter must reconstruct the way in which the play expresses meaninglessness. Rather than translate the play's meaning into philosophical terms, the interpreter must understand the play's incomprehensibility.

Precisely because it refuses to spout philosophical doctrines, *Endgame* challenges philosophy to give an interpretation. Indeed, Adorno finds this challenge nearly definitive for the relevance of contemporary philosophy: "The interpretive word . . . cannot recuperate Beckett, even though his dramaturgy, by virtue of its enigmatic character, . . . points toward interpretation. One could almost designate as the criterion of relevant philosophy today whether it is up to that task."[5] The reason for this lies in Adorno's view of philosophy's historical character. Writing elsewhere on the contemporary tasks of philosophy, Adorno endorses Hegel's claim that philosophy "is its own time apprehended in thoughts."[6] According to Adorno, this "astonishing claim" presents a task that neither existentialism nor logical positivism fulfills. His own effort is to devote thought to phenomena in which contemporary society is exposed for what it is.[7]

Adorno does not share Hegel's confidence in the rationality of reality, however, nor does he retain early Marx's optimism that, through a proletarian revolution, philosophical interpretation will help change the world.[8] Instead, Adorno introduces his criterion of relevant philosophy with a comment on the difficulty of understanding contemporary society: "The irrationality of bourgeois society on the wane resists being understood: those were the good old days when a critique of political economy could be written which took this society by its own *ratio*. For in the meantime it was thrown this *ratio* on the junkheap and virtually replaced it with direct control."[9] While this comment reflects the shift in ideology discussed in chapter 4, it also suggests that philosophy's attempt to apprehend its own time has become deeply problematic.

For Adorno's readers, the first problem of interpretation is to understand the connection between the difficulty of understanding contemporary society and the challenge of interpreting Beckett. The solution lies in some missing premises that help explain Beckett's significance for Adorno's philosophy. According to W. Martin Lüdke, Beckett's significance can hardly be overestimated. For Adorno, advanced capitalism contains the emerging thrust of history in general, authentic modern art expresses the core of the history of art, and the reciprocation of progressive philosophy and modern art generates comprehensive knowledge of both historical processes. In order for this knowledge to be gained, however, modern art must also express the essence of advanced capitalist society.[10] And here lies a premise omitted from the *Endgame* essay: Whereas philosophy can no longer confidently criticize academic disciplines such as economics and sociology when trying to understand its own time, authentic artworks such as *Endgame* contain a penetrating apprehension of contemporary society. To the extent that philosophy wants to be a thoughtful apprehension of its own time, *Endgame* calls for philosophical interpretation. The difficulty of interpreting this play is that it exposes the irrationality of contemporary society while resisting rational exposition. *Endgame* is an enigmatic organon for a philosophy that has transformed Hegel's *Phenomenology* and Marx's *Capital* into a critical phenomenology of culture after Auschwitz. Authentic works of modern art are their own time apprehended for philosophy.[11]

Beckett's Meaning

Given a close connection between the difficulties of understanding contemporary society and of interpreting *Endgame*, Adorno's attempt to comprehend the play's incomprehensibility is also an attempt to grasp society's irrationality. According to Adorno, *Endgame* upstages Sartre's traditional dramatizations of existentialist doctrine. Beckett's avant-garde form "absorbs what is expressed and changes it."[12] When *Endgame* parodies the three Aristotelian unities, it simultaneously pokes fun at existentialist philosophy. Adorno's essay first shows how Beckett reduces various staples of existential ontology, such as historicity, the human condition, Heidegger's *Befindlichkeiten*, and Jasper's "situations," to a minimal existence. Then the essay analyzes Beckett's parody of the traditional categories of drama, and it concludes by interpreting *Endgame*'s import as the history of the subject's end.[13] In this way Adorno demonstrates that Beckett's play does not present the abstract idea of absurdity. Instead it expresses the real absurdity of all culture, including existential philosophy, after World War II. By carrying this historical experience into the details of dramatic form, Beckett raises social critique to the level of aesthetic form (371/ 354).

Adorno suggests that Beckett completes the tendency in Kafka, Proust, and Joyce to wed reflection with pure presentation. The harder it becomes to find real events meaningful, the more illusory becomes the idea of an aesthetic configuration binding the artist's intention with the artwork's meaning. Beckett gets rid of the illusion. His self-conscious parodies use thoughtful reflection both to establish the artwork's meaning and to express the absence of meaning. *Endgame* faces up to the historical absence of a metaphysical meaning sufficient to support overarching forms of dramatic unity. If its dramatic structure and language remained meaningful in a traditional manner, the play could not express the absence of meaning. If the play did not cohere, nothing significant would be expressed. Beckett achieves aesthetic meaning while expressing metaphysical absurdity, and he does so by rigorously negating the traditional forms of dramatic meaning (*Sinnzusammenhang*). Metaphysical meaninglessness becomes the meaning of *Endgame* because its aesthetic meaninglessness acquires meaning as a determinate negation of the dramatic forms that used to *affirm* metaphysical meaning.[14]

In giving this interpretation of Beckett's incomprehensibility, Adorno deliberately transforms the traditional concept of meaning evidenced in the work of Beethoven, Goethe, and Hegel. Adorno says that traditional aesthetics expects the artwork to be a meaningful whole. The interaction of whole and parts is supposed to generate an artistic meaning (*Sinn*) that coincides with the artwork's metaphysical import (*Gehalt*). This traditional concept of meaning remains partially valid for Adorno. He agrees that an artwork's meaning is constituted by the interrelating of all the work's phenomenal moments. But he sees that the sum total of artistic meaning does not coincide with the metaphysical import of a work such as *Endgame*. So too the metaphysical and the aesthetic do not coincide in Adorno's transformed concept of meaning, although the two dimensions remain closely related (516–17/476–77).

This transformation helps Adorno explain how "absurd" works can remain understandable. They can remain understandable so long as their intention and meaning are neither equated nor divorced. According to Adorno, confusing the artist's intention with the artwork's objective meaning is the "most fatal" source of mistakes in art criticism. Yet subjective intentions are not irrelevant for understanding the artwork. They help organize the artwork and become part of its objectivity. The artwork's objective meaning synthesizes and carries the artist's intentions (226–27/216–17). The same approach makes for better interpretations of older works. Adorno gives the example of a play by Goethe. Although "humanity" was originally an idea that Goethe intended to express, this idea has entered the language of *Iphigenie auf Tauris* and hence become relevant for any interpretation. Humanity is the meaning, not simply the intention, of Goethe's drama (227/217–18).

There are some problems with Adorno's reference to *Iphigenie*. Kaiser, for example, criticizes this illustration for ignoring the play's plot and characters.[15] A larger problem, however, is Adorno's equivocation with the term *Sinn*. *Sinn* can indicate either aesthetic or metaphysical meaning, and (aesthetic) meaning can refer to either the import of an artwork or its constructed coherence. Often it is difficult to tell whether such equivocations are "occasional" or "serious," to use a distinction Adorno applies to Hegel.[16] Be that as it may, Adorno wishes to argue that the intended absence of meaning affects both the form and the import *(Gehalt)* of Beckett's plays; meaninglessness has become *Endgame*'s objective meaning (516–17/476–77). Beckett's incomprehensibility can be understood, provided intention and meaning are properly distinguished and the concept of meaning is reconceived.

Final History

The fact that Beckett's incomprehensibility can be understood does not guarantee that Adorno's interpretation is comprehensible. The *Endgame* essay makes it hard to distinguish between the meaning to be found in *Endgame* and the meaning Adorno finds. What he finds in *Endgame* is the final history *(Endgeschichte)* of the human subject. Beckett's play lets this history seem like an infinite catastrophe rather than an ontological condition.[17] According to Adorno, the following scene parodies human autonomy:

Hamm: Take me for a little turn. (Clov goes behind the chair and pushes it forward.) Not too fast! (Clov pushes chair.) Hug the walls, then back to the centre again. (Clov pushes chair.) I was right in the centre, wasn't I?

Clov: (pushing). Yes.

Hamm: We'd need a proper wheel-chair. With big wheels. Bicycle wheels! (Pause.) Are you hugging?

Clov: (pushing). Yes.

Hamm: (groping for wall). It's a lie! Why do you lie to me?

Clov: (bearing closer to wall). There! There!

Hamm: Stop! (Clov stops chair close to back wall. Hamm lays his hand against wall.) Old wall! (Pause.) Beyond is the . . . other hell. (Pause. Violently.) Closer! Closer! Up against!

Clov: Take away your hand. (Hamm withdraws his hand. Clov rams chair against wall.) There! (Hamm leans towards wall, applies his ear to it.)

Hamm: Do you hear? (He strikes the wall with his knuckles.) Do you hear? Hollow bricks! (He strikes again.) All that's hollow! (Pause. He straightens up. Violently.) That's enough. Back!

Clov: We haven't done the round.

Hamm: Back to my place! (Clov pushes chair back to centre.) Is that my place?

Clov: Yes, that's your place.

Hamm: Am I right in the centre?

Clov: I'll measure it.

Hamm: More or less! More or less!

Clov: (moving chair slightly). There!

Hamm: I'm more or less in the centre?

Clov: I'd say so.

Hamm: You'd say so! Put me right in the centre!

Clov: I'll go and get the tape.

Hamm: Roughly! Roughly! (Clov moves chair slightly.) Bang in the centre!

Clov: There![18]

Adorno comments that Beckett's imbecilic ritual pays back the "hubris of idealism, the enthroning of humanity as creator in the center of creation."[19]

Later, the blind master Hamm orders his lame servant Clov to view the earth for him. Clov asks, "Any particular sector you fancy? Or merely the whole thing?"[20] In one rational question that sounds like nonsense, Adorno writes, Clov shows the absurdity in a pure positing of the human subject. Clov's master is the great-grandson of Fichte, whose "absolute subjectivism" elicited Jacobi's charge of nihilism. The ham-handed master is also Schopenhauer's second cousin, whose sole hope is "the cosmic night" he invokes with quotes of poetry.[21]

Hamm's power is impotent. Clov's servile subtlety has turned the table and has hit the nail on the head.[22] Clov's absurdly rational "Or merely the whole thing?" exposes the absurdity of Hamm's *ratio*.

On Adorno's interpretation, the subject that strives for complete autonomy turns reason into a mere instrument of domination. Eventually reason ignores its purposes and disregards what it has disqualified into a mere object of domination. Then the subject must ask about the meaning that reason itself has eliminated. No answer remains but the nothingness that purely instrumental rationality already is. "Any particular sector . . .? Or merely the whole thing?" Yet the apparent absurdity of reason is historical, not ontological. The development of purely instrumental reason is a historical process, although this process lets reason's absurdity seem ontological. Beckett's drama shatters the semblance. Beckett's negative ontology is the negation of ontology. The possibility of something true but inconceivable is decisively opened by the immanent contradiction in which Beckett shows reason terminating.[23] Blind instrumental reason is a historical fetish that could be superseded.

Endgame and Adorno's interpretation converge in a critique of the irrational rationality of today's society. Adorno tries to show that, despite the advance of science and technology, there has not yet been a decisive change in the "existentials" of human prehistory—domination, slavery, and suffering. "In view of the concrete possibility of utopia, dialectics is the ontology of the wrong state of things."[24] A negative ontology is still an ontology, however. Is there a difference between an infinite catastrophe and an ontological condition? Is there a difference between Beckett's final history and Adorno's critique of the human subject? Does Adorno affirm Beckett's "pictureless picture of death"? Or does the convergence of Beckett and Adorno become a separation?

According to Adorno, both Clov and Hamm live toward death:

Clov: I love order. It's my dream. A world where all would be silent and still and each thing in its last place, under the last dust.

And, a little later,

Hamm: If I can hold my peace, and sit quiet, it will be all over with sound, and motion, all over and done with.[25]

Beckett's blank picture of death presents an ambiguous suspension of the historical dialectic. In *Endgame* the difference disappears between absolute domination—the completely static hell—and utopia, where everything would be in its right place. Adorno writes: "The ultimate absurdity is that the repose of nothingness and that of reconciliation cannot be distinguished from each other. Hope creeps out of a world in which it is no more conserved than pap and pralines, and back where it came from, back into death."[26] But *Endgame* cannot even accept the hope that there will be nothing anymore. The play's only comfort is that of stoically carrying on.

Adorno finds something in Beckett's nothingness. By presenting the final history of human autonomy in an exchange society, *Endgame* offers the only fitting reaction to Auschwitz: "Such nihilism implies the opposite of identification with nothingness. To Beckett, as to the Gnostics, the created world is radically evil, and its negation is the possibility of another world not yet in existence. . . . The slightest difference between nothingness and what has come to rest would be the haven of hope, a no man's land between the border posts of being and nothingness."[27] Adorno's philosophy tries to wrest hope from the slight difference between the emptiness of absolute domination and the peace of reconciliation. What remains to be seen is the substance of this hope, and the ability of Adorno's philosophy really to deliver.

7.2 Reification and Reconciliation

Adorno's reading of *Endgame* does not simply emerge from the play when it is interpreted. His reading is informed by a philosophy of history whose claims go well beyond modern art and contemporary society. Although Adorno has dispensed with the Lukácsian notion of a historical meta-subject, he has not given up the assumptions of unity and continuity in the sociohistorical process. Only these assumptions let Adorno locate the historical meaning of modern artworks in their carry-

ing a truth that is itself historical. If Adorno did not assume
that the dialectical course of human history is one process with
interconnected stages, he could hardly describe the truth content of modern works as a "crystallization of history," nor could
he find historical meaning in such crystallizations.

It is true, of course, that Adorno has little use for the Enlightenment's faith in progress. It is also true that he finds
Hegelian universal history deeply problematic: "No universal
history leads from savagery to humanitarianism, but there is
one leading from the slingshot to the megaton bomb."[28] Yet
he does not give up the notion of what Jay calls "longitudinal
totality."[29]

History is the unity of continuity and discontinuity. Society stays alive,
not despite its antagonism, but by means of it; the profit interest and
thus the class relationship make up the objective motor of the production process, on which everyone's life depends, and the primacy
of which has its vanishing point in the death of all. This also implies
the reconciling side of the irreconcilable; since nothing else permits
human beings to live, not even a changed life would be possible
without it. What historically made this possibility may as well destroy
it.[30]

Adorno construes human history as an antagonistic unity in
which advances are not purely progressive and in which the
obstacles to progress are not simply regressive. This construal
proceeds from the present in light of a possible but not inevitable future.

Adorno's philosophy of history can be described as a "dialectic of enlightenment," with all that this implies for the
subject's relationships to nature, culture, society, and the future. W. Martin Lüdke says that "Trying to Understand Endgame" provides a "model" in which Adorno develops his theory
of the dialectic of enlightenment. Beckett's play functions as a
"chief witness" for this dialectic's "logic of disintegration."[31]
Although the "logic of disintegration" has several dimensions,
the most important one in Adorno's reading of Beckett is that
between the formation of an autonomous self and the loss of
genuine autonomy: "We are dealing here . . . with a basic
premise of Adorno's philosophy. Once installed as the precondition for the constitution of identity over against overpower-

ing Nature, the principle of self-preservation restricts the identical subject to an expression of compulsive identity, which, having become independent, maintains itself even when Nature is almost completely controlled."[32] Peter Dews notes a similar theme when he compares critical theory with poststructuralist "logics of disintegration." He says that Horkheimer and Adorno turn Weber's theory of rationalization "into a world-historical process of reification, in which the calculating, instrumental rationality required of the subject in its struggle to gain independence from the overwhelming powers of external nature requires a corresponding repression of the spontaneity of inner nature. The culmination of this process is an empty, adapted subjectivity which has lost that very autonomy for whose sake the conquest of nature was initiated."[33] If Adorno finds hope in Beckett's blank picture of death, however, this must indicate that the "world-historical process of reification" is also something else, and that the use of instrumental rationality to achieve autonomy does not simply result in "an empty, adapted subjectivity." In other words, the dialectic of enlightenment must be a genuine dialectic, and not simply a logic of disintegration.

Nature and Culture

One can hear another side of the historical narrative by imagining how Hegel might criticize Adorno's reading of Beckett. Hegel could pose the same objections he raised against "the unhappy consciousness." For "the unhappy consciousness," he says, the hope of becoming one with "the beyond" must remain "without fulfillment and present fruition." Between the hope and its fulfillment stands "the absolute contingency or inflexible indifference" that is involved in something transcendent assuming definite shape and providing a basis for hope.[34] To Hegel, Adorno's reading of *Endgame* would seem to pry hope loose from an almost skeptical stoicism, despite Adorno's sharing Hegel's critique of stoicism and skepticism. Can this hope be more than the unfulfilled wish of an "unhappy consciousness" that cannot ground its hope in the historical process?[35]

Hegel's criticism embodies confidence in human autonomy

and in intellectual culture, especially in Hegel's own "absolute knowledge." Because of where Hegel's hope lies, the manifest failures of twentieth-century culture cast doubts on his criticism of unhappy consciousness. Indeed, Adorno regards unhappy consciousness as "the one authentic dignity" that spirit received when it separated from the body. It serves as a negative reminder to the spirit about its corporeal aspect. Only an ability to suffer "gives spirit whatever hope it has."[36]

Adorno's hope is directed not toward becoming one with "the beyond" but toward "corporeal resurrection."[37] This hope overturns the self-satisfied culturalism of Hegel's "belly turned spirit."[38] Adorno recognizes with Hegel that any "freedom of self-consciousness" presupposes the dialectic of master and slave. Whereas *Endgame* mocks that dialectic, Adorno reinterprets it as a regressive progress in experience and intellect throughout the prehistory of humanity.[39] The price of achieving autonomy has been a reification of consciousness, although autonomy could not have been achieved in any other way. The question is whether reification can be surpassed without a loss of autonomy. Given the way in which Adorno ties reification to the principle of exchange, this question is simply another version of the problem of human agency for social transformation.

The problem of human agency intensifies when Adorno claims that discursive thought works against corporeal resurrection by repressing the material and the nonidentical. The mere thought of hope transgresses hope and works against it.[40] Yet to think this about the thought of hope would be impossible without hope. Adorno's thought ties hope to the experience of suffering. *Weh spricht: vergeh.* Suffering calls for the transformative praxis that would resolve the antagonisms registered by suffering.[41] To the extent that discursive thought ignores suffering, Adorno's hope requires that he think against thought and express the suffering both disguised and multiplied by instrumental rationality.

Adorno's critique of thought belongs to a larger critique of culture, not a condemnation of culture but a reflection of culture upon itself. In this self-reflection lies a complement to corporeal resurrection. For the body to be revived, culture must be reconciled with nature. To be reconciled, culture must reflect on its own tendency to repress nature, particularly that which is internal to the human subject. Self-reflection is the key to a possible conversion in the dialectic of enlightenment. Because culture can still reflect on itself, there is still reason to expect a resurrection of the flesh, even though the decisive change would have to take place in the structure of society.

The importance of self-reflection is clear from *Dialectic of Enlightenment*. In this fragmentary phenomenology of spirit, Horkheimer and Adorno find a potentially fatal flip in the early stages of Western civilization. The flip occurs during the time of patriarchal myths. Myth modulates toward enlightenment in a phase, marked by Olympian and Hebraic religions, when "bourgeois" society replaces nomadism, thought becomes independent, magic turns into rational praxis, and the human subject awakens as the world's rational ruler. By locating the image of God in human cultural power, both Archilochos and Genesis deify rational domination. The task for Horkheimer and Adorno is to demythologize that deification.[42]

The outcome depends on a crucial distinction in origins that many commentators have overlooked. The distinction can be expressed in three contrasts: retribution or grace, liquidation or sublation, repression or conciliation. Olympian myth portrays the world as an endless no-exit where everything has its comeuppance under the natural relations of retribution, equivalence, and fate. According to Horkheimer and Adorno's chapter on anti-Semitism, however, the God of Judaism confronts nature as nature's other principle. This God "does not merely guarantee nature's blind cycle." Unlike Olympian deities, the God of Judaism "can liberate from this cycle." While entangling creation in a net of guilt and merit, this God remains gracious, covenanting with human beings and promising them a Messiah.[43] The Hebrew religion implies a possible exit from the natural cycle: the world might not always remain the way it is.

Olympian myth represents eternal retribution by itself punishing tribal religions. When a martial master race established its rule over indigenous peoples, its patriarchal gods annihilated the various local spirits, conceptual unity dissolved diffuse representations, and the self tabooed mimetic magic in order to rule nature by rational means. The Jews, by contrast, out-lawed mimesis and deprived magic of power not so much through eradication as through conciliation. Judaism lets pagan sacrifices be transformed into the sanctified rhythm of social life.[44] Judaism makes no repressive claim to truth, and its promise of salvation is not guaranteed. Salvation lies in avoiding all beliefs that substitute themselves for salvation and in maintaining the idea of undeserved blessing. Rather than turning rational domination into the pure truth at the basis of a dominated world, Judaism clings to the hope of reconciliation without bringing it about by force. Whereas Greek mythology installs fate and domination as the truth and deprives the world of hope, reconciliation is the "highest concept" of Judaism, and expectation is the entire sense of that concept.[45]

Reconciliation is also the idea that guides Adorno's critique of Western culture. Adorno thinks of reconciliation as a process bringing nature and culture together without arbitrarily imposing culture on nature. His allegorical interpretation of Judaism leaves open the question whether this idea preserves or destroys the Judaic concept of reconciliation. It is more important in the present context to note that there is a historical basis for Adorno's idea, and that the historical process is not one-dimensional. The dialectic of enlightenment occurs in a tension between reification and reconciliation.

Synthesis and Rescue

The point of Adorno's idea of reconciliation is directed against Hegel, who considered reconciliation a cultural accomplishment. The idea derives from a determinate negation of Hegel's notion of synthesis, and it emphasizes a rescue of nature. Adorno opposes Hegel's teaching that a negation of the negation is an affirmation. So long as society is antagonistic, thought is as well. Thought can neither directly identify the nonidentical nor grasp it indirectly by means of a conceptual negation of the negation. The need to negate a negation shows that the previous negation was insufficiently negative. To transform the later negation into an affirmation fosters indifference

to what was first negated. "Irreconcilably, the idea of reconciliation bars its affirmation in a concept."[46]

Yet Adorno does not see negative dialectic as no more than
an increasingly negative negation. The dialectic is simultaneously retrograde. Refusing to affirm reconciliation does not
mean giving up the notion of synthesis. For Adorno, conceptual synthesis defines the difference that "disappeared" in the
concept; without a synthesis, the difference between contradictory moments would not become apparent.[47] But he refuses to
transform accomplished conceptual synthesis into the supposed reconciliation of reality. His concept of conceptual synthesis mediates the difference between Hegel's "sublation" and
Hölderlin's "anamnesis of doomed naturalness,"[48] and it makes
apparent the transient negativity of Adorno's own idea of
reconciliation.

The same transient negativity surfaces when *Aesthetic Theory*
rescues the category of "natural beauty" from its dismissal in
Hegel's aesthetics (74–121/68–115). Adorno's rescue does not
merely revive Kant's aesthetics, nor does it simply recall early
Marx's goal of "naturalizing" human beings and "humanizing"
nature.[49] Adorno rejects the Kantian notion that beauty is
governed by a subjective principle, thereby intensifying the
indeterminacy noted by Kant's definition of beauty. Furthermore, Adorno's recollection of early Marx is largely ironic.
Paraphrasing Nietzsche, Adorno would say human beings already are natural, all too natural, and nature is unavoidably
human, all too human. Human beings carry out domination
as if they were beasts of prey, and nature has become a mere
object of human control.

The rescue of "natural beauty" belongs to Adorno's metacritique of Hegel. For Hegel "spirit and its artistic beauty stands
higher than nature."[50] The indeterminacy of natural beauty is
a deficiency, and this deficiency makes artistic beauty necessary.
Adorno agrees with Hegel that natural beauty is indeterminate.
He also agrees that, as nature's enigmatic language, natural
beauty needs to be sublated by art (117/111). This is needed
not because natural beauty is inferior, however, but because
thought is deficient. Natural beauty would never become ac-

cessible for discursive thought were it not objectified by art (114/107–8). The beauty of art imitates the beauty of nature, but the determinacy of art surpasses that of nature.

Whereas Hegel emphasizes that natural beauty is beautiful only for conscious apprehension,[51] Adorno stresses that natural beauty reminds us of something nonidentical, something not merely "for others" (116/110). Natural beauty is "the residue of non-identity in things, in an age when they are otherwise spellbound by universal identity" (114/108). Natural beauty promises the nonidentical, but, as a consciously experienced phenomenon, simultaneously denies it (99/93, 104/97–98, 114/108). Art tries to keep this promise by breaking it (103/97). Whereas aesthetic experience of natural beauty dissipates into the amorphous, the labor of art gives rise to form. Far from being a mere means of controlling the nonidentical, form is also connected to the idea of reconciliation (104/98, 120/113–14). In different ways, and in polar mediation, both natural beauty and artistic beauty encipher the nonidentical. If culture were reconciled with nature, the nonidentical would be subject to neither irrational chaos nor rational domination, the two historical shapes of myth (115/109–110, 120/114).

Adorno's attempt to rescue "natural beauty" from Hegelian dismissal makes it clear that "reconciliation" is not simply a future condition in which all domination would cease. It is easy to misinterpret his talk of reconciliation in this way. For example, Lüdke, who correctly identifies natural beauty as Adorno's paradigm for the nonidentical, says that Adorno's concept of reconciliation indicates "a social condition without domination."[52] It would be more accurate to say that reconciliation indicates a historical process in which blind domination gives way to enlightened synthesis. The problem with reification is not that identity is achieved but that the nonidentical is repressed. So, too, Adorno criticizes Hegel's aesthetics not for insisting that natural beauty needs to be sublated by art, but for dismissing natural beauty because of its indeterminacy. The implications of all this for Adorno's stance toward modern art emerges from his critique of "formalism."

Substantial Formalism

As part of his attempt to historicize aesthetic norms, Adorno argues that the category of beauty records a transition to the primacy of form. The search for variegated unity arises with an emancipation from a fear of nature, but the category of beauty preserves this fear in a formal compulsion toward isolation from immediate existence (82–84/75–78). Hence the category has an ambiguous status. Beauty is a spell on the mythic spell of fearful nature. Whenever that which cannot be made beautiful is suppressed as something "ugly," beauty prolongs the mythic spell, and it falls short of the idea of reconciliation that arose with this category at the dawn of human subjectivity (76–77/70–71).

For Adorno the formalism of Hellenic classicism and eighteenth-century neoclassicism epitomizes mythic beauty. By carrying out unification as an act of violence, such formalism prevents the harmony attempted (78/71). This criticism recalls Nietzsche's *Birth of Tragedy* (1872), where, in the conflict between Dionysius and Apollo, the force of formless frenzy is fully necessary for the form-giving power that triumphs. Or, to use the terms of Freud, the more modern ego needs the more ancient id.[53] Adorno says that form needs the archaic giants in order not to succumb to the myth prolonging itself in any form that simply rejects myth.

As was indicated by the discussion of formal liberation in the previous chapter, Adorno does not deny the importance of form in art. Instead he adopts a position that could be called "substantial formalism." Just as *Negative Dialectics* does not discount concepts when it thinks against thought, so *Aesthetic Theory* does not discount form when it criticizes formalism. Just as successful conceptual synthesis is said to disclose the differences between contradictory moments, so successful artistic synthesis is said to disclose the differences within content. But as concepts must respect the object if they are to have content, so form must emerge peacefully from mimetic impulses if form is to be substantial (213/205). The best works of art respect the unique identity of the nonidentical and do not force an identity of form and content (263/253). They achieve a peaceful and fragile reconciliation of the one with the many (242–43/232, 455/425). In such works artistic form is a nonviolent synthesis preserving divergent and contradictory impulses, sometimes even suspending itself for the sake of disparate content (215–16/206–8). Adorno thinks of artistic form as an identity that makes the nonidentical less alien but lets it remain distinct.

Against Hegel, however, Adorno insists that neither successful conceptual syntheses nor the best works of art achieve full and real reconciliation. So long as society remains antagonistic, no artwork will achieve complete reconciliation. Until the conciliatory identity of identity and the nonidentical is actualized in society, all artworks are forced to posit a mere semblance of reconciliation (219/210). The artistic relation of form to content embodies both the potential presence and the actual absence of reconciliation. Although both Hegel and Adorno give art the task of presenting reconciled contradictions, Hegel thinks that reconciliation is already accomplished in culture, while Adorno thinks it remains to be accomplished in society. Complete reconciliation remains a possibility in Adorno's aesthetics. Authentic artworks promise that this possibility is still possible.

Indeed, Adorno repeatedly emphasizes that artistic form participates in domination as well as in reconciliation (120/113–14, 237–40/227–30, 453–54/423–24). There are two reasons for this emphasis. On the one hand, art needs a dose of civilization's toxin in order to resist civilizing repression. Modern art is virtually an identification with the aggressor, a mimesis of reification. On the other hand, because this mimesis occurs within a separate artistic sphere, artworks can heal the wound with the poisonous spear that inflicted it. Instead of forcing the word to become flesh, authentic works let the flesh become word: form lets each impulse become expressive within the whole (216–17/207–9). When aesthetic unity appears to have done no violence to amorphous nature, unity, which really disunites, shades into reconciliation (202/194). Culture is no longer the old enemy of nature. Instead of simply identifying the nonidentical, culture identifies itself *with* the nonidentical.

Hence form's participation in domination is necessary for art's participation in reconciliation, provided formal unification

is conciliatory rather than harsh. Participation in both domination and reconciliation enables modern art to offer a negative naming of the concrete (203/195). According to Adorno,
the concrete has yet to exist; it would be the peaceful identity
of what exists. What currently exists is subject to imposed
identity. Artworks anticipate the concrete by recollecting what
was. In artistic constellations, what exists becomes something
that has already been. Something that has existed no longer
exists, something that no longer exists might yet come to exist.
By rearranging what exists, artworks both recollect what no
longer exists and anticipate what does not yet exist (200–205/
192–96).

According to Adorno, flexible and individualized form enables modern works of art to recollect and anticipate what
would differ from the present world, where blind domination
and exchange prevail. Reconciliation acquires an artistic shape
by means of conciliatory domination. As reconstellations of
what exists, the best modern works are determinate negations
of contemporary social reality. They recollect what society represses, and they anticipate what society and its members could
become if domination would really turn into reconciliation.
Even though the prevailing relations of production continually
thwart utopian possibilities, modern art gives a negative testimony for the possibility of the possible (204/196). An artwork
such as *Endgame* carries out an irreconcilable reconciliation.

Because art lacks actuality, however, such a testimony is ambiguous. The possibility of reconciliation is promised, but art
pretends that reconciliation already exists (203/195). Hence
modern art must also be criticized. The idea of reconciliation
may not detract from the corporeal resurrection to which hope
clings.[54] The point of reconciliation would be the satisfying of
material needs. Until society really changes, dialectical philosophy and authentic art will remain negative, even toward themselves. They cannot really accomplish reconciliation. The most
they can contribute are models of conciliatory praxis arising
from opposition to a dominative exchange from which neither
philosophy nor art is exempt. Hegel's hubris has been
humbled.

7.3 Adorno's Endgame

Adorno's revision of Hegel continues the Enlightenment tendency to anchor historical meaning in rational autonomy, but in a post-Enlightenment fashion. Like twentieth-century positivists, Adorno questions the traditional concept of meaning. Like the existentialists, Adorno doubts the efficacy of autonomous agents and products. And in anticipation of poststructuralism, Adorno challenges the cultural dominance of instrumental rationality. Paradoxically, his philosophy of history raises all these caveats, yet continues to anchor historical meaning in human autonomy and rationality. On Adorno's interpretation, this is also the central paradox of works such as *Endgame*. In both cases there seems to be an irresolvable tension between the claims of autonomy and the need for historical meaning.

Meaning and Autonomy

According to *Philosophy of Modern Music*, the dilemma of modern music resembles that of unhappy consciousness: it achieves freedom by means of emptiness.[55] In resisting the social control exercised by the culture industry, modern music rejects the public hearing it needs. The more it insists on autonomy, the more it hardens itself against the social context from which music's autonomy stems. Modern music cannot escape the dilemma that now confronts all intellectual culture in the West: the emancipation of spirit coincides with its emasculation. In 1949 Adorno's solution was to urge progressive musicians to keep insisting on isolated autonomy instead of feigning a false humaneness. It is better to use organized emptiness to deny the meaning of an irrational society, he says, than to go hunting for positive meaning.[56]

When commenting on the modern "crisis of meaning" two decades later, *Aesthetic Theory* continues to assume a historical dialectic with economic underpinnings, but it places more weight on the relation between metaphysical and aesthetic meaning than on the relation between social context and artistic import (229–35/219–25). This shift in emphasis reflects the fact that disputes about abstraction in painting had become passé, and serialism and chance had moved avant-garde music beyond the problems of dodecaphony and atonality. For Adorno, however, the conflict between autonomy and meaning had not become less intense.

Aesthetic Theory argues that positive meaning cannot simply be posited by the autonomous subject, since the subject's emancipation cancels positive meaning. Yet the "subjectivizing" of art enables artworks to confront "the general state of mind" and attain "a historically timely truth" (506/467). By challenging "the idea of meaning in art works and [their] meaning-constitutive categories" (229/219–20), a work such as *Endgame* presents the truth about a society whose organization makes life meaningless. The ever-increasing tension between human autonomy and social absurdity puts in question the legitimacy of artistic meaning. Artists such as Beckett recognize this situation without giving philosophical explanations. In their artworks the inexorable testing of synthesis has turned against the artwork's meaning-constitutive coherence and against meaning in general (229–30/219–21).

This discussion of "meaning" in art is tied to Adorno's reconception of "meaning" in history. *Negative Dialectics* connects the concept of meaning with a dialectic in the development of human autonomy, described by various authors as a process of secularization, modernization, or rationalization. Adorno says the development of human autonomy undermines metaphysical concepts such as meaning that seem necessary for achieving autonomy. Against historical romanticism, however, he argues that the truth of metaphysical views should not be deduced from their collective validity in closed cultures. Adorno's own position is clear: "The autonomous Beethoven is more metaphysical, and therefore more true, than Bach's *ordo*."[57]

Yet this position is puzzling. On the one hand, Adorno associates the possibility of metaphysical experience with the possibility of freedom, and he claims that subjects must be liberated from the old collective bonds to be capable of freedom. On the other hand, he recognizes that Beethoven's humanism belongs to an age when the laws of the "free market" were supplanting the authority of church and state. Hence it is unclear why Beethoven's autonomous music should be considered more true than Bach's *ordo*. Adorno's claim about Beethoven seems no less apologetic than theological attempts to praise Bach's *soli Deo gloria* while ignoring his feuds with church authorities. The binding power of authorized doctrines does not guarantee their truth, but secularization does not automatically usher in human freedom, not even freedom from starvation and destruction. One could just as easily argue that since Bach's pietist music expresses suffering and Beethoven's humanist music expresses domination, Bach's music is more true than Beethoven's.

Indeed, Adorno's own essay on Bach contains a full awareness of the mixed character of "progress" and "autonomy."[58] Secularization might not be a curse, but neither is it an automatic blessing. In fact, the very concept of autonomy contains the ambiguity confronted by Beckett's plays and Adorno's philosophy. The hope for a more humane existence has become inseparable from rigorously autonomous culture, but this culture keeps imitating the old Adam. The achievement of autonomy is inconceivable apart from a society where emancipation has progressed hand in hand with domination, and where hope for humanity has become incompatible with the experience of absurdity after Auschwitz.[59]

Not even this experience makes the concept of meaning meaningless, however. If Beckett's plays crystallize aesthetic meaning by negating metaphysical meaning (403/381–82), then Adorno's meditations on metaphysics acquire historical meaning by negating the metaphysical concept of meaning. As a "refuge of fading theology" (229/219), the concept is suspect because of its ideological functions rather than because of its theological origins. It easily cuts short a critique of society's irrationality. According to Adorno, the question about the meaning of life usually assumes that human beings can "make sense" of life. But the concept of meaning involves an objectivity beyond all human "making." Meaning that is "made" is already fictitious: it duplicates the human subject.

With this claim, Adorno begins in his own way to "make sense" of the concept of meaning. He says it calls for subjective reflection on how far human beings can see beyond themselves toward the objectivity involved in the concept of meaning.[60] The concept is not to be declared meaningless, but meaning must not be reduced to the outcome of authentic existential choices. Neither positivism nor existentialism suffices. Schopenhauer could not have despaired about the world's grayness if there were no concept of a different color whose traces remain in the negative whole. Bergson could not have taken life to be meaningful if he had really faced irrevocable death. One should neither declare life meaningless nor call it meaningful.[61] According to Adorno, the theological consciousness of nothingness corrects the affirmation of life's meaning. Yet the emptiness of human life would not be cured by our having a change of heart but only by removing the principle that governs the cycle of self-preservation.

The principle Adorno has in mind is the principle of dominative exchange. If metaphysics and the structure of society are as inseparable as Adorno claims,[62] then one may expect the problem of social transformation to return in Adorno's meditations on meaning. The problem is one of human agency. Can the emptiness of human life be cured in the way proposed if human beings do not have a change of heart? Will anyone really change so long as the principle of exchange remains in effect? If metaphysics and social structure intertwine, and if Adorno skirts the questions just raised, then his attempt to find the objectivity in "meaning" might turn the metaphysical concept of meaning into a negative utopia: although the concept of meaning seems necessary if we are to keep hoping for an undamaged life, we seem unable to attain the object of hope. Is there a difference between declaring life meaningless and saying the principle of exchange must be abolished without saying how? Another look at Adorno's reading of *Endgame* may provide an answer.

Authentic Negation

One task of *Aesthetic Theory* is to explain and justify the negative meaning that remains in artworks such as *Endgame*. Adorno knows that, for the varieties of positivism he opposes, it makes little sense to ask the existentialist *Sinnfrage* he questions. To the extent that the idea of meaning does not make empirical or linguistic sense, it falls under the positivists' taboo on metaphysics. Because Adorno thinks metaphysical and aesthetic meaning are closely related, he cannot avoid asking whether the artistic demolition of meaning throws art into the arms of "positivist" or "reified" consciousness. A related but more vulgar question would be why Beckett's plays have been lionized if everyday consciousness is so reified.

Without raising the second question, *Aesthetic Theory* develops a distinction between authenticity and resignation in answer to the first. In an authentic artwork, the negation of meaning takes shape as a negative quality of the work itself (*als Negatives sich gestaltet*); in a resigned artwork, the negation of meaning is simply replicated (*positive sich abbildet*). Everything depends on whether the negation of meaning is determinate or abstract, on whether the negation has intrinsic meaning or whether it simply conforms to the status quo. Hence, avoiding the arms of reified consciousness depends on whether substantial forms are achieved. So-called absurdist works of the "highest formal level" are not merely meaningless because import accrues to their negation of meaning (231/221, 379/361–62).

Adorno does not give an example in this context of a "resigned" work of art, thereby creating the impression that he is mainly interested in works that retain meaning in however negative a fashion. Be that as it may, a clear case of authentic negation is that of Beckett's *Endgame*. According to Adorno, Beckett's play carries the negation of meaning into the traditional categories of drama (230/220). From categories that once established meaning, other categories are extrapolated. The *Endgame* essay shows how Beckett's drama carries out a parody of traditional categories.[63] Humor becomes black. The hero becomes an anti-hero. Plot is decomposed. The catastrophe is replaced by Clov's announcing "There's no more painkiller." In addition, this negation of traditional categories carries forward the work of a previous generation. Beckett's parody draws consequences from Kafka's novels in a way that resembles the serial extension of Schönberg's dodecaphony. Both Beckett and Stockhausen invert the earlier generation's contribution.[64]

In general, *Aesthetic Theory* argues that negation of meaning becomes aesthetically meaningful when it is realized in the material with which the artist works. Because such a realization requires form, authentic negation requires formal emancipation, not emancipation from form. Adorno does not hide his aversion to dadaist negations of meaning, which amount to frontal attacks on art as art. Beckett's absurd plays are still plays. They do not lack all meaning. They put meaning on trial. To do this as determinately as traditional artworks express positive meaning, modern artworks must be consistent in their negation of meaning. Consistency obligates a play such as *Endgame* to achieve the density and unity that once were supposed to constitute meaning. Although the achievement of unity cannot rely on traditional artistic categories, and although consistent modern works must negate those categories, consistency in the negation of meaning gives "absurd" artworks a historical meaning. Through consistent negation of meaning, such works become complexes of meaning (230–31/221).

Yet there is a puzzle here which Adorno himself recognizes. Artistic meaning has shown itself to be arbitrary (234–35/224–25). Even the inevitable and true development toward determinate negation of meaning is accompanied by a movement toward indeterminacy where aesthetic subjectivity is eliminated by virtue of its own logic. According to Adorno, the composer György Ligeti has accurately described the tendency and dilemma of recent avant-garde art: complete determination converges with complete contingency. Complete domination becomes arbitrary, empty, and impotent.

Adorno's hope for transformation rests in part on the fact that domination is not yet complete, nor is the human subject completely impotent. In *Endgame,* the negation of meaning is not a complete determination. Authentic negation generates a complex of meaning that preserves the category of meaning. Here one finds a crucial enigma for Adorno's aesthetics: every authentic negation of meaning ends up seeming meaningful. To Adorno's way of thinking, this enigma confirms the illusory character of art: "Art is illusion in that it cannot escape the hypnotic suggestions of meaning amid a general loss of meaning" (231/222). But the illusory character of art is precisely what prevents it from becoming merely ideological.

One enigma for Adorno's readers is that his philosophy and aesthetics continue to make sense despite their recognizing the impotence and complicity of autonomous intellectual culture toward a society that prolongs exploitation. Adorno's attempt to preserve the concept of meaning is a historically necessary attempt to recall the hope without which a praxis of liberation would lose its point. In a society that surrounds everyone with images of success and dreams of instant pleasure, one of the most difficult tasks, and one of the most crucial, is to recall genuine needs that remain unfulfilled.

It would be mistaken to consider Adorno's negative dialectic "nihilistic" just because it exposes the emptiness of life under consumer capitalism. If Adorno were simply saying everything is nothing, his philosophy would not merit our consideration. Adorno attempts to carry out a determinate negation even when he defends Beckett against the charge of nihilism. Adorno looks for something in the nihilist's "nothing." What he finds in *Endgame* is the final history (*Endgeschichte*) of the human subject. It would also be mistaken to consider Adorno's aesthetic theory merely "utopian" just because it does not say how a structural transformation is to occur. If Adorno were simply saying everything must change somehow, his claims would not hold our attention. Adorno attempts to carry out a determinate negation even when he wrests hope from *Endgame*'s blank picture of death. What must be broken is the grip of blind domination and exchange. In this sense the final history of the human subject can be more than an ending. It can also be a beginning.

Adorno's endgame demonstrates that autonomous human subjects can carry out a critique of the subject on behalf of a society in which human beings would be neither the oppressors nor the oppressed. It does not say how such a society can come into existence. Adorno's endgame demonstrates that autonomous intellectual culture can criticize itself without losing sight of the need for structural transformation. It does not say how this need is to be met. Yet even the silence suggests questions of relevance to the praxis of liberation. Which would fully liberated people be able to discard: the claim of autonomy or the concept of meaning? And if such liberation were to occur, would the negations of meaning in *Endgame* and *Aesthetic Theory* turn out to be true?

8

Truth and Illusion

Adorno's paradoxical descriptions of modern art all point in the same direction. Whether as defetishizing fetish or as disalienating alienation, whether as impractical praxis or as meaningless meaning, modern art provides an illusion of truth. The truth to which modern art testifies is a social, political, and historical truth. Adorno views modern art as an illusion (*Schein*) that is socially necessary.

It will become apparent that in Adorno's account art is doubly illusory and doubly revelatory. This complex doubling shows up as antinomies in authentic works of art. Despite these antinomies, and because of them, authentic works of art constitute semblances of truth in contemporary society. But so long as this society remains untrue, artistic semblances of truth will be as paradoxical as Adorno's attempt to redeem them. I shall argue that Adorno's critical appropriation of Hegelian philosophy is crucial to understanding his concept of artistic truth content. In rejecting Hegel's claim to an absolute knowledge of the truth, Adorno's aesthetics seems to preserve Hegel's deepest metaphysical impulses.

8.1 Antinomies of Illusion

According to Adorno, the illusory character of art arises from its demand for unity. To be a determinate negation of society, an artwork must achieve its own unity (235/225), but achieving unity makes it illusory in two ways. First, the artwork's unity is usually feigned rather than fully achieved. Second, such unity covers up societal antagonisms, which include the artwork's opposition to society.

A pivotal norm in Adorno's aesthetics requires the unity of a work to emerge from disparate elements and honor their individuality (166/159, 234/224). If, as Adorno claims, persistent analysis can discover imposed unity or prearranged elements in nearly every work of art, then artistic unity is fictitious, and, compared to the complete "aesthetic reconciliation" that artworks desire, these are an illusion (160–61/154–55). Though required for authenticity, unity makes artworks doubly illusory. It lets artworks pose as integral and autonomous entities, even though they have absorbed heterogeneous moments, and it lets artworks suggest that contemporary society is not antagonistic, even though it is. Aesthetically meaningful works feign a unity that cannot be fully achieved so long as society remains antagonistic.

At the same time, however, unified works of art are doubly revelatory: denunciation and anticipation are "syncopated" in art (130/124). Authentic works make apparent the antagonistic essence (*Wesen*) of social reality, an essence concealed by social appearances. By condemning this *Wesen* as an *Unwesen*, authentic artworks simultaneously posit the possibility of an essentially different reality. The unity in authentic works reveals and criticizes the divisive unity of an administered society. Because of the disunity within artistic unity, however, unified works disclose true unity as a possibility rather than as something actually achieved. As an illusory revelation and a revelatory illusion, every authentic artwork is a *tour de force* trying to actualize what is actually impossible at present. Hence the highest aim of artistic performances is to expose the antinomy of the *tour de force*.[1]

One aim for a reading of *Aesthetic Theory* is to expose antinomies within Adorno's account of artistic illusion. His account is an amazing combination of disparate matters: the concepts of mimesis and imagery; the distinctions among artifact, entity, and phenomenon; and the crisscrossing of artistic image and apparition with relations between reality and art and between the actual and the possible. These divergent elements can be unified by pointing to two antinomies in a double illusion that is doubly revelatory.

In the first place, there is a contradiction between sublating social reality and imitating the objective ideal inside an emergent work. The contradiction is unavoidable: external sublation is a precondition of artworks, and internal imitation is their law. The contradiction is also necessary: it prevents artworks from either becoming mere illusion or posing as *the* truth. Nevertheless artworks do pose as autonomous entities, ones whose essential reification conflicts with their participation in processes of production and consumption.

In the second place, artworks are cumulative images of sociohistorical reality that oppose themselves as instantaneous apparitions of another reality. This opposition is necessary: the instant of apparition is mediated by historical imagery, and the image acquires its full significance only in the instant of apparition. Artworks contain clues for resolving the tensions between dialectic and utopia, between an antagonistic society and the possibility of perpetual peace, but they remain antinomous so long as the tensions are not actually resolved.

Sublation and Imitation

The first antinomy of artistic illusion occurs between sublation and imitation. According to Adorno, the forms and materials of art enter artworks from social reality. Although this reality is shed upon entering the artwork, the work always constitutes an afterimage (*Nachbild*) of society. The artwork constantly walks a tightrope, as it were, between art and society. The artwork would collapse if either end were cut. By becoming pure art and eliminating every reference to reality, the artwork would cancel its own precondition, the source of its forms and materials. By becoming a mere likeness of reality, the artwork would neither protest how things are nor point to what is possible (158–59/151–52, 271/260). Politically committed artworks act as if they are not artistic, even though they are. Hermetic artworks pose as pure art, even though they are not. Both types are as illusory as all other works of art. Their illusory character arises from an antinomy between the precondition of artworks and their law. Their necessary sublation of external reality inevitably conflicts with their necessary imitation of an internal and objective ideal.

Adorno says "the law of ever art work" is that it resemble its own objective ideal. The artwork must seek mimetic identity with itself (159/153, 190/183, 202/194). An artwork's "objective ideal" is not a Platonic form of beauty, but the *telos* of that artwork alone. "Objective" means "not posited by the artist," and "ideal" means "what an art work itself wants to be and become." Adorno's phrase captures the challenge facing an artist when an artwork begins to take shape. The first line of a composition carries implications for every subsequent line. As the other lines appear, they unfold and modify those implications. In the end, all lines ought to cohere as this particular composition. The composition has been trying to mime itself, rendering each moment expressive as a moment of this composition.

Sometimes Adorno seems to prefer the necessary imitation of an objective ideal over the necessary sublation of external reality. Indeed, he reverses the argument of Plato's *Sophist* (129/123). In Plato's dialogue the "Stranger from Elea" distinguishes two kinds of images (*eidola*): a likeness (*eikon*) is like the original, whereas a semblance (*phantasma*) only seems to be a likeness. As images, both likenesses and semblances are imitations, but only semblances, including the "arts," involve an element of deceit. Adorno agrees that the illusory character (*Scheincharakter*) of artworks constitutes their difference from empirical reality. One reason for their illusory character, however, is that they still imitate (*Nachahmung*) reality (158/152). The more an artwork becomes a mere likeness (*Abbild*) of reality, the more illusory that work becomes. In a sense, the artwork could shed its illusory character if it would rid itself of all likeness to a false reality. For this to happen, society would have to become true.

Plato considered art's weakness to be its imitative distance from the really real. Adorno replaces this weakness with the strength of self-imitation. Similarity with itself separates the artwork from a false reality, where nothing is really real because everything obeys the law of exchange. He views the recognition of this strength as a progressive contribution of the "art for art's sake" movement, in contrast to nineteenth-century moralism (160/153). The artwork never fully lives up to its own objective ideal, however. Hence the strength of art is also its weakness. The law of every artwork amounts to a prohibition on imaging the absolute. The obligation to self-identity forbids any symbolizing of "the nonidentical that would not emerge until after the dissolution of the compulsion of identity."[2] At the same time, the weakness of art is also its strength. There is truth in the artwork's failure to achieve complete identity with itself: only the absolute could have complete self-identity. "To that extent aesthetic illusion . . . represents the truth" (159/153). The artwork's attempt and failure at self-imitation tell us two things: not only is mimetic self-identity still possible, but also the artwork is not *the* truth, despite its relative truth amid the false reality it sublates.

The artwork does pose as an autonomous entity (*Ansich-seiendes*), however, and Adorno considers this pose illusory. In the first place, the artwork is never a pure thing in itself. It is always a thing for others. Although a work becomes independent from its own genesis by being fixed in a script or score, it remains something produced and consumed as a commodity. In the second place, the artwork is not merely a thing. It is also a process continuing in space and time. Thus artworks have a double character, like Kant's concept of a "thing." The Kantian concept can refer to either a subjectively constituted object or the thing in itself (153/146–47, 190/183, 288/276–77). Kant's concept has entered *Aesthetic Theory* via Lukács's theory of reification, however. Unlike Kant, Adorno conceives things as commodities and as congealed processes. By posing as autonomous entities, artworks partake in the same commodity fetishism that Marx unmasked in *Capital*.

This pose is a double bind, one that captures the way autonomous works operate within advanced capitalism. In the first place, "reification belongs to the essence of art works, although it contradicts their appearing essence" (153/146). That is to say, artworks are both produced as artifacts and experienced as phenomena. Both characteristics are essential to the artwork, and they contradict each other. Artworks are artifactual phenomena. In the second place, artworks are essentially dynamic but also essentially static. While containing a continual conflict among disparate moments, the work can not become a field of conflicting forces unless it is a self-contained entity. Otherwise the forces would not join in conflict (263–64/253). A self-contained entity cannot be an ongoing process, yet an artwork must be both. Artworks are dynamic entities.

Adorno's polarity of artifact and phenomenon can be elucidated in terms of the musical work. Philosophers of music have long debated which is the actual work, the symphony as composed or the symphony as performed or heard. If it is the symphony as composed, then performances would seem never to give us the actual work known as Beethoven's *Eroica* Symphony. If the actual work is the symphony as performed or heard, then there would seem to be as many *Eroica* Symphonies as there are performances or aural experiences that go by that name. The polarity of artifact and phenomenon points to this debate but reformulates it as a tension inherent to every work.

This tension contains a further polarity between the work's character as an entity and its character as a process. As an entity the work exists both as a finished product and as an experienced object. As a process the work carries the impulses and intentions that went into its production, and it continually changes its appearance during the history of its reception. Thus the finished product is also incomplete, and the experienced object has its own experience, as it were.

Furthermore, the artifact is experienced as more than a mere artifact, and the phenomenon presents itself as more than a mere phenomenon. Perhaps we can put matters like this: The musical composition tends to cloak itself in the guise of a performance, even when the composition is intended to call attention to its own artifactual character. The musical performance tends to present itself as the composition itself, even when the performance is intended to call attention to its own phenomenal character. Yet these two poles always remain in tension, as can be documented from any rehearsal of a Beethoven symphony.

For Adorno such tension insures that the work is not simply an inert thing among inert things, a dead product among dead

products, a superficial commodity among superficial commodities. Rather the work has an internal process through which
it can bring forth the surrounding social process. Both the
process and the fact that is arrested are necessary for revelatory
opposition to the world that enters the work. If artworks were
not internal processes resulting from external processes, artworks would not move in and against society. If the processes
were not reified, artworks would not achieve the autonomy
that allows them to surpass the social "world of things," becoming appearances of its essence, and suggesting a transformed
reality (125/119).

Image and Apparition

The second antinomy in artistic illusion occurs between the
image-character and apparitional quality of artworks as phenomena. Adorno conceives artworks as "imageless images" condensed from "configured" historical experiences (421–22/396–
97). In such images appears a universal structure that forcibly
holds society together. The universal structure seems inaccessible to ordinary experience, and it tends to elude analysis.
Artworks make this structure apparent without covering up its
contradictory character. The social totality shows up more directly in artistic monads than in discursive concepts, Adorno
claims.

The social universal imaged by artworks is the "historical
antagonism of subject and object" (130/124). This antagonism
penetrates consciousness in the shape of a difference between
the particular and the universal.[3] In a world where consumers
are deceptively soothed by culture industry products, the image-character of art exposes the alienation of subject and object. Authentic works bring to the surface the irrationality of
society's seemingly rational order.

To do this, artworks must be carried by the sociohistorical
experiences of individual artists. The exposure of alienation
presupposes both an experience of alienation and a mediated
difference between objective imagery and subjective imagination (132–33/126–27). Developing a suggestion from Husserl's
Cartesian Meditations,[4] Adorno argues that art and experience

intersect by way of collective images housed in individual experience. Collective images enter the artwork and give it a latent collectivity despite contingent individuation. The mediated difference between individual imagination and collective imagery reproduces the historical antagonism of subject and object, and this difference reproduces itself in a tension within artworks as images. They are imaginary because they are autonomous, but they are actual because they have a historical substance. Artworks become "imageless images" when their condensations of external history begin to "converse," until they erupt in an apparitional instant of appearance (132–33/126–27).

Adorno's "instant of appearance" (*Augenblick des Erscheinens*, 124/118) recalls the idiomatic expression "the truth dawned on me" ("*die Wahrheit ging mir auf*").[5] He says that questions about the truth of art come into view "when a non-existent is seen to rise as if it were real" (128/122). The artistic instant of appearance resembles the preternatural apparition (*Himmelserscheinung*), which bursts upon human beings beyond the reach of their intention. Prototypical for the artistic apparition is the firework, itself a prototypical apparition. The firework fleetingly appears, a humanly produced, celestial sign. It flashes and fades without letting its meaning be understood (125/119–20). It is empirical, yet more than empirical; humanly planned, yet more than planned; instantaneous, enigmatic. According to Adorno, every significant artwork catches one by surprise (123/118). The spirit of an artwork suddenly appears, promising sensuous happiness to adequate recipients, almost despite their will. Spiritualized sensuousness is an artistic epiphany (125/119). Even in *Endgame* there is a magic moment, full of expectation, when the curtain rises. Recent art, though ashamed of its aura, cannot do without it.[6]

The instant of appearance is the moment of mediated transcendence when objectified mimesis begins to speak as spirit. When in its compositional context a chord has an enormous effect, the devoted listener shudders, and the marriage of eros and knowledge is consummated.[7] Organized sensuousness becomes pregnant with transcending spirit. Unactualized possibility joins absorbed actuality. The stored-up nonidentical breaks into an exchange society without becoming fungible, and the possibilities of reconciliation and resurrection appear. As apparitions, artworks hint at what life would be like were it emancipated from imposed identity (128/122–23).

If artworks as images are concrete appearances of a universal that usually remains inaccessible, then artworks as apparitions are expressions of a concrete individual that usually remains mute. As in experience, so in art, the universal is individually registered, and the individual is universally mediated. Both universal and individual become concrete as that which speaks from a particular monad. Each artistic monad is both a process and an instant (154/147). As images, artworks are the duration of transience. As apparitions, they are instantaneous explosions of their objectified process. As both process and instant, the artwork is social history, productively frozen into an imageless image, and receptively thawed in a mediated moment. In this moment, possibility appears to be actual. Experiencing art amounts to becoming aware of an immanent process in the instant when it is suspended (130–31/124–25).

For Adorno, phenomenal artworks are cumulative images of an historical reality that oppose themselves as instantaneous apparitions of something that does not exist. Such self-opposition is unavoidable and necessary. The antinomies of art cannot be resolved in an antagonistic world (131–32/125–26). Only through opposition to their apparitional quality do artworks become imageless images (126/120), but the apparition always destroys their image-character. The movement objectified in artworks is immortalized in the instant of appearance and simultaneously annihilated by being reduced to an instant. The instantaneous explosion can burst the continuity of the artwork's condensed history only because apparition itself is essentially historical. The instant of apparition is mediated by the process of the image, and the image acquires its full significance only in the instant of apparition. There is no transcendence without that which is being transcended. There is no mediation without that which is mediated. Utopia would be a transformation of historical society. Today's reality would first show its real colors in the dawn of a new world.

Hieroglyphic Script

Clearly the dialectic of apparition and image intersects the relation between possibility and actuality in Adorno's aesthetics. This intersection changes the meaning of the traditional aesthetic category of illusion (*Schein*). According to Gerhard Kaiser, Adorno's concept of "illusion" no longer emphasizes references within this world or from within this world to something outside it. Instead, it stresses a relation to this world from something else.[8] Kaiser's interpretation needs to be broadened. Though the artwork as apparition lets something more and something else relate to this world, the artwork as image simultaneously lets this world relate to something more and something else. Possibility and actuality are bound together just as tightly as the apparition and the image. Adorno makes the traditional category of illusion more complicated, more dialectical, more paradoxical.

Adorno's description of artworks as "hieroglyphic scripts" (189/182) summarizes the paradoxical relation between actuality and possibility in art. The same description captures the dialectical relation between phenomenal artworks and their conceptual interpretation. The phrase stems from Benjamin's concept of "allegory," as reworked in *Dialectic of Enlightenment*. Horkheimer and Adorno consider myths to be symbolic rather than allegorical. Myths are symbols in two ways: the sign (*Zeichen*) and the image (*Bild*) are one, and myths present something as being eternal because it recurs in mythic rituals. According to *Dialectic of Enlightenment*, myths lost their symbolic character when they underwent a division of labor. Science and words as signs separated from the various arts and from words as tone, image, and "word proper." Though inescapable, this separation can have serious consequences. When the separation is simply endorsed, "each of the two isolated principles tends toward the destruction of truth." Science tends to become mere calculation, and art tends to become mere copying (*abbilden*).[9]

Horkheimer and Adorno cite hieroglyphs as evidence that language originally functions as both sign and image. Hieroglyphs are scripts-turned-image and images-turned-script. As images, hieroglyphs have intrinsic meaning. As scripts, they refer beyond themselves.[10] Adorno assumes this double function when he states that "only *qua* handwriting do [works of art] have a language" (189/182). Artworks resemble hieroglyphs because their internal meaning and external reference are closely connected, and because this connection keeps them relatively close to nature. Artworks are enigmatic codes of nature that invite conceptual interpretation but defy it.

The internal meaning (*Sinn*) of artworks resides in their coherence (*Sinnzusammenhang*). By entering an artwork's coherence, the moments of an artwork are able to suggest more than they are. Although mediated by the artwork's coherence, this "more" or "plus" (*das Mehr*, 122/116) differs from such coherence. The plus incorporates the indeterminate expression of natural beauty, which itself is what in nature appears to be more than nature literally is—an enigmatic language that discursive thought is too weak to understand (105/99, 111/104–5, 122/116). Adorno claims that art attempts to rescue the plus seemingly expressed by natural beauty. Artworks try to rescue this plus from its indeterminacy, making it accessible to discursive thought, which usually treats nature as a mere object of domination (114/107–8). Nature's plus turns into the artwork's own plus—a spirit, through which artworks become more than they are.[11] Artworks are hieroglyphs with a veiled but definite meaning (122/116).

Adorno uses "hieroglyphic script" to describe how, as humanly produced aesthetic objects, artworks hint at more than can be pinned down in their organized sensuousness, even though they make their suggestions only in their sensuousness and organization. In every genuine artwork, says Adorno, something appears that exceeds what the work empirically is. Transformed elements of reality cohere in a new constellation that turns into a cipher. What is inscribed, though conceptually indeterminate, is made nonconceptually determinate by the coherence from which it emerges and from which it differs. The plus is definitely suggested, but only suggested (127–28/ 121–22).

By suggesting that something nonexistent exists, artistic hieroglyphs paradoxically posit a transcendence that they may not posit: a merely posited transcendence does not transcend (122/ 116–17, 128–29/122–24). True transcendence would require a social praxis honoring the nonidentical that is negatively present in the plus of nature and art. Artistic hieroglyphs are caught between a real need to rescue the nonidentical and an inability to actualize that rescue; between a real need to suggest a transformed society and the inability actually to transform it (129/123–24). The tension between need and inability would be resolved only if transcendence were truly actualized.

Artworks suggest transcendence by mediating actuality and possibility, but they fail to transcend insofar as they only suggest. Yet, in mediated instants of artistic expression, the plus does appear as the other, and the artwork's spirit seems to be true (123–24/117–18). If an artistic image is history made possible, and if an artistic apparition is possibility made historical, then the task for an Adornian critic is to decide whether the spirit of an artistic monad is an actual possibility. In a false society, is this artwork's spirit true?[12]

Contradictory Spirit

Adorno regards the spirit (*Geist*) of an artwork as a continual contradiction between external sublation and internal imitation, between entity and process, between artifact and phenomenon, between image and apparition, between internal meaning and external reference. Spirit is the "immanent mediation" of an artwork, the process of tension that converts each moment into its own opposite. For example, the artwork's spirit dwells within both artifactual and phenomenal moments, mediates them, transcends them (134–35/128–29). In a similar way, Adorno's concept of artistic spirit mediates and transcends the concepts of Kandinsky and Hegel.

Adorno argues against Kandinsky that spirit could not qualify the artwork to be art if spirit lacked a foundation in configured sensuous moments. Against the *Jugendstil* that Kandinsky opposed, however, Adorno holds that all sensuousness in artworks is spiritually mediated (134–36/129–30). The sensuous appearance and the appearing spirit form each other in the configuration of sensuous moments. The appearance becomes a phenomenon in the deepest sense of the word (135/129); the spirit becomes tied to that specific phenomenon (136/130). According to Adorno, an artwork's spirit must arise from the work's configuration and must mediate the configured sensuous moments.

The contradictory character of Adorno's "artistic spirit" is close to Hegel's concept of spirit. Adorno has three objections to Hegel's concept, however. First, artistic spirit is neither an absolute spirit nor a guarantee of the absolute. Second, the sensuous moments of an artwork are not merely contingent. Third, the artwork's spirit remains one moment among many and does not become identical with the artistic whole.[13] The third objection constitues Adorno's most important break with Hegel and "aesthetic Idealism" (137/131). The spirit of an artwork is not identical with the work's sensuous moments and their configuration. In its unity with the artistic phenomenon, spirit is simultaneously other than the phenomenon. At the same time, Adorno places greater emphasis than Hegel did on particular artworks in their particularity. The spirit of an artwork is an import (Gehalt) peculiar to that work (135/129).

For Adorno, this spirit is immanent to an artwork, yet it can truly be spirit only if, in contradiction, it transcends the artwork. Although inhering in the work's configuration and constituting itself through this configuration, the spirit is spirit only to the extent that its immanence is countered by an artwork's tendency to interrupt its own configuration.[14] Artistic spirit cannot achieve a pure identity with the artistic configuration. What opposes spirit remains in constant opposition, precisely because spirit is a process of opposition that opposes even itself. By opposing itself, artistic spirit transcends the artwork of which it is the spirit. The spirit of an artwork can simultaneously be illusion and more than illusion.

Adorno nevertheless holds that "the illusion of works of art originates in their spiritual essence" (165/158). Whereas, like much of Western philosophy, Hegel ties art's illusory character to its sensuousness, Adorno claims that spirit makes art illusory. Separated from corporeal nature and manual labor, spirit becomes a fetish. Art presents spirit as something that exists in artistic entities. A nonexistent abstraction is elevated to the status of something that exists (165/158). Spirit comes to seem like a fully autonomous being even though artworks are human artifacts (274/263). The spirit of artworks compels them to be illusory.

At the same time, spirit is not merely illusory; it is also true. Spirit is not just the illusion of an autonomous being, but it also negates every false autonomy. By constituting itself through the interrelating of sensuous elements, the spirit of an artwork displays the nonexistence, the negativity, the derivative character of spirit (166/159). By making itself definite in particular works, spirit breaks with its own principle of separation (348/333). Indeed, artistic spirit tries to rescue that which in nature surpasses nature's identity as an object of conceptual control.

Adorno sees this attempted rescue as necessary but illusory. Only if the spirit in artworks is more than illusory can the rescue be more than illusory. But artworks are something made, and therefore their spirit is illusory. How, then, can artistic spirit be true? This, for Adorno, is "the paradox of aesthetics as a whole: namely, how the act of making can cause the apparition of a thing that is not made; how something can be true which is not true in terms of its own concept" (164/157). Clearly artistic spirit or import must be distinct from illusion, even though no artwork has import except through illusion. As Adorno puts it, art sheds illusion only to the extent that its import is "literally true."

Since no artwork has import except through illusion, the redemption of illusion becomes central to Adorno's aesthetics. On that redemption depends art's "emphatic right, the legitimation of its truth" (163–64/157). Art's illusory character is philosophically justified as art's participation in truth (166/159). Even though Adorno's philosophy sees itself as a socially necessary illusion, his aesthetics attempts a paradoxical rescue of a paradoxical illusion and refuses to rest with a merely illusory rescue. The crux to this rescue lies in the philosophical redemption of artistic import, a redemption that has great significance for all of Adorno's work.[15]

8.2 Redemption of Import

The desire to redeem artistic import is an underlying impulse of *Aesthetic Theory* (12–14/4–6, 506–510/467–70). The desire arises from a sense that art is under attack and from a conviction that art is still needed. Adorno's articulation of this desire poses what will be called the double paradox of artistic truth. To address this double paradox, Adorno employs a concept of truth content and related notions of materialization, suspension, and transcendence.

Double Paradox

According to *Aesthetic Theory*, Hegel's disputed prognosis about the death of art has become a real possibility (503–6/464–67). The opening pages describe various conflicts that threaten art's existence. These boil down to a contradiction between artistic freedom and the abiding unfreedom of society as a whole. Because of that contradiction, art has come close to destroying itself. The continuing life of art in society depends on art's being interpreted and understood. But now nothing about art is readily understood: not art itself, not its relation to society, not even its right to exist (9/1). One task of *Aesthetic Theory* is to understand art's current lack of intelligibility.

On Adorno's interpretation, revolutionary art movements in the early twentieth century strove for absolute freedom, but they restricted their pursuit to art itself. Inevitably they were foiled by the continuing lack of freedom in society as a whole: in an unfree society, artistic freedom cannot be fully attained. The quest for artistic freedom led to an imprisonment of art within itself, where it has begun to destroy the materials and forms received from society. At the same time, the idea of humanity, which once nourished art's autonomy, has faded as society failed to become humane. Locked in the social prison of its own autonomy, modern art has begun to attack itself. Art after Auschwitz can no longer accept what Marcuse called "the affirmative character of culture" (10/2), for every autonomous work sanctions an inhuman status quo. In opposing contemporary society, art must oppose itself, raising the specter of art's demise. Is art even possible? Or has isolated emancipation fatally severed art from its social preconditions?

The demise of art would not necessarily be for the better. In Adorno's opinion, the culture industry contributes to a "false liquidation of art."[16] It closes off any perspective of social change, and it prompts people to turn artworks into vehicles for emotional projection. There are also misguided attempts to do away with art within autonomous art: happenings, performance art, and various neo-dadaist attacks on art as art. For Adorno, the demise of art would not be for the better unless society attained the utopia whose possibility is still suggested in works such as *Endgame*.[17]

All of this assumes that there is a continuing need for art, which Adorno's aesthetics tries to articulate—despite the barbarism of writing poetry after Auschwitz;[18] despite the societal mechanisms that falsify human needs (34–35/26–27); despite the fact that assertions about the need for art are usually ideological (361–62/345). According to *Aesthetic Theory*, the genuine need for art is what *Negative Dialectics* calls a "condition of all truth." The genuine need for art is a need to express suffering.[19] It is a need to maintain a consciousness of objective needs. To this need, as old as human history, the best modern art answers (47/40, 533/492). To meet this need, art's expression must be inexorably negative. So long as society remains inhuman, art must be "inhumane" in its service to humanity (35/27–28, 293/281). Otherwise suffering, art's "humane content" (*der humane Gehalt*, 387/369), will not be expressed.

Adorno's explanation of a genuine need for art implies the historical necessity of a philosophy to articulate this need and to lend conceptual weight to art's expression. His aesthetics tries to help disclose the truth of authentic art despite art's self-negation in social isolation. Part and parcel of this attempt are critical interpretations aimed at the truth content of particular works. It is because of the need for modern art that Adorno raises the central question of his "metaphysics of art": How can something cultural (*ein Geistiges*) be true? It is because of the need for aesthetics that this question implies a second: "To ask how an artifact can be true is to pose the question of how illusion—the illusion of truth—can be redeemed. Truth content cannot be an artefact. Therefore every act of making in art is an endless endeavour to articulate what cannot be made, namely spirit" (198/191).

Adorno's way of posing both questions indicates a refusal to equate cultural authenticity with objective truth. He also refuses to equate the redeeming of illusion with an unqualified defense of modern art. His questions transfer the antinomies of artistic illusion into the paradox of artistic truth. This is a double paradox. First, truth content, which cannot be something made, must be expressed through human making. Second, truth, which seems to be a unity, must appear in many particular works of art. Art never directly meets the truth. Art can reach the unmade truth only through the making of particular plays or poems or compositions (199/191). Adorno tries to redeem truth from artistic illusion by extrapolating nonartifactual truth content from artistic artifacts.

Truth Content

The discussion of the concept of truth content in Adorno's *Aesthetic Theory* recalls the "Epistemo-Critical Prologue" in Walter Benjamin's *The Origin of German Tragic Drama*. According to Benjamin, truth is an unintentional unity that is not open to question. "Truth is an intentionless state of being (*Sein*), made up of ideas."[20] While retaining Benjamin's emphasis on unity and the lack of intention, Adorno sees a dialectical relation between truth and human intentions, and he connects the unity of truth with the multiplicity of the nonidentical. Human intentions are the vehicles art needs to rescue nature (121/115). According to Adorno's critique of instrumental reason, "nature" is more than it is, more than an object of technological control for exploitative profit. By remembering the nonidentical, art liberates spirit from its "repressive aims" (173/166) and points to the truth in which human intentions would be fulfilled. In the concept of artistic truth content, the extremes of Adorno's philosophy meet: the nonidentical, which would be qualitatively individual and more than an object of blind domination; and truth, which in its fullness would be beyond instrumental rationality and mediated through it.[21]

Adorno uses an analogy to suggest this connecting of the nonidentical and truth. As the nonidentical in "nature" is manifold (*ein Vieles*), so artistic truth is tied to many artworks in various media (198–99/191). Just as Adorno opposes Hegel's view of nature, so Adorno resists Hegel's tendency to turn artistic truth into a general concept floating free from particular works. At the same time, however, Adorno conceives the truth of art and of artworks as one truth. Another analogy, one pertaining to art and the arts, illuminates his view of how artworks relate to unitary truth. According to Adorno, the concept of "art" does not unite all the various arts, yet art moves toward unity, in opposition to empirical reality, and through the multiplicity of the arts.[22] In a similar way the concept of "truth content" does not unite all the moments of the truth in various artworks, yet truth content moves toward unity, in opposition to artistic illusion, and through the multiplicity of particular works.

Such analogies indicate that the concept of truth content is hard to pin down. The difficulty increases when one notes what seems to be an unintended contradiction between two passages only a few pages apart. According to the first passage, "Great works of art are unable to lie. Even when their content [*Gehalt*] is illusory, it does represent truth because it is a necessary illusion. It is only the botched . . . ones that are untrue" (196/188). In the second passage, Adorno claims that at art's pinnacle, where its "truth transcends illusion," "art is most vulnerable. By giving expression to the superhuman notion of being beyond deceit, art [must] perpetrate an act of deception" (200/192–93). Given the necessity of their illusory import, great artworks cannot lie; yet when artistic truth transcends illusion, art must be false. Adorno's concept of truth content lurks somewhere in this tangle of truth and illusion.

In a discussion with Lucien Goldmann, Adorno once said "The idea of the truth . . . probably can be grasped only in a fragmentary manner."[23] Thus it is not surprising that his reflections on the concept of truth content seem slippery. Indeed, *Aesthetic Theory* tends to conceive truth content in terms of what it is not. There are two reasons for this tendency. First, Adorno is developing "second reflections" on a category that has already been decisive in his interpretations of various artworks and oeuvres. Whereas his interpretations spell out the character and mediations of truth content in specific phenomena, *Aesthetic Theory* develops the category of truth content as such.[24] Second, negative definition is especially appropriate for a boundary concept, a *Grenzbestimmung*, to use Kant's term.[25] According to Adorno, the truth content in artworks is something negative (*ein Negatives*) (200/193). To discover truth content, one must follow all the ways it is mediated in particular works of art. In a similar way, to define the category of truth content itself, one must say what truth content is not.

A negative definition is necessary because "truth content" mediates the nonidentical in empirical existence with the precondition of the possibility of identification. When defending Kantian boundary concepts such as the *Ding-an-sich* against the "plausible critique" of Fichte and Hegel, Adorno says "the construction of thing-in-itself . . . is that of a nonidentity as the precondition of the possibility of identification; but it is also the construction of that which eludes categorial identification."[26] The background to this defense lies in Adorno's revision of Hegel's notion that every immediacy is internally mediated. According to Adorno, particular objects are internally mediated by historical communication with other objects, despite conceptual attempts isolate them and reduce them to their universal identity. "What is, is more than it is."[27] Truth, as Adorno conceives it, is ambiguously nonexistent. That is to say, truth does not now exist, but it could exist and it could have existed. Just as what is, is more than it is, so what does not now exist, is more than its present nonexistence. The existing possibility of truth is the precondition for all Adorno's identifications, just as the nonidentical in empirical existence is the aim of his identifications.

Both the nonidentical and the possibility of truth are contained in the truth content of artworks. Their truth content is what artworks are not and what they nevertheless express. "Truth content cannot be identified directly. It is mediated in itself, and if it is to be known, calls for mediation by philosophy" (195/187). So too, a positive definition of truth content would have to identify the precondition for identifying how artworks are more than they are. The only way to define the category of artistic truth content is to spell out the ways in which truth content is not what artworks are.

The negative definition of truth content refers to processes discussed in previous chapters. The truth content of an artwork is not the experiences and thoughts that enter an artist's intentions, nor is it the materials and procedures with which the artist works. But there would be no truth content if there were no interaction between intentions and technique during the production of artistic artifacts.[28] Truth content is neither content and form nor their dialectic. But there would be no truth content if there were no dialectic of content and form in artistic entities.[29] Truth content is not sensuous elements and their configuration, nor is it identical with the spirit that mediates them. But there would be no truth content if there were no configured elements and no spirit in artistic phenomena. Such processes make possible philosophical extrapolations that touch on a region resembling Kant's "intelligible world."[30] The three processes from which Adorno extrapolates truth content can be described as materialization, suspension, and transcendence.

Materialization and Suspension

In the process of materialization, the artist's intentions and interactions with artistic material become relevant to the emergence of truth content. Although intention and achievement are not to be confused, nor their relation overemphasized, the discerning of a work's truth content can begin by asking whether the artist's intentions were actually achieved (222–23/ 212–14, 420–21/395–96). There is an ambiguity, however, in Adorno's understanding of relations between intentions and truth content. On the one hand, he describes truth content as the materialization of the most advanced consciousness of contradictions within the horizon of possible reconciliation. This consciousness is true (285/274). On the other hand, Adorno describes truth content as the complete presentation of false consciousness and regards his own book on Wagner as a redemption of the truth of false consciousness (196/188).

This ambiguity becomes problematic because of Adorno's reason for the second description. He argues that truth as such should not be separated from the presentation of false consciousness because true consciousness has never existed. But he must also think that true consciousness does exist. Otherwise there would be little point in talking about false consciousness, whether completely presented or not, and there would be no basis for describing truth content as the materialization of true consciousness. Adorno owes us an account of how truth content as the materialization of true consciousness relates to truth content as the complete presentation of false consciousness.

The closest he comes to this is when he says the falsity of an artist's intended idea often betrays itself in technical inadequacy (195/187). Judgments about the truth of an artwork require countless technical judgments, for artworks have objective import only insofar as this surfaces via artistic technique (280–82/269–71, 317/304, 420/395–96). Not every technical failure signals false intentions, however, nor can judgments about the truth of what was intended rely completely on immanent technical criticism.

The missing link between Adorno's two descriptions of truth content lies in his theory of the material unconscious. The notions of spontaneity and sensation let him connect artistic truth content with technical adequacy and historical modernity without reducing truth content in either sense to either of these. The process of determinate negation conditions artistic truth, but truth content does not boil down to technical success or historical progressiveness. Truth content is mediated by a material unconscious registering both technical problems and social contradictions. The artist's material unconscious lets history crystallize in artworks, and truth content itself is an "unconscious historiography" (200/193, 286/274). Hence truth content can surface despite the falsity of an artist's consciousness, but it can also surface by way of the truth of an artist's consciousness.

In the case of Wagner, Adorno considers the objectified consciousness both true and false.[31] It is "true" insofar as Wagner's technique adequately expresses experiences that register the technical and social problems of his day. The objectified consciousness is "false" insofar as it embodies a regressive social stance and Wagnerian operas try to cover contradictions. If correct, this reading of Adorno mitigates the unintended contradiction noted earlier. Great artworks cannot lie, not even when their import is false, because an artistically valid presentation of false consciousness tells us something true about society and its conflicts. At the same time, artworks whose import is true cannot but be false because the reconciliation they posit has not actually been achieved.

This last point implies, however, that truth content is more than the materialization of consciousness. There is more to extrapolating truth content than merely reconstructing the process of materialization. One must also evaluate the artwork's qualitative success in carrying out an internal dialectic of content and form, regardless of the artist's intentions. Adorno employs two general criteria of qualitative success, both of them connected to his viewing nature as the indirect contrary and artistic truth content as the direct contrary of human intentions (121/114–15). For an artwork to be successful, its form must preserve traces of the amorphousness that form tends to repress (80/74). For a work to be decisively successful, its form must flow directly from its truth content (281/270).

The first criterion has attached to it more specific criteria, all of them relevant for the extrapolation of truth content from an artwork's internal dialectic. As the dialectical unity of form and content, the import (*Gehalt*) of an artwork can turn into its truth content (*Wahrheitsgehalt*), provided the work possesses integrality, intensity, and articulation. For Adorno, each of these criteria is normative for the mediation of content and form and the evaluation of an artwork's status. In an integral artwork, unity emerges from the work's impulses and keeps them alive. The difficulty of achieving integrality arises both from the disparate impulses, which tend to diffuse, and from formal unity, which inevitably cuts the impulses down to size. Given the procrustean tendencies of "great" art, fragmentary works sometimes have preeminence (217/208, 221/212, 277–79/266–67, 283/271). According to Adorno, the aim of form is to make every detail eloquent within the artistic whole. In an intense artwork, mimesis transfers from the details to the totality, so that the whole intensifies the details (216–17/207–8, 279–80/268). Intensity, in turn, requires articulation, the disposition of an entire work according to the complexes within it. Lack of articulation means the complexes are insufficiently distinct or their unification is artificial. In general, the more abundant and full the complexes, the more articulate the whole, and the better a work's overall quality (219–21/210–12, 284–85/272–73).

Yet integrality, intensity, and articulation do not suffice for determining an artwork's rank. Depth is a more decisive criterion, especially with respect to truth. One must determine whether the work confronts antagonisms (283/271). The profound artwork highlights its contradictory moments, neither eliminating them nor leaving them disconnected. In a profound artwork, antagonisms are brought to the surface and placed in the horizon of a possible reconciliation. By virtue of a nonrepressive synthesis of antagonisms, profound artworks oppose a world where antagonisms are forcibly integrated—although their opposition returns as a conflict within the works themselves, for they let society remain antagonistic. A profound work carries out society's contradictions by carrying out this most ominous and fruitful contradiction of art in general.[32]

A work's ultimate status depends on its truth content (285/273). In order to flow directly from truth content, the form of a work must suspend itself on behalf of that which exceeds the dialectic of content and form (73–74/67, 216/207). Subjectively mediated consistency, the uncompromising elaboration of an artwork (73/67), must serve objective truth (420/395). Art's corrective artistic sublation of society's incorrect categories must culminate in a correction of artistic consistency. Truth content amounts to a dialectical suspension of the dialectic of content and form. At the same time, the criteria of qualitative success remain crucial for determining a work's truth content. Miscarried artworks cannot be true: they fail to achieve the integrality, intensity, articulateness, and depth that are required for them to have significant import. Miscarried works do not achieve consistency, not to mention a correction of consistency. In fact, says Adorno, "botched art is no art at all" (280/269).

If Adorno's insistence on qualitative success gives short shrift to substandard art, then his conception of dialectical suspension gives special status to works he would call "sublime." Examples of sublimity occur in Kafka's prose and in Beethoven's final string quartets.[33] Such works carry the suspension of the artistic totality into artistic form. Under the pressure of truth content, sublime artworks perforate their own thorough logicality, just as Adorno's negative dialectic thinks against thought. Sublime art suspends itself on behalf of a truth content that is not illusory, even though this suspension does not rid art of its illusory character (292/280).

Mediated Transcendence

The dialectical suspension of the dialectic can also be thought of as a mediated transcendence of the artwork's spirit. The relation between spirit and truth is complex. At one point Adorno says the spirit of an artwork is not coterminous with truth content (136/130). Artworks participate in truth content by way of their spirit, but their spirit can also be false. In one of the "Additions," however, Adorno writes that the spirit of artworks is their truth content (423–24/398). Does this mean spirit and truth content are in fact coterminous? The identity and difference of spirit and truth content can be explained by the notion of mediated transcendence.

The passage just mentioned implies that an artwork's truth content is present in a negative fashion, as something that is constitutively other than the work of art. The concept of spirit gets at this negative presence from a different angle. Spirit dialectically emerges within the work and refers beyond it. In the Adagio movement of Beethoven's Piano Sonata op. 31, no. 2 in D minor, says Adorno, hope dawns in such an authentic way that it points beyond the piece in which it appears. Hope is the sonata's emerging spirit, but, by being beyond the work itself, hope is also the sonata's truth content. Truth content is that which is not illusory in the artistic illusion. Truth content is that which transcends via that which is transcended. Truth content is neither independent of the configured sensuous moments nor immanent to them, but mediated by the configuration it transcends. For a qualified interpreter, technique and form point the way. As both the result and the transcendence of the artistic totality whose mediation is spirit, truth content is the mediated transcendence of spirit (280/268, 423–24/398).

Adorno claims that a nonconceptual spirit makes artworks commensurable to philosophical concepts. Proper philosophical interpretations will elicit spirit from an artistic configuration and confront the configured elements with their spirit, thereby moving to this spirit's truth or falsity beyond the work of art. "Truth content is not what art works denote, but the criterion which decides if they are true or false in themselves. It is this . . . truth content . . . alone which is [compatible with] philosophic interpretation . . . [and which] corresponds to . . . philosophical truth" (197/190). Immanent philosophical critique transcends its object by way of its object.[34] To become aware of the truth content of an artwork is to become conscious of the entire process from which truth content arises. Philosophy has the special task of comprehending both the artistic process and artistic truth. Philosophical interpretation is required in order to attain artistic truth content (193–94/186–87), and a philosophical redemption of illusory spirit is required to legitimate art's claim to truth (164/157).

Commensurability with philosophical concepts does not mean that the truth content of artworks is conceptual, however (199/191). In their movement toward truth, artworks need concepts, but for the sake of their truth, they resist conceptualizing (201/193). At the same time, the truth content of art is not merely artistic. Although it can appear only in works of art, truth content negates the works in which it appears (199/191). Artworks both have truth content and do not have it; they definitely suggest the truth, but only suggest it (194/187, 201/193). The truth content of artworks is located in a reciprocation between philosophical concepts and artistic phenomena.

According to Adorno, art lets something nonexistent seem to exist. In authentic works this something appears not to be fabricated. If this something is the truth, then, when artworks are experienced and interpreted, they and their semblance are sublated by the truth (199/191). Art has truth in an illusory import, and this can be a semblance of truth.[35] Yet artworks can only testify for the possibility of the possible; they cannot actualize this possibility. So long as authentic works let something seemingly existent *appear* as if it cannot be fabricated, even the most authentic artworks are feigning truth. The most authentic semblance can still dissemble, even when it is a semblance of truth (200/192). That is why art needs philosophy: philosophy must determine whether artistic import is indeed a semblance of truth.

8.3 Modern Art and Negative Dialectic

Adorno's claims about truth content compel one to question the philosophy that insists on the truth of artistic truth. More specifically, they compel one to reexamine the relationship between modern art and negative dialectic as reciprocal vehicles of truth. This can be done by first locating Adorno's claims in the history of philosophical aesthetics and then exploring their implications.

Self-Negation

Aesthetic Theory locates modern art in a negative dialectic that is both historical and philosophical. The book thereby crystallizes conflicts about rationality no less fundamental to modern society than to modern philosophy. It is apparent from Adorno's aesthetics that a struggle over rationality lies at the heart of philosophical aesthetics, at least in the German tradition. This struggle can be traced back to Kant's attempt to locate the origin and solution of "the antinomy of taste" in a noncognitive but rational concept of the harmony between nature and freedom. With this concept, Kant's *Critique of Judgment* indirectly sanctions autonomous art as a symbol of morality, and it desperately tries to bridge the gap between what is, which reason can determine, and what ought to be, which reason obligates us to pursue. Ten years later Schelling proclaimed art to be the only true organon of philosophy, one that reveals the unknown identity of subject and object before their alienation.

The problem with Kant's moralism and Schelling's aestheticism, according to Hegel, is that they overlook the comprehensive and progressive rationality of history as a whole. Hegel says that polar opposites such as "is and ought" or "subject and object" lack truth in isolation from each other. Instead, the truth lies in their mediation, which "is absolutely accomplished and is ever self-accomplishing." Art is no mere symbol of morality, nor is the identity of subject and object unknown: art has the task of disclosing truth in sensuous form and setting forth the reconciled opposition between subject and object.[36] Indeed, the unfolding of reason in history has made culture more important than morality. Because Hegel places philosophy at the pinnacle of culture, however, art becomes, in effect, a gloriously autonomous servant of philosophic truth.

Aesthetic Theory tries to defend art against this sort of servitude, just as Negative Dialectics opposes Hegel's claim that the reconciliation of subject and object is absolutely accomplished. Yet Adorno does not exempt art from the task of disclosing historical truth, nor does he revert to Schelling's aestheticism. The truth to be disclosed is primarily social rather than primarily philosophical or artistic. What needs to be expressed is the suffering of socialized individuals. The subject-object opposition to be presented is an antagonism in society's structure. Suffering and antagonism can only be removed through social praxis, not through merely cultural reconciliation. In a sense, Adorno has revived Kant's "symbol of morality." Art stands in for a truly rational praxis in a truly rational society.

For Kant, the antinomy of taste has its origin and resolution in reason. For Hegel, the rational resolution of Kant's antinomy is also a real historical resolution. For Adorno, the dilemmas of art and their possible resolution derive from sociohistorical developments in which scientific, artistic, and philosophical rationality play crucial roles. His philosophy tries to expose the antagonisms in these developments and point to their possible outcome, but without locating their ultimate resolution in art or philosophy. His philosophy has taken on the burden of an antagonistic society.

In this society a dialectic within philosophical aesthetics has turned into a negative dialectec that thinks against thought.[37]

Turning against its own participation in a false society, Adorno's philosophy tries to conceptualize its own impossibility. Faced with the temporarily impossible possibility of a true society, Adorno's negative dialectic tries to negate itself, recognizing its own limits, and dedicating itself to the object that takes precedence over the subject. This attempt is deeply paradoxical. On the one hand, Adorno demonstrates the limits of thought. He shows what it means to think in the light of liberation without acting as if our thinking is either fully liberated or directly liberating. On the other hand, Adorno continues to tie the possibility of freedom to the limiting power of thought. Whereas the task of Kantian reason was to restrict scientific rationality for the sake of rational morality and reasonable taste, the task of negative dialectic is to restrict the restricter for the sake of nonrestrictive identity and unrestricted nonidentity.[38]

The final section of *Negative Dialectics* is not the only place where this task is performed. Adorno's philosophy contains neither a final negation of the negation of the negative nor a final appearance of the possible liberation that illumines a negative world. Hegel's absolute knowledge has not turned into an absolute negation of knowledge. In a paradoxical way, liberation is both present and absent at any instant. The ongoing process of theoretical negation is supposed to make possible the instantaneous appearance of liberation, just as in art the image makes possible the apparition. The idea of reconciliation requires that dialectical thought repeatedly negate its own antagonistic self. Such self-negation is concealed and revealed throughout the major works of Adorno's final decade.[39]

Adorno seems to have stripped Nietzsche's "free spirits" of any remaining illusions about the liberating power of reason. Like few other philosophers in our century, Adorno has internalized the fact that, in a supposedly rational society, the calculated extermination of human beings was rationalized by misreading Nietzsche's critique of metaphysics. In criticizing Nietzsche's critique of metaphysics, Adorno indicts the hope in reason still latent in Nietzsche's critique.[40] Yet Adorno's own critique of reason assumes that human beings can achieve a rational reordering of what has been rationally disordered, and this assumption seems to make thought supremely responsible for its own order and for the order of society. Having disordered thought and society, thought must now restrict itself for the sake of that which thought and society have come to dominate. Hence a question arises concerning the limits of the thought that limits thought. What provides such limits, other than the order that needs to be changed and the nonidentical on which thought has imposed order?

A struggle with this question takes Adorno's successors in two different directions. Some retain the strongly negative cast of Adorno's critique of reason while surrendering the assumption that human beings can achieve a rational reordering of what has been rationally disordered. Such followers gravitate toward poststructuralism and deconstruction. Other of Adorno's successors take nearly the opposite tack. They retain the assumption about rational reordering, but give up the negative cast of Adorno's critique. Such followers include some thoughtful critics of poststructuralism and deconstruction.[41]

Common to both camps, however, is a tendency to find Hegel's totalizing approach to reason in history even more problematic than it is for Adorno. Not surprisingly, Adorno's insistence on a philosophical knowledge of artistic truth comes under attack from both sides. Adorno is vulnerable to criticism in two respects. One has to do with the relationship between art and philosophy, which can be described as a dialectic of nonidentity. The other has to do with the apparent presumption of Adorno's philosophy to have an absolute knowledge of the truth, which can be described as a broken promise.

Dialectic of Nonidentity

Although religion has vanished from Hegel's familiar triad, Adorno retains a close reciprocation between art and philosophy. They share, he says, "a mode of conduct that forbids pseudomorphosis."[42] Whereas philosophy is primarily conceptual, and art is not, both of them engage in expression and negation, and they need each other to carry out this common task. Unlike science, which aims for a correspondence between propositions and facts, both art and philosophy seek a progressive expression of deeply socialized experience.[43] To give expression, both art and philosophy must carry out determinate negation or, in the words of *Philosophy of Modern Music,* "determinate contradiction."[44] They must contradict a contradictory world.

Negative Dialectics describes contradiction as "the nonidentical under the aspect of identity," and dialectic as "the consistent consciousness of nonidentity."[45] Adorno's assigning art the task of contradiction makes one wonder about the consistency of his own consciousness of nonidentity. There is something odd about applying the single concept of contradiction to qualitatively different media of negation. Given the nonconceptual character of art, "contradiction" cannot be the same process in art as it is in philosophy. Are modern works of art inherently "contradictory," or do they first become contradictory when a philosopher places them "under the aspect of identity"?

Adorno's reply involves his provocative reconception of the Hegelian problem of defining the nonidentical. As a conceptual attempt to honor the nonidentical, Adorno's negative dialectic requires that the definiteness of the nonidentical not depend on conceptual definition. Otherwise his own negation of Hegel's "accomplished reconciliation" would remain a mere postulate of nonidentity in a philosophy that cannot escape conceptual identity. At this point, art acquires great significance for Adorno's own philosophy. Artworks are said to define the nonidentical in a nonconceptual fashion, and their defining remains nonconceptual even when they receive conceptual interpretations. Technique and form enable art to place the nonidentical under the aspect of identity without imposing conceptual identity.

Because Adorno wants to respect the nonidentical, his aesthetic theory must emphasize the difference between art and philosophy, and his interpretative practice must extrapolate truth content rather than impose it. His stress on technique and form counters Hegel's tendency to read philosophical ideas into art. Yet Adorno's categories seem vague in a way that threatens the difference he wishes to uphold. As used by Adorno, "definition" is an indefinite term, "determinate negation" has an indeterminate meaning, and "contradiction" covers many contraries that are qualitatively distinct. Perhaps both art and philosophy "define" the nonidentical, but surely not in the same sense. Even if both art and philosophy "contradict" a "contradictory" world, they do so in such different ways that applying "contradiction" to all instances forces identity on the nonidentical. Two potential problems arise. On the one hand, art might be theorized and interpreted as if it were philosophy. On the other hand, philosophy might be presented as the savior of art and of the nonidentical.

Adorno tries to avoid the first problem by appealing to the nonconceptual character of art. He says, for example, that concepts and claims lose their usual logic when they enter art, and that art provides a nondiscursive form of knowledge. Nevertheless, his explanation of such knowledge makes art seem conceptual, discursive, and even philosophical. Two questions illustrate this problem. First, do artworks display a logic, as Adorno claims, or do they simply have more or less articulate forms and structures? Second, do artworks criticize society, or do they merely stand in relationships of tension and opposition? The problem comes to a head in Adorno's view of art as a process of determinate negation. The concept of determinate negation derives from the history of discursive argumentation, especially as this occurs in philosophy. Can art be viewed as a process of determinate negation without being treated as if it were a mode of discursive, indeed philosophical knowledge?

Adorno tries to avoid the problem of presenting philosophy as art's savior by insisting on the conceptual character of philosophy. Even when describing his philosophical ideal as "full, unreduced experience in the medium of conceptual reflection," he calls attention to the prominence of concepts. This means, among other things, that philosophical interpretations of art will not try to establish an identity between artworks and philosophical concepts, even though "it is through such interpretation that the truth of the work unfolds."[46]

In one of his more emphatic moments, however, Adorno claims that "aesthetic experience must pass over into philosophy or else it will not be genuine" (197/190). Such a claim gives philosophy a prerogative on the awareness of truth and falsehood that rightly characterizes full participation in art. Consider as well Adorno's claim that "the progressively unfolding truth of [the] work of art is none other than the truth of the philosophic concept" (197/189). He does not say that the truth of the philosophic concept is none other than the truth of the work of art. Combined with Adorno's concern about a philosophical redemption of artistic import, this example points to a Hegelian tendency to make art's ultimate significance depend on philosophy. To the extent that the disclosure of artistic truth requires philosophical interpretation, it is ultimately because of philosophy that art can express social antagonisms and suggest the possibility of reconciliation.

One implication of this tendency is that philosophy becomes a privileged, albeit paradoxical, redeemer of the nonidentical. According to Adorno, no other mode of knowledge in contemporary society can mediate within itself between mimesis, which provides access to the nonidentical, and discursive rationality, which has become increasingly instrumental. Although art performs a similar mediation, its rationality is not discursive: "Art works talk like fairies in tales: if you want the absolute, you shall have it, but only in disguise. [The true is undisguised to discursive knowledge, but for this reason also unattained; artistic knowledge attains the truth, but as something incommensurable to art]" (191/183).[47] Unlike science, philosophy deliberately retains a rhetorical element in its conceptual medium, crossing the divide between artistic and discursive knowledge. It thereby bridges the gap between the nonidentical, which art makes definite, and identity, which discursive knowlege tries to impose.

Hence the philosophical interpretation of artistic truth content acquires metaphysical significance. As the "objective solution" to the enigma of every work, truth content cannot be attained by discursive knowledge in general, but only by "philosophical reflection." According to Adorno, "this alone is what legitimates aesthetics" (193/186). As we shall see, such a legitimation of aesthetics threatens to delegitimate Adorno's negative dialectic. For by striking the pose of redeemer, Adorno's philosophy apparently presumes to have an absolute knowledge of the truth, a presumption that would violate his refusal to impose identity on the nonidentical.

Broken Promise

The final section of *Negative Dialectics* asks whether metaphysical knowledge of the absolute is possible without Hegel's presumption of absolute knowledge.[48] If truth is conceived dialectically, then dialectical thought poses as a form of absolute knowledge, in conflict with the idea of negative dialectic. If truth is conceived as something completely incommensurable with dialectic, then one resorts to a theory of double truth, contrary to the idea of truth. Thus negative dialectic must oppose its own tendency toward absolute knowledge, and, in this opposition, make room for contingent knowledge of a possible absolute. This absolute "would be the nonidentical that would not emerge until after the dissolution of the compulsion of identity."[49] Adorno envisions a migration of metaphysics into micrology, where existences are brought into a constellation that turns them into a script of the truth. "The smallest intramundane traits would be of relevance to the absolute, for the micrological view cracks the shells of what, measured by the subsuming cover concept, is helplessly isolated and explodes its identity, the delusion that it is but a specimen."[50]

Adorno's use of the conditional (*das Absolute wäre*) suggests that Hegel's presumption might be disguised rather than abandoned. An attempt at contingent knowledge of the absolute faces its own aporia, one recalling the previous choice between making dialectic absolute or resorting to a double truth. If the micrological view is a type of conceptual thought, then the absolute disappears from view: conceptual thought cannot grasp the nonidentical, which would not emerge until after the compulsion of identity dissolves. If the micrological view is not a type of conceptual thought, then the absolute seems incommensurable to conceptual thought, and a new theory of double truth emerges. If the micrological view is a new kind of thought, one neither conceptual nor nonconceptual, then, unless the structure of society has changed, this thought makes special claims for itself and seems to presume an absolute knowledge. Can any kind of thought legitimately claim that its micrological view would assist truth's emerging from what exists?

Perhaps this question does not count as an argument against micrological metaphysics. In any case, Adorno's turn to micrology is not motivated by an argument but an "experience." He appeals to the experience of how thought "that does not decapitate itself" flows into the transcendent idea of a world in which "not only extant suffering would be abolished but also the suffering that is irrevocably past would be revoked." Such thought converges in the concept of something different from this "unspeakable world," a concept pointing to a goal that would also be the origin of history.[51]

Adorno avoids Hegel's theodicy: the concept of the "humanly promised 'other' of history" is not real, and it does not rationalize human suffering. Instead, he transforms ontological proofs for God's existence into an argument from experience for a secularized eschatology. The "other" does not exist just because it can be thought, yet it could not be conceived if something in reality did not urge this concept upon us.[52] Adorno's idea of utopia is not a Kantian postulate that is subjectively necessary. All our marred moments of happiness and all the breaches in history's dialectic are continually broken promises of human well-being in a different world. In its turn to micrology, Adorno's negative dialectic risks the "folly" of relying on these promises.

According to *Negative Dialectics*, truth takes the shape of folly when, amid untruth, human beings refuse to surrender truth. This claim helps explain the paradoxes of modern art. Artworks such as *Endgame* say that not everything is just nothing. If everything were nothing, whatever exists would be colorless, and our resisting the exchange society would lose the help of the eye that does not want the world's colors to fade. Art receives its illusion from what is not illusion. Truth is promised in illusion.[53]

According to *Aesthetic Theory*, the lack of color in recent art is a negative "apotheosis" of color (204/196). Though such art may disillusion an eye expecting a rainbow, it is not for art itself to decide whether its negativity is its barrier or its truth (201/193). Art has no power over the possibility that, in the end, everything might come to nothing, even though art posits the possibility of the possible as if it were more than merely possible (200/192–93). Art can only constitute a semblance of truth.

Nowhere, however, does Adorno say why anyone should rely on promises made in an inefficacious gray. Who besides a micrological metaphysician can tell whether truth is being promised in modern art or, for that matter, in negative dialectic? Adorno asserts that "art is the promise of happiness, a promise that is constantly being broken" (204/196). Artworks trace the neediness inscribed in historical reality, and, insofar as what is in need unconsciously attracts its restoration, they point to objective truth. Art's expressing the will for a different world is as substantial as this will (199/192). But the questions Adorno does not address are how substantial this will is in contemporary society, and where, outside art and philosophy, it is to be found.

In Adorno's conception, artworks give a secular anticipation of a messianic condition (16/8, 208/200); they "demonstrate" a fundamental change for society (199–200/192). *Aesthetic Theory* tries to redeem art's illusory import as a semblance of truth. Despite art's illusory character, art can testify for the possibility of the possible. But to do this, art must transcend itself in cooperation with a philosophy intent on redeeming illusion for the sake of truth. According to that philosophy, authentic modern works reassemble historical reality into a negative testimony for a possible possibility. Utopia does not actually exist just because it can be artistically suggested, yet it can be extrapolated from modern art. Since the extrapolating is carried out by a philosophy within today's reality, the apparent aporia of micrological metaphysics turns into the unanswered question of Adorno's eschatology. One wonders exactly how the possible possibility would differ from current reality.

This question returns us to contemporary society and to the tasks of art and philosophy today. On Adorno's reading, negation and expression enable artistic illusion to anticipate a true society in which damaged life would be restored. In today's society, however, philosophy must negate artistic negation and rearticulate what art expresses. Truth would be falsified if it were merely conceptualized, but truth would be impotent if it could not be conceptually communicated. Art needs a philosophy that needs art. In their truth content, the two converge (197/189). Although art and philosophy cannot exempt themselves from a false society, together they disclose social truth. While critically justifying autonomous art in a false society, Adorno's aesthetics justifies itself as a vehicle for the truth of art. Compared to Hegel's aesthetics, this vehicle is the paradoxical carrier of a broken promise.

If art and philosophy can disclose social truth, then the false totality cannot be totally false, and the possibility arises that modern art and negative dialectic have overlooked truth that is unfolding beyond their confines. The final three chapters pursue this possibility. They use various criticisms of Adorno's thought to evaluate his contributions to philosophical aesthetics. The criticisms pertain to Adorno's autonomism, modernism, and cognitivism. I shall argue that each emphasis harbors valid insights, but each must be modified in order to appropriate Adorno's contributions under current conditions.

III
Criticism

9
Models of Mediation

Agreeable arts are those whose purpose is merely enjoyment. . . . Fine art, on the other hand, is a way of presenting that is purposive on its own and that furthers, even though without a purpose, the culture of our mental powers to [facilitate] social communication.
Kant[1]

Adorno's *Aesthetic Theory* develops a complex model of the social mediation of art, and it provides a sustained argument for the social significance of autonomous art. In these ways the book carries the Marxist tradition to a level of sophistication not easily matched by other paradigms for the study of art. Yet both Adorno's model and his argument have left sympathetic critics unconvinced. Several important criticisms occur in Peter Bürger's *Theory of the Avant-Garde*. Bürger claims that, by improperly assuming the validity of the principle of autonomy, Adorno skews his approach to art's social significance. As I shall show, however, Bürger's criticisms are undermined by some of his own assumptions.

This chapter argues that neither Adorno nor Bürger has given a satisfactory account of art's social significance. In *Aesthetic Theory*, Adorno misreads the autonomy of art and neglects heteronomous art. In *Theory of the Avant-Garde*, Bürger misreads the avant-garde's attack on autonomy and abandons normative aesthetics. This argument provides a more precise evaluation of Adorno's autonomism than was attempted in chapters 4 and 5.

9.1 Adorno and Bürger

Despite their differences, Adorno and Bürger have a shared position about the autonomy of art. This position involves six claims. (1) Art has become independent from other institutions in bourgeois society. (2) Art's independence, and claims concerning its independence, depend on developments in other institutions, especially political and economic ones; the autonomy of art has always been relative to bourgeois society as a whole. (3) The relative independence of *art* has become increasingly tied to the production and reception of *artworks* whose intent has not been to accomplish purposes directly served by other institutions, whether economic, political, religious, or academic. The primary functions of these works have been somewhat peculiar to art—maintaining an image of humanity, expressing "irrational" needs and desires, satisfying aesthetic contemplation, or attacking the autonomy of art. (4) Autonomous art both affirms and criticizes the society to which it belongs, and this combination of affirmation and criticism is inextricable from its autonomy. (5) Because of external pressures and developments within art itself, the autonomy of art has become increasingly problematic in advanced capitalist societies. (6) Nevertheless, autonomy remains crucial for art's contributions within advanced capitalist society. Autonomous art, by virtue of its autonomy, has a special social significance. Although Bürger is less enthusiastic about this last claim, he too suggests that autonomy may be legitimate and necessary so long as advanced capitalist societies have not been fundamentally transformed.

Together these six claims make up a powerful and persuasive position. The position has profoundly troubling aspects, however. These appear in the qualifications Adorno and Bürger introduce at strategic points in their arguments. Adorno defends the principle of autonomy, only to undermine it with his penetrating comments on the fetishism of artworks. Bürger attacks the same principle, only to resign himself to its inescapability. In both cases the autonomy of art is viewed as an "evil" necessary for some greater good. Indeed, Adorno's version sometimes resembles a theodicy of autonomous art.

Artwork as Monad

As was shown earlier, Adorno's model of social mediation can best be located within the Marxist tradition, with its emphasis on relations between base and superstructure. For Adorno, as for other Marxists who share an internalist paradigm, the loci for social mediation are tendencies within art that intersect nonartistic tendencies. One of Adorno's contributions to the Marxist tradition is to give a detailed account of art as a type of production, rather than merely an ideological arena in the superstructure of a capitalist social formation. At the same time, he, like Lukács, develops an expressivist version of the internalist paradigm. He tries to show that artistic phenomena express not simply the economic base as such but the inner dynamic of an entire social formation. His model of social mediation is an internalist theory that encourages expressive accounts of artistic phenomena.

The central phenomenon in Adorno's model is the work of art. Accordingly, when Adorno writes on art, he tends to develop tensions within particular works that echo tensions in society as a whole. Obviously this description must be qualified; Adorno does address the social position of art as a whole, and he does comment on the production and consumption of art. Nevertheless his focus remains on tensions within the work of art. The main claim in the section titled "The Mediation of Art and Society," for example, is that works of art express the social totality: "The process that occurs in art works and which is arrested in them has to be conceived as being the same as the social process surrounding them. In Leibnizian terminology, they represent this process in a windowless fashion. . . . All that art works do or bring forth has its latent model in social production" (350–51/335). To ask about the structure of Adorno's model of social mediation, then, is to ask about the structure of the artwork as a social monad whose internal process brings forth the social process surrounding it.

In Adorno's model, autonomy and social character mark the position of artworks within advanced capitalist societies. Artworks are defetishizing fetishes. Their autonomy is conditioned by society as a whole, but is itself a precondition for truth in art. The notions of autonomy and truth, in turn, motivate Adorno's claims about social significance. Although he locates the social significance of artworks in both their import and their social functions, he understands their social functions as primarily cognitive functions, and he regards the significance of these functions as directly dependent on artistic import. And, although import consists of both social content and truth content, truth provides the ultimate criterion for the social significance of a work's import and, by extension, for the social significance of the work's social functions. Autonomy, then, is a precondition for that which ultimately determines an artwork's social significance.

Adorno's concept of import and his emphasis on import have three implications for his approach to the social functions of a work of art. First, he does not think these functions can be fully explained by empirical methods. To the extent that social functions are informed by the work's import, they exceed the grasp of empirical techniques. Second, he tends to consider significant only those functions that stem from the import of a work. Third, his assessment of the significance of a work's social functions is governed by more than an account of the work's social content. In the final analysis, his assessment is governed by an interpretation of the work's truth content.

Art as Institution

Peter Bürger has challenged Adorno's account of autonomy and social significance.[2] He uses some of Adorno's own assumptions to criticize Adorno's account and to propose an alternative. Bürger's targets include Adorno's emphases on autonomous works and on import. By implication, Adorno's concept of truth content also falls under the critic's scalpel. Whereas Adorno focuses on the import of autonomous works, Bürger emphasizes what he calls the institution of art.

He comes to this emphasis by historicizing Adorno's aesthetic theory.[3] Bürger explains that to historicize a theory is to grasp the connection between the unfolding of the theory's subject matter and the elaboration of its categories. To historicize an aesthetic theory is to grasp the connection between the history of art and the history of philosophical reflections on art. Bürger's historicizing thesis is this: Because "the avant-garde movements" first made recognizable "certain general categories of the work of art," the aesthetician must understand the development of art in bourgeois society "from the standpoint of the avant-garde."[4]

According to Bürger, Adorno is mistaken when he subsumes historical avant-garde movements such as futurism, constructivism, dadaism, and early surrealism under the concept of "modern art." The avant-garde is a distinct historical phenomenon. It goes beyond the modernist assault on traditional genres and techniques to attack the entire bourgeois institution of art. This attack is an institutional "self-criticism" whose aim is "to reintegrate art into the praxis of life." According to Bürger, the avant-garde exposes and challenges the principle of autonomy at work in the history of bourgeois art and in Adorno's aesthetic theory.[5]

The central category in Bürger's own model is the "institution of art," which he thinks of as a historical category. Made possible in part by the avant-garde's "self-criticism" of art, this category is most directly applicable to phenomena in Western societies since the late 1700s, even though it also helps explain phenomena from other social formations.[6] In its most general meaning, "the institution of art" refers to "the productive and distributive apparatus and also to the ideas about art that prevail at a given time and that determine the reception of works."[7] Bürger's approach emphasizes governing ideas about the purpose of art, along with the aesthetic norms whereby such ideas take hold in production and reception.[8] This general approach assumes a more specific meaning of "art as an institution," namely, those ideas which govern the production and reception of artworks in bourgeois society and which compose the concept of autonomy.

Bürger says "the autonomy of art" is an ideological category of bourgeois society, one that "both reveals and obscures an actual historical development." On the one hand, it describes the real "detachment of art as a special sphere of human activity from the nexus of the praxis of life." On the other hand, the category of autonomy simultaneously obscures how this detachment occurs as a sociohistorical process. The category becomes a distortion when "the relative dissociation of the work of art from the praxis of life in bourgeois society . . . becomes transformed into the (erroneous) idea that the work of art is totally independent of society."[9]

According to Bürger, this ideological category originated with the rise of philosophical aesthetics at a time when an economically strong bourgeoisie was seizing political power. As consolidated in the writings of Kant and Schiller, the concept of autonomy indicates how the art of bourgeois society differs in purpose, production, and reception from "sacral art" of the High Middle Ages and "courtly art" during the reign of Louis XVI. Bourgeois art serves neither as a cult object within the life of the faithful nor as a self-portrayal of artistocratic society. Instead it serves as a "portrayal of bourgeois self-understanding . . . in a sphere that lies outside the praxis of life."[10] Furthermore, whereas collective production characterizes sacral art, and collective reception characterizes both sacral and courtly art, both production and reception are individual acts in bourgeois art.

The detachment of art from life praxis became complete during the latter half of the nineteenth century when aestheticism rejected bourgeois life praxis and gave up the claim that art interprets life. By letting distance from life praxis become the import of autonomous works, aestheticism set the stage for avant-garde self-criticism of the institution of autonomous art. Avant-garde movements rejected both aestheticism and bourgeois life praxis, trying "to organize a new life praxis from a basis in art" while eliminating autonomous art as an institution.[11] "Avant-gardiste manifestations" undermined the notion of art's intended purpose, negated the categories of individual creation and individual reception, and challenged the distinction between producer and recipient.

The avant-garde's attack on autonomy failed, however, only to be institutionalized as art by a more recent "neo-avant-garde."[12] These developments leave Bürger with two questions: first, whether it is possible or even desirable to integrate art into the praxis of life within bourgeois society, and second, whether the culture industry has not already provided a "false elimination of the distance between art and life" and a "false sublation of autonomous art."[13]

Bürger's Criticisms

Such questions do not keep Bürger from criticizing Adorno's model of social mediation. He has three criticisms. The first pertains to Adorno's emphasis on autonomous works, the second to his emphasis on import, and the third to his understanding of social significance. Concerning the emphasis on autonomous works, Bürger argues that Adorno is unable to criticize art as an institution because he takes this institution for granted.[14] Adorno focuses on autonomous works without recognizing how his focus is itself governed by an institutional framework whose doctrine of autonomy the avant-garde has decisively challenged. Indeed, Adorno elevates one type of work to normative status while rejecting popular art and older styles of autonomous art such as literary realism. Even though the type elevated is what Bürger calls the "avant-gardiste" or "nonorganic" work, the historical avant-garde has undermined Adorno's claim that this is the only legitimate style in advanced capitalist society. They have destroyed "the possibility that a given school can present itself with the claim to universal validity. . . . The meaning of the break in the history of art that the historical avant-garde movements provoked does not consist in the destruction of art as an institution, but in the destruction of the possibility of positing aesthetic norms as valid ones."[15]

Bürger's second criticism concerns Adorno's emphasis on import. In nineteenth-century aestheticism, according to Bürger, the relative independence of bourgeois art from other social subsystems became fused with the increasingly asocial and apolitical import of individual works. The anti-aestheticism of the avant-garde exposed bourgeois art as a social institution whose principle of autonomy meant the social impotence of autonomous works. Because Adorno thinks within this institution, he has little to say about the social functions of artworks. Instead of analyzing the institutional framework that largely determines a work's social functions, Adorno is led by the doctrine of autonomy to derive such functions from the import of works in themselves. Ideology critique comes at the expense of functional analysis.[16] As a result, Adorno tends to ignore the sociohistorical context in which the work arises and the history of reception in which the work operates.[17]

Once the theoretical implications of the avant-garde become clear, however, a normative focus on import will be replaced "by a functional analysis, the object of whose investigation would be the social effect (function) of a work, which is the result of the coming together of stimuli inside the work and a sociologically definable public within an already existing institutional frame."[18] The work will undergo a functional analysis, not so much of the work's supposed functions in society at large, but of the work's changing functions within the evolving institution of art.

Bürger's third criticism addresses Adorno's understanding of the social significance of individual works. It was noted earlier that Adorno locates the social significance of the artwork in both its import and its social functions, but that the work's social significance ultimately hinges on the truth or falsity of the work's import. The problem with such an understanding of social significance, according to Bürger, is that it dehistoricizes the work. Adorno's approach makes it difficult to distinguish between the historical meaning (*Sinn*) and the contemporary relevance (*Deutung, Gehalt*) of the work. For example, when Goethe's *Iphigenie* is interpreted as prophesying the flip of enlightenment into mythology, Adorno is attributing experiences to the work that Goethe could not have had. The result is what Gadamer might call a "fusion of horizons" between the past and the present.

Bürger thinks such a fusion dissolves the historical specificity of a particular work. He calls for an "institution-sociological approach" that separates these horizons in order to place them in a dialectical relation. The sociologist should try to determine the position of Goethe's drama within the institution of literature in Goethe's day. This position should then be related to the work's later acceptance into the literary canon and its potential significance today. In this way the "interpretation" of individual works becomes a "production of significance" (*Be-*

deutungsproduktion) that self-consciously proceeds from a different historical experience and a different conception of literature than those of Goethe and his contemporaries.[19]

Bürger wishes to replace Adorno's emphasis on the import of autonomous works with an emphasis on the changing function of the work within a changing institution of art. Whereas Adorno makes the social significance of the work of art depend on the truth of its import, Bürger seems to make this depend on the work's potential contribution to the eventual integration of art and life. Bürger has rendered problematic Adorno's monadic model of social mediation. At the same time, however, Bürger's criticisms of Adorno raise questions about a claim both authors share. It is the sixth claim mentioned earlier, namely, that autonomy is crucial for art's contributions within advanced capitalist society. This claim deserves further attention.

9.2 Autonomy, Truth, and Popular Art

Several questions can be raised about the claim that autonomy is crucial for art's contributions within advanced capitalist society. One might wonder, for example, whether art can or does make contributions in any society. One might also reexamine the notion of "advanced capitalist society." For present purposes such questions will be set aside in favor of a closer look at "autonomy" and the emphasis Adorno places on this concept.

We should note in passing that there are many different applications of the concept of autonomy. Göran Hermerén distinguishes no fewer than twelve theses about art's autonomy, some pertaining to the history and characteristics of art as an institution, others to the character, functions, and reception of works of art. While some theses are descriptive, others are prescriptive. Hermerén also asks that we "distinguish clearly between the autonomy of art and our ideas about the autonomy of art."[20]

If all these distinctions were rigorously applied, however, we would soon lose sight of what is most interesting in the debate between Bürger and Adorno. Both of them think that the autonomy of art and the autonomy of works are inextricable from each other. Neither author accepts a clear distinction between descriptive and prescriptive theses about autonomy. Each author claims that the actual autonomy of art and dominant ideas about autonomy belong together, and that we cannot adequately understand the one without understanding the other. Bürger and Adorno share the claim that the autonomy of art and of works, both actual and ideational, is crucial for art's contributions within advanced capitalist society. They simply draw different conclusions from this claim.

In Adorno's account, the claim in question implies a strong notion of truth. Unlike Bürger, who says little about truth, Adorno views autonomy as a precondition for truth in art. To make sense of this view, one must assume with Adorno that the attainment of truth is a historical process whose precondition is also historical. Moreover, this historical precondition must be irreversible, at least until society as a whole undergoes a fundamental transformation.

Yet it is not clear why the assumption of irreversibility must be granted. Could it not be, for example, that in a consumer capitalist society enough changes will occur, short of a fundamental transformation, that art's relative independence from other social institutions will become a thing of the past? There are many indications that the institution of autonomous art is headed in such a direction. Would the completion of this process mean that truth could no longer be attained in art? Although Adorno might not be claiming that autonomy is *the* precondition for truth in art, he nonetheless considers it *a* precondition, and a crucial one at that.

Another way to put such questions would be to ask whether truth has been attained in art prior to the development of autonomy. Here one is struck by how little Adorno has to say about art prior to the eighteenth century. This fact need not deter us, however, since either a yes or a no would be instructive. If Adorno granted that truth has been attained prior to the development of autonomy, then autonomy would seem less crucial for the attainment of truth. If Adorno denied that truth has been attained prior to the development of autonomy, then his idea of truth in art might appear as little more than a sophisticated justification for autonomous art, perhaps in the age of its demise.

The waters become even more muddy when we turn to heteronomous art in the twentieth century. By "heteronomous art" I mean art that has not become relatively independent from other institutions of bourgeois society and whose products are produced and received to accomplish purposes that are directly served by other institutions. The term covers both traditional folk art and contemporary popular art. Examples of heteronomous art include everything from liturgical dance to tribal masks, from advertising jingles to commercial movies. If such art lacks autonomy, a crucial precondition for artistic truth, then one wonders about the legitimacy of measuring it according to the criterion of truth. Yet Adorno's critique of the culture industry makes little sense apart from the criterion of truth. If heteronomous art does not lack this precondition, then the distinction between autonomy and heteronomy disappears. Yet the focus of *Aesthetic Theory* presupposes a clear distinction. The book focuses almost exclusively upon autonomous art.

The obvious fact that *Aesthetic Theory* has little to say about heteronomous art seems entirely consistent with Adorno's claims about autonomous art. He regards autonomy as a precondition for truth in art, and truth as the ultimate criterion for the social significance of any work of art. An aesthetics primed in this way toward truth and social significance can hardly be expected to pay much attention to heteronomous art. Since such art lacks a precondition for truth, it probably cannot meet Adorno's ultimate criterion for social significance.

Adorno's stance can prompt three responses from those who are dissatisfied with the systematic neglect of heteronomous art in *Aesthetic Theory*. One would be to question whether the neglect of heteronomous art is truly in keeping with the deepest intentions of his aesthetics. A second response would be to challenge his tight connections between autonomy, truth, and social significance. A third would be to surrender the pivotal notion of truth in art. Unlike the third response, which seems premature, the first and second responses look promising.

Purpose and Function

One way to begin a response is to argue that Adorno's concept of autonomy is misconceived. This is different from Bürger's claim that Adorno improperly assumes the principle of autonomy. My argument is that Adorno confuses two aspects of autonomy that are both actually and ideationally distinct. The first aspect is one of purpose. The other is one of function. "Purpose" pertains to the fulfillment of human needs and desires within a society. "Function" pertains to the institutionalized operations and practices whereby human purposes are met or denied. Although purposes and functions are connected, they are also distinct.

Adorno's concept of autonomy loses sight of this distinction. Consider, for example, the dual use of "function" (*Funktion*) in his provocative claim that "if any social function can be ascribed to [art works] at all, it is . . . to have no function" (336–37/ 322). As an empirical claim about how art actually operates in society this would be patently incorrect. No one, and certainly not Adorno, would want to deny that even supposedly "autonomous" works operate as market commodities and find all sorts of uses in situations where economic transactions are taking place. As a claim about purposes Adorno's formulation also is problematic. It suggests, contrary to his own intent, that works of (autonomous) art fail to fulfill human needs and desires. His paradoxical statement trades on an ambiguity in the term "function." What he intends to say is that insofar as autonomous works fulfill human needs and desires within advanced capitalist society, they do so by refusing to operate in the manner dictated by other institutions. Autonomous works must be more or less useless within other institutions in order to serve the purpose of social critique and utopian memory.

Even such a construal of autonomy is too simple. Works of so-called autonomous art have many uses within other institutions. If they did not, they could not serve any purpose, not even that of social critique and utopian memory. Such works are used, for example, as agents of employment, socializing, corporate image-building, and civic pride. They function in many institutions, and they must function in some of these institutions in order to serve any purpose. How could we be overwhelmed by the onset of the reprise in Beethoven's Ninth Symphony (363/347) if there were no musicians' unions, concert halls, corporate foundations, or government grants? How could we critically reflect on the truth of this passage (364/347) if publishers and record companies did not produce scores, records, tapes, or compact discs? These questions might seem to take Adorno's approach too lightly, but apparent trifles can be instructive. By concentrating on the monadic work of art, Adorno seems to discount the entwinement of autonomous art with other social institutions. Even if other institutions frustrate human purposes, this would not eliminate the entwinement that does in fact exist.

I am not suggesting that the concept of autonomy be abandoned. Instead I am proposing to refine the concept by distinguishing between purposes and functions. The fact that art has become a relatively independent institution in society does not mean that the products of this institution have shed all their functions within other institutions. The claim that "autonomous art" serves a purpose thwarted by other institutions need not entail the claim that art has no social functions. At best the concept of autonomy will imply that at least some of what is called art has come to serve certain human purposes more directly than have other institutions in society. Furthermore, the functions whereby this occurs, although entwined in other institutions, are not exhausted by the operations of those institutions.

Consider, for example, a concert performance of Beethoven's Ninth Symphony. The performance may present a powerful gesture of human self-affirmation in ways that few nonartistic events can match. Although the performance helps provide employment, gives an occasion for socializing, or builds corporate images and civic pride, these facts do not exhaust its functions. The performance is also and simultaneously functioning as an object of attention and interpretation for both the performers and the audience, and is doing so at various levels of perception, technique, cultural memory, and social import. Yet, as Adorno would agree, it would be much too simple to say this performance instantiates autonomy only to the extent that it functions as an aesthetic object for aesthetic purposes. Not only are the primary purposes for undertaking such a performance more than merely aesthetic, the functions of this performance also include much more than merely aesthetic functions.

This account of autonomy raises the question whether an illuminating distinction can still be drawn between autonomous and heteronomous art. Although the distinction seems to be fading, both in actuality and in thought, one contrast bears pointing out. The processes and structures that have come to characterize autonomous art are such that its products tend to be self-referential. The tendency toward self-reference has become increasingly evident in the twentieth century. For products of autonomous art, a primary means of serving this institution's purposes is to affirm and reject other products of autonomous art.[21] The functions of these products in other institutions tend to be secondary means subservient to self-referential functions. One can see a rough parallel here with the institution of academic scholarship, whose products also tend to be self-referential, unlike research and teaching outside the modern academy. By contrast, products of heteronomous art tend not to be self-referential. For products of heteronomous art, the primary means of serving its purposes are functions within other institutions.[22]

By way of illustration, think of the contrast between a piece of concert music, say Stravinsky's *Symphony of Psalms,* and a piece of liturgical music, say a contemporary setting of Psalm 39 for congregational singing. Stravinsky's symphony was written as a tour de force, one that tackles various compositional problems and deliberately inserts itself into a concert tradition. Performers approach the symphony primarily in terms of its musical challenges. Audiences listen to it in terms of how well those challenges are met relative to other compositions and to other performances of the same composition. The psalm setting, by contrast, was written to meet a need for new liturgical actions, and it is sung as a way of carrying out such actions. Both pieces very well fulfill similar purposes, such as the expression of suffering and hope, but the means to such an end are somewhat different, with a corresponding difference in the primacy of their functions within nonartistic institutions. It is no easier to imagine an event of public worship in which Stravinsky's symphony would be liturgically appropriate than to imagine a concert in which congregational singing of the psalm setting would be aesthetically appropriate.

The contrast between autonomous and heteronomous art is fluid, however, and it certainly is no longer so firm as to support Adorno's strong preference for autonomous art.[23] Yet the critical thrust of Adorno's approach has not lost its relevance. Perhaps the best way to honor his intentions without accepting his formulations would be to loosen the connections between autonomy, truth, and social significance. This move can employ two counterclaims: (1) that autonomy is not a precondition for truth in art; and (2) that truth in art is not the ultimate criterion for the social significance of art, even though the criterion of truth does apply to art, both autonomous and heteronomous. These counterclaims allow one to argue for the truth and social significance of heteronomous art.

Truth and Social Significance

For present purposes, "truth in art" will be taken to mean the way in which the status quo is challenged and human aspirations are disclosed. Although Adorno might have found this description insufficiently negative, it does capture some of his idea of truth content. Now let us ask whether in an advanced capitalist society a work of art must be autonomous in order to challenge the status quo and to disclose human aspirations. It is hard to imagine why this would have to be so. Perhaps relative independence from other institutions would allow the work to present its challenge and disclosure in a more concentrated and sophisticated way, but the self-referential tendency of autonomous works could just as easily prevent this challenge and disclosure. Autonomy might make truth possible in some works and make it impossible in others.

By the same token heteronomy need not keep a work from challenging the status quo and disclosing human aspirations. The lack of relative independence could allow the work to present its challenge and disclosure in a more diffuse and accessible way, even though the absence of self-reference could also derail this challenge and disclosure. Heteronomy might make truth possible in some works and make it impossible in others. To claim that autonomy is a precondition for truth in art is to ignore the ability of heteronomous works and events to challenge the status quo, sometimes in ways that are more effective than those available to autonomous works.

The reference to effectiveness introduces the second counterclaim: truth in art is not the ultimate criterion for the social significance of art. There are two reasons for claiming this. One is that social significance depends just as much on institutions outside art as it does on the import of works within the institution of art. The second is that the reasons for finding a work or event socially significant are so varied that the question of truth or falsity can become relatively unimportant.

To illustrate the first reason, think of the social significance of political cartoons, whether those of Honoré Daumier in the nineteenth century or those of Garry Trudeau in our own. Commentators of various political persuasions would probably agree that "Doonesbury" had greater social significance in the 1980s than "Blondie." The basis for such an assessment could hardly be restricted to the import of Trudeau's series. Crucial considerations would have to be the prominence given this series in the print media and the way "Doonesbury" became part of the American political landscape. If the series had not become syndicated and notorious, it would have less social significance, regardless of its import. The social significance of "Doonesbury" is heavily dependent on the contemporary operations of the print media and the American political system.

The second reason for denying that truth is the ultimate criterion for social significance is the variety of reasons for finding a work or event of art socially significant. The reasons for finding a television series such as "Dallas" socially significant probably have little in common with the reasons for finding a performance by Laurie Anderson socially significant. The first set of reasons would have to do with the power of public image-making; the second set of reasons would pertain to the erasure of boundaries between autonomous and heteronomous art. This illustration does not mean that "social significance" is a categorical chameleon whose content changes for each phenomenon. Instead the point is that, given the great variety in reasons for finding artistic phenomena socially significant, it hardly makes sense to posit an ultimate criterion for social significance. Positing truth as the ultimate criterion usually assumes or implies that "major works" of "autonomous art" have greater social significance than lesser works of autonomous art and than any works of heteronomous art. Such an assumption or implication makes little sense, however, unless the reasons for assigning social significance are of the same kind. This homogeneity does not exist, not even in Adorno's own discussions of phenomena ranging from swing jazz to Beckett's *Endgame*.

If autonomy is not a precondition for truth in art, and if truth is not the ultimate criterion for art's social significance, then the criteria of truth and social significance need not be restricted to autonomous art. To the extent that Adorno's own critique of the culture industry applies these criteria to heteronomous art, our counterclaims serve to honor his intentions without sharing his strong preference for autonomous art. Yet the arguments given for these counterclaims might seem to undercut the critique of any art, whether heteronomous or autonomous. For if the social significance of artistic phenomena depends on the operations of other institutions, and if the reasons for assigning social significance lack homogeneity, then how can we make coherent global judgments about art in contemporary society?

This question is particularly urgent in view of popular art's increasingly prominent role in societies around the world. Philosophers who wish to address the central issues of our day will need to develop a philosophy of popular art.[24] Yet the traditional tools of aesthetics are inadequate for this task. More specifically, the assumptions and categories of traditional aesthetics are inappropriate for analyzing, interpreting, and evaluating popular art. The inadequacy of Adorno's *Aesthetic Theory* in this regard is not that it fails to revise traditional aesthetics but that it fails to do this with a view to art that is not autonomous. Hence the question about coherent global judgments suggests a need to reconsider the relationship between traditional aesthetics, which gives rise to such judgments, and popular art, which seems to render such judgments inappropriate.

Traditional Aesthetics and Popular Art

The failure to give an account of heteronomous art is common to most of traditional aesthetics. Since its eighteenth-century formation as a subdiscipline of philosophy, traditional aesthetics has had two domains. The first is the aesthetic dimension of life and reality. Traditional categories attached to this domain include natural beauty, taste, and aesthetic experience. The second domain is that of "fine art" or "high art" or Art with a capital A. This domain became the more prominent one after Hegel declared it the primary subject matter of aesthetics. Much of twentieth-century aesthetics concentrates on questions pertaining to high art, and, when discussing the aesthetic dimension, does so in terms of high art. Although increasing discussion of the aesthetics of the environment, fashion, and sport indicates a revival of attention to the aesthetic dimension, traditional aesthetics has shown little interest in folk and popular art.

Indeed, the main assumptions of traditional aesthetics sit uneasily with the realities of popular art. Such assumptions include the following three: (1) that the proper attitude toward works of art is one of disinterested contemplation; (2) that what R. G. Collingwood calls "art proper" is autonomous, having unique purposes and peculiar norms; and (3) that aesthetic norms are the most important or the only relevant norms for art. As Bürger indicates, it is the second of these assumptions that Adorno has done the least to challenge. At the same time, elements of the first and third assumptions also remain in Adorno's aesthetics.[25]

The presence of these assumptions renders Adorno's aesthetics inadequate with respect to popular art. Traditional emphases on disinterested contemplation, artistic autonomy, and aesthetic normativity clash with the realities of popular art. In the first place, disinterested contemplation is hardly the attitude to take if one wants to enjoy a rock concert, nor does rock music consistently generate aesthetic delight in the way things look or sound. The appropriate attitude is more desirous of sensual gratification, and the resulting pleasure is more visceral than what has traditionally been understood as aesthetic delight. In the second place, popular art makes little or no pretense at autonomy. It does not purport to have a unique purpose or to meet peculiar norms. It serves purposes of entertainment, communication, and narration that could just as well be fulfilled in other ways, and it embodies standards of technique and popularity not much different from ones pertaining to other products on the market. In the third place, even when popular art measures up to aesthetic norms such as originality or authenticity, these hardly seem like the most important or only relevant norms for popular art. No matter how original or authentic, for example, a movie that proves unpopular has less merit as a product of popular art.

When one compares the realities of popular art with the categories of traditional aesthetics, three gaps appear. These have to do with the limited focus of traditional aesthetics. Traditional attention to individual aesthetic experiences, creative works of art, and the quality or merit of such experiences or works, on the one hand, seems incompatible with the industrial organization, process-orientation, and popularity of popular art, on the other. These gaps are already implicit in Kant's distinction, quoted above, between "fine art," which unintentionally promotes mental culture, and "agreeable arts," whose sole intent is entertainment. I will briefly describe each of the three gaps before proposing some categories to help bridge them.

First, traditional attention to the individuality of aesthetic experiences seems incompatible with the industrial organization of popular art. Traditional aesthetics tries to say what is required for an individual to find a particular object "beautiful" or "aesthetically satisfying." This attempt assumes that there are individual perceivers seeking unique experiences toward discrete objects. The industrial organization of popular art undermines such assumptions. Standardization is crucial to popular art production, especially that which is mass-mediated;[26] the marketing of popular art leaves little to the vagaries of individual choice; and the consumption of popular art is self-consciously mass consumption—id est, an important part of enjoying products of popular art is to experience one-self as part of a larger population. The products of popular art are intentionally generic, even when they flaunt their "in-dividuality." Indeed, the operations of the culture industry make attention to the individuality of aesthetic experiences seem quaint.

The second gap is that the dominance of mass production, distribution, and consumption in popular art makes the tra-ditional emphasis on the work of art seem odd. The notion of autonomy leads traditional aesthetics to concentrate on the work of art as a product of individual creativity. Traditional aesthetics tries to analyze the nature of the work of art as well as the place of the artist in society. Although Adorno drops the essentialism of traditional aesthetics and voices suspicions about individual creativity, he continues to emphasize the au-tonomous work. In popular art, by contrast, the particular product is less important than the general processes of pro-duction, distribution, and consumption within which the prod-uct operates. Furthermore, each process is much more complex than the traditional emphasis suggests. This is particularly clear in the case of production. Whereas traditional aesthetics might worry about the relevance of the artist's intentions for inter-preting the work, the theorist of popular art must ask who "the artist" of a movie or record or television program is. Is the artist of a movie the producer, the director, the editors, the author of the screenplay, the actors, or the film crew?[27] Perhaps the entire notion of "the work of art," with its ties to individual creativity, is incompatible with popular art.

The third gap occurs between traditional concerns about the quality of aesthetic experiences and the aesthetic merit of art-works, on the one hand, and the importance of popularity, on the other. Traditional aesthetics claims that peculiar aesthetic norms hold for art, and that these norms are the most impor-tant or the only relevant norms for art. Traditional aesthetics expects us to rely on these aesthetic norms in order to deter-mine the quality of aesthetic experiences and to evaluate the merit of artworks. It is a truism of traditional aesthetics that the "best" or "greatest" works of art need not be the best-liked or the most widely received, for what decides their merit is their ability to meet aesthetic norms, not their popularity. In popular art, by contrast, popularity is a primary consideration. Although some commentators might suggest a correlation between aesthetic merit and popularity, this is hardly plausible with regard to high art, and it seems unlikely in the case of popular art. Hence the importance of popularity renders problematic the traditional concern about aesthetic merit.

The gaps between traditional aesthetics and popular art make it desirable for philosophers to find ways to bridge them. Several sets of categories may be needed to do this. If properly constructed, these categories will apply to both autonomous and heteronomous art, to the extent that this distinction is still useful. Their employment would revise traditional aesthetics beyond what Adorno has accomplished, thereby not only bringing aesthetics closer to popular art but also highlighting aspects of "fine art" that philosophers have neglected in the past. At the same time, the normative dimension in Adorno's aesthetics would be retained.

9.3 Normative Aesthetics

Categories

The first set of categories pertains to the social formation within which we are trying to understand both traditional aesthetics and popular art. The categories in question—"system" and "lifeworld"—derive from the social philosophy of Jürgen Habermas.[28] Habermas says a clear bifurcation has occurred between a systemic and an intersubjective level in modern societies. At the systemic level, which includes legal, economic, and administrative systems, "steering media" such as money and power operate independently of the orientations of individual agents. At the intersubjective level of the lifeworld, individuals continue to pursue various orientations in their actions. Although social institutions can channel the influence of the lifeworld upon formally organized systems, in the history of capitalism social institutions have tended instead to channel the influence of the system upon the lifeworld.

Habermas's distinction suggests a framework for understanding the place of art in societies that have become capitalist,
industrial, and formally democratic. We can view art as a social
institution tied to both a politico-economic system and an intersubjective lifeworld. This allows one to distinguish between
art as an operational component in the societal system and art
as an ensemble of practices and experiences in the lifeworld of
individuals. When explaining traditional emphases on individual aesthetic experiences, creative works of art, and aesthetic
merit, for example, one can point out that traditional aesthetics
has focused on art in the lifeworld and neglected art in the
societal system. One can also observe that theories of popular
art which recognize the prominence of industrial organization,
economic processes, and popularity thereby call attention to
art's place in the societal system, without providing an adequate
account of art as an ensemble of practices and experiences.
Whereas traditional aesthetics must learn to locate art in the
societal system, theories of popular art may have to learn to
locate art in the lifeworld.

In either case, the locating of art in society will rely on the
category of "social institution," with its correlates, already discussed, of "function" and "purpose." By "social institution" is
meant a durable, relatively distinct, and cross-culturally instantiated mode of organizing life in society. The category is broad
enough to encompass science, education, economic markets,
and families, to name a few. Although differing from Bürger
on the precise meaning of the term, I agree that art should be
thought of as a "social institution." Art can indeed be described
as a durable, relatively distinct, and cross-culturally instantiated
mode of organizing life in society. Obviously it changes over
time, it shades off into other institutions, and it looks different
in various cultures. Yet there is significant continuity throughout the changes, there are significant differences from other
institutions, and the specificity of art in one culture is never
totally unique to that culture.

I have suggested that the institution of art in contemporary
Western societies participates in both the societal system and
the lifeworld. Here there is no telling difference between high
art and popular art. Together they make up a network of

processes and structures that is a somewhat self-regulating component in the politico-economic system. At the same time, both types of art make up an ensemble of practices and experiences having relative cohesiveness and identity. They are ways of organizing our contemporary lifeworld. As was suggested earlier, even the highest of "autonomous" artworks has many functions, both in the societal system and in the lifeworld. Such a work functions as economic commodity, legal possession, and curatorial object, as well as an object of perception, enjoyment, discourse, and social interaction. The crucial question for philosophers to ask is not whether autonomous artworks have social functions, but which purposes the works' functions are fulfilling, and whether these purposes are desirable.

Pursuing answers will point up the limitations of looking at art as artworks rather than as institution. Traditional aesthetics picks out features and merits of the work of art, whether as the product of art making or as the object of art reception or as an entity in its own right, but it has difficulty seeing the social functions of artworks as well as of art making and art reception. Hence Bürger is right to criticize Adorno's emphasis on autonomous artworks. At the same time, however, Bürger's turn to the work's functions *within* the "institution" of art continues the traditional emphasis in a slightly different guise. Much more attention must be given to the functions of artistic phenomena in other institutions and to the operations of the art institution in both the societal system and the intersubjective lifeworld. Otherwise substantive questions about the human purposes of art might be ignored. Given the prominence of popular art in contemporary society, such questions need to be raised, not only about high art but also about popular art.

A third set of categories will be useful in asking about the human purposes of art. The categories to be considered—structures, standards, and criteria—should help bridge the gap between the traditional emphasis on aesthetic merit and the importance of popularity. Traditional aesthetics, with its focus on high art, tends to evaluate the merits of the work of art according to aesthetic norms. Popular art, with its emphasis on popularity, seems to undermine any concern about normative

evaluation, whether aesthetic or otherwise. By distinguishing
structures, standards, and criteria, one can show that all art,
and all reflection upon art, has an inescapable normative dimension in contemporary Western societies. Before elaborating
these categories, however, let me indicate the problems that
might arise if, in criticizing Adorno's aesthetics, one simply
abandons the traditional concern for normative evaluation.
Such potential problems surface in Bürger's stance toward normative aesthetics.

Social History and Aesthetic Norms

Like Adorno, Bürger thinks the importance of artistic phenomena ultimately depends on their contribution to a utopian future. Unlike Adorno, however, Bürger holds that the historical
avant-garde movements have destroyed "the possibility of positing aesthetic norms as valid ones."[29] It is no longer possible
for the theorist to elevate one type of work to a norm for
evaluating all works of art. The post-avant-garde philosopher
faces a vast array of materials, styles, and traditions, with none
being preferable. Indeed, normative aesthetic theory might no
longer be possible: "Whether this condition of the availability
of all traditions still permits an aesthetic theory at all, in the
sense in which aesthetic theory existed from Kant to Adorno,
is questionable. . . . Where the formal possibilities have become
infinite, not only authentic creation but also its scholarly analysis become correspondingly difficult."[30] The historicizing of
Adorno's aesthetic theory seems to have ended in Bürger's
abandoning normative aesthetics.

If normative aesthetics were indeed abandoned, this would
have troubling implications for Bürger's own theory. In the
first place, it would be difficult to establish the validity of his
historicizing Adorno's aesthetics. Bürger historicizes from the
standpoint of the avant-garde. If valid aesthetic norms can no
longer be posited, it becomes hard to determine why Bürger's
stance toward Adorno's norms is any more valid than any
other. It also becomes unclear why one should bother to take
Adorno's aesthetics seriously enough to historicize it.[31] In the
second place, the abandoning of normative aesthetics would

raise the question whether Bürger has an adequate basis for a critique of autonomous art and autonomous works. Bürger's "patient, dialectic critique"[32] would risk becoming locked into its object. In the third place, even if we granted the need to turn from normative aesthetics to functional analysis, the impossibility of normative aesthetics would raise methodological problems for the functional analysis of artistic phenomena. It would become difficult to decide which phenomena deserve analysis, and even more difficult to justify this decision in the face of criticisms.[33]

These potential problems, to be explored in more detail, would be forestalled by the normative character of Adorno's aesthetics. For all its historicizing of traditional norms such as "beauty," *Aesthetic Theory* does not abandon the normative character of traditional aesthetics. Instead it unmasks the pretense that such norms are eternal and immutable. Adorno's troubled genius has been his refusal either to divorce aesthetic norms from a larger sociohistorical process or to accept whatever aesthetic norms have taken shape in the sociohistorical process.

One must say "troubled" because this double refusal helps generate the difficulties Bürger has noted. Adorno tends to derive his aesthetic norms from modern nonorganic works within the institution of autonomous art; he tends to use such works as a standard for rejecting popular art as well as literary realism; and his interpretation of older works such as Goethe's *Iphigenie* tends to dissolve their historical specificity. Nevertheless Adorno's aesthetics gives us a basis for assessing the legitimacy and validity of his own historicizing project. His approach entitles us to ask whether he has indeed shed light on all art from a contemporary perspective and whether he has succeeded in releasing a new truth content in traditional aesthetic categories. In addition, Adorno's idea of truth content provides both a definite basis for his critique of art and a criterion for making defensible decisions about which works deserve analysis.

Bürger, by contrast, seems to have dismissed the labor of normative aesthetics by radicalizing the connection between aesthetic norms and social history. He seems to have given up the second half of Adorno's refusal. This move is puzzling, however, for now there seems to be no normative basis within Bürger's theory for assessing his own historicizing project. How should one commend or criticize the results of his critique of Adorno's aesthetics? Bürger is not releasing the truth content of Adorno's normative claims. Instead Bürger uses the historical fact of avant-garde anti-autonomy to render Adorno's claims invalid for post-avant-garde art. Indeed all positing of aesthetic norms seems to have become invalid in post-avant-garde aesthetics. If this were so, however, then what would be the point of criticizing Bürger's historicizing critique? If he is not himself making normative claims about art, then his "theory" can only be treated as a more or less imaginative and illuminating historical narrative.

Yet Bürger is suggesting normative claims. By implication, at least, he is positing as a valid norm the historical impact of artistic phenomena on aesthetic theory. This is what a critique of Bürger would have to address. One could question, for example, whether the historical avant-garde movements actually did destroy the possibility of theoretically positing valid norms for art. Furthermore, even if the avant-garde has had some such impact, there is no obvious reason why the historical impact of specific historical movements should operate as the norm whereby normative aesthetics is invalidated.

Besides raising questions about the validity of historicizing Adorno's aesthetics, Bürger's implicit norm renders problematic his own critique of art. Whereas Adorno's idea of truth content provides a definite basis for his critique of art, the appeal to historical impact leaves little room for critical evaluations of the phenomena said to have this impact. One of the few conceivable modes of evaluation along these lines would be to say which phenomena have had or can have greater impact than others. Perhaps Bürger has this in mind when he calls for interpretations that are a "production of significance." Unless Bürger posits norms beyond historical impact, however, he will have no more basis for distinguishing between better and worse works than does Pierre Bourdieu, who considers such distinctions an arbitrary reinforcement of social status.[34]

Given Bürger's claim that the avant-garde had destroyed the possibility of positing valid norms for works of art, he can posit norms beyond historical impact only at the price of inconsistency. To be consistent he would have either to soften his claim about the avant-garde's impact or to give up the norm of historical impact. If Bürger insisted on both the claim and the norm, then there would be little basis for deciding whether the impact of the avant-garde has been significant or worthwhile. The lack of such a basis would then raise the question why aesthetics should take the avant-garde as its own standpoint, especially when Bürger himself acknowledges that the avant-garde failed to destroy the institution of autonomous art. Silence on this question would indicate that there is no reason to prefer Bürger's critique of autonomous art over Adorno's or Bourdieu's.

The apparent abandonment of normative aesthetics also poses methodological problems for the functional analysis of artistic phenomena. As we have seen, Bürger wishes to replace Adorno's emphasis on the import of autonomous works with an emphasis on the changing function of the work within a changing institution of art. Although this move holds considerable promise, two methodological problems arise.

The first concerns the justification for analyzing certain works rather than others. Functional analysis must decide which works deserve analysis and must justify this decision in the face of criticism. Why, for example, would someone decide to do a functional analysis of Goethe's *Iphigenie*? If scholars decided this for the reason that *Iphigenie* has been prominent within the institution of literature, they would be following whatever the institution dictates. If they decided this for the reason that *Iphigenie* has contemporary significance, they would be relying on judgments that go beyond the work and its functions. The criteria of such judgments could not simply be the norm of historical impact. This is especially evident in the case of works ignored in the past that may have contemporary significance, such as those that feminist artists and scholars have repeatedly discovered.

The second methodological problem concerns the interpretation of a work's functions. It seems that Bürger wishes to place his interpretations in the horizon of a utopian future by updating the work's function for the contemporary situation.

The potential problem with this mode of interpretation is that it could easily become arbitrary. Unlike Adorno's interpretations, Bürger's functional analysis seems to lack ways to test the interpretation of a work's functions against the work's intrinsic merits. His functional analysis also seems to be locked into the bourgeois institution of autonomous art in its current form. The "theory of the avant-garde" has little to say about the culture industry or about indigenous and transitional art forms outside the immediate orbit of consumer capitalism. Because of this narrow focus, there are few ways to form comparative judgments in a larger sociohistorical context. Both the reference to intrinsic merits and the comparison with phenomena outside bourgeois art require judgments for which Bürger has no normative criteria. It becomes difficult to avoid arbitrary intepretations.

Complex Normativity

By pointing out potential problems in Bürger's approach, I am not suggesting that Adorno's revision of normative aesthetics is beyond criticism. An admirable refusal to divorce aesthetic norms from social history has led both authors to an insufficient account of normativity. Perhaps the categories of structures, standards, and criteria will make for a more nuanced account and help reestablish a philosophical basis for the critique of art.

"Structures" refer to relatively stable patterns that govern a social institution. In Western societies the mesh between the structures of art and economic and technological structures is particularly tight, as is apparent from the emphasis on popularity in popular art. "Standards" refer to dominant expectations shared by practitioners with respect to actions and outcomes in an established social institution. For example, technical competence is a minimal standard for all practicing artists in Western society's institution of art, one that artists and their public assume. "Criteria" refer to the standards as they are formulated when an institution's practitioners make normative claims in public discourse. While implicit in much talk about art, criteria become explicit in the discourse of art critics, educators, and scholars. They are not simply imported from the ivory tower, however, but occur in ordinary discourse about art. One of the philosopher's tasks is not simply to say which structures, standards, and criteria prevail, but to ask why they prevail and whether their prevalence is desirable.

In this connection the assumptions of traditional aesthetics can help raise questions in critique of popular art. One such question pertains to "popularity," a dominant standard and criterion in contemporary popular art. Adorno's critique of the culture industry places this question high on the philosophical agenda. His critique makes one wonder whether "popularity" is simply a euphemism for "cash value for the owners of the culture industry." An affirmative answer could make one ask why this norm should have any more weight than other norms, including aesthetic norms. One could also consider what the dominance of "popularity" as a standard and criterion tells us about the structure of popular art relative to the politico-economic system.

There are good reasons to think that public discourse about popular art has gradually come to equate "popularity" with commercial success.[35] If this meaning has become dominant in public discourse, then an emphasis on popularity could very well steer an apparently populist and democratic impulse in an antidemocratic and elitist direction. Those who prize popularity, while equating it with the number of albums or tickets sold, say in effect that whatever rings up the most private profit also best represents what the people need and desire. In this context, the supposedly elitist concern for aesthetic merit could help us rethink the criterion of popularity, thereby serving in some small measure to liberate popular art from culture industry bondage.

Although it seems best to take distance from Adorno's emphasis on autonomy and truth, simply dismissing aesthetic norms and the traditional concern for normative evaluation would demolish any basis for a philosophical critique of art, both popular and otherwise. To abandon normative aesthetics seems premature. There are holes in Adorno's theory, but the ship is still afloat. Bürger is on target when he criticizes *Aesthetic Theory* for elevating one type of work to an aesthetic norm, but he misses the mark when he concludes that it has become impossible to posit valid aesthetic norms. So long as one's theory of art includes a critique of art, the positing of norms is unavoidable, even if the norm is one of historical impact. Bürger's conclusion makes sense only if one assumes with Adorno that certain works are the source of aesthetic norms. If one drops this assumption, the impact of the avant-garde begins to look somewhat different. By attacking the institution of autonomous art, perhaps the avant-garde has helped make possible a more complex normativity rather than simple anormativity.

"Complex normativity" refers to a network of norms, no one of which has preeminence, and many of which apply to phenomena outside autonomous art. Some of the norms apply to the functions of works within art as an institution. Others apply to the functions of works within other institutions. Still others apply to what Adorno calls the import of the work. With suitable extensions and revisions these various norms could also be shown to hold for related actions, events (for example, concerts), and processes (for example, the reception of a novel). A partial list of such norms could include technical excellence, formal depth, aesthetic expressiveness, social scope, political effectiveness, and historical truth. Rarely would a particular work meet all these norms, nor would very many works display exceptional merit with respect to every norm that they do meet. Philosophical aesthetics would have the task of spelling out the contents of such norms in the context of a critical understanding of social history.

If this were done in the proper manner, we could circumvent some of the problems Bürger has noted in Adorno's aesthetics. Certainly one style, tradition, or type of work could no longer be made the standard whereby all others are found deficient. A work with formal depth, for example, could be found politically ineffective. So too a work that is technically excellent could be found inappropriate to its situation and therefore lacking in social scope. Complex normativity would also counteract the tendency to dissolve the historical specificity of older works. Because the historical truth of a work would not be considered the ultimate criterion, there would be much less pressure to fuse its historical horizon with that of the interpreter. At the same time, in contrast to Bürger's tendency, the actual or imputed historical impact of a work would not be decisive for determining its various merits.

Still, there is something dissatisfying about pursuing complex normativity in aesthetic theory. We seem to have surrendered the claim, shared by Adorno and Bürger, that the social significance of artistic phenomena ultimately depends on their contribution to a utopian future. On this topic more will be said in the following chapters. For now, two points must suffice.

In the first place, the question of utopia is not a normative question. It puts all normative claims in question. No matter what norm one applies to artistic phenomena, the question of their contribution to utopia remains. The same question holds for one's normative claims, including any claims on behalf of complex normativity.

In the second place, claiming that the social significance of artistic phenomena ultimately depends on their contribution to a utopian future is not the same thing as showing what this claim means for specific phenomena. It is in the showing that *Aesthetic Theory* retains the speculative dimension that *Theory of the Avant-Garde* lacks. Without this dimension, this critical fantasy, if you will, a model of social mediation easily becomes just one more part of the status quo. There is no way to build critical fantasy into a theoretical model. Without it, however, our criticisms of Adorno will lose their point, and the employment of a different model will fail to result in a genuine critique of art.

10

Politics of Postmodernism

The tradition of all the dead generations weighs like a nightmare on the brain of the living. And just when they seem engaged in revolutionizing themselves and things, . . . they anxiously conjure up the spirits of the past to their service and borrow from them names, battle-cries, and costumes in order to present the new scene of world history in this time-honoured disguise and this borrowed language.
Marx[1]

The Echternach dancing procession is not the march of the World Spirit; limitation and reservation are no way to represent the dialectic. Rather, the dialectic advances by way of extremes. . . . The prudence that restrains us from venturing too far ahead . . . is usually only an agent of social control, and so of stupefaction.
Adorno[2]

The heroic tone of Adorno's instructions for dialectical writing has come to sound quaint. In the decades since the publication of *Minima Moralia*, an atmosphere of pluralism and eclecticism has begun to affect every intellectual tradition. We have entered an age when traditions no longer weigh like a nightmare on the brain of the living, when people conjure up the spirits of the past in order to amuse themselves in the present. Whereas Adorno attempted to mediate Marxism and modernism, neither Marxism nor modernism has prevailed. Adorno's successors must ask whether Marxism can thrive in a postmodern culture, and what political strategies are appropriate under current conditions.

Were it not for the dance of Fredric Jameson, Marxism and

postmodernism might well seem incompatible. Both as story-telling and as the story being told, postmodernism subverts the central claims of Marxism. This is particularly so of Western Marxism, whose critique of capitalism relies on claims about totality and history. Such claims are of little use to a movement that celebrates the particularity of the present moment. Jameson is not about to join the celebration, but he is not ready to condemn it either. He wishes to tell a Marxist story about the postmodernist feast, but give a new choreography to Marxist storytelling. By examining Jameson's attempt to update Marxist categories for a postmodern culture, one gains a new appreciation for the limits and contributions of Adorno's cultural politics.

This chapter shows that reinterpretative dances can be problematic. More specifically, Jameson's attempt to update Western Marxist aesthetics threatens to become self-referentially incoherent, and some reasons for the threat lie in a category he shares with Adorno. Contrary to Adorno's advice, my presentation here mimics the dance of Echternach, in form if not in content. Taking three steps forward, the chapter first discusses some implications of the Adorno-Lukács debate, presents Jameson's view of this debate, and examines his attempt to reconstruct the Western Marxist notion of "import" into the notion of "symbolic act." Stepping backward, it then discusses Jameson's attitude toward postmodernism and reads the notion of "reification" as a code he shares with Adorno and Lukács. The final section argues that this code must be revised if one wants to appropriate Adorno's cultural politics under current conditions. This argument will extend the evaluation of Adorno's paradoxical modernism that began in chapters 6 and 7.

10.1 Deprivileged Subject

"Postmodernism" indicates our context for reading Jameson and rereading Adorno. In part a sign of academic fashion, the concept styles itself after "modernism," itself a multivalent concept. Rather than review recent debates about how the two concepts connect, I will pick out an aspect that links Adorno and Jameson. This aspect is the dialectic between subject and object in Western culture since the seventeenth century. "Subject" refers to the human knower or agent, whether individual or collective. "Object" refers to whatever the human knower or agent is thought to constitute or generate.

The relevance of the subject-object dialectic is suggested by a comment on the "hyperspace" of postmodernism in Jameson's conversation with Anders Stephanson: "We used to talk about this in terms of subject-object dialectics; but in a situation where subjects and objects have been dissolved, hyperspace is the ultimate of the object-pole, intensity the ultimate of the subject-pole, though we no longer have subjects and objects."[3] "Postmodernism" can be regarded as a movement toward abandoning the subject-object dialectic.

Deep in this movement is the impulse to deprive the subject of its privileged position. In philosophy, this impulse opposes the constitutive knower first clearly articulated in Descartes's *cogito ergo sum*. In the arts, the impulse toward deprivation either destroys the privileged position of the artist or highlights a destruction that has already occurred. In literary criticism, the deprivation of the subject undermines both the authority of the author and the criteria of the critic.

The tendency to deprivilege the human subject is neither sudden nor arbitrary. It emerges gradually from modern Western culture, which is itself tied to the history of capitalism and industrialism. Perry Anderson and Martin Jay point to a similar tendency growing within Western Marxism.[4] If they are correct, then a struggle over the subject's position may well be central to Western Marxism—central, not as in "the center," but as an unavoidable struggle upon which depends much of its credibility and vitality. Given the emphasis on subjective agency in traditional Marxist politics, the question of the subject's position has implications far beyond the fields of philosophy, art, and literary criticism. The implications become clearest at an intersection called "cultural politics."

Lukács and Adorno

The transition from middle Lukács to late Adorno is particularly instructive in this regard. According to Martin Jay, Western Marxism begins by emphasizing a sociohistorical totality and by privileging a collective subject that can transform this totality. Lukács's *History and Class Consciousness* gives the classic presentation of this approach. Although spawned in part by Lukács's book, Adorno's *Negative Dialectics* appears to demolish both the emphasis on totality and the privileging of a collective subject: "No longer could a Western Marxist defend an expressive view of the whole in which a meta-subject was both the subject and object of history. No longer could history itself be seen as a coherent whole with a positive conclusion as its telos. No longer could totality ignore the non-identity of the historical and the natural and subordinate the latter to human domination."[5] As Jay's comments suggest, Adorno's work deprivileges the collective subject with respect to nature, culture, and society, both in the present and in the future.

Yet one cannot ignore Adorno's expectation of a human transformation of culture and society and his hope for a new relationship with nature. His abandonment of Lukács's meta-subject does not entail a complete rejection of the collective subject. In paradoxical fashion, Adorno tries to give an immanent critique of the privileged subject, "to use the strength of the subject to break through the fallacy of constitutive subjectivity."[6] The subject is to be deprivileged, but a privileged subject must carry this out. Adorno's cultural politics is one of paradoxical modernism, one that attributes unusual political merits to authentic modern art.

The preceding chapters suggest that Adorno has three reasons for taking this political position. First, by expressing that nature could be more than an object of rational control, modern art challenges a narrowly rationalized relationship between human beings and nature. Whereas technology and science make a fetish of the latest techniques and methods, modern art recalls the unfulfilled needs and purposes without which production becomes absurd. Second, modern art exposes the pseudo-objectivity of the social system. Whereas an administered society makes social institutions and the social system seem natural and unchanging, modern art uncovers the historical contradictions underlying this facade. Third, modern art refuses to surrender a utopian impulse. Whereas the dominant forms of ideology in advanced capitalism encourage resignation, modern art reminds us that nothing has to remain the way it has come to be.

These three reasons give only partial descriptions of Adorno's position. Although they suggest that he locates modern art outside the modern world, this is by no means the case. Modern art is "the social antithesis of society," and hence part of the sociohistorical totality he considers false. The recollection of unfulfilled needs depends on advanced artistic technique; the exposure of sociohistorical contradictions is itself contradictory; and the glimpses of utopia in modern art are negative signs of hope. The political merits of modern art lie not only in its providing an alternative vision but also in its providing an immanent critique of the contemporary social formation.

Moreover, because Adorno sees advanced capitalism as the product of a long historical process, modern art participates fully in the dialectic of enlightenment. As was seen earlier, this participation has two sides. On the one hand, modern art gives critical expression to what has been lost or missed in the historical process. This is not a mere expression, however, but a critical expression achieved by rejecting what prevented certain possibilities from becoming actual. On the other hand, modern art gives a negative image of what could still be achieved if the social structure and historical process were fundamentally transformed. Again, this is not a mere image, but a negative image emerging from art's own failure to actualize what could still be achieved.

Combining these two sides, and using the Lukácsian concepts that Adorno revises, we can say that modern art provides an oppositional but conciliatory expression of reification and a fragmentary but reified image of reconciliation. Even this formulation must be qualified, however. Not all of modern art, and not every work of modern art provides such an expression and image, but those works which engage in an immanent critique of their own materials, traditions, artifactual character, and aura. Only such works, exemplified by Beckett's *Endgame*, are authentic in their critical expression and negative imaging.

A good example of Adorno's cultural politics, and a relevant one for understanding Jameson, occurs in the Adorno-Lukács debate mentioned in chapter 2. When it occurred in the late 1950s, this debate concerned the political merits of modernism and realism in twentieth-century literature. Read from the vantage point of Jameson's recent writings, however, the debate also enacts a struggle over the position of the epistemic subject relative to the import of the literary work. Behind the debate lie different understandings and evaluations of the import of twentieth-century literature. For Lukács, the import of modernist works embodies an incorrect view of humanity. For Adorno, by contrast, the import of modernist works does not embody any worldview. Nor does he consider import to be "form-determinative."[7] Although seeming to share the category of import, Lukács and Adorno construe it differently. Both construals concern the manner in which a work presents social reality; both provide overarching standards of literary criticism; yet the two are incompatible, with Adorno's construal being much less subject-centered than that of Lukács.

As others have noted, Lukács's approach to literary import is problematic. Adorno registers some of the problems without pinpointing their source. These problems do not result from Lukácsian blindness to form or technique. Instead they stem from what Adorno vaguely identifies as inadvertent subjectivism.[8] More precisely put, the main difficulties arise from a double expectation that literary import originates in the knowing subject and that this epistemic subject provides the key to interpreting literary import.

One can label this expectation a version of epistemic subjectivism. "Epistemic subjectivism" refers to a tendency to privilege the human knower as the ultimate source of "meaning," literary or otherwise. This privileged epistemic subject may be either individual or collective. The epistemic subject in literature may be the author, the reader, or the critic. While it is not entirely clear which of these Lukács considers most important, it is plain that he locates the ultimate source of literary import in the human knower. For Lukács, literary import originates in subjective worldviews; mediated by literary works, subjective worldviews provide the key to interpreting literary import.

Lukács's emphasis on worldview embodies a nineteenth-century expectation that meaning can ultimately be found in the subject's global outlook on life and society. His assessments of twentieth-century literature continually assume that authentic works will express such a global outlook. Adorno does not share this expectation. His emphasis on technique embodies a typically twentieth-century concern, and he rejects any attempt to locate the ultimate source of meaning in the epistemic subject. Adorno does not privilege the epistemic subject as a constituter of meaning, nor does he think of literary import as deriving from a subject's worldview. Hence the realism-modernism debate enacts a struggle over the position of the epistemic subject relative to the import of a literary work, and thereby presents a crucial issue in the cultural politics of Western Marxism.

Empty Chair

This struggle reaches a new stage in Fredric Jameson's *The Political Unconscious*. Jameson's work as a literary theorist and cultural critic owes much to both Lukács and Adorno, as well as to other prominent Western Marxists such as Bloch, Benjamin, Marcuse, and Sartre.[9] In recent years Jameson has also been in conversation with structuralist Marxists such as Louis Althusser and various French poststructuralists such as Jacques Derrida, Michel Foucault, Jacques Lacan, Jean Baudrillard, Gilles Deleuze, and Jean-François Lyotard.[10] Along with this conversation has come a turn toward popular art and the culture of postmodernism.[11] Jameson retains a traditional Western Marxist concern with the political implications of twentieth-century culture. Unlike Lukács and Adorno, however, he does not privilege either realist or modernist works. Instead, he resists assigning unusual political merit to any past or present cultural phenomena.

Jameson's criticisms of Lukács and Adorno take their cues from an orientation toward the future. *The Political Unconscious* concludes by trying to set the stage for "conceiving those new forms of collective thinking and collective culture which lie beyond the boundaries of our own world." This staging reserves "an empty chair . . . for some as yet unrealized, collective,

and decentered cultural production of the future, beyond realism and modernism alike."[12] Jameson's general stage directions prompt three observations. First, he is announcing a
political task not fulfilled in *The Political Unconscious*. While
saying there is an urgent need to project a vital political culture,
Jameson steps back to explore preconditions for making such
a projection. Second, no existing works seem to count as elements of a vital political culture. "An empty chair" is reserved
for some future cultural production. Third, this vital political
culture will be "beyond realism and modernism."

Recalling earlier debates, one surmises that Jameson wants
to go beyond both Lukács and Adorno. Lukács tries to reinstate
realism and dethrone modernism; Adorno, to install certain
modernist works; Jameson, to unseat both realism and modernism. Whereas Lukács and Adorno see realism and modernism respectively as the best political culture for the present,
Jameson wishes to hold the position open for some future
culture. His book does not indicate how this culture would be
connected with past and present cultural phenomena, nor does
it say what kind of culture is politically preferable under current conditions.

Jameson's hesitation on the last score contrasts strongly with
Adorno's militant tone in "Commitment." Indeed, Jameson
calls Adorno's essay an "anti-political revival of the ideology of
modernism."[13] Although Adorno correctly notes how consumer capitalism turns even the most subversive didactic works
into mere commodities, Jameson asserts that this fact cuts more
than one way. It also speaks against seeing modernist works as
prototypically political, since consumer capitalism has rendered
modernism innocuous.

Having thus begun to dethrone modernism, Jameson uses
"reification" in *The Political Unconscious* to "transcode" literary
modernism and social life within monopoly capitalism.[14] Not
only has consumer capitalism rendered modernism innocuous,
but modernism has always had reification as its precondition.
In principle, then, no modernist work will be more capable
than any other work to penetrate the facades of contemporary
society. One cannot assign special political merit to authentic
modernist works.

At the same time, Jameson questions Lukács's use of "reification" to repudiate modernist styles. According to *The Political Unconscious*, no literary work, no matter how "reactionary" in intent, is "mere ideology" in the sense of being false consciousness pure and simple. The Marxist critic should examine the "strategies of containment" whereby all sorts of works repress deeply political impulses. When it comes to such strategies, modernism and realism are more intricately interwoven than Lukács thinks. In fact, realism has its own strategies of containment.[15]

Even when acknowledging an affinity with Lukács, Jameson takes distance from *Realism in Our Time:*

We must . . . place some distance between our use of the concept [of reification] and that to be found in Lukács' various later accounts of modernism, in which the term reification is simple shorthand for value judgment and for the repudiation by association of the various modern styles. Yet Lukács was not wrong to make the connection between modernism and the reification of daily life: his mistake was to have done so ahistorically and to have made his analysis the occasion for an ethical judgment rather than a historical perception.[16]

According to Jameson, Lukács's failure to historicize lets him ignore the "Utopian vocation" of modernist phenomena. The increasing abstraction of visual art, for example, does more than express the reification of daily life. Such abstraction "also constitutes a Utopian compensation for everything lost in . . . the development of capitalism" such as the place of quality, feeling, and sheer color and intensity.[17] Here Jameson comes close to a notion of art as "the promise of happiness, a promise that is constantly being broken," even while he refuses to privilege those modernist works whose colorlessness Adorno considers a "negative apotheosis" of color (204–5/196). The presence of a utopian impulse is not peculiar to modernism nor to any specific works of modern art. One may expect to find a utopian impulse in every literary work: "All ideology in the strongest sense . . . is in its very nature Utopian."[18]

Jameson's concern in *The Political Unconscious* is not to promote those recent works that have greatest political merit, but to hold open a chair for some future culture beyond realism and modernism alike. This culture will be "collective and decentered" in ways that realism and modernism, with their links to capitalism, never could have been. Having come earlier in the development of capitalism, realism may not have had modernism's elaborate strategies for containing the utopian impulse. Realism may also not have had reification as its precondition. Yet realism is no less ideological than modernism, just as modernism is no less utopian than realism. Besides, both realism and modernism are dated literary movements, their political implications conditioned by earlier stages of class struggle and cultural revolution. To ask which movement has greater merit today would be to misunderstand current conditions. Today is the age of postmodernism and consumer capitalism.

10.2 Jameson's Ambivalent Postmodernism

Jameson's criticisms of Adorno and Lukács mark a clear departure from their emphases on literary import and indicate a new phase in the struggle over the epistemic subject. One way to illustrate the shift is to consider Jameson's category of "the symbolic act," which upstages the category of import in Lukács and Adorno. Despite their disagreements about the political merits of realism and modernism, both Lukács and Adorno promote comprehensive evaluations of the import of specific works. For Lukács, who favors realism, the key to such evaluations is the work's literary worldview. For Adorno, who favors modernism, the key to evaluating import is the work's literary technique. Rather than coming down on either side, Jameson proposes a three-horizon model for literary criticism where each horizon of interpretation is nested within the next.

Symbolic Act

On Jameson's model, any literary text can be read as a symbolic act within a class discourse that occurs within a more or less revolutionary social formation. The relationship between the symbolic act and its referent is one of text and subtext. There is a social reality from which the text emerges. When emerging, however, the text draws social reality into its own texture and transforms it into a subtext, thereby hiding the independent existence of the text's own social situation. Hence a literary critic must rewrite the literary text "in such a way that the latter may itself be seen as the rewriting . . . of a prior . . . *subtext*" which "must itself always be (re)constructed after the fact."[19]

Jameson affirms with Kenneth Burke that the symbolic act is both a genuine *act*, albeit symbolic, and a genuine *symbol*, albeit active. "Symbolic" has the force of "projective," in the manner of dreams when subjected to psychoanalysis. The projection is of the political history of a specific time and place. Within the first horizon of interpretation, a Balzac novel, for example, would be read as a projective resolution of social contradictions in France after the failure of the Napoleonic revolution, during the demise of the country aristocracy, etc. Formal or aesthetic contradictions in the text itself would be taken as imaginary and unavoidably incomplete resolutions of social contradictions in nineteenth-century France. Like a dream hiding the unconscious, the text hides its subtext until successfully analyzed.[20] As a symbolic act, the text tends to deny what it projects.

If one now asks whether there is an actor for this act, a projector for this projection, it seems the only actor is the act itself. In Mohanty's words, both text and author are seen "as a node of interaction, as the criss-crossings of ideology, desire and the intransigence of history."[21] Jameson shares with structuralist Marxism a tendency to disregard questions of subjective agency. This tendency continues in his account of the other two horizons of interpretation, where the text is linked to the structure of class discourse and portrayed as the intersection of impulses from contradictory modes of cultural production. Despite talk of class conflict and cultural revolution, Jameson makes little attempt to address the traditional problems of human agency for these processes.

What counts for Jameson's interpretations is not the comprehensive evaluation of some import tied to an author's worldview (Lukács) or to an author's social experience and expertise (Adorno). What counts is a self-activating act, which interpretation reactivates. Texts are like dreams that occur and await interpretation. The author seems to have vanished, along with the task of specific political evaluation. The text and its interpreter remain. On a larger scale, the epistemic subject seems to have not merely lost its privileged position but faded altogether from the scene.

Jameson's reasons for upstaging the category of import and playing down the role of the author are linked to his understanding of current historical imperatives. Two imperatives are especially high on his agenda. One is "the need to transcend individualistic categories and modes of interpretation."[22] Jameson argues that "only the dialectic provides a way for 'decentering' the subject concretely, and for transcending the 'ethical' in the direction of the political and the collective."[23] The notion of a symbolic act is one way to transcend the apparently individualistic category of import and to move beyond the "ethical" judgments traditionally attached to this category. The second imperative, closely related to the first, is to maintain a sense of collective agency without reviving Lukács's meta-subject. The notion of import, with its implication of representative expression or effort, is either outdated or premature.[24]

Although Lukács and Adorno disagree over the political merits of modernist works, they agree that these merits must be evaluated and that such evaluations hinge on literary import. The notion of symbolic act lets Jameson change the rules of their game. He uses the debate about modernism to show how he would historicize individualistic, ethical categories, such as good/bad and progressive/regressive, by looking for the "ideological" and "Utopian" features of any given phenomenon.[25] A similar procedure governs his interpretations of postmodernist phenomena. He points out their ideological and utopian features, but he does not assess their relative political merits.

Given the need to replace individualistic categories, to transcend ethical judgments, and to maintain a sense of collective agency, one might wonder why Jameson does not give up the project of interpretation, which emphasizes the interpreter as an individual center of judgment. Must not a decentering dialectic itself be decentered? Jameson's criticism of postmodernist "ideologies of the text" makes clear that he wishes to retain the project of interpretation.[26] He tries to retain it by uncoupling his historiographic analysis of ideological and utopian features from specific evaluations concerning the political merits of cultural phenomena. Nevertheless, these uncoupled approaches tend to coalesce in claims about his own project of interpretation, claims of a sort that Jameson refuses to make about other cultural phenomena. He assigns priority to the political perspective in interpretation,[27] even though he hesitates to do something similar with respect to literary production. So too, whereas Jameson expects that his own interpretations will prove to be "stronger" than others,[28] he seems not to expect something similar with respect to specific literary texts. He reserves an empty chair for some future culture, even though he is not willing to give up making this reservation in the present. The result is a cultural politics—call it "ambivalent postmodernism"—within which lurks a strong potential for incoherence.

Political Culture

The potential for incoherence in Jameson's cultural politics concerns three problems, all of them related to the apparent evaporation of the epistemic subject. These problems can be seen by returning to his reasons for rejecting Adorno's "antipolitical revival of the ideology of modernism." The first reason is that consumer capitalism has rendered modern art innocuous. The second is that modern art employs reifying strategies of containment. The third reason is that the presence of a utopian impulse is not peculiar to modern art. At first these reasons seem convincing. Upon further reflection, however, one wonders whether any of these facts is peculiar to modern art.

Jameson's writings on postmodernism suggest a negative answer. His path-breaking article on "Postmodernism, or The Cultural Logic of Late Capitalism" identifies postmodernism as the cultural dominant of consumer capitalism.[29] Jameson follows Ernest Mandel in positing three dialectical stages of capitalism: market capitalism, monopoly capitalism, and late, multinational, or consumer capitalism. Parallel to these stages are the cultural stages of realism, modernism, and postmodernism. Just as consumer capitalism is the purest stage of capitalism, so postmodernism is the virtual apotheosis of reification in culture. Such a periodization seems to imply that current conditions fatally weaken all oppositional forms of culture, which must employ reifying strategies of containment simply to survive. Furthermore, even if utopian impulses can be found within an oppositional form, their existence will not be peculiar to such a form. Hence Jameson's grounds for rejecting Adorno's modernism also seem like reasons for expecting little genuine and effective opposition within postmodern culture, an undesirable consequence for a Marxist cultural politics. The question is whether Jameson has found ways to avoid this conclusion.

To show that genuine and effective opposition can be expected, Jameson would have to solve three problems tied to his reasons for rejecting Adorno's modernism. The first concerns the relationship of Jameson's interpretation to the postmodern culture in which it takes place. This is the problem of preconditions for a critique of postmodern culture. The second problem concerns the relationship of Jameson's interpretation to whatever oppositional forces exist within postmodern culture. This is the problem of the relation of theory to praxis within cultural politics. The third problem, which encompasses the other two, pertains to the possibility of a new political culture within the space of postmodernism. This is the problem of the empty chair.

An illustration of the first problem occurs in "The Politics of Theory," Jameson's discussion of recent debates about postmodernism in architecture.[30] Jameson distinguishes four different positions. There are critics such as Charles Jencks and Tom Wolfe who are anti-modernist but pro-postmodernist, in contrast to Manfredo Tafuri, who opposes both modernism and postmodernism. There are others such as Jean-François Lyotard who are both pro-modernist and pro-postmodernist, in contrast to Jürgen Habermas and Hilton Kramer, who oppose postmodernism for pro-modernist reasons. Jameson regards all such positions as ethical judgments rather than historical perceptions. Since "we are *within* the culture of postmodernism," the point is neither to condemn nor to celebrate postmodernism but to give it "a genuinely historical and dialectical analysis."[31] Jameson's approach is one of ambivalent postmodernism—postmodernist in the sense that it locates itself within postmodern culture, but ambivalent in the sense that it refuses to condemn or celebrate that culture. He insists on his own location within postmodern culture but takes distance from postmodernist affirmations of that culture.

The problem here is that Jameson's location within postmodern culture is ill-defined. His desire to give "a genuinely historical and dialectical analysis" is not a postmodern impulse. According to his own analysis, postmodern culture displays sheer discontinuity and a loss of historical depth. If Jameson's analysis is correct, then are there any sources or tendencies within postmodern culture that make such an analysis possible? Perhaps the analysis is living on borrowed time, so to speak, drawing upon a Marxist tradition amid the death of all traditions. If so, then the political prospects for such an analysis seem bleak. Or perhaps the analysis is made possible by certain oppositional forces alive within postmodern culture. If this were so, however, one would expect Jameson to show more sympathy for the traditional Marxist project of specifically evaluating the relative political merits of existing cultural phenomena. The inappropriateness of condemning or celebrating postmodernism as a whole need not mean that the Marxist interpreter should refrain from a political critique of specific phenomena.

Here a second problem emerges, not unlike one facing Adorno's paradoxical modernism, namely, the problem of relating theory to praxis within cultural politics. What exactly is the relationship between Jameson's interpretation and existing oppositional forces? Jameson posits a certain homology between his theoretical project and the artistic task of "cognitive mapping."[32] He also suggests that his empathetic critique of postmodernist "theories" is analogous to a homeopathic critique which, like Doctorow's work, would "undo postmodernism by the methods of postmodernism."[33] Nevertheless, homologies do not establish an interaction between the two homologous fields, nor do analogies establish exactly how such an interaction would proceed.

The first two problems both express the problem of the empty chair. Given the space of postmodernism, which Jameson has analyzed in such an instructive fashion, what are the possibilities of a new political culture? This question encompasses both the preconditions for a critique of postmodern culture and the preconditions for oppositional forms of postmodern culture. To the question of oppositional forms, Jameson's article on postmodernism gives an excruciatingly tentative answer:

> The new political art—if it is indeed possible at all—will have to hold to the truth of postmodernism, that is, to say, to its fundamental object—the world space of multinational capital—at the same time at which it achieves a breakthrough to some as yet unimaginable new mode of representing this last, in which we may again begin to grasp our positioning as individual and collective subjects and regain a capacity to act and struggle which is at present neutralized by our spatial as well as our social confusion. The political form of postmodernism, if there ever is any, will have as its vocation the invention and projection of a global cognitive mapping.[34]

Jameson's answer is like a minuet, calling for a new political culture while declaring it all but impossible under current conditions. The answer revives the theme of subjectivity while pointing out what blocks subjective initiative. The problem of the empty chair remains.

Jameson is not unaware of this problem; much of his energy in recent years has gone into addressing it. What is still needed, however, is a systematic reexamination of certain tendencies that make this problem a potential source of incoherence for Jameson's project. The move in *The Political Unconscious* to reserve an empty chair may be more than a promise to project a vital political culture in subsequent writings. The reservation might also be an inevitable outcome of troublesome tendencies noted by various commentators on Jameson's book.[35] One tendency of particular importance in the present context is the tendency to absolutize the concept of reification. After observing this tendency at work in *The Political Unconscious*, one can see Jameson's ambivalent postmodernism as setting a new stage for Western Marxism's struggle over the subject's position. One can also suggest ways in which this staging must be modified if Jameson's project is not to become incoherent.

Master Code

Jameson's book describes the concept of reification as a mediation. By "mediation" he means the analyst's inventing of a code that is applicable to two distinct objects or structural levels.[36] Jameson considers "reification" a highly useful device for transcoding literary modernism and social life. Reification is not "a mere methodological fiction," however; society is assumed to be "a seamless web" despite its fragmented and multidimensional appearance. At the same time, this assumption about society has a "merely formal" appeal, except insofar as it provides "the philosophical justification" for the analyst's "local practice of mediations."[37]

There are some troubling aspects to Jameson's account of reification. One is the weakness of his rationale for using this specific mediation rather than others. The assumption of totality, which justifies the practice of mediations, needs some justification beyond the fact that mediations require this assumption. Besides, even if Jameson successfully gives additional justification, the assumption of totality does not in itself justify the specific mediation of "reification." It is not clear that Jameson ever does argue convincingly for using "reification." Since this concept yields insightful results in specific interpretations, however, the apparent lack of a convincing argument may not be a serious problem.

A more troublesome aspect of Jameson's account of reification is its circularity. When Jameson explains the need for mediations, of which reification is one, he does so in ways that already employ reification as a mediation. Consider the following passage: "Mediations are thus a device of the analyst, whereby the fragmentation and autonomization, the compartmentalization and specialization of the various regions of social life . . . is at least locally overcome, on the occasion of a particular analysis."[38] In positing that social life has undergone fragmentation, autonomization, and so on, Jameson is already invoking a global theory of reification. Although he never clearly presents this theory, Jameson continually aligns such phenomena as the "privatization of contemporary life" and the dehistoricizing of contemporary consciousness with reification. He also subsumes psychic fragmentation and the "autonomization of sexuality" under the dynamic of reification. Similar alignments or subsumptions occur with respect to professionalization, Taylorization, scientific specialization, the autonomizing of artworks, the rationalizing of social institutions, and the instrumentalizing of "values."[39] From a purely methodological perspective, it seems disingenuous to explain the need for mediations in terms that already suppose the legitimacy of an assumed theory of reification. In addition, because the theory is assumed rather than elaborated, there is a strong possibility that the concept will become a master code for twentieth-century culture under capitalist conditions, even though reification is supposed to be just one mediation among many. The tendency of such a master code is to become more suggestive than precise.

The most troublesome aspect of Jameson's use of "reification," however, is that it tends to make irrelevant all attempts to decide which phenomena are more or less resistant to reification. The long-range effect is to render problematic any attempt to give a political critique of contemporary culture. In this respect, the problems in Jameson's ambivalent postmodernism stem from a code he shares with Adorno's modernism and Lukács's anti-modernism but takes one step further. The code is "reification."

Both Lukács and Adorno see reification as the central mechanism whereby the commodity form permeates the entire culture of capitalism. Both authors also treat certain works of art as privileged opponents of reification. For Lukács, realism provides the requisite works. The literary worldview in realist works ensures that these maintain a grasp on the sociohistorical totality and penetrate reified social life under capitalist conditions. For Adorno, certain modernist works have sufficient experiential depth and technical progressiveness to resist the commodification of consciousness and to expose the hidden contradictions of capitalism.

Jameson also sees reification as a central mechanism in the culture of capitalism. Under the conditions of consumer capitalism, however, reification seems to have reached the point where no works and no authors provide a strategic challenge to reification. For Jameson, one structural peculiarity of consumer capitalism is the nearly total colonization of consciousness by the process of commodification. His book assumes that we live in a society where reification has become nearly total on both the subject's and the object's side. In the hyperspace of postmodernism, "subjects and objects have been dissolved."[40] It is understandable, then, why the evaluation of relative political merits has become problematic. The difficulty for Jameson is to explain the possibility of any political consciousness today, whether in the producer, the consumer, or the text itself. The attempt to balance "ideology" and "Utopia" in all cultural phenomena indicates precisely this difficulty. In consumer capitalism no specific "strategy of containment" has greater political liabilities than any other. So too no specific "perspective on the future"[41] has greater political prospects than any other. The reservation for something beyond realism and modernism is made from a highly reified present.

Here the question of the subject's position returns with a vengeance. If the present is as highly reified as Jameson suggests, one must wonder about the viability and legitimacy of any attempt to give a political interpretation of contemporary phenomena, including Jameson's own effort. If the interpreter does indeed stand squarely within the highly reified culture of postmodernism, how can the interpreter maintain political consciousness and make defensible claims about the legitimacy of the interpreter's own construal of culture? The same reasons for reserving an empty chair for some future culture argue for vacating the present chair of political interpretation. Jameson's project threatens to become self-referentially incoherent.

Rather than accept this conclusion, one could just as easily argue against assuming that reification has become as pervasive as Lukács, Adorno, and Jameson think. This argument need not claim that "reification" is a bogus concept. The concept can function as an illuminating theoretical construct with a basis in empirical research. Problems arise when this construct is made the key to a totalizing theory of sociohistorical reality. When this occurs, the specificity of Marx's economic critique evaporates, and cultural critique gradually loses its political point, whether through dogmatism, irrelevance, or indifference.

Dogmatism is clearly visible in Lukács's a priori rejection of modernist literature because of the supposedly reified and reifying character of its worldview. Dogmatism is also evident in his inattention to the socioeconomic basis of realist literature, whose worldview supposedly penetrates reified social life. Adorno's approach is less dogmatic but no less problematic. The irrepressible question raised by his paradoxical praise of modernist works is "So what?" Why is it important, for example, that Beckett's *Endgame* powerfully presents the final history of subjectivity? What real contribution can such a work make to the raising of political consciousness, if capitalist culture is as monolithic as Adorno assumes?

Jameson avoids the dogmatism of Lukács and the irrelevance of Adorno, but at the price of indifference. Jameson's use of the concept of reification makes it seem no longer meaningful to discriminate among phenomena that are more or less resistant to reification. Given the three problems noted earlier, however, it is hard to see how Jameson's project of political interpretation can avoid incoherence unless the concept of reification is relativized. The presumed pervasiveness of reification in postmodernism would eliminate the preconditions for a critique of postmodern culture, interrupt the relationship of Jameson's interpretation to oppositional forces, and prevent the growth of a new political culture within the space of postmodernism.

Obviously the concept of reification cannot be relativized by fiat. This would require an empirically based structural and historical analysis of consumer capitalism and its culture. In principle, however, one can think of two ways to proceed. The first way would be to restrict the concept's scope to a primarily economic meaning and to adopt a more refined vocabulary for analogues or extensions of the commodity form outside the strictly economic arena. Another way would be to suggest that reification either has not become as pervasive as Jameson thinks or has reversed itself in important respects during recent years.

Either way would require a rethinking of the role of the subject in cultural politics, as well as a movement beyond reification in both theory and praxis.

10.3 Beyond Reification

Unfinished Project

Jameson himself has begun to relativize the concept of reification, as is indicated by his article on *"History and Class Consciousness* as an 'Unfinished Project.' "[42] This article argues that Lukács's defense of realism has the theory of reification as its philosophical basis. Realism bears the force of dereification in Lukácsian aesthetics, just as the consciousness of the proletariat did in *History and Class Consciousness.* Jameson finds particularly significant the way Lukács connects the logic of capitalism with the possibility and necessity of a counter-logic: "This allows us to imagine a collective project not merely capable of breaking the multiple systemic webs of reification, but which *must* do so in order to realize itself."[43] Equally significant is the fact that Lukács pursues this connection in the direction of a collective subject's dereifying "aspiration to totality" rather than a conventional subject-object synthesis.

These matters are significant, says Jameson, because of two implications for a postmodern context. One is that the aspiration to totality points toward "a collective possibility which very much presupposes a collective project."[44] The second implication is that particular social groups, classes, or class fragments have an epistemological priority in a capitalist society. Both implications point toward the reprivileging of a collective subject, albeit not the proletarian consciousness on which Lukács counted for a systemic transformation of capitalist society.

According to Jameson, distinctive "moments of truth" can be found in feminist theorizing as well as in the group experiences of women, blacks, and Central European Jews. To grasp a group's "moment of truth" is not only to see how the group's social constraints make possible an otherwise unavailable experience of society but also to translate such experience "into new possibilities of thought and knowledge."[45] Under current conditions, then, Lukács's theory turns into a "principled relativism" with a specific presupposition:

The presupposition is that, owing to its structural situation in the social order and to the specific forms of oppression and exploitation unique to that situation, each group lives the world in a phenomenologically specific way that allows it to see, or better still, that makes it unavoidable for that group to see and to know, features of the world that remain obscure, invisible, or merely occasional and secondary for other groups.[46]

Does Jameson's "principled relativism" relativize the concept of reification sufficiently to save his project of political interpretation from incoherence? At one level, the answer seems to be yes. Lukács's "reification" and "proletarian consciousness" give way to "the variable structures of 'constraint' lived by . . . various marginal, oppressed or dominated groups." The dereifying aspiration to totality makes room for the way each group's experience produces its own view and its own "distinctive truth claim."[47] The task now is to make an inventory of the variable structures of constraint, always acknowledging distinctive truth claims. Translated into cultural politics, such language suggests that various cultural phenomena arising from various group experiences can provide strategic challenges to what was once called reification. It also suggests that a political interpretation of postmodern culture will receive instruction from such groups, even while it tries to provide a cohesive framework for understanding their experience.

At the same time, however, Jameson refers to "late capitalism" as the "absent common object of such 'theorization' from multiple 'standpoints,' "[48] thereby once again indirectly invoking a nonrelativized concept of reification. He also fails to discuss how the truth of various claims will be determined and how the relative merits of conflicting truth claims will be adjudicated. An answer to either question would have to appeal to a systematic theory of postmodern culture. Inevitably the question would then arise as to the political basis for such a theory. More pointedly, from what group standpoint will the distinctive truth claims of various groups be grasped? Does the systematic theory itself arise from the experience of a genuine collective subject—genuine in the sense of living common constraints in a way that produces shared illumination?

A nonrelativized concept of reification appears to continue operating at the level of this last question. Jameson seems to hold that reification permeates postmodern culture but releases various types of dereifying consciousness in groups occupying marginal or oppressed positions. A dialectic occurs between the reifying structure of capitalism and various subsidiary structures. These subsidiary structures exist by virtue of the structure of capitalism, but they render transparent its reifying tendencies. It is to such groups or subsidiary structures that one must look for the vision and initiative to accomplish systemic transformation. One no longer sees an empty chair, but rather several that are occupied. But the position from which one sees these occupants is not yet transparent.

Jameson's appeal to a plural collective subject alleviates the threat of incoherence but does not eliminate it altogether. The preconditions for a critique of postmodern culture must still be illuminated, and the relationship between such a critique and various oppositional forces within postmodern culture must still be spelled out. Even if many chairs replace the chair of modernism, the positioning of these chairs remains a crucial question. Their place relative to each other, their contributions within postmodern culture, and their references to a postcapitalist culture must still be decided. This is an unfinished project, and it is a collective project, one for which Jameson's reinterpretative dance is emblematic.

Political Evaluation

In retrospect, Jameson's ongoing attempt to update Western Marxist categories for a postmodern context underscores both the limitations and contributions of Adorno's paradoxical modernism. More specifically, Jameson's criticisms raise two questions about Adorno's cultural politics. The first is whether modern art has special political merits. The second question is whether it is necessary to make philosophical claims about the relative political merits of cultural phenomena.

With respect to the first question, one should note that refusing to assign special political merits to any particular group of cultural phenomena would be no less problematic than failing to expect distinctive "moments of truth" from any particular group in society. Jameson's adoption of a "principled relativism" with respect to the political consciousness of oppressed groups suggests that a similar stance should be adopted toward cultural phenomena. This means, however, that it is inadequate simply to say that "all ideology in the strongest sense . . . is in its very nature Utopian."[49] The utopian impulses in modern or postmodern art should not be considered Utopian *überhaupt* but specified for particular phenomena, in terms of a historical context, and with reference to prevailing political conditions.

It is precisely such specificity that gives limited validity to Adorno's paradoxical modernism. Adorno has successfully articulated the negative utopia in modern works of art without displacing them from the sociohistorical process. Given the course of Western societies since the eighteenth century, it is indeed politically important that modern works have presented an alternative vision of nature, culture, and society, and have done so without divorcing themselves from the contemporary social formation. To the extent that their presentation is tied to the conditions under which modern works have been produced and received, one would not expect to find the same vision in premodern or postmodern works. At the same time, Adorno's critical endorsement of a work such as *Endgame* makes specific reference to the political conditions for which the work is relevant. Although one might question Adorno's reading of the work's relevance and his understanding of prevailing political conditions, the specificity of his evaluation makes its political dimension unmistakable.

Unfortunately Adorno's cultural politics has more to do with mounting an intellectual opposition to the capitalist system than with aligning such opposition with groups whose social position predisposes them toward structural transformation. A similar inattention to questions of political alignment characterizes much of the modern art whose political merits Adorno praises. The shortcomings of Adorno's paradoxical modernism lie in the autonomist and cognitivist assumptions of his cultural politics. By insisting on autonomy as a precondition of import and truth, Adorno pays too little attention to the political functions artworks actually have in the social system and cultural lifeworld. By locating the political relevance of artworks in their artistic import, Adorno ignores the question of how people actually experience such works and how import arises in the interaction between experience and art.

Hence, although Adorno gives insightful criticisms of the political inappropriateness and ineffectiveness of committed art, he does not argue convincingly that autonomous art is any more appropriate or effective. His arguments in favor of autonomous works assume that their import will "get through" to people, changing their political attitudes, and thereby changing their political behavior. As he says in the passage quoted earlier from the essay on "Commitment," "Kafka's prose and Beckett's plays . . . have an effect by comparison with which officially committed works look like pantomime. . . . The inescapability of their works compels the change of attitude which committed works merely demand."[50] Adorno fails to consider in detail the effect of existing political attitudes and behavior on the reception of artistic import. A theater audience may indeed be temporarily disturbed by Beckett's plays. Unless there is a predisposition toward social transformation, however, the overall effect might be to confirm the audience in its comfortable position.

It is doubtful that artistic import can have a genuinely political impact unless extra-artistic factors make for appropriate receptivity. This suggests that the political truth of an artwork depends in part on the way it functions in the lives of its recipients. To think of truth content as something inherent to the artwork is to have a restricted notion of truth. In such a conception, questions of reception become largely irrelevant for the project of evaluating an artwork's political truth. The result is a divorcing of art from politics, contrary to Adorno's intention. The theoretical politics of autonomy supports the practical autonomy of politics.

My criticisms do not discount the political merits of modern art, but they do limit the validity of Adorno's claims on this score. Even though he does not wish to foreclose on future possibilities, and even though he wishes to judge modern works in light of future possibilities, he sometimes writes as if modern art is the last conceivable refuge for utopian impulses. He also sometimes appears to suggest that the importance of premodern works resides in their prefiguring the import of modern works. These tendencies are tied to a philosophy of history that reads peculiarly modern phenomena such as reification back into the dawn of human civilization. By clearly specifying the historical period to which modern art belongs, and by making reference to the political consciousness of specific social groups, Jameson helps correct such tendencies.

To suggest that the validity of Adorno's claims is limited does not imply, however, that it is no longer necessary to make philosophical claims about the relative political merits of cultural phenomena. No doubt current conditions militate against venturing such claims. Not only does the culture of postmodernism make all past phenomena seem equally unimportant, but also some postmodernist theories make all current rankings seem equally arbitrary. Unless one wishes to accept whatever poses as acceptable, however, one can hardly avoid saying certain cultural phenomena are better or worse than others in certain respects. Unless one takes the position that all cultural phenomena are politically neutral, certain cultural phenomena will seem more desirable than others with respect to their political import and impact. Philosophical claims along these lines are necessary in order to place front and center what much of postmodern culture tries unsuccessfully to marginalize.

Admittedly, there is always the danger of doing what Jameson finds objectionable in Lukács's anti-modernism. One runs the risk of substituting ethical judgments for historical perceptions. The converse is also a danger, however, namely the substituting of historical perceptions for ethical judgments. While claims about political merits require solid historical grounds, they cannot avoid being political evaluations. They cannot be reduced to historical perceptions without losing their point. Despite all the reservations one might have toward Adorno's claims concerning the political merits of authentic modern works, his claims retain their own merit as political evaluations. They recall the legitimacy, indeed, the necessity of criticizing or commending specific cultural phenomena for political reasons. The heroic tone of his pronouncements reminds postmoderns that prudence is not always a virtue.

11
History, Art, and Truth

Art's vocation is to unveil the *truth* in the form of sensuous artistic configuration, to set forth the reconciled opposition just mentioned, and so to have its end and aim in itself, in this very setting forth and unveiling. For other ends, like instruction, purification, bettering, financial gain, struggling for fame and honour, have nothing to do with the work of art as such, and do not determine its nature.
Hegel[1]

Adorno's paradoxical modernism, like Hegel's view of art's vocation, raises fundamental issues in the philosophy of history. Indeed, some readers have thought that Adorno's aesthetics is necessitated by his philosophy of history, almost as if he would not have needed to write *Aesthetic Theory* were it not for insoluble problems in his philosophy of history.[2] There are two historical reasons for resisting such a conclusion. First, Adorno's philosophy of history is itself inspired in part by his reflections on art and aesthetics. Second, the close connection between philosophy of history and aesthetics is deeply embedded in the German philosophical tradition since Kant. German aesthetics implies questions of *Geschichtsphilosophie*, and vice versa.

Nowhere is this connection more striking than in questions about reason in history, which figure prominently in Adorno's writings and remain central for his successors. As was suggested earlier, Adorno's successors have two contrasting responses to his critique of rationality. Some retain the strongly negative cast of his critique but surrender his assumption that human beings can achieve a rational reordering of what has been rationally disordered. Others retain the assumption about rational reordering, but give up the negative cast of Adorno's critique. Albrecht Wellmer is among those who give up the negative cast of Adorno's critique. Yet he remains receptive to the concerns of the other camp, perhaps more so than his close colleague Jürgen Habermas. Wellmer's critical commentary on the nexus of history, art, and truth in Adorno's aesthetics can help one evaluate Adorno's stance on some of the issues raised in chapters 7 and 8.

11.1 Wellmer's Stereoscopic Critique

Wellmer's criticisms take the form of a "stereoscopic" reading. He wants "to set free the truth content of Adorno's aesthetics" from "an overly narrow construction of history," "to develop it through critique and interpretation," and thereby to arrive at "a three-dimensional picture" revealing "the latent depth" of Adorno's texts.[3] As was noted in chapter 1, Wellmer criticizes Adorno's reduction of rationality to instrumental reason and rejects the resulting gap between historical society and utopia. By replacing Adorno's totalizing critique of reason with a pluralizing reconstruction of rationality, Wellmer is able to give a differentiated account of discursive truth claims and artistic truth potential.

Wellmer's reconstruction of rationality appeals to Habermas's revision of critical theory. According to Wellmer, Habermas avoids both the radical negativism and the abstract utopianism of Adorno's philosophy of history. Habermas makes a clear categorial distinction between instrumental rationality and action, on the one hand, and communicative rationality and action, on the other. Against Marx, Habermas shows that bourgeois forms of morality and law do not simply mirror the capitalist mode of production but also express "an irreversible collective learning process" categorially distinct from scientific and technological progress. Against Weber, Habermas argues that the emergence of universalist morality and law is categorially distinct from formal and bureaucratic rationalization. Against Horkheimer and Adorno, Habermas

demonstrates that the idea of a rational society is already embodied and recognized in the democratic institutions, legitimacy principles, and self-interpretations of modern societies.
Consequently Habermas can give an immanent critique of
modern societies and avoid Adorno's chasm between utopia
and history. Habermas's critique not only shares a "common
normative ground" with modern societies but also indicates
how these can continue moving toward a truly rational
organization.[4]

On Wellmer's analysis, as on Habermas's, the fundamental
constraint in Adorno's aesthetics is that it embodies a perfor-
matively contradictory critique of reason. Wellmer identifies
three specific problems connected with this constraint. First,
instrumental rationality is wrongly set in opposition to aesthetic
rationality. Second, the work of art is overloaded as a model
of reconciliation. Third, the notion of artistic truth becomes
esoteric. To get around these problems, and to develop his own
"three-dimensional picture," Wellmer replaces Adorno's dialectic of reification and subjectification with a model of differentiation and integration in rationality. He also replaces the
notion of reconciliation with one of uncompelled communication, and he connects the concept of artistic truth with validity
in everyday speech.

Plural Rationalities

According to Wellmer, the opposition between aesthetic and
instrumental rationality arises from a dialectic of reification
and subjectification in Adorno's critique of reason. In this dialectic, reason appears to be infected with domination and the
will to self-preservation from its earliest beginnings.[5] Developed to liberate, reason becomes a way to dominate inner and
outer nature. By means of reason, nature has become a mere
object of control, people have become manipulable things, and
society has turned into an opaque functional system.

Like Lukács, says Wellmer, Adorno characterizes modern
rationalization as a process of "reification" in which formal and
instrumental rationality become amalgamated. Unlike Lukács,
however, Adorno considers this modern amalgamation as the

extreme case of a unity to be found in the prehistory of reason. "Formal rationality" refers to the tendency to establish unified and consistent systems of knowledge, explanation, or action. "Instrumental rationality" refers to the tendency to develop knowledge for the purpose of controlling natural and social processes. Adorno combines these two forms of rationality in his notion of "identifying thought," "identity-logical thinking," or "discursive reason."

"Subjectification" indicates the other pole in Adorno's critique of reason. According to Wellmer, Adorno reinterprets the traditional triad of subject, object, and concept "as a relationship of repression and domination, where the instance of repression—the subject—at the same time becomes the overpowered victim."[6] The unified self forms to preserve itself over against threatening nature, but it forms at the price of repressing inner nature, with its anarchic desire for happiness. Identity-logical thinking arises as a tool for self-preservation, but it boomerangs on the subject of thought, making the latter forgetful of its natural origins and original desire.

From all of this, says Wellmer, comes Adorno's call for a self-transcendence of identity-logical thinking. *Negative Dialectics,* which characterizes this self-transcendence as the incorporation of a mimetic moment into conceptual thought, tries to achieve it through "configurative" or "trans-discursive" philosophizing.[7] By depicting art and philosophy as the two spheres where a rational-mimetic wedding can shatter reification, Adorno places art and philosophy in antithesis to the world of instrumental reason.[8] Hence the opposition between aesthetic and instrumental rationality is fundamental to Adorno's critique of reason. It stems from critical theory's need "to defend an idea of reason which . . . it can no longer defend in the medium of discursive thought." Certain works of art become "virtually . . . the last residue of reason in a rationalized world." Adorno conceives society's transformation into a truly rational society "in terms of a sublation of instrumental into aesthetic rationality." Because Wellmer considers such a conception implausible, Adorno's defense of "reason" strikes him as "an impotent protest against Max Weber's negative verdict about the fate of reason in the modern world."[9]

Following Habermas, Wellmer wishes to "give up the thesis of a dialectical relationship between subjectification and reification."[10] The thesis makes it impossible to explain "how a self-transcendence of reason . . . is to be thought as a historical project."[11] More specifically, opposing aesthetic to instrumental rationality fails to provide a model of social transformation. It fails because these two types of rationality "cannot possibly signify alternative forms of social integration."[12]

Wellmer's reasons for this last claim are anchored in Habermas's model of differentiation and integration in rationality. Habermas's model emphasizes communicative rationality and validity claims. "Communicative rationality" refers to a mode of raising and accepting validity claims. The person who raises intersubjective validity claims must be ready to give and receive arguments. Implicit in the very structure of human speech, the notion of communicative rationality indicates the standard of rationality shared by competent speakers in modern societies. According to this notion, no intersubjective validity claim can be "exempt in principle from possible critical examination." The notion presupposes a clear differentiation of "the validity dimensions of objective truth, normative rightness, and subjective sincerity"—a process that reaches completion in modern societies, where traditional worldviews have lost their grip and relatively autonomous validity spheres have developed.[13] According to Habermas, intersubjective validity claims now occur in the three distinct "moments" of cognitive-instrumental, moral-practical, and aesthetic-practical rationality, and these moments prevail in the three domains of science and technologies, law and morality, and art and eroticism, respectively.[14]

Wellmer thinks that the notion of communicative rationality provides a normative basis for social critique and social transformation. The notion suggests that a rational society would display a new openness among relatively autonomous domains. For example, the formalized processes of administration and legislation "would become permeable to the need-interpretations, moral impulses or aesthetic experiences articulated beneath the level of formal organizations." So too, the arts would reenter the life process by becoming "a medium of communication" for individuals in society.[15]

The Habermasian model provides Wellmer with two reasons for saying that aesthetic and instrumental rationality cannot signify alternative forms of social integration and therefore should not be set in opposition à la Adorno. In the first place, the historical differentiation of aesthetic and instrumental rationality is irreversible and intrinsically unproblematic. Adorno's projected sublation of instrumental into aesthetic rationality wrongly assumes that the process of differentiation is both reversible and intrinsically problematic. Only this assumption allows him to project a social transformation in which one type of rationality—aesthetic rationality—provides the model for all types of rationality. In the second place, as construed by Adorno, aesthetic rationality lacks the dialogical dimensions that would be required for a genuine transformation of society in its highly differentiated state. Aesthetic synthesis in works of art "cannot possibly prefigure the open rules of dialogue with *many* voices" that is required for a new integration of system and lifeworld.[16]

Wellmer wishes to replace Adorno's dialectic of aesthetic and instrumental rationality with a differentiated interplay of plural rationalities. Just as the differentiation of instrumental, moral, and aesthetic rationality reminds one of Kant's distinction among understanding, practical reason, and reflective judgment power, so the picture of interplay recalls a Kantian free play of cognitive faculties in aesthetic experience.[17] According to Wellmer, because the unity of instrumental rationality does not exist, instrumental rationality does not have to be superseded by aesthetic rationality. What is needed instead is a reciprocal opening of various types of discourse with their particular rationalities. Aesthetic, moral, and "factual" discourses "are bound together in multiple ways—even if aesthetic, moral or cognitive validity claims represent different categories of validity, which cannot be reduced to a *single* category of *validity*. What is at stake here is not a 'reconciliation of the language games' in Adorno's sense but the mutual 'openness' of the discourses to each other: the 'sublation' of the *one* reason in the interplay of plural rationalities."[18] As Wellmer acknowledges, such an approach is both familiar and foreign to Adorno.

Reconciliation and Communication[19]

Closely related to Wellmer's picture of plural rationalities is his objection to Adorno's emphasis on reconciliation. Wellmer thinks the gap between utopia and historical society in Adorno's philosophy of history forces Adorno to overload the work of art as a model of reconciliation. Adorno's aesthetics does not bridge the gap, but simply reinstates it as a "dialectic of aesthetic semblance." The "moving principle of *Aesthetic Theory,*" in Wellmer's opinion, is the "mutual intertwining" of this dialectic with that of reification and subjectification.[20]

To describe Adorno's dialectic of aesthetic semblance, Wellmer distinguishes between two meanings of "aesthetic truth": aesthetic validity (*Stimmigkeit,* truth$_1$) and presentational truth (*gegenständliche Wahrheit,* truth$_2$). Adorno holds that art can give us the truth$_2$ about reality only by virtue of the truth$_1$ of an artwork's synthesis. At the same time, the artwork's synthesis can be true$_1$ only if it allows reality to come to appearance (truth$_2$). Because reality is antagonistic, art can be true$_2$ only to the extent that it presents reality as unreconciled. Yet to present reality as unreconciled, artworks must achieve a "nonviolent aesthetic synthesis of the diffuse" whose validity places reality in the light of reconciliation. Such a synthesis produces the appearance of reconciliation, whereas reality remains unreconciled. Hence aesthetic synthesis can be true$_1$ only by "turning against itself and calling its own principle into question—it must do this for the sake of truth which may not be had except by means of this principle."[21]

In this way the gap between utopia and historical society gets inscribed at the core of aesthetic rationality as the antinomy of a synthesis that must simultaneously be both reconciled and unreconciled. In Wellmer's words, "The modern work of art must, in one and the same movement, produce as well as negate aesthetic meaning, balance itself as it were on the razor's edge between affirmative semblance and illusionless anti-art."[22] This must be so because Adorno fuses two mixtures of ideas in his idea of reconciliation. The first mixture includes mimesis and redemption. The second mixture includes synthesis and peace. Adorno sets these fused mixtures in opposition to the processes of reification and subjectification and thereby to history as a whole.

In the first place, Adorno's idea of reconciliation connects the notions of mimesis and redemption. According to Wellmer, Adorno's "mimesis" refers to a sensuously receptive, expressive, and communicative mode of conduct among living things. By preserving mimesis, art and philosophy prefigure a "resurrection of the flesh" redeeming nature from the violence of identifying thought. Such redemption would affect both external nature, which would become more than an object of human control, and internal nature, which would no longer be repressed. Wellmer describes this first mixture as a utopian combination of sensualism and eschatology, and he claims that only this combination lets "aesthetic synthesis become for Adorno the prefiguration of a reconciled relationship of people, things, and creatures of nature."[23]

In the second place, Adorno's idea of reconciliation connects the notions of synthesis and peace. Art and philosophy shatter reification not simply by preserving mimesis, but by wedding the mimetic with a rational moment. Both art and philosophy can achieve syntheses that respect the particularity upon which identifying thought imposes systematic unity. Common to both spheres is a "reconciling" spirit that projects within itself the possible reconciliation of all living things.[24] The projected reconciliation would mean peace not only among human beings but also between human beings and nature.

Wellmer finds Adorno's idea of reconciliation unduly "messianic." By fusing mimesis, redemption, synthesis, and peace in an idea of reconciliation, Adorno "allows the gap between historical reality and the state of reconciliation to become so profound that bridging it can no longer be a meaningful goal of human praxis." At the same time, the "immensity of the gap . . . means that reality, prior to all experience . . . is pinned to negativity."[25] A "materialist deciphering" will have to extract Adorno's aesthetics from his larger philosophy of reconciliation.

Wellmer's crucial move in this regard is to separate the idea of a humane society, which he considers genuinely materialist, from the idea of a redemption of nature, which he regards as a remnant of outmoded theology and metaphysics. This move lets him read Adorno's philosophy of reconciliation as an implicit attempt to conceptualize an actual self-transcendence of modern culture in the direction of a postmodern culture, a postrationalistic form of rationality, and a decentered subject. Adorno's allegedly "other-worldly" utopia becomes "innerworldly," and artworks become media of communication rather than models of reconciliation.[26]

In taking the fissure between materialist and messianic motifs as his clue, Wellmer explicitly follows the lines of Habermas's *The Theory of Communicative Action*. Habermas replaces the subject-object paradigm of a philosophy of consciousness with the subject-subject paradigm of a philosophy of language. He argues that all culture, being tied to language, displays "a symmetrical, communicative relationship between subject and subject" just as much as "an asymmetrical, distancing relationship between subject and object." Indeed, to be properly understood, even instrumental rationality, which highlights the subject-object relationship, must be incorporated into a more comprehensive communicative rationality, which emphasizes the subject-subject relationship.

Wellmer claims that the subject-object paradigm of a philosophy of consciousness makes Adorno unable to perceive the communicative preconditions behind language's objectifying functions. Instead Adorno takes "mimesis," as he calls communicative behavior, to be extraneous to ordinary and scientific language. Once one sees communicative behavior as constitutive for all culture, however, Adorno's utopian projection of a nonviolent synthesis can emigrate "to the sphere of discursive reason itself" and discursive reason can attain elements of this utopian projection "from the conditions of its own foundation in language." Although discursive rationality cannot dispense with the identity-logical dimension preconditioning all language, it also cannot dispense with either the plurality of usages and users or the need to achieve consensus. Such plurality and need inhere in all communicative practices. Any modern use of language to communicate, whether in science, philosophy, political debate, or everyday speech, must appeal, however implicitly, to the norm of noncompulsory discourse for all participants. The appeal and the norm are Wellmer's "inner-worldly" utopia.[27]

Translated into aesthetics, the turn to a subject-subject paradigm means that the work of art should be construed as a *medium* of *communication* rather than a *model* of *reconciliation*. Hence "aesthetically experiencing, communicating, and acting subjects" must be inserted into Adorno's "categorial schema of art, reality, and utopia."[28] The artwork's aesthetic synthesis "is no possible model for a state of society free from repression." It "can only signify a trans-human state of affairs, but not a life form of speaking and interacting individuals." Wellmer, by contrast, sees aesthetic synthesis as a means to generate aesthetic experiences promoting "unblocked communicative relationships," both among individuals and of individuals with themselves. By "illuminating our life praxis and our self-understanding," such art-generated aesthetic experience "*is*, as Adorno thought, the presence of a utopian perspective."[29] Indeed, "without aesthetic experience and its subversive potentials, our moral discourse would necessarily become blind and our interpretations of the world empty."[30]

Wellmer does not completely dismiss the notion of aesthetic synthesis as a model. He says that modern aesthetic syntheses may point to a new form of subjectivity. Modern art's open forms signal a new attitude subjects can take toward their own decentered state. Such forms may stand for a form of subjectivity no longer displaying the rigid unity of the bourgeois subject but having the more flexible structure of what Habermas calls a "communicatively fluid" ego-identity. In a sense, then, aesthetic synthesis in modern art does give a *model* for non-aesthetic synthesis.[31] At the same time, however, Wellmer insists that aesthetic synthesis be seen as a *medium* of intersubjective communication. To "catalyze changes in forms of individuation and socialization," works of art must actually function in connection with "forms of non-aesthetic communication." They cannot "point towards an emancipation of communication" by virtue of their "intrinsic being," but only "by virtue of their *effect*," their intervention in the "attitudes, feelings, interpretations, and value judgments" that subjects bring to their relationships.[32] This insistence on the pragmatics of communication, which points to decentered subjects for a postrationalistic rationality, has a significant impact on the concept of artistic truth.

Artistic Truth Potential

A reconstructed concept of truth is central to Wellmer's break with Adorno's totalizing critique of rationality. This reconstructed concept is a postmodernist replacement for the Hegelian notion of a "self-completing truth," a notion Adorno retains despite his objections to Hegel's totalizing tendencies. In an attempt to elucidate "the dialectic of modernism and postmodernism," Wellmer describes his own "postmodernist dialectic" as not having the connotations of a "self-completing truth." This description comports well with his characterization of postmodernism as "a kind of explosion of the modern episteme, in which reason and its subject—as source of 'unity' and of the 'whole'—are blown to pieces."[33]

According to Wellmer, Adorno's idiosyncratic use of a Hegelian notion of truth to criticize capitalist rationalization owes as much to Nietzsche as to Marx. Adorno thinks that reason develops within the process of human labor upon nature. Unlike Marx, however, Adorno sees this process as evidence of reason's illusory and violent character, not of its truth. This view recalls Nietzsche, who says that logic stems from the will to power, not from the will to truth. Unlike Nietzsche, however, Adorno frames his view in a Marxist way: the illusory character of identifying thought indicates its ideological character, and the concept of ideology presupposes a notion of truth that Nietzsche rejects. Adorno maintains "an emphatic concept of truth," even though he must conceive it "as something foreign, as it were, to the world of identifying thought, to the delusory nexus of instrumental rationality."[34]

While not rejecting the concept of truth as such, Wellmer wishes to make it less esoteric by returning it to the sphere of normal discourse. Following Habermas's consensus theory of truth,[35] Wellmer treats "truth" as one of the norms implied by any use of language for purposes of intersubjective communication. The result for Wellmer's aesthetics is that the notion of artistic *truth content* gives way to a notion of artistic *truth potential*. The latter notion is supposed to alleviate two problems in Adorno's approach to truth in art. It will be useful to review Wellmer's account of both problems before summarizing his alternative.

The first problem has to do with the relationship between art and philosophy. Adorno's concept of artistic truth presupposes an aporetic relationship between art and philosophy: both art and philosophy aim at complete knowledge of the truth, but neither one can grasp more than a complementary and fragmented form of truth. Although Adorno's position seems to necessitate the "performative contradiction" of stating philosophically what cannot be stated philosophically, Wellmer's criticism concerns a different but related problem. According to Wellmer, Adorno's concept of artistic truth makes works of art depend on philosophical interpretation for disclosure of their truth content. Without philosophical interpretation, artworks cannot really fulfill their cognitive functions. The problem is that Adorno "has to conceive of aesthetic knowledge as philosophical insight and the truth of art as philosophical truth."[36] Wellmer suggests two reasons why this is a problem: it privileges the presentational dimension of artistic truth above other dimensions, and it denigrates art's truth potential in ordinary aesthetic experience.

The second problem in Adorno's approach to artistic truth pertains to the relationship between art and history. Wellmer maintains that Adorno turns a utopian idea of reconciliation into "a central moment" of the truth content of the work of art. As a result, all efforts to unravel the truth content in particular works of art become a single attempt to rescue the idea of reconciliation that art as a whole is supposed to make available.[37] Wellmer does not clearly explain why this is a problem. His reason seems to be that the actual function and import of a particular work get swallowed up in a utopian generalization having little direct bearing on the historical situation for which a work's truth content is supposed to be important.

To circumvent both problems, Wellmer introduces a distinction between "truth" and "truth potential." This distinction relies on Habermas's "language-pragmatic differentiation of the everyday concept of truth."[38] Wellmer identifies three different dimensions of validity in the everyday concept of truth: "apophantic," "endeetic," and moral-practical or normative truth, all three of which all speakers have at their disposal. These dimensions correspond roughly to the cognitive-instrumental, aesthetic-practical, and moral-practical types of rationality noted earlier. Other terms for the three dimensions of validity are "truth" (*Wahrheit*), "truthfulness" or "sincerity" (*Wahrhaftigkeit*), and "rightness" or "appropriateness" (*Richtigkeit*). Although Wellmer does not point this out, the use of "truth" to indicate the "apophantic" dimension may make this the privileged dimension from which the "endeetic" and "normative" dimensions derive their meaning *as* dimensions in ordinary "truth."

Be that as it may, Wellmer wishes to deny the literal ascription not only of apophantic truth but also of endeetic truthfulness and normative rightness to the work of art. "Truth" can be ascribed to art, he says, but only in a metaphorical manner. Art does not literally contain or present truth. Nevertheless, a basis exists for the metaphorical ascription of truth to art, since artworks do have a "truth potential." To explain why "truth" can only be metaphorically ascribed to art, Wellmer discusses the close connection between "aesthetic validity" (*Stimmigkeit*) and "truth potential" (*Wahrheitspotential*) in the work of art. He also examines the relation between aesthetic discourse and aesthetic experience.[39]

By "aesthetic validity" Wellmer means a kind of fittingness internal to the work of art. It corresponds to what was earlier discussed as the "truth$_1$" of a work's aesthetic synthesis. Although Wellmer does not say exactly how the concept of "aesthetic validity" relates to the concept of "validity" dimensions in ordinary discourse, it seems to indicate a prelinguistic type of normativity. The "truth potential" of an artwork, by comparison, seems to indicate a prelinguistic type of apophantic truth claim. It corresponds to what was earlier discussed as the artwork's presentational "truth$_2$." To the extent that both aesthetic validity and truth potential are prelinguistic, they can be normative and apophantic only in a metaphorical sense.

"Truth potential" refers to the potential artworks have for

disclosing truth, rather than to their "truth content" as such. Indeed, Wellmer wishes to replace the notion of truth content with that of truth potential. The question for him is not what makes an artwork's import true or false, but rather what makes it capable of carrying truth potential. His answer requires an explanation of the relationship between aesthetic validity and truth potential.

According to Wellmer, metaphors such as "disclosing" or "showing" reality capture the intuitive core to the traditional apophantic concept of artistic truth. The metaphors indicate that we can recognize (*erkennen*) what is being disclosed only if we are already familiar (*kennen*) with it as something that is undisclosed. At the same time, every detail is crucial in a traditional work of art: the reality being disclosed would be different if the work's sensuous configuration were changed. Thus there is an intimate connection between the disclosive power or "truth potential" of the work of art and the "rightness" or "aesthetic validity" of the work's construction.

"Truth" gets ascribed to art because of how aesthetic discourse relates to aesthetic experience. Where there is controversy about what a work discloses (truth potential) and how well it makes the disclosure (aesthetic validity), our discourse points to aesthetic experience in a correcting and expanding manner. The aesthetic validity of the work must be perceived, and this perception involves both the work's being perceived as reality's self-disclosure and reality's being recognized as disclosing itself. In such situations, aesthetic discourse simultaneously addresses both the aesthetic validity of the work and the "authenticity" of its "presentation." Moreover, to discuss these matters, the participants must mobilize their own experience, and they must do so in the three dimensions of truth, truthfulness, and normative rightness all at once.

Because of intimate connections between truth potential and aesthetic validity, on the one hand, and aesthetic discourse and aesthetic experience, on the other, it is easy to ascribe "truth" to art, even though a strictly literal usage would limit the term to discursive claims made about art: "Neither truth *nor* truthfulness may be attributed *unmetaphorically* to the work of art. . . . That truth and truthfulness—and even normative rightness—are instead *metaphorically* bound up with each other in the work of art may only be explained by the fact that the work of art, as a symbolic construct with an aesthetic validity claim, is at the same time the object of an *experience* in which the three dimensions of truth are linked *unmetaphorically*."[40] The consequence of this approach is that Adorno's dialectic of artistic truth gives way to Wellmer's more differentiated account of how the artwork's aesthetic validity and truth potential function in aesthetic experience and aesthetic discourse. Adorno's allegedly emphatic and antirational concept of truth seems to have been tamed and rationalized. Utopian generalizations no longer threaten to swallow particular works of art. The philosophical disclosure of artistic truth content is no longer crucial, for everyday experience and ordinary discourse will suffice to uncover artistic truth potential.

In retrospect, one can see that Wellmer's domestication of "artistic truth" informs both his general criticisms of Adorno's philosophy of history and his specific revisions of Adorno's aesthetics. Having criticized the reduction of rationality to instrumental reason, Wellmer wishes to replace Adorno's opposition between aesthetic and instrumental rationality with a differentiated interplay among aesthetic, moral, and instrumental rationality. Having rejected the gap between utopia and historical society, Wellmer proposes to treat the artwork as a medium of intersubjective communication rather than as a paradoxical model of reconciliation. The main project is to replace Adorno's totalizing critique of reason with a pluralizing reconstruction of rationality. The domestication of Adorno's concept of artistic truth is crucial for this project. But the price of domestication remains to be determined.

On the one hand, the historical truth content of *Aesthetic Theory* culminates in its conception of truth. Adorno's conception holds considerable promise for an age in which many philosophers find traditional ideas of truth no longer valid. *Aesthetic Theory* returns the question of truth to the center of philosophical aesthetics without reducing truth to a mere correspondence between propositions and facts, or simply existentializing truth into authentic decisions, or baldly pragmatizing truth into the test of consequences. At the same time, Adorno shows how theoretical interpretations can honor cultural phenomena without isolating them from their social and historical settings; he emphasizes the importance of social consciousness for artistic truth; and he opens aesthetics itself to the test of exegetical fruitfulness rather than entrenching it behind a rigid methodology.

On the other hand, Wellmer's criticisms indicate problems in Adorno conception of truth. Further reflection is needed on several topics, including the concept of artistic truth, the status of philosophical claims about artistic truth, the historiographic patterns surrounding such claims, and the language in which Adorno couches his conception of truth. Restricting the discussion to the last three topics, I will develop alternatives, partially derived from both authors, that reclaim some of Adorno's approach.

11.2 Philosophical Truth Claims

Wellmer's concept of truth potential is supposed to deprivilege the presentational dimension of artistic truth and recognize art's cognitive functions in ordinary experience. In developing this concept, however, Wellmer not only ignores the question of how aesthetic experience relates to philosophical interpretation but also counts all ascriptions of truth to art as metaphorical. In both respects new questions arise about the status of claims about artistic truth.

There is something odd about using the everyday concept of truth to reconceptualize ascriptions of truth to art. Although such ascriptions occur in ordinary discourse, rarely do they display the precision one expects of philosophical discourse. What seems "metaphorical" from the perspective of ordinary language might not be metaphorical from the perspective of philosophical language. In any case, an equally good starting point for understanding such claims would seem to be philosophical discourse, which always has something extraordinary about it, even among ordinary language philosophers. To the extent that ascriptions of truth to art occur in philosophical discourse, the relationship of such discourse to aesthetic experience is crucial for understanding claims about artistic truth.

Examining this relationship will help raise the question whether philosophical truth claims about art are merely metaphorical.

Philosophical Discourse

Wellmer's discussion of truth potential helps one understand how aesthetic experience informs philosophical truth talk. Wellmer holds that controverted claims about a work's presentation of reality must appeal to the participants' experience of the work's disclosive power (truth potential) and internal fittingness (aesthetic validity). This suggests that no amount of talking and writing will suffice to establish philosophical truth claims about art in the absence of looking and seeing or listening and hearing or reading and rereading the phenomena in question. An empirical basis is necessary for philosophical aesthetics, even though philosophy lacks the experimental and statistical methods of many of the natural and social sciences.

The pervasiveness of such a basis in Adorno's aesthetics helps account for the seriousness with which its truth claims must be taken, especially by philosophers in the English-speaking world. Adorno emphasizes the necessity of aesthetic experience for philosophical aesthetics, and his own aesthetics embodies an intense engagement with modern art. Perhaps the necessity of aesthetic experience also indicates why analytic aesthetics has sometimes become no less dreary than the traditional approaches it was supposed to replace. Analytic aesthetics conceives of its task as a clarifying exercise in second-order discourse. The philosopher is supposed to sort out the concepts and claims contained in the aesthetic discourse of critics and audiences, and, to a lesser extent, in the aesthetic discourse of scholars and educators in the arts. While the contributions of such an approach are undeniable, various limitations have become increasingly apparent over the years. Some of these limitations inhere in the way analytic aesthetics conceives its task.[41]

The analytic philosopher assumes that aesthetic discourse should meet the criteria of clarity and consistency. Yet the experience to which aesthetic discourse belongs is not of a sort that emphasizes clarity and consistency in the use of language.

Consequently the philosophical search for clarity and consistency puts a demand on aesthetic discourse that the latter can hardly be expected to meet so long as it continues to render discussable the experience to which it belongs. Moreover, by proceeding at one remove from aesthetic discourse itself, the search tends to forget its obligation to submit philosophical claims about aesthetic discourse to the test of aesthetic experience. The result is all too often a philosophical discourse that is irrelevant for art critics, audiences, scholars, and educators because it lacks discernible references to art as experienced. The analytic philosopher who says that "truth" cannot properly be applied to art may thereby be ratifying the distance from art of an aesthetics that restricts itself to second-order discourse.

An emphasis on the necessity of aesthetic experience for philosophical aesthetics need not discount the importance of second-order discourse, however. If properly conceived and executed, second-order discourse can help shape aesthetic discourse and the practices of art. A crucial criterion here is the ability to tune the categories of aesthetic discourse to their peculiar subject matter without restricting their range to the subject matter itself. Adorno's discussion of "technique" is highly instructive in this regard. By conceiving technique to be simultaneously artistic and social, and by treating it in this manner, Adorno indicates how critics and scholars can concentrate on artistic phenomena without losing sight of their social implications. In fact, one of Adorno's most important contributions has been to develop new categories that apply to contemporary artistic phenomena and incorporate a keen social consciousness. These categories can help shape aesthetic discourse and artistic practice.

Philosophical discourse concerning artistic truth can inform aesthetic experience in three ways. First, philosophical truth talk serves to highlight the peculiarly allusive references in even the least representational art. Philosophical attempts to judge the truth or falsity of a work's import bring to mind what aesthetic experience often overlooks, namely that art discloses something about ourselves and our world, something hard to pin down but nonetheless crucial. Second, philosophical talk about artistic truth or falsity indicates the social and historical limits of aesthetic experience. It serves as a reminder that no matter how good the object, the experience, and its articulation, a question remains as to the point of it all. Where is it all headed, and is this direction desirable? Third, philosophical truth talk points to the social and historical possibilities of aesthetic experience. Such talk signals that the script is not finished and the performance is not over once an artistic phenomenon has been perceived and discussed. The phenomenon and the experience will be absorbed into larger patterns and processes, where they will be more or less significant, more or less important.

By highlighting art's allusiveness and indicating the sociohistorical limits and possibilities of aesthetic experience, philosophical talk about the truth of art reinserts aesthetic experience into the sociohistorical world from which it only seems to depart. Philosophical truth talk destroys the illusion of distance that clings to aesthetic experience and to first- and second-order discourse about art. Paradoxically, talk that itself seems so distant from everyday experience and ordinary language serves to bring these home.

"Metaphorical" Ascriptions

This suggests that philosophical ascriptions of truth to art are not merely metaphorical. In a trivial sense, such ascriptions should not be considered merely metaphorical because it is extremely difficult to make out a firm distinction between "metaphorical" and "literal" uses of language. Wellmer's claim that truth may not be attributed unmetaphorically to the work of art assumes such a distinction without saying exactly what it comes to. Beyond this rather obvious point, however, the suggestion that philosophical ascriptions of truth are not merely metaphorical should be understood as making three assertions. First, philosophical truth claims about artworks and other artistic phenomena are no more metaphorical than some other philosophical truth claims. Second, philosophical truth claims about art make meaningful reference to the import of art and aesthetic experience in the modern world. Third, philosophical

truth claims about art provide part of the basis for a philosophical theory of truth.

The first assertion can be illustrated by reference to philosophical claims about the truth of claims in science. At one
level, such philosophical claims are fairly straightforward. The
philosopher simply makes the claim P that scientific claim S is
true. At another level, however, a philosophical claim about
the truth of a scientific claim is less straightforward, for the
philosophical claim P might itself be true in a sense that is
somewhat different from the way in which the scientific claim
S is true. The difference could have to do with either the nature
of the claims or the context of their justification. At this level
the "truth" of philosophical claim P calls for a philosophical
theory as to the criterion of truth. In elucidating whether claim
P is true in the same sense as claim S, the philosopher must
put forward additional claims (P_n) that might be true, but perhaps not in the exactly same sense as either P or S. If by "metaphorical" one means that a claim does not apply in a straightforward sense, then, compared with scientific claims, philosophical claims P_n about the truth of philosophical claims relative
to scientific claims could well be metaphorical. This need not
mean, however, that such philosophical claims P_n must be untrue. It would simply mean that, being highly mediated, they
might not be true in exactly the same sense that scientific claims
are true. To say that philosophical claims P_n can be true only
if they are true in the same sense as scientific claims would be
to put forward another philosophical claim, one which might
itself violate the strict sense of scientific "truth."

Of course there is an important difference between the "metaphorical" character of philosophical truth claims about scientific claims and the "metaphorical" character of philosophical
truth claims about works of art. The philosopher who ascribes
truth to an artwork is not ascribing it to propositions, claims,
or other discursive entities.[42] It would be a mistake, however,
to conclude from this fact that the work of art and a philosophical truth claim about it cannot both be true. It would also
be incorrect to conclude, as Wellmer seems to say, that the
"truth" of the artwork and the "truth" of the philosophical
truth claim must both be *merely* metaphorical. Rather, the philo-

sophical truth claim cannot be "true" in exactly the same sense as the artwork is "true," and in each case the "truth" belongs to the same family or constellation of meanings. This family or constellation, to which the concept of truth applies, allows philosophical truth claims to refer meaningfully to the import of art and aesthetic experience in the modern world. If there were no diversity of truths, there could be no reference, and if there were no unifying concept of truth, the reference could not be meaningful.

One plausible reply to this general line of argument would be to grant that some philosophical truth claims about art are not metaphorical but to say that this does not mean that artworks themselves (or their import) can actually be true or false. Suppose, for example, that Wellmer's thesis (T) about metaphorical ascriptions is not itself metaphorical. Suppose he is making the nonmetaphorical claim T that truth can only be ascribed metaphorically to art. This claim is nonmetaphorical, and it is a philosophical truth claim about art. Moreover, if this nonmetaphorical truth claim T were justified, then it would be wrong to ascribe truth unmetaphorically to art.[43]

Leaving aside the question whether Wellmer has adequately justified T, let's examine what this reply comes to. In the first place, one needs to distinguish between first-order and second-order philosophical truth claims. First-order claims ascribe truth to the import of a particular work of art, for example, "Beckett's *Endgame* shows the truth about human autonomy." Second-order philosophical truth claims say in general whether such first-order truth claims are meaningful, legitimate, metaphorical, and the like. Wellmer's thesis T is a second-order claim, and hence not one of those claims whose supposedly metaphorical status is in dispute.

In the second place, whether or not first-order philosophical truth claims about art are metaphorical depends on whether works of art or other artistic phenomena can themselves be true in some sense. Wellmer wishes to deny that they can. His apparent reason for this denial is that artworks do not normally contain or convey truth claims. The assumption supporting this reason seems to be that only claims and other discursive entities can be true or false. But I see no reason to grant this assumption. We often say, for example, that an insight is true without thereby requiring that the insight be put forward in discourse in order to be true. Why could not artworks contain or convey insights rather than claims or propositions, and why could not such insights be called true or false? Moreover, a second-order claim to the effect that truth *can* be unmetaphorically ascribed to art would be just as unmetaphorical as Wellmer's second-order claim to the contrary. It would also need adequate justification, which I do not pretend to have given.

Nondiscursive Truth

I do hold, however, that first-order truth claims refer meaningfully to the import of art and aesthetic experience in the modern world. Meaningful references provide a second reason for saying that philosophical ascriptions of truth to art are not merely metaphorical. Truth talk about art is not simply the figment of a Hegelian imagination, no more than artworks are merely physical, perceptual, and artifactual objects. Artworks in the modern world are also cultural and sociohistorical objects whose production and reception unavoidably involve prelinguistic stances toward truth and falsehood. These stances do not have to be spelled out in claims and propositions in order to be stances on the truth or falsehood of some cultural practice, social pattern, or historical tendency. They can take shape in works of art, not as a "message" or "idea" somehow separate from these works, but as their import, as that which in the work the work is all about. Philosophical truth talk does not simply impose truth claims on the work or reconstruct the work in philosophy's image. Rather, to use Adorno's language, philosophical truth talk extrapolates from the work that which in the work the work is all about. What gets extrapolated exists independently from its extrapolation, but not in separation from the work from which it is extrapolated.

As Wellmer notes, such language easily makes artistic truth content seem esoteric. The advantage to Wellmer's speaking about truth potential, it seems to me, is that this calls attention to art's cognitive functions in ordinary experience and discourse. The advantage to Adorno's speaking about truth content, by contrast, is that this recognizes the peculiarities of art as an allusive location of insight. Perhaps both notions are needed to provide a basis for first-order philosophical truth claims about artistic phenomena. The notion of truth content is needed in order to point to that which acquires cognitive functions in everyday life. The notion of truth potential is needed to remind us that ordinary experience and discourse are required in order for these cognitive functions to be acquired. Perhaps the employment of both notions would provide a path past the esoteric tendencies of Adorno's emphatic claims about philosophy and art, but without dissolving artistic truth into the process of discursive communication.

Philosophical claims concerning the relationship of a philosophical truth claim to the truth content of a particular work have a status similar to philosophical claims P_n concerning the truth of a philosophical claim P about the truth of a scientific claim S. In the end, such high-level claims call for a philosophical theory of truth. What philosophers often fail to consider, however, is the extent to which philosophical truth claims about art provide part of the basis for such a theory. By making this connection explicit, Adorno provides us with a third and final reason for saying that philosophical ascriptions of truth to art are not merely metaphorical. They are not merely metaphorical because what philosophers take "truth" to mean is informed in part by the philosophical truth claims they make about art.

Consider, for example, the philosopher who not only denies that a particular artwork displays truth content but also denies that "truth" can be meaningfully ascribed to any work of art. Usually the latter denial will commit one to a theory of truth according to which only discursive entities such as sentences, claims, and propositions can properly be called true. An argument for such a theory would not consult works of art but rather the very discursive entities already declared prime candidates for truth or falsehood. If one then pointed out that there exists a type of discourse, namely philosophical discourse, in which truth is regularly ascribed to art, the reply would probably be that such ascriptions are surely metaphorical or imprecise.

Consider, by contrast, the philosopher who not only makes truth claims about particular works but also holds that in general such claims are meaningful. Here too the philosopher is usually making a commitment to a philosophical theory of truth, but to a theory in which things other than discursive entities can properly be called true. Such a theory allows one to consider philosophical ascriptions of truth to art as more than merely metaphorical.

To argue against considering philosophical truth claims merely metaphorical does not establish whether and in what sense art itself can be true or false. The argument as presented pertains primarily to philosophical ascriptions of truth to art and does not purport to give an account of the truth of art as such. No more has been attempted than a metaphilosophical clearing operation. Yet the argument does suggest a promising line for future investigation. It should be worthwhile to examine the extent to which philosophical theories of truth are themselves informed by the absence or presence of reflections on what some philosophers call artistic truth. Whether one calls it truth content, truth potential, or something else, the nondiscursive but experience- and world-disclosing capacities of art seem relevant for what philosophers try to capture when they put forward a theory of truth. What this relevance comes to is far from clear, however, as is the content of philosophical claims that ascribe or deny truth to art. Because of the close connection between philosophical truth claims about art and philosophical theories of truth, it becomes extremely difficult to adjudicate the conflict between philosophers who do and philosophers who do not think that such claims are merely metaphorical.

11.3 Historical Truth Content

The difficulty of adjudication is compounded when one takes Adorno's position that the truth of art is historical. Not only does this position conflict with some traditional notions of truth in Western philosophy and religion, but also it commits one to making comprehensive claims about history of a sort that contemporary historians are loathe to make. Faced with traditional notions of truth as eternal, one must give a plausible case for the legitimacy of making philosophical claims about the historical truth of cultural phenomena. Faced with contemporary skepticism, one must indicate the fruitfulness of making such claims. Actually the case for legitimacy and the indication of fruitfulness are closely linked, since current conditions militate against making philosophical claims about historical truth. Both the legitimacy and fruitfulness of such claims depend in part on their providing ways to maintain critical consciousness within the postmodern culture of consumer capitalism.

Patterns of Historiography

Adorno's own historico-philosophical evaluations of modern art provide influential examples of the sorts of claims that are needed. At the same time his concept of an artistic "context of problems" holds considerable promise as a category to guide such evaluations. This category helps one highlight artistic contributions without foreclosing on future possibilities. It also helps one construct lines of continuity and discontinuity without imposing an empty unity on the historical process.

To locate cultural phenomena in a "context of problems" is to avoid both the narrowness of technical historiographies and the imprecision of global philosophies of history. To evaluate the contributions of cultural phenomena within their context of problems is to avoid both the positivism of merely descriptive accounts and the idealism of strongly prescriptive accounts. To argue for the legitimacy of such evaluations is to take issue with both the historical relativism of poststructuralism and the historical dogmatism of orthodox Marxism. In all these respects Adorno's approach has much to offer.

His approach is problematic, however, insofar as it fails to give a systematic account of its own construction of specific contexts of problems. Despite his emphasis on import and technique, for example, Adorno does not provide the periodizations and classifications warranted by historical patterns in import and technique. Instead he gives unrepeatable, exemplary treatments of preselected works. As a result, his constructions seem arbitrary, even though they rely on hidden historiographic patterns. What is needed, then, is a more explicit presentation of the historiographic patterns within which cultural phenomena are being evaluated.

Without presenting such patterns, which would make little sense apart from an actual historiographic account, I can at least mention the sorts of patterns that need to be presented. I will label them synchronic, diachronic, and "perchronic" patterns.[44] Synchronic patterns pertain to problems widely shared by practitioners at a certain time. Diachronic patterns pertain to changes in these problems and their solutions from one generation or era to the next. Perchronic patterns pertain to relatively long-lived traditions that inform a cultural practice and intersect both synchronic and diachronic patterns.

Accordingly, to give a precise and comprehensive historical account of cultural phenomena requires the construction of a three-dimensional context of problems. The string quartets of Béla Bartók, for example, should be located with respect to twentieth-century challenges of composition and performance. They should also be inspected as giving new solutions to older problems in this genre as well as providing new challenges for subsequent practitioners. And they should be situated in a tradition of purely instrumental music going back several centuries. All three dimensions should be explored if one wants to give a defensible evaluation of the historical truth of Bartók's string quartets.

If one wishes to avoid the narrowness of technical historiographies, however, one must also read behind the lines, as it were, of the patterns mentioned. Adorno's readings treat works of art as sociohistorical "monads," thereby suggesting that one must go beyond strictly literary, musical, or artistic patterns in order to make sense of literary, music, or art history. As is clear from Adorno's own interpretations, to go beyond these patterns one must have a larger narrative of the historical process. Despite the problems inherent in a global philosophy of history, something like this is needed for any historiography of the arts that wishes to exceed the writing of technical monographs.

Comprehensive Judgments

Adorno's reflections on the history of philosophy shed an indirect light on the problem of making comprehensive judgments in art historiography. Within the history of philosophy, he asserts, there appears something of the movement of history as a whole.[45] Adorno's own studies of Kierkegaard, Husserl, and Hegel attempt to disclose something of this larger historical movement. Most important in the present context is Adorno's assertion, not his attempts at carrying it out.

The assertion is instructive in several regards. First, it suggests that the history of philosophy has acquired its own integrity, which is not to be equated with specialization or professionalization. This integrity motivates both philosophy's historical unfolding and philosophers' historiographic accounts of this unfolding. Second, Adorno refuses to separate the history of philosophy from the histories of other phenomena. Instead he emphasizes how internal to philosophy's history is the entire movement of history. By implication, comprehending the history of philosophy requires grasping something of the entire movement of history within the history of philosophy. The best way to do this, according to Adorno, is to engage in philosophical critique of other philosophies.[46] If sufficiently rigorous and imaginative, such critique will disclose something of the entire movement of history. Although treated philosophically, philosophical problems will not be approached as merely philosophical problems. Third, Adorno does not say that the philosopher's historiographic account of the history of philosophy suffices for comprehending the entire movement of history. "Something" of that movement appears, but full comprehension would require more than philosophical historiography.

Going beyond Adorno's own account, one can suggest two reasons why philosophical historiography will not suffice. One reason is that, from the side of the historical process, even more is taking place than what all the various general and specialized historiographies study. Even the most comprehensive historiography cannot avoid the fact that history continually writes itself behind our backs. In the words of Karl Marx,

"[Human beings] make their own history, but they do not make it just as they please."[47] The other reason is that, from the side of historiography itself, no study and no combination of studies will be complete and self-contained. Even the most technical of historiographies cannot avoid the fact that historiography remains a derivative life practice, one which shapes and receives shape from the historical dialectic. Historiography is always subject to reorientation by way of the other life practices and institutions to which it is tied. In this sense, history not only writes itself *behind* our backs but also writes itself behind *our* backs.

Adorno's assertion about the history of philosophy helps illuminate what has been described as reading behind the lines of strictly artistic patterns. To the extent that the arts have become integrated into an institution of art in Western society, the history of art can be said to have acquired its own integrity. As was observed concerning the history of philosophy, this integrity should not be equated with professionalization or specialization. If the history of art does have its own integrity, then this can be thought to provide impetus to both the historical unfolding of art and historiographic attempts to grasp art's unfolding. One need not generalize speciously from more technical historiographies in order to write a general historiography of the arts, nor need one impose inappropriate theorems of philosophical historiography. The general history of art is neither a convenient fiction nor an ideological imposition. It is an actual process that calls for a general historiography of the arts, one which reads across the lines of strictly literary, musical, and other patterns.

Furthermore, the history of art need not be studied as if it were separate from the histories of other phenomena, whether these be political, economic, philosophical, or religious. One can emphasize how internal to the history of art is the entire movement of history, and one can expect that comprehending art's history will require some grasp of the entire movement of history internal to it. As Adorno's own writings demonstrate, a good way to achieve this grasp is through immanent but critical analyses of artistic phenomena. At the same time, Adorno's assertion about the history of philosophy suggests that, no matter how comprehensive, one's historiographic account will not suffice for comprehending the entire movement of history. Both the history of art and history as a whole continually elude our grasp and reorient our historiography.

None of this means, however, that philosophical claims about the historical truth of cultural phenomena are doomed to failure. Instead, such claims are crucial to any historiography of art that wishes to respect both the integrity of art history and its connection with history as a whole. Philosophical truth claims are the most comprehensive historiographic judgments that one can make about artistic phenomena. Such claims encompass an evaluation of the phenomena in a context of problems and an understanding of the history informing this evaluation. To say of a work of art that its import is true is to make a discussable judgment concerning its contributions in a particular time and tradition as well as over the years. To say this is also to make explicit how one thinks the artwork stands in the entire movement of history. If one acknowledges that even this claim is caught up in history, and if one does not pretend that a truth claim is itself the truth, then the claim can be legitimate and fruitful. Such an understanding of philosophical truth claims is one of Adorno's most important insights, one that Wellmer's reconstruction of rationality deconstructs.

As comprehensive historiographic judgments, philosophical truth claims are unacceptable both to those who think truth is eternal and to those who consider it unknowable. Compared with traditional absolutism and contemporary skepticism, however, there is a double advantage to the practice of making philosophical truth claims as comprehensive historiographic judgments. On the one hand, this practice does not try to elevate critical consciousness above current conditions. On the other hand, critical consciousness is not surrendered to the push and pull of contemporary culture. The legitimacy and fruitfulness of making historico-philosophical truth claims about art are linked to the need to maintain critical consciousness within a culture that makes all truth claims seem presumptuous or irrelevant. It is in providing means to resist the glitzy culture of consumer capitalism that much of Adorno's challenge and legacy lie.

Languages of Suffering

The final move in a critique of Adorno's aesthetic should be to compare it with his philosophy's vision and motive. Adorno envisions a philosophy that is "full, unreduced experience in the medium of conceptual reflection."[48] His own philosophy does not always live up to this vision. As Adorno himself sees, the dialectical concepts at his disposal cannot do justice to the qualitative variety of experience.[49] Yet he modifies these concepts and their connections for the sake of a historical experience rendering traditional categories inadequate, in the face of all the unmet needs and unfulfilled desires both multiplied and disguised in a supposedly rational society. It is in such a society that Adorno states the motive of his philosophy: "The need to lend a voice to suffering is a condition of all truth."[50] He tries to fulfill this condition by uniting spontaneous experience and stringent thought in highly expressive language.

Adorno's aesthetics, like a commentary on it, cannot avoid making metaphilosophical claims about philosophical claims concerning artistic truth. Although unavoidable, such metaphilosophical claims draw attention to the language in which a conception of truth is couched. In the case of *Aesthetic Theory*, this is the language of suffering,[51] a language somehow slighted by Wellmer's emphasis on truth potential, communication, and the interplay of plural rationalities. Adorno's metaphilosophical claims are not simply claims about the connections of history, art, and truth. They are part of an attempt to lend a voice to unmet needs and unfulfilled desires.

The vision and motive of Adorno's philosophy make it insufficient to criticize *Aesthetic Theory* because its systematic aspects are "rigid" and "artificial" or because Adorno's aesthetic judgments exhibit a "latent traditionalism."[52] More to the point is to ask whether these systematic aspects hinder the voicing of unreduced experience and whether Adorno's aesthetic judgments block the expression of suffering. Compared with any other attempt of the past two hundred years, Adorno's aesthetics stands out for its eloquent integration of systematic theory with expressive concerns. Like other of his writings, *Aesthetic Theory* lends a voice to suffering.

Yet the acknowledging of Adorno's vision and motive does not exempt one from reexamining his contribution. Adorno's metaphilosophical claims seem to reserve for his own philosophy a decisive knowledge of the truth about falsity. His language leaves the impression that the real meaning of suffering and the complete disclosure of the truth depend on the interpretation given in his own philosophy. Such impressions give Adorno's critics a double task. On the one hand, one must recognize what is expressed in Adorno's philosophy. One cannot merely note the fact of suffering, but must continue Adorno's attempt to comprehend it and to expose easy explanations as potential ways to perpetuate a massive destruction of nature and human life. On the other hand, one must also question the truth of Adorno's contribution—both the truth of his apparent claim to speak decisively about falsity, and the truth of his interpretation of suffering.

Adorno's metaphilosophical claims make it seem that he, like Hegel, fails to challenge philosophy's decisive claim to truth. Understandably, this apparent failure incites rejection from various participants in postmodernist culture. Yet there is something peculiar about rejecting a philosophy because it makes, or seems to make, a decisive claim to truth. Those who pass a negative philosophical judgment on this claim act as if they have philosophical knowledge of a truth that challenges the decisive claim to truth. They seem to be making or implying another decisive truth claim. When Adorno's critics charge his philosophy with the hubris of claiming to know the truth about falsity, the charge tends to fall under its own accusation.

If one does not wish to perpetuate what seems to be a fundamental failure, then the question must be left in question form. One must simply ask whether Adorno reserves for his own philosophy a decisive knowledge of truth. In this way Adorno's philosophy makes evident the perplexing position of philosophy itself. Philosophy takes place within a damaged life, whose reparation is a mutual task, and in a misdirected society, whose redirection is a shared responsibility. As Adorno has demonstrated, philosophy must remain radically open to the other without giving up the attempt to make true claims about truth and falsity and without reducing truth and falsity to mere matter of discursive rationality.

Even though *Aesthetic Theory* expresses suffering in an incomparable way, those who share Adorno's concerns cannot avoid raising questions about this expression. The experience of suffering, direct and pervasive though it be, cannot directly illuminate itself. It must be interpreted. The need to express suffering, clearly urgent and significant, cannot be self-evident as a condition of truth. The need must also be met in ways that are true. The philosophical recognition of this need, no matter how compelling, cannot be self-contained. The recognition must also represent those for whom the suffering is expressed and interpreted.

Adorno suggests that philosophy makes its efforts on behalf of many who cannot see what is at stake in contemporary society.[53] In this "representative" effort, Adorno's philosophy comes close to the stance of prophecy. Although prophets should not be called elitist just because their message is prophetic, those whom prophets claim to represent are entitled to ask about the status of the prophets' calling, the character of their burden, and the insightfulness of their message. Adorno's readers may legitimately ask how his philosophy received its commission to speak truth about a dissonant world. They may also ask whose suffering is being expressed, and whether this expression is true. They may even wonder whether Adorno's aesthetic theory does more to ensure the continuation of a negative dialectic than to encourage transformations that would eliminate the need for a negative dialectic.

Yet these questions, no matter how legitimate and unavoidable, should not blind us to the need that conditions the historical truth of Adorno's philosophical aesthetics. As Adorno experienced it, that need is to express an inexpressible suffering that has been concealed and multiplied in countless ways. According to the conclusion of Adorno's unfinished aesthetics, the same need conditions the historical truth of modern art:

Surely it would be better for art to vanish altogether than to forget suffering, which is art's expression and which gives substance to its form. Suffering, not positivity, is the humane content of art. If the art of the future were to become positive once again, one would be justified in suspecting that negativity had not been obliterated. [That suspicion is always there; the threat of relapse is constant; and freedom, being freedom from the principle of possession, cannot be possessed. What sort of historiography would art be,] if it wiped out the memory of accumulated suffering (386–87/369).

The need for modern art is the need for a negative dialectic. If modern art is a language of suffering, then *Aesthetic Theory* is a second language for modern art. The truth of these languages cannot be ignored.

Notes

Introduction

1. The centrality of "truth" in Adorno's aesthetics is evident from several German monographs. Listed chronologically, these include: Gerhard Kaiser, *Benjamin. Adorno. Zwei Studien* (Frankfurt: Anthenäum Fischer Taschenbuch, 1974). Friedemann Grenz, *Adornos Philosophie in Grundbegriffen. Auflösung einiger Deutungsprobleme* (Frankfurt: Suhrkamp, 1974). Wolff Rehfus, "Theodor W. Adorno. Die Rekonstruktion der Wahrheit aus der Ästhetik" (Cologne: Universität zu Köln, Inaugural-Dissertation, 1976). Martin Zenck, *Kunst als begriffslose Erkenntnis. Zum Kunstbegriff der ästhetischen Theorie Theodor W. Adornos* (Munich: Wilhelm Fink, 1977). Lucia Sziborsky, *Adornos Musikphilosophie. Genese—Konstitution—Pädagogische Perspektiven* (Munich: Wilhelm Fink, 1979). Peter Christian Lang, *Hermeneutik, Ideologiekritik, Ästhetik. Über Gadamer und Adorno sowie Fragen einer aktuellen Ästhetik* (Königstein: Forum Academicum, 1981). The most important article on this topic is Albrecht Wellmer, "Truth, Semblance, Reconciliation: Adorno's Aesthetic Redemption of Modernity," *Telos*, no. 62 (Winter 1984–85), pp. 89–115, which is discussed in chapter 11 below. For a critical study in the tradition of analytic aesthetics, see Anthony Savile, "Beauty and Truth: The Apotheosis of an Idea," in *Analytic Aesthetics*, ed. Richard Shusterman (Oxford: Basil Blackwell, 1989), pp. 123–46.

2. George Lichtheim, *From Marx to Hegel* (New York: Herder & Herder, 1971; Seabury Press, 1971), pp. 43–44, n. 15. Though the German term *Problematik* has no precise equivalent in English, the transliteration "problematic" has become common in postmodern academic discourse.

3. Section 2.2 in the bibliography lists several reviews of the English translation of *Aesthetic Theory*.

4. For a useful discussion of various models of critique, see Charles Taylor and Alan Montefiore, "From an Analytical Perspective," in Garbis Kortian, *Metacritique: The Philosophical Argument of Jürgen Habermas*, trans. John Raffan (Cambridge: Cambridge University Press, 1980), pp. 1–21.

5. See Kortian, *Metacritique*, pp. 28–29.

6. Contemporary philosophers who continue the attack on Descartes and Kant include Richard Rorty, Hans-Georg Gadamer, and Jacques Derrida, despite the marked differences in their philosophical orientations. The later Ludwig Wittgenstein presents an obvious exception, since he challenges foundationalism without significant recourse to Hegel. For a survey of what can be called the problem of critique in twentieth-century philosophy, see *After Philosophy: End or Transformation?*, ed. Kenneth Baynes, James Bohman, and Thomas McCarthy (Cambridge, Mass.: MIT Press, 1987).

7. Robert J. Antonio, "Immanent Critique as the Core of Critical Theory: Its Origins and Developments in Hegel, Marx and Contemporary Thought," *British Journal of Sociology* 32 (September 1981): 330–45; the quote is from p. 330.

8. The classic English language discussion of artistic truth is John Hospers, *Meaning and Truth in the Arts* (1946; Chapel Hill: University of North Carolina Press, 1974). Two books that serve to connect German and Anglo-American traditions on this topic are Susanne K. Langer, *Feeling and Form: A Theory of Art Developed from "Philosophy in a New Key"* (New York: Charles Scribner's Sons, 1953), and Albert Hofstadter, *Truth and Art* (New York: Columbia University Press, 1965).

1 Historical Positions

1. The short biography in this section relies mainly on the more complete accounts in Carlo Pettazzi, "Studien zu Leben und Werk Adornos bis 1938," in *Theodor W. Adorno*, ed. Heinz Ludwig Arnold (Munich: Edition Text + Kritik, 1977), pp. 22–43; Susan Buck-Morss, *The Origin of Negative Dialectics: Theodor W. Adorno, Walter Benjamin, and the Frankfurt Institute* (Hassocks, Sussex: Harvester Press, 1977), pp. 1–23; Eugene Lunn, *Marxism and Modernism: An Historical Study of Lukács, Brecht, Benjamin, and Adorno* (Berkeley: University of California Press, 1982); and Martin Jay, *Adorno* (Cambridge, Mass.: Harvard University Press, 1984), pp. 24–55. See also Richard Wolin, *Walter Benjamin: An Aesthetic of Redemption* (New York: Columbia University Press, 1982).

2. *Geschichte und Klassenbewusstsein: Studien über marxistische Dialektik* (Berlin: Malik Verlag, 1923; Darmstadt/Neuwied: Sammlung Luchterhand, 1968); trans. as *History and Class Consciousness: Studies in Marxist Dialectics* by Rodney Livingstone (London: Merlin Press, 1971).

3. Ernst Bloch, *Geist der Utopie* (Munich: Duncker & Humblot, 1918), 2d ed., rev. (Berlin: Paul Cassirer, 1923), reprinted (Frankfurt: Suhrkamp, 1964); various sections now in Ernst Bloch, *Man on His Own: Essays on the Philosophy of Religion*, trans. E. B. Ashton (New York: Herder and Herder, 1970), and in Ernst Bloch, *Essays on the Philosophy of Music*, trans. Peter Palmer, intro. David Drew (Cambridge: Cambridge University Press, 1985). Georg Lukács, *Die Theorie des Romans: Ein geschichtsphilosophischer Versuch über die Formen der grossen Epik* (Neuwied: Luchterhand, 1971); trans. as *The Theory of the Novel* by Anna Bostock (Cambridge, Mass.: MIT Press, 1971). Lukács's study first appeared in the journal *Zeitschrift für Ästhetik und Allgemeine Kunstwissenschaft* (1916). It was published as a book a few years later (Berlin: Paul Cassirer, 1920).

4. "Goethes Wahlverwandtschaften," written 1921–1922, first published by Hugo von Hofmannsthal in *Neue Deutsche Beiträgen* (1924–1925), reprinted in Walter Benjamin, *Illuminationen: Ausgewählte Schriften* (Frankfurt: Suhrkamp, 1977), pp. 63–135.

5. *Ursprung des deutschen Trauerspiels* (Berlin: Ernst Rowohlt, 1928), rev. ed. (Frankfurt: Suhrkamp, 1978); trans. as *The Origin of German Tragic Drama* by John Osborne

(London: NLB, 1977). The book was begun in 1923 and submitted unsuccessfully as a *Habilitationsschrift* at the university in Frankfurt in 1925. The revised edition of 1978 contains the text of the critical edition of Benjamin's *Gesammelte Schriften*, 6 vols., ed. Rolf Tiedemann and Hermann Schweppenhäuser (Frankfurt: Suhrkamp, 1972–).

6. Adorno's correspondence with Krenek is contained in *Theodor W. Adorno und Ernst Krenek: Briefwechsel*, ed. Wolfgang Rogge (Frankfurt: Suhrkamp, 1974). Adorno's acquaintance with Hanns Eisler would later lead to their collaboration on *Composing for the Films* (New York: Oxford University Press, 1947), which appeared only under Eisler's name until published in Germany as *Komposition für den Film* (Munich: Rogner & Bernhard, 1969). The text of the German version is contained in GS 15 (1976): 7–155. For bibliographies of Adorno's writings, see the introduction to the bibliography below.

7. Buck-Morss, *Origin of Negative Dialectics*, p. 15.

8. This apt description of Adorno's dialectical, antisystematic writings comes from Georg Picht, "Atonale Philosophie," in *Theodor W. Adorno zum Gedächtnis*, ed. Hermann Schweppenhäuser (Frankfurt: Suhrkamp, 1971), pp. 124–28.

9. "Der Begriff des Unbewussten in der transcendentalen Seelenlehre" ("The Concept of the Unconscious in the Transcendental Theory of Mind"), written in Frankfurt 1926–1927, rejected by Adorno's mentor Hans Cornelius, and published posthumously in GS 1 (1973) 79–322.

10. Buck-Morss, *Origin of Negative Dialectics*, pp. 20–23, 90–101, and passim.

11. GS 1 ("Die Aktualität der Philosophie," –1931): 325–44, trans. as "The Actuality of Philosophy," *Telos*, no. 31 (Spring 1977), pp. 120–33; and GS 1 ("Die Idee der Naturgeschichte," –1932): 345–65, trans. as "The Idea of Natural History," *Telos*, no. 60 (Summer 1984), pp. 111–24. Neither lecture was published during Adorno's lifetime, but both of them announce themes and concerns that were to remain prominent in his subsequent writings.

12. "Zur gesellschaftlichen Lage der Musik," *Zeitschrift für Sozialforschung* 1 (1932): 103–124, 356–78; trans. as "On the Social Situation of Music," *Telos*, no. 35 (Spring 1978), pp. 128–64.

13. *Kierkegaard. Konstruktion des Ästhetischen* [Tübingen: J. C. B. Mohr (Paul Siebeck), 1933]; 2d and 3d eds. (Frankfurt: Suhrkamp, 1962, 1966); now in GS 2 (1979); *Kierkegaard: Construction of the Aesthetic*, trans., ed., and with a foreword by Robert Hullot-Kentor (Minneapolis: University of Minnesota Press, 1989). The book is a revision of Adorno's second *Habilitationsschrift*, which was sponsored by Paul Tillich and successfully defended in 1931.

14. "Über den Fetischcharakter in der Musik und die Regression des Hörens," *Zeitschrift für Sozialforschung* 7 (1938): 321–55; revised version in *Dissonanzen. Musik in der verwalteten Welt* (Göttingen: Vandenhoeck & Ruprecht, 1956); now in GS 14 (1973): 14–50. The revised version is translated as "On the Fetish-Character in Music and the Regression of Listening" in *The Essential Frankfurt School Reader*, ed. Andrew Arato and Eike Gebhardt, introduction by Paul Piccone (New York: Urizen Books, 1978), pp. 270–99. Adorno gives a more accessible statement of his position in "On Popular Music," written with the assistance of George Simpson, *Studies in Philosophy and Social Science* 9 (1941): 17–48.

15. Max Horkheimer and Theodor W. Adorno, *Dialektik der Aufklärung. Philosophische Fragmente* (Amsterdam: Querido, 1947), 2d ed. (Frankfurt: S. Fischer, 1969); trans. John Cumming (New York: Seabury Press, 1972). The original manuscript was first published as a mimeograph in 1944. GS 3 (1981) contains the 1969 edition, supplemented by "Das Schema der Massenkultur" (GS 3: 299–335), which expands the chapter on the culture industry.

16. By T. W. Adorno, Else Frenkel-Brunswik, Daniel J. Levinson, and R. Nevitt Sanford in collaboration with Betty Aron, Maria Hertz Levinson, and William Morrow (New York: Harper & Brothers, 1950). *The Authoritarian Personality* is the first volume in *Studies in Prejudice*, a series begun in 1944, sponsored by The American Jewish Committee, and edited by Max Horkheimer and Samuel H. Flowerman. Adorno's contributions to this massive and controversial volume are reprinted under the title *Studies in the Authoritarian Personality* in GS 9.1 (1975): 143–509.

17. *Philosophie der neuen Musik* [Tübingen: J. C. B. Mohr (Paul Siebeck), 1949]; subsequent editions in 1958, 1966, and 1972; 5th ed. in GS 12 (1975); trans. Anne G. Mitchell and Wesley V. Blomster as *Philosophy of Modern Music* (New York: Seabury Press, 1973). *Minima Moralia. Reflexionen aus dem beschädigten Leben* (Frankfurt: Suhrkamp, 1951), 2d ed. (1962), reprint (1969), now in GS 4 (1980); trans. E. F. N. Jephcott as *Minima Moralia: Reflections from Damaged Life* (London: NLB, 1974). *Versuch über Wagner* (Frankfurt: Suhrkamp, 1952), 2d ed. (Munich/Zurich: Droemer Knaur, 1964), now in GS 13 (1971): 7–148; trans. Rodney Livingstone as *In Search of Wagner* (London: NLB, 1981).

18. *Prismen. Kulturkritik und Gesellschaft* (Frankfurt: Suhrkamp, 1955), subsequent editions in 1963 and 1969, now in GS 10.1 (1977): 9–287; trans. Samuel and Shierry Weber as *Prisms* (London: Neville Spearman, 1967; Cambridge, Mass.: MIT Press, 1981).

19. GS 10.1 (P, "Kulturkritik und Gesellschaft," 1951): 30; *Prisms*, p. 34.

20. "Einleitung," in *Zur Metakritik der Erkenntnistheorie. Studien über Husserl und die phänomenologischen Antinomien* (Stuttgart: W. Kohlhammer, 1956), GS 5 (1970): 12–47; "Introduction," in *Against Epistemology: A Metacritique; Studies in Husserl and the Phenomenological Antinomies*, trans. Willis Domingo (Cambridge, Mass.: MIT Press, 1983), pp. 3–40. For another translation of this introduction, see "Metacritique of Epistemology," *Telos*, no. 38 (Winter 1978–79), pp. 77–103.

21. "Der Essay als Form," in *Noten zur Literatur* I (Frankfurt: Suhrkamp, 1958), GS 11 (1974): 9–33; trans. as "The Essay as Form," *New German Critique*, no. 32 (Spring-Summer 1984), pp. 151–71.

22. Collections on music include *Dissonanzen. Musik in der verwalteten Welt* (Göttingen: Vandenhoeck & Ruprecht, 1956) ("Dissonances: Music in the Administered World"); *Klangfiguren. Musikalische Schriften* I (1959) ("Tone Configurations: Musical Writings I"); *Einleitung in die Musiksoziologie. Zwölf theoretische Vorlesungen* (1962), trans. E. B. Ashton as *Introduction to the Sociology of Music* (New York: Seabury Press, 1976); *Der getreue Korrepetitor: Lehrschriften zur musikalischen Praxis* (Frankfurt: S. Fischer, 1963) ("The Loyal Musical Coach: Pedagogical Writings on Musical Praxis"); *Quasi una fantasia. Musikalische Schriften* II (1963); *Moments musicaux. Neu gedruckte Aufsätze 1928 bis 1962* (1964) ("Musical Moments: Newly Published Essays from 1928 to 1962"); *Impromptus. Zweite Folge neu gedruckter musikalischer Aufsätze* (1968); *Nervenpunkte der neuen Musik (Ausgewählt aus "Klangfiguren")* (Reinbek bei Hamburg: Rowohlt, 1969) ("Nerve Points of the New Music, Selected from *Tone Configurations*"). Books for which no publisher is listed were published by Suhrkamp. *Dissonanzen* and *Einleitung in die*

Musiksoziologie are now contained in GS 14 (1973); *Der getreue Korrepetitor* in GS 15 (1976); *Klangfiguren* and *Quasi una fantasia* in GS 16 (1978); and *Moments musicaux* and *Impromptus* in GS 17 (1982).

23. *Noten zur Literatur* ("Notes on Literature") I (1958), II (1961), and III (1965). GS 11 (1974) contains all three volumes plus *Noten zur Literatur* IV, which was published posthumously.

24. *Mahler. Eine musikalische Physiognomik* ("Mahler: A Musical Physiognomy") (Frankfurt: Suhrkamp, 1960), now in GS 13 (1971): 149–319; *Mahler: A Musical Physiognomy*, trans. Edmund Jephcott (Chicago: University of Chicago Press, 1988). *Berg. Der Meister des kleinsten Übergangs* ("Berg: The Master of the Smallest Transitions") (Vienna: Verlag Elisabeth Lafite; Österreichischer Bundesverlag, 1968), now in GS 13 (1971): 321–494.

25. *Drei Studien zu Hegel* ("Three Studies on Hegel") (Frankfurt: Suhrkamp, 1963), now in GS 5 (1970): 247–381.

26. *Eingriffe. Neun kritische Modelle* (1963) ("Interventions: Nine Critical Models"), now in GS 10.2 (1977): 455–594. *Ohne Leitbild. Parva Aesthetica* (1967, 1968) ("Without Guidelines: Parva Aesthetica"), now in GS 10.1 (1977): 289–453. *Stichworte. Kritische Modelle 2* (1969) ("Keywords: Critical Models 2"), now in GS 10.1 (1977): 595–782. All three books were published by Suhrkamp.

27. The main documents in this dispute are collected in *Der Positivismusstreit in der deutschen Soziologie* (Neuwied and Berlin: Hermann Luchterhand, 1969); trans. Glyn Adey and David Frisby as *The Positivist Dispute in German Sociology* (London: Heinemann, 1976). David Frisby's "Introduction to the English Translation" (pp. ix–xliv) gives a helpful survey of the debate. Adorno's contributions to this volume are also contained in GS 8.

28. GS 8 ("Einleitung zum *Positivismusstreit in der deutschen Soziologie*," 1969): 309; "Introduction," in *The Positivist Dispute in German Sociology*, p. 27.

29. *Negative Dialektik* (Frankfurt: Suhrkamp, 1966), 2d ed. (Suhrkamp, 1967), now in GS 6 (1973): 7–412; trans. E. B. Ashton as *Negative Dialectics* (New York: Seabury Press, 1973). A closely related work is *Jargon der Eigentlichkeit. Zur deutschen Ideologie* (Frankfurt: Suhrkamp, 1964), now in GS 6 (1973): 413–526; trans. Knut Tarnowski and Frederic Will as *The Jargon of Authenticity* (London: Routledge & Kegan Paul, 1973).

30. Perhaps one should speak of a conference and a counter-conference. The proceedings of the first, which was held in Frankfurt, are collected in *Adorno-Konferenz 1983*, ed. Ludwig von Friedeburg and Jürgen Habermas (Frankfurt: Suhrkamp, 1983). The proceedings of the second, which was held in Hamburg, are collected in *Hamburger Adorno-Symposion*, ed. Michael Löbig and Gerhard Schweppenhäuser (Lüneburg: Dietrich zu Klampen, 1984). Of particular interest in this second collection is the "Kritik der Frankfurter 'Adorno-Konferenz 1983'" (pp. 148–69) coauthored by Christoph Türcke, Claudia Kalász, and Hans-Ernst Schiller. An anthology devoted to Adorno's aesthetics appeared ten years after his death: *Materialien zur ästhetischen Theorie Theodor W. Adornos. Konstruktion der Moderne*, ed. Burkhardt Lindner and W. Martin Lüdke (Frankfurt: Suhrkamp, 1979). Other anthologies are listed in section 2.1 of the bibliography below.

31. Jay, *Adorno*, p. 22.

32. Quoted by Thomas Baumeister, "Theodor W. Adorno—nach zehn Jahren," *Philosophische Rundschau* 28 (1981): 1–26; the quote is from p. 25. Baumeister's article reviews books by Beier, Düver, Figal, Sauerland, Schmucker, Sziborsky, Tichy, and Zenck, as well as the anthology *Materialien zur ästhetischen Theorie Theodor W. Adornos*.

33. The most important books in this regard include Perry Anderson's *Considerations on Western Marxism* (London: NLB, 1976; Verso Edition, 1979) and *In the Tracks of Historical Materialism* (Chicago: University of Chicago Press, 1984); Alvin W. Gouldner's *The Two Marxisms: Contradictions and Anomalies in the Development of Theory* (New York: Seabury Press, 1980); Russell Jacoby's *Dialectic of Defeat: Contours of Western Marxism* (Cambridge: Cambridge University Press, 1981); and Martin Jay's *Marxism and Totality: The Adventures of a Concept from Lukács to Habermas* (Berkeley: University of California Press, 1984). Useful anthologies include Dick Howard and Karl E. Klare, eds., *The Unknown Dimension: European Marxism Since Lenin* (New York: Basic Books, 1973); *Western Marxism: A Critical Reader*, ed. *New Left Review* (London: NLB, 1977); and *An Anthology of Western Marxism: From Lukács and Gramsci to Socialist Feminism*, ed. Roger S. Gottlieb (New York: Oxford University Press, 1988). A concise history of Marxism is given in David McLellan, *Marxism after Marx: An Introduction* (Boston: Houghton Mifflin, 1979). See also the parallel anthology *Marxism: Essential Writings*, ed. David McLellan (Oxford: Oxford University Press, 1988).

34. For a summary of these attacks and Korsch's reply to his critics, see "The Present State of the Problem of 'Marxism and Philosophy'—An Anti-Critique" (1930), in Karl Korsch, *Marxism and Philosophy*, trans. with intro. Fred Halliday (New York and London: NLB, 1970), pp. 98–144.

35. Jay, *Totality*, p. 1.

36. Maurice Merleau-Ponty, *Adventures of the Dialectic* (1956), trans. Joseph Bien (Evanston: Northwestern University Press, 1973).

37. Anderson, *Considerations*, p. 92.

38. Jay, *Totality*, p. 80.

39. Ibid., p. 537.

40. Ferenc Fehér, "Grandeur and Decline of a Holistic Philosophy," *Theory and Society* 14 (July 1985): 873.

41. William Hackman, review of *Dialectic of Defeat*, in *Theory and Society* 13 (March 1984): 274–80.

42. Douglas Kellner, "Remarks on Alvin Gouldner's *The Two Marxisms*," *Theory and Society* 10 (March 1981): 266. In *The Two Marxisms*, pp. 159–62, Gouldner points out three problems in Anderson's approach: Anderson ignores the substantial differences among so-called Western Marxists, overlooks the pessimism in Lenin's view of working-class consciousness, and treats unavoidable contradictions within Marxism as mere intergenerational conflicts to be solved by reverting to a purified Trotskyism.

43. Martin Jay makes a similar point in "For Gouldner: Reflections on an Outlaw Marxist," *Theory and Society* 11 (November 1982): 759–78. Jay proposes "to introduce a second axis to bisect that created by Gouldner's dichotomy [of critical and scientific Marxism], an axis whose poles are Western and Eastern Marxism" (p. 771).

44. David McLellan, *Marxism after Marx*, pp. 298–306.

45. Anderson, *Considerations*, p. 42. This assessment of the failure is partially corrected in Anderson's "Afterword" (pp. 109–121), which points to some weaknesses in classical Marxism.

46. Jay, *Totality*, p. 7.

47. Helmut Dubiel, *Theory and Politics: Studies in the Development of Critical Theory* (1978), trans. Benjamin Gregg, with an introduction by Martin Jay (Cambridge, Mass.: MIT Press, 1985). As Dubiel points out, this research program was first labeled "Critical Theory" during the second phase of its development (1937–1940). It makes sense, however, to apply the label to all phases (i.e., 1930–1945) of "early Critical Theory" as well as to later permutations of the same research program.

48. The classic account of the Institute's history is by Martin Jay, *The Dialectical Imagination: A History of the Frankfurt School and the Institute of Social Research, 1923–1950* (Boston: Little, Brown, 1973). The most comprehensive account in German is Rolf Wiggershaus, *Die Frankfurter Schule* (Munich: Hanser, 1986).

49. Volumes 1–7 (1932–1938) were published as the *Zeitschrift für Sozialforschung* by Librairie Félix Alcan in Paris. Volumes 8–9 (1939–1941) were published as *Studies in Philosophy and Social Science* by the Institute of Social Research in New York City. The journal was reprinted in 1970 by Kösel-Verlag in Munich. A paperback edition of this reprint appeared ten years later (Munich: Deutscher Taschenbuch Verlag, 1980). Volume 1 of the reprint edition contains an excellent introduction by Alfred Schmidt, "Die *Zeitschrift für Sozialforschung*: Geschichte und Gegenwärtige Bedeutung." See also Jürgen Habermas, "The Inimitable Zeitschrift für Socialforschung: How Horkheimer Took Advantage of a Historically Oppressive Hour," *Telos*, no. 45 (Fall 1980), pp. 114–21.

50. Two anthologies of writings by critical theorists are *The Essential Frankfurt School Reader*, ed. Andrew Arato and Eike Gebhardt, intro. Paul Piccone (New York: Urizen Books, 1978), and *Critical Theory and Society: A Reader*, ed. Stephen Eric Bronner and Douglas MacKay Kellner (New York: Routledge, 1989).

51. Martin Jay, "Introduction," in Dubiel, *Theory and Politics*, p. xi. Adorno's version of the research program is mentioned by Wolfgang Bonss and Norbert Schindler, "Kritische Theorie als interdisciplinärer Materialismus," and discussed by Martin Jay, "Positive und Negative Totalität. Adornos Alternativentwurf zur interdisciplinären Forschung," in Wolfgang Bonss and Axel Honneth, eds., *Sozialforschung als Kritik: Zum sozialwissenschaftlichen Potential der kritischen Theorie* (Frankfurt: Suhrkamp, 1982). For an English version of Jay's article, see "Positive and Negative Totalities: Implicit Tensions in Critical Theory's Vision of Interdisciplinary Research," in Martin Jay, *Permanent Exiles: Essays on the Intellectual Migration from Germany to America* (New York: Columbia University Press, 1985), pp. 107–119.

52. Two anthologies of critical interpretation have appeared in English: *On Critical Theory*, ed. John O'Neill (New York: Seabury Press, 1976); and *Foundations of the Frankfurt School of Social Research*, ed. Judith Marcus and Zoltán Tar (New Brunswick, N. Y.: Transaction Books, 1984). For anthologies in German, see section 2.1 in the bibliography below. I do not discuss a fourth and more recent type of criticism, which can be termed deconstructive. In this connection, see Michael Ryan, *Marxism and Deconstruction: A Critical Articulation* (Baltimore: Johns Hopkins University Press, 1982).

53. The most significant exception to this pattern in American scholarship has been the work of Fredric Jameson. A shift toward systematic studies will occur as younger members of this group become established scholars. See, for example, Douglas Kell-

ner's *Critical Theory, Marxism, and Modernity* (Cambridge: Polity Press, 1989) and Seyla Benhabib's *Critique, Norm, and Utopia: A Study of the Foundations of Critical Theory* (New York: Columbia University Press, 1986), which attempts "the reconstruction of the history of theories from a systematic point of view" (p. x). The questions raised by Benhabib's approach are discussed in Benjamin Gregg, "Modernity in Frankfurt: Must a History of Philosophy Be a Philosophy of History?" *Theory and Society* 16 (January 1987): 139–51, and in an exchange between Benhabib and Gregg in the same issue, pp. 153–63.

54. For an overview of the American reception of critical theory up to 1981, see Douglas Kellner and Rick Roderick, "Recent Literature on Critical Theory," *New German Critique*, no. 23 (Spring-Summer 1981), pp. 141–70. On the reception of Adorno's work, see Martin Jay, "Adorno in America," *New German Critique*, no. 31 (Winter 1984), pp. 157–82. A German version of Jay's article is contained in *Adorno-Konferenz 1983*, pp. 354–87.

55. Anderson, *Considerations*, p. 78. It should be noted that, in coming to this assessment, Anderson simply ignores the political and economic writings of Friedrich Pollock, Karl August Wittfogel, Franz Borkenau, Franz Neumann, and Otto Kirchheimer, all of whom at some point were members of the Frankfurt School.

56. Göran Therborn, "The Frankfurt School," *New Left Review*, no. 63 (September-October 1970), pp. 65–96; the quote is from p. 94. Therborn's article also appears in *Western Marxism: A Critical Reader* and in *Foundations of the Frankfurt School of Social Research*. For a rebuttal to Therborn's attack, see Martin Jay, "The Frankfurt School's Critique of Marxist Humanism," *Social Research* 39 (Summer 1972): 285–305; reprinted in Jay's *Permanent Exiles*, pp. 14–27.

57. George Friedman, *The Political Philosophy of the Frankfurt School* (Ithaca: Cornell University Press, 1981), pp. 299–300.

58. Kellner and Roderick, "Recent Literature," p. 146, summarizing a point made by Andrew Arato and Eike Gebhardt in *The Essential Frankfurt School Reader*.

59. Kellner and Roderick, "Recent Literature," pp. 152–53 and 168–69, summarizing the criticisms of David Held, Helmut Dubiel, and Axel Honneth.

60. Arato, "Political Sociology and Critique of Politics," in *The Essential Frankfurt School Reader*, pp. 3–25. In his "General Introduction" to the same anthology, Paul Piccone states that the intellectual-historical reason for failing to uncover oppositional forces is not that critical theory jettisoned Marxist tenets nor that Marxism showed its inherent emptiness. Instead there was an "unwarranted retention of too much traditional Marxist baggage" (p. xvii).

61. David Held, *Introduction to Critical Theory: Horkheimer to Habermas* (Berkeley: University of California Press, 1980), pp. 364–74.

62. "The concept of critique is compromised by its ties with the myth of Enlightenment, the view of history as one all-embracing process in which a historical subject attains its essence, autonomy. And the critique of political economy is comprised by a vision of heteronomy peculiar to German social theory, issuing from its characteristic conflation of features specific to the capitalist process of production and features specific to instrumental rationality." Paul Connerton, *The Tragedy of Enlightenment: An Essay on the Frankfurt School* (Cambridge: Cambridge University Press, 1980), p. 131.

63. Ibid., pp. 135–39.

64. Lichtheim, *From Marx to Hegel*, p. 5.

65. In this connection see Andrew Feenberg, *Lukács, Marx and the Sources of Critical Theory* (Totowa, N. J.: Rowman and Littlefield, 1981). For a perceptive commentary, see the review essay by Robert D'Amico, "Feenberg on Lukács," *New German Critique*, no. 26 (Spring-Summer 1982), pp. 173–83.

66. Phil Slater, *Origin and Significance of the Frankfurt School: A Marxist Perspective* (London: Routledge & Kegan Paul, 1977), pp. xiv, 53–93, 144.

67. Günter Rohrmoser, *Das Elend der kritischen Theorie: Theodor W. Adorno, Herbert Marcuse, Jürgen Habermas* (Freiburg: Rombach, 1970), pp. 24, 28.

68. Arnold Künzli, *Aufklärung und Dialektik: Politische Philosophie von Hobbes bis Adorno* (Freiburg: Rombach, 1971), pp. 147–55.

69. Friedman, *Political Philosophy of the Frankfurt School*, pp. 154–67, 201, 246, 262–76.

70. See, for example, the following articles by Martin Puder: "Die Frankfurter Schule und die Neue Linke," *Neue Deutsche Hefte* 18 (1971) 1: 113–22; "Zur 'Ästhetischen Theorie' Adornos," *Neue Rundschau* 82 (1971): 465–77; "Adornos Philosophie und die gegenwärtige Erfahrung," *Neue Deutsche Hefte* 23 (1976): 3–26. See also the chapter titled "Kritiek op de Kritische Theorie" in Willem van Reijen, *Filosofie als Kritiek: Inleiding in de Kritische Theorie* (Alphen aan den Rijn/Brussels: Samson Uitgeverij, 1981), pp. 311–20.

71. Jürgen Habermas, *Theorie und Praxis. Sozialphilosophische Studien* (1967), 4th ed., revised and expanded (Frankfurt: Suhrkamp, 1971); trans. John Viertel (abridged ed.) as *Theory and Practice* (Boston: Beacon Press, 1973).

72. Held, *Introduction to Critical Theory*, pp. 398–400.

73. Rüdiger Bubner, *Modern German Philosophy*, trans. Eric Matthews (Cambridge: Cambridge University Press, 1981), pp. 169–202.

74. Bubner, "Theory and Practice in the Light of the Hermeneutic-Criticist Controversy," *Cultural Hermeneutics* 2 (1975): 337–52. This paper gives a précis of the argument developed in *Modern German Philosophy*. Earlier versions of the argument occur in Bubner's "Was ist kritische Theorie?" and " 'Philosophie ist ihre Zeit, in Gedanken erfasst' " in the anthology *Hermeneutik und Ideologiekritik* (Frankfurt am Main: Suhrkamp, 1971), pp. 160–209 and 210–43; "What Is Critical Theory?" and "Philosophy Is Its Time Comprehended in Thought," in Bubner's *Essays in Hermeneutics and Critical Theory*, trans. Eric Matthews (New York: Columbia University Press, 1988), pp. 1–35 and 37–61. For another hermeneutical critique of critical theory on theory and practice, see Michael Theunissen, *Gesellschaft und Geschichte: Zur Kritik der kritischen Theorie* (Berlin: Walter de Gruyter, 1969).

75. Jay, *Dialectical Imagination*, p. 4.

76. This point, or one like it, is made by Russell Jacoby, "Marxism and the Critical School," *Theory and Society* 1 (Summer 1974): 231–38; Douglas Kellner, "The Frankfurt School Revisited: A Critique of Martin Jay's *The Dialectical Imagination*," *New German Critique*, no. 4 (Winter 1975), pp. 131–52; and Phil Slater, *Origin and Significance of the Frankfurt School*, pp. xiv–xv. For Jay's response to Jacoby and Jacoby's reply to Jay, see

"Marxism and Critical Theory: Martin Jay and Russell Jacoby," *Theory and Society* 2 (1975): 257–63.

77. Dubiel, *Theory and Politics*, pp. 3–10 and passim.

78. Dubiel assumes that critical theory's "historical significance lies not so much in its political effect (which is in any case slight) or in its academic influence (which is declining) as in the enduring relevance of its theory-constitutive political and historical self-consciousness" (p. 6).

79. Lucio Colletti, *Marxism and Hegel* (1969), trans. Lawrence Garner (London: NLB, 1973; Verso, 1979), pp. 173–75. For a discussion of Colletti's attack, see Martin Jay, *Totality*, pp. 451–61.

80. Tom Bottomore, *The Frankfurt School* (New York: Tavistock Publications, 1984), pp. 35–49.

81. Ibid., pp. 23–24.

82. Therborn, "Frankfurt School," pp. 79, 84.

83. Leszek Kolakowski, *Main Currents of Marxism*, vol. 3, pp. 376–79. Related arguments occur in Zoltán Tar's *The Frankfurt School: The Critical Theories of Max Horkheimer and Theodor W. Adorno* (New York: John Wiley, 1977). Tar's general thesis "seems to be that Horkheimer and Adorno are better left unread," according to Charles Dyke's review in *The Journal of Aesthetics and Art Criticism* 37 (Winter 1978): 222–23. The book has been harshly criticized by Paul Harrison in *Telos*, no. 37 (Fall 1978), pp. 220–26, and by Martin Jay, "Critical Theory Criticized: Zoltán Tar and the Frankfurt School," *Central European History* 12 (March 1979): 91–98. Similar reactions have been provoked by Axel van den Berg's claim that the critical theorists' "greatest failure" is their inability "to understand that 'positivism' (i.e., empiricism and simple straightforward logic) is not at all inimical or irrelevant to practical concerns." See his "Critical Theory: Is There Still Hope?," *American Journal of Sociology* 86 (November 1980): 449–78, as well as the comments by Philip Wexler, Lawrence Parker, and David Ashley and the reply by van den Berg in *American Journal of Sociology* 88 (May 1983): 1250–70.

84. Friedman, *Political Philosophy of the Frankfurt School*, pp. 279–301. In this connection see Russell Jacoby's scathing review of Friedman's book in *Telos*, no. 49 (Fall 1981), pp. 203–5.

85. Because Wellmer has done the most to carry his criticisms into the area of aesthetics, I shall focus on his account. I shall also omit the objections of hermeneutical critics, which were indicated in the earlier discussion of culture and capitalism. Habermas has been devoting more attention to aesthetics in recent years. His aesthetics, such as it is, is discussed by several essays in *The Aesthetics of the Critical Theorists: Studies on Benjamin, Adorno, Marcuse, and Habermas*, ed. Ronald Roblin (Lewiston, N.Y.: Edwin Mellen Press, 1990). See in particular David Ingram, "Completing the Project of Enlightenment: Habermas on Aesthetic Rationality" (pp. 359–421), Margaret Rose, "Habermas and Postmodern Architecture" (pp. 422–39), Stephen K. White, "Foucault's Challenge to Critical Theory" (pp. 440–75), and Thomas L. Dumm, "The Politics of Post-Modern Aesthetics: Habermas Contra Foucault" (pp. 476–510).

86. Albrecht Wellmer, "Communications and Emancipation: Reflections on the Linguistic Turn in Critical Theory," in *On Critical Theory*, ed. John O'Neill (New York: Seabury Press, 1976), pp. 231–63. See also the chapter on "The Latent Positivism of

Marx's Philosophy of History" in Wellmer's *Critical Theory of Society* (1969), trans. John Cumming (New York: Herder and Herder, 1971), pp. 67–119.

87. Ibid., p. 245.

88. Wellmer, "Reason, Utopia, and the Dialectic of Enlightenment," *Praxis International* 3 (July 1983): 83–107. This article has been republished in Richard J. Bernstein, ed., *Habermas and Modernity* (Cambridge, Mass.: MIT Press, 1985), pp. 35–66.

89. Ibid., p. 92.

90. Jürgen Habermas, "The Entwinement of Myth and Enlightenment: Max Horkheimer and Theodor Adorno," in *The Philosophical Discourse of Modernity: Twelve Lectures* (1985), trans. Frederick Lawrence (Cambridge, Mass.: MIT Press, 1987), pp. 106–130; the quotes are from p. 119. For an earlier version of this article, see "The Entwinement of Myth and Enlightenment: Re-Reading *Dialectic of Enlightenment*," *New German Critique*, no. 26 (Spring-Summer 1982), pp. 13–30.

91. Raymond Geuss, *The Idea of a Critical Theory: Habermas and the Frankfurt School* (Cambridge: Cambridge University Press, 1981), p. 95.

92. Robert Hullot-Kentor, "Back to Adorno," *Telos*, no. 81 (Fall 1989), pp. 5–29.

2 Aesthetic Debates

1. Stefan Morawski, "Introduction," *Karl Marx/Frederick Engels on Literature and Art*, ed. Lee Baxandall and Stefan Morawski (New York: International General, 1973), pp. 3–47. The list in Eugene Lunn's *Marxism and Modernism*, pp. 9–32 is similar: art as a production for human purposes; the alienation and commodification of artistic labor under capitalist conditions; the ideological and utopian functions of art within a base/superstructure model of society; and the value of literary realism in the context of a form/content distinction.

2. There is much more literature on Marxian and Marxist aesthetics than standard anthologies in Anglo-American aesthetics would indicate. A recent anthology on critical-theory aesthetics is *The Aesthetics of the Critical Theorists* (Edwin Mellen Press, 1990). Two fine accounts of Marxian aesthetics are Mikhail Lifschitz, *The Philosophy of Art of Karl Marx* (London: Pluto Press, 1973), and Margaret Rose, *Marx's Lost Aesthetic: Karl Marx and the Visual Arts* (Cambridge: Cambridge University Press, 1984). Useful historical surveys of Marxist aesthetics include Henri Arvon, *Marxist Esthetics* (1970), trans. Helen R. Lane (Ithaca: Cornell University Press, 1973), and Dave Laing, *The Marxist Theory of Art* (Sussex: Harvester Press; Atlantic Highlands, N. J.: Humanities Press, 1978). For two contrasting approaches to Marx's legacy in aesthetics see Ernst Fischer, *The Necessity of Art* (1959), trans. Anna Bostock (Harmondsworth: Penguin Books, 1963), and Adolfo Sánchez Vásquez, *Art and Society: Essays in Marxist Aesthetics* (1965), trans. Maro Riofrancos (New York: Monthly Review Press, 1973). Three influential attempts to develop a Marxist literary theory in an Anglo-American context are Raymond Williams, *Marxism and Literature* (Oxford: Oxford University Press, 1977); Fredric Jameson, *The Political Unconscious: Narrative as a Socially Symbolic Act* (Ithaca: Cornell University Press, 1981); and Terry Eagleton, *Literary Theory: An Introduction* (Minneapolis: University of Minnesota Press, 1983). Standard bibliographies of publications in English include *Marxism and Aesthetics: A Selective Annotated Bibliography*, comp. Lee Baxandall (New York: Humanities Press, 1968), and *Guide to Marxist Literary Criticism*, comp. Chris Bullock and David Peck (Bloomington: Indiana University Press, 1980).

3. Jürgen Habermas, "Walter Benjamin: Consciousness-Raising or Rescuing Critique" (1972), in *Philosophical-Political Profiles*, trans. Frederick G. Lawrence (Cambridge, Mass.: MIT Press, 1983), pp. 131–65; the quote is from p. 155.

4. This focus on the Adorno-Benjamin debate has shaped much of the English language reception of Adorno's aesthetics. The debate is used to assess Adorno's aesthetics in Susan Buck-Morss's *The Origin of Negative Dialectics* (1977), Eugene Lunn's *Marxism and Modernism* (1982), and Richard Wolin's *Walter Benjamin: An Aesthetic of Redemption* (1982). See also Peter U. Hohendahl, "Autonomy of Art: Looking Back at Adorno's *Ästhetische Theorie*," *German Quarterly* 54 (March 1981): 133–48, and Sabine Wilke, "'Torn Halves of an Integral Freedom': Adorno's and Benjamin's Readings of Mass Culture," in *The Aesthetics of the Critical Theorists*, pp. 124–51.

5. The main writings in dispute were "The Work of Art in the Age of Mechanical Reproduction" (–1935+1936), in Walter Benjamin, *Illuminations*, pp. 217–51; and two essays derived from Benjamin's larger *Passagenarbeit* and titled "Paris, The Capital of the Nineteenth Century" (1935, also known as the Arcades Exposé) and "The Paris of the Second Empire in Baudelaire," both contained in *Charles Baudelaire: A Lyric Poet in the Era of High Capitalism*, trans. Harry Zohn (London: NLB, 1973), pp. 155–76 and 9–107 respectively. One could add to these writings "Some Motifs in Baudelaire" (1939), in *Charles Baudelaire*, pp. 107–154, although Buck-Morss says this essay abandons the positions that had elicited Adorno's objections (*Origin*, pp. 159–63). The most important correspondence between Adorno and Benjamin concerning these essays is translated in *Aesthetics and Politics*, ed. Ronald Taylor (London: NLB, 1977; Verso, 1980), pp. 110–41. German versions of Adorno's letters are contained in his *Über Walter Benjamin* (Frankfurt: Suhrkamp, 1970).

6. The translation in *Illuminations*, pp. 217–51, of "Das Kunstwerk im Zeitalter seiner technischen Reproduzierbarkeit" follows the so-called "Zweite Fassung" in Benjamin's *Gesammelte Schriften* 1:2, pp. 471–508. For details on the drafts and revisions of this essay, see Buck-Morss, *Origin*, pp. 286–87, n. 98; and Wolin, *Walter Benjamin*, pp. 183–84. The essay's title is correctly retranslated as "The Work of Art in the Age of Its Technical Reproducibility" in the excerpt in *Art and Its Significance: An Anthology of Aesthetic Theory*, 2d ed., ed. Stephen David Ross (Albany: State University of New York Press, 1987), pp. 527–39.

7. "Über den Fetischcharakter in der Musik und die Regression des Hörens," in GS 14 (D 1956): 14–50; trans. in *The Essential Frankfurt School Reader*, pp. 270–99. The preface to the third edition of *Dissonanzen* (1963) describes the essay as the first distillation of Adorno's American experiences when he was working on the Princeton Radio Research Project under the direction of Paul Lazarsfeld. Adorno also reports that the essay was intended as a response to Benjamin's "Work of Art" essay. See GS 14: 9–10. See also Adorno's "Scientific Experiences of a European Scholar in America" and Lazarsfeld's "An Episode in the History of Social Research: A Memoir" in *The Intellectual Migration: Europe and America, 1930–1960*, ed. Donald Fleming and Bernard Bailyn (Cambridge, Mass.: Harvard University Press, 1969). A German version of Adorno's article is contained in GS 10.2 (S, "Wissenschaftliche Erfahrungen in Amerika," 1968/1969): 702–738.

8. My summary does not emphasize contrasts in subject matter, methodology, and political orientation, even though these play a large role in the dispute. Benjamin's essay is a meditative discourse on the visual arts and film whose political orientation is the struggle of the working class against fascism. Adorno's essay is a dialectical critique of mass mediated music whose political orientation is an opposition to advanced capitalism. Whereas Buck-Morss emphasizes contrasts in methodology and political orientation, Lunn emphasizes contrasts between Benjamin's artistic orientation

to symbolism and surrealism and Adorno's orientation to expressionism. The importance of "structural differences in medium and genre" is mentioned by Fredric Jameson, "Reflections in Conclusion," *Aesthetics and Politics*, p. 197.

9. Benjamin, *Illuminations*, p. 229.

10. Ibid., p. 234.

11. GS 14 (D, "Fetischcharakter," 1938/1956): 46–47; trans., pp. 295–96.

12. Benjamin, *Illuminations*, pp. 223–25.

13. Ibid., p. 231.

14. Ibid., p. 241.

15. GS 14 (D, "Fetischcharakter," 1938/1956): 24–26; trans., pp. 278–79.

16. Ibid., p. 34; trans. p. 286.

17. Ibid., pp. 47–50; trans., pp. 296–99. Adorno's claim that modern music liquidates the aura of traditional art comes out more clearly in his letter of 18 March 1936 to Walter Benjamin, in WB 126–34; trans. in *Aesthetics and Politics*, pp. 120–26.

18. Letter of 18 March 1936 to Walter Benjamin, in WB 129; trans. in *Aesthetics and Politics*, p. 123. A related formulation occurs in the "Fetish-Character" article: "The unity of the two spheres of music is thus that of an unresolved contradiction. . . . The whole can not be put together by adding the separated halves, but in both there appear, however distantly, the changes of the whole, which only moves in contradiction. . . . Between incomprehensibility and inescapability, there is no third way; the situation has polarized itself into extremes which actually meet." GS 14 (D, "Fetischcharakter," 1938/1956): 20–21; trans., p. 275.

19. Representative of these reactions are Slater's *Origin and Significance of the Frankfurt School* (1977) and Lunn's *Marxism and Modernism* (1982). In his "The Frankfurt School in the Development of the Mass Culture Debate (*The Aesthetics of the Critical Theorists*, pp. 26–84), however, Eugene Lunn defends Adorno from charges of elitism made by pluralistic defenders of popular culture such as Herbert Gans.

20. For varying accounts of the realism controversy see Werner Mittenzwei, "The Brecht-Lukács Debate," in *Preserve and Create: Essays in Marxist Literary Criticism*, ed. Gaylord C. LeRoy and Ursula Beitz (New York: Humanities Press, 1973), pp. 199–230; the anthology *Aesthetics and Politics*, pp. 60–99; and Eugene Lunn, *Marxism and Modernism*, pp. 73–145.

21. Leon Trotsky, *Literature and Revolution* (1923) (Ann Arbor: University of Michigan Press, 1960), p. 14.

22. For an introduction to radical art groups after the October Revolution and their impact on Brecht, see Arvon, *Marxist Esthetics*, pp. 56–82; for a survey of Trotsky's criticisms of these groups, see Laing, *The Marxist Theory of Art*, pp. 20–45.

23. Trotsky, *Literature and Revolution*, p. 236.

24. Lunn, *Marxism and Modernism*, pp. 73–145, gives an excellent account of these political differences in the context of the Lukács/Brecht controversy.

25. See, for example, the books by Slater and Buck-Morss cited above.

26. GS 11 (NL III, "Engagement," 1962): 409–430; trans. "Commitment," *The Essential Frankfurt School Reader,* pp. 300–318; also in *Aesthetics and Politics,* pp. 177–95. Translation citations will be from *The Essential Frankfurt School Reader.* Adorno reports that this essay originated as a talk broadcast on Radio Bremen, 28 March 1962 (GS 11: 699).

27. In *The Essential Frankfurt School Reader,* pp. 255–69; also in Walter Benjamin, *Understanding Brecht,* trans. Anna Bostock (London: NLB, 1973; Verso Edition, 1977), pp. 85–104. Citations will be from *The Essential Frankfurt School Reader.* Buck-Morss, *Origin,* p. 143, notes that the essay originated as a lecture to the Paris *Institute pour l'étude du fascisme,* a "Communist front organization." Although Adorno did not see the text of this lecture at the time, he was highly critical of Brechtian themes in other of Benjamin's writings, including the "Work of Art" essay.

28. Ibid., p. 256.

29. Ibid., p. 257.

30. Ibid., p. 261.

31. Ibid., pp. 266–67.

32. Ibid., pp. 267–69.

33. GS 11 (NL III, "Engagement," 1962): 430; trans., p. 318.

34. Ibid., pp. 417–18; trans., p. 308.

35. Ibid., p. 421; trans., p. 310.

36. This factor helped prompt Adorno's famous claim, reformulated in "Commitment," that writing lyric poetry after Auschwitz is barbaric. See GS 10.1 (P, "Kulturkritik und Gesellschaft," 1951): 30; *Prisms,* p. 34. Cf. GS 11 (NL III, "Engagement," 1962): 422–27; trans., pp. 312–15, and GS 10.2 (E, "Was bedeutet: Aufarbeitung der Vergangenheit," 1960): 555–72.

37. GS 11 (NL III, "Engagement," 1962): 429; trans., p. 317.

38. Ibid., p. 430; trans., p. 318.

39. Ibid., p. 426; trans., pp. 314–15.

40. Cf. Jameson, "Reflections in Conclusion," *Aesthetics and Politics,* pp. 208–9.

41. In "The De-aestheticization of Art: On Adorno's *Aesthetische Theorie*," *Telos,* no. 41 (Fall 1979), pp. 105–127, Richard Wolin portrays Adorno's book as "a monumental effort to vindicate modernism, to authenticate its 'right to exist' from a historico-philosophical point of view, however precarious that right might appear in contrast with the grandeur of classical works of art" (p. 106). In "Adorno's Aesthetics of Illusion," *Journal of Aesthetics and Art Criticism* 44 (Winter 1985): 181–89, Thomas Huhn also interprets *Aesthetic Theory* as "a weighty defense of modern art" (p. 181), although he argues against Wolin that the crisis of the avant-garde should be described as a crisis of illusion rather than a crisis of identity. Janelle Reinelt, "Approaching the Postmodernist Threshold: Samuel Beckett and Bertolt Brecht," in *The Aesthetics of the*

Critical Theorists, pp. 337–58, points out both modern and postmodern tendencies in Adorno's approach to Beckett and Brecht as well as in both Beckett and Brecht.

42. Adorno, "Erpresste Versöhnung. Zu Georg Lukács: 'Wider den missverstandenen Realismus,' " *Der Monat* 11 (November 1958): 37–49; republished in *Noten zur Literatur* II (Frankfurt: Suhrkamp, 1961); now in GS 11 (1974): 251–80; trans. as "Reconciliation under Duress" in *Aesthetics and Politics*, pp. 151–76.

43. Lukács, "Preface" (1962), *The Theory of the Novel*, p. 22.

44. Georg Lukács, *Realism in Our Time: Literature and the Class Struggle*, trans. John and Necke Mander, Preface by George Steiner (New York: Harper & Row, 1964); first published under the title *The Meaning of Contemporary Realism* (London: Merlin Press, 1962). The book originated in lectures given at the Deutsche Akademie der Künste in January 1956 and repeated several times in Poland, Italy, and Austria. The book's German title—*Wider den missverstandenen Realismus* (Hamburg: Claassen Verlag, 1958)—has been replaced with the original title—"Die Gegenwartsbedeutung des kritischen Realismus"—in Georg Lukács, *Essays über Realismus, Probleme des Realismus I*, *Werke*, vol. 4 (Neuwied: Luchterhand, 1971), pp. 457–603.

45. Lukács, "Die Gegenwartsbedeutung," *Werke* 4: 551; trans., p. 93.

46. GS 11 (NL II, "Erpresste Versöhnung," 1958): 259–62; trans., pp. 158–62.

47. Ibid., pp. 265, 273–74; trans., pp. 163, 171–72.

48. Ibid., pp. 265–66, 278–79; trans., pp. 163–64, 175–76.

49. The methodological contrasts between Lukács and Adorno are discussed at greater length in the author's "Methodological Shadowboxing in Marxist Aesthetics: Lukács and Adorno," in *The Aesthetics of the Critical Theorists*, pp. 244–90.

50. Among the many discussions of this topic, the following are most instructive: Burkhardt Lindner, "Der Begriff der Verdinglichung und der Spielraum der Realismus-Kontroverse" (pp. 91–123) and Peter V. Zima, "Dialektik zwischen Totalität und Fragment" (pp. 124–72), in *Der Streit mit Georg Lukács*, ed. Hans-Jürgen Schmitt (Frankfurt: Suhrkamp, 1978); Dieter Kliche, "Kunst gegen Verdinglichung: Berührungspunkte im Gegensatz von Adorno und Lukács," in *Materialien zur ästhetischen Theorie Theodor W. Adornos*, pp. 219–60; the chapter "The Lament over Reification" in Gillian Rose, *The Melancholy Science*, pp. 27–51; and the chapter "Theodor W. Adorno and the Collapse of the Lukácsian Concept of Totality" in Martin Jay, *Marxism and Totality*, pp. 241–75.

51. Burkhardt Lindner, "Der Begriff der Verdinglichung," pp. 91–123.

52. GS 11 (NL II, "Erpresste Versöhnung," 1958): 263; trans., p. 161.

3 Philosophical Motivations

1. Jay, *Adorno*, p. 11.

2. Fredric Jameson, "T. W. Adorno; or, Historical Tropes," *Marxism and Form: Twentieth-Century Dialectical Theories of Literature* (Princeton: Princeton University Press, 1971), p. 3.

3. Rose, *The Melancholy Science,* pp. ix–x.

4. These uncompleted changes and the history of Adorno's manuscript are described in the "Editors' Epilogue" (AT 537–44/493–98). The woes of the translator were compounded by wrangling between the German and English publishers. In *Telos,* no. 65 (Fall 1985), see Bob Hullot-Kentor, "Adorno's *Aesthetic Theory:* The Translation" (pp. 143–47), and Christian Lenhardt, "Reply to Hullot-Kentor" (pp. 147–52).

5. Weber, in *Prisms,* pp. 12–13.

6. Rose, *The Melancholy Science,* p. 12.

7. Ibid., p. 25.

8. ND 44/33–34.

9. "Ohne Leitbild" originated as a radio address and was first published in *Neue Deutsche Hefte* (1960); it was republished as the lead essay in the collection *Ohne Leitbild. Parva Aesthetica* (1967, 1968); it is now in GS 10.1: 291–301. "Wozu noch Philosophie" also originated as a radio address; it was first published in *Merkur* in 1962; after being revised it became the lead essay in *Eingriffe. Neun kritische Modelle* (1963); now in GS 10.2: 459–73. "Parataxis. Zur späten Lyrik Hölderlins" was presented to the annual conference of the Hölderlin-Gesellschaft in June 1963; an expanded version was published in *Neue Rundschau* (1964); it was reprinted in *Noten zur Literatur* III (1965), and is now in GS 11: 447–91.

10. GS 5 (ME 1956): 3/12. See also the author's review of *Against Epistemology* in *Canadian Philosophical Reviews* 4 (April 1984) 2: 49–52.

11. Ibid., pp. 15–16/7. Similar formulations occur throughout the writings of Adorno's last decade.

12. GS 5 (H, "Skoteinos oder Wie zu lesen sei," 1963): 330, 354–55.

13. ND 114/108.

14. In this connection see Matthias Tichy, *Theodor W. Adorno: Das Verhältnis von Allgemeinem und Besonderem in seiner Philosophie* (Bonn: Bouvier Verlag Herbert Grundmann, 1977).

15. GS 11 (NL I, "Der Essay als Form," 1958): 31–32; trans., pp. 169–70.

16. ND 148/144–45.

17. ND 17/5.

18. See, for example, ND 16–21/4–8.

19. ND 58/48.

20. ND 22/11.

21. MM, sec. 98, p. 171/152.

22. ND 39–42/28–31.

23. Compare MM, sec. 153, p. 281/247 with ND 385–86/393 and 396–97/404–5.

24. ND 21/9–10 and 114–16/108–110.

25. GS 11 (NL I, "Der Essay als Form," 1958): 21; trans., p. 161.

26. Buck-Morss, *Origin of Negative Dialectics*, pp. 186, 190. For similar reasons Adorno would have questioned Gillian Rose's claim that "the philosophical and sociological principles which structure his criticism of philosophy, sociology, music and literature are always the same" (*The Melancholy Science*, p. 10).

27. Cf. PM 32–35/24–28; MM 14–15/16; GS 5 (ME 1956): 12–15/3–6.

28. ND 349/356.

29. MM, sec. 29, p. 55/50: "The whole is the untrue." Hegel's dictum was "The True is the whole." Cf. Georg Wilhelm Friedrich Hegel, *Phänomenologie des Geistes* (1807), 6th ed., ed. Johannes Hoffmeister (Hamburg: Felix Meiner, 1952), p. 21; *Phenomenology of Spirit*, trans. A. V. Miller (Oxford: Oxford University Press, 1977), p. 11.

30. In a line dropped from Lenhardt's translation, Adorno says: "Art exists only in relationship to its other; art is the process with its other" (GS 7: 12).

31. Adorno's thesis in *Philosophy of Modern Music* illuminates all of his writings on the arts. There he claims that contemporary philosophy of music is possible only as the philosophy of modern music because only in such music can one still pursue "the disclosure of truth in aesthetic objectivity" (PM 19/10).

32. The translation "to conceptualize categories of perdition as categories of transition" does not capture the sense of Adorno's "die untergehenden Kategorien als übergehende zu denken." Perhaps a better translation would be "to conceptualize irrelevant categories as transitional categories"—i.e., as categories that participate in a necessary historical development and that can taken on new meanings in the current situation.

33. One thinks in this connection of Pierre Bourdieu, *Distinction: A Social Critique of the Judgement of Taste* (1979), trans. Richard Nice (Cambridge, Mass.: Harvard University Press, 1984).

34. This is the subtitle of *Materialien zur ästhetischen Theorie Theodor W. Adornos: Konstruktion der Moderne*, the German anthology published ten years after Adorno's death. See especially the editors' "Kritische Theorie und ästhetisches Interesse: Notwendige Hinweise zur Adorno-Diskussion" (pp. 11–37) and Burkhardt Lindner's " 'Il faut être absolument moderne.' Adornos Ästhetik: Ihr Konstruktionsprinzip und ihre Historizität" (pp. 261–309).

35. Buck-Morss, *Origin of Negative Dialectics*, pp. 90–110.

36. GS 5 (H, "Skoteinos oder Wie zu lesen sei," 1963): 334.

37. For passages illustrating the mixture of Benjaminian, Hegelian, and Husserlian elements in Adorno's "phenomenology," see GS 1 ("Die Aktualität der Philosphie," –1931): 325–44, trans. as "The Actuality of Philosophy"; GS 1 ("Thesen über die Sprache des Philosophen," –1931): 366–71; and ND 61–64/52–55 and 163–74/161–72. For cautious appreciations of Husserl and the "material phenomenology" of Hed-

wig Conrad-Martius and Max Scheler, see GS 5 (H, "Skoteinos," 1963): 337–41; PT 1: 197; and ND 21–25/9–14.

38. ND 62–63/52–53 and 163–66/161–63.

39. A classic and widely anthologized statement of the anti-essentialist position is by Morris Weitz, "The Role of Theory in Aesthetics," *Journal of Aesthetics and Art Criticism* 15 (September 1956): 27–35. For refinements of Weitz's position, see his article on "Art as an Open Concept" in *Aesthetics: A Critical Anthology*, ed. George Dickie, Richard Sclafani, and Ronald Roblin, 2d ed. (New York: St. Martin's Press, 1989), pp. 152–59. The same anthology (pp. 653–55) contains a useful bibliography on the debate over defining art in analytic aesthetics since the 1950s.

4 Society's Social Antithesis

1. Marcia Muelder Eaton, *Basic Issues in Aesthetics* (Belmont, Calif.: Wadsworth, 1988), pp. 76–103.

2. Karl Marx, *A Contribution to the Critique of Political Economy* (1859), trans. S. W. Ryazanskaya, Introduction by Maurice Dobb (New York: International Publishers, 1970), pp. 19–23. The central passage is reprinted in *Marx/Engels on Literature and Art*, ed. Lee Baxandall and Stefan Morawski (New York: International General, 1973), pp. 85–86.

3. This usage is compatible with the "functional sense" of "ideology" in Marx's writings, as described by Allen Wood, *Karl Marx* (London: Routledge & Kegan Paul, 1981), pp. 117–20. Wood distinguishes this sense from "historical idealism" and "ideological illusion."

4. This is the way Lunn construes the opening pages of Marx's *Eighteenth Brumaire of Louis Bonaparte* in *Marxism and Modernism*, pp. 18–20. The limitations of such a construal for understanding race and gender oppression are illustrated and criticized by Douglas Kellner, "Critical Theory and Ideology Critique," in *The Aesthetics of the Critical Theorists*, pp. 85–123.

5. Fredric Jameson, *The Political Unconscious: Narrative as a Socially Symbolic Act* (Ithaca: Cornell University Press, 1981), pp. 23–58. Althusser applies these labels to three historical forms of causality or "effectivity."

6. Ibid., p. 36.

7. Terry Eagleton, *Marxism and Literary Criticism* (London: Methuen, 1976), p. 75. Eagleton's approach in this book fuses a Brechtian Benjamin with the Althusserian structuralism of Pierre Macherey's *Pour une théorie de la production littéraire* (Paris, 1970); *A Theory of Literary Production*, trans. Geoffrey Wall (London: Routledge & Kegan Paul, 1978).

8. Karl Marx, *Capital: A Critique of Political Economy*, vol. 1: *The Process of Capitalist Production*, trans. Samuel Moore and Edward Aveling, ed. Frederick Engels (New York: International Publishers, 1967), pp. 71–83.

9. Ibid., pp. 193–98.

10. Ibid., p. 8.

11. Ibid., p. 72.

12. Ibid., p. 81.

13. Ibid., p. 78.

14. Lukács, *History and Class Consciousness*, pp. 83–85.

15. Ibid., p. 84.

16. Ibid., p. 93.

17. Ibid., p. 168.

18. ND 190–93/189–92.

19. GS 14 (D, "Über den Fetischcharakter in der Musik und die Regression des Hörens," 1938/1956): 321–56; trans. in *The Essential Frankfurt School Reader*, pp. 270–99.

20. See in this connection Adorno's "Veblen's Attack on Culture: Remarks Occasioned by the Theory of the Leisure Class," *Studies in Philosophy and Social Science* 9 (1941): 389–413. A German version published in 1953 is reprinted in GS 10.1 (P, "Veblens Angriff auf die Kultur"): 72–96; trans. in *Prisms*, pp. 75–94.

21. Rose, *The Melancholy Science*, pp. 27–51. For another discussion of Adorno's reception of the theory of reification, see Friedemann Grenz, *Adornos Philosophie in Grundbegriffen* (Frankfurt: Suhrkamp, 1974), pp. 35–56.

22. GS 14 (D, "Fetischcharakter," 1938/1956): 24–25; trans., pp. 278–79. Cf. AT 33, 39.

23. Benjamin, *Illuminations*, pp. 222–23, 230–32, 239–41.

24. GS 14 (D, "Fetischcharakter," 1938/1956): 25–27; trans., pp. 279–80.

25. See Adorno's essay on changes in ideology and in its concept, SE (1956, "Ideologie"): 162–81/182–205. An earlier version can be found in GS 8 ("Beitrag zur Ideologienlehre," 1954): 457–77.

26. Concerning the political and economic theories behind Adorno's social theory, see Giacomo Marramao, "Political Economy and Critical Theory," *Telos*, no. 24 (1975), pp. 56–80; a different translation of this article appears in *Foundations of the Frankfurt School of Social Research*, pp. 323–39.

27. See Adorno's letter dated 18 March 1936 in WB 126–34; trans. in *Aesthetics and Politics*, pp. 120–26.

28. SE (1956, "Ideologie"): 178–79/202–3.

29. Ibid., p. 176/198–99.

30. For an extended discussion of the "pure immanence of culture industry" and the "monadological character of autonomous music" as complementary extremes, see Martin Zenck, *Kunst als begriffslose Erkenntnis*, pp. 60–92.

31. Adorno, letter dated 1 February 1939, WB 157–60.

32. Paul Connerton, *The Tragedy of Enlightenment* (1980), p. 51. Connerton's entire chapter on "The Critique of Ideology" (pp. 42–59) is worth reading in this connection.

33. DA 141–91/120–67.

34. Christel Beier, *Zum Verhältnis von Gesellschaftstheorie und Erkenntnistheorie. Untersuchungen in der kritischen Theorie Adornos* (Frankfurt: Suhrkamp, 1977), pp. 93–94.

35. ND 149–50/146–47.

36. GS 10.1 (P, "Kulturkritik und Gesellschaft," 1951): 25; *Prisms*, p. 30.

37. Adorno's mature social theory is contained in three articles on society and two essays on the social sciences: GS 8 ("Gesellschaft," 1966): 9–19, trans. as "Society," *Salmagundi*, no. 10–11 (Fall 1969—Winter 1970), pp. 144–53; GS 8 ("Spätkapitalismus oder Industriegesellschaft?" 1968): 354–70, trans. as "Is Marx Obsolete?", *Diogenes*, no. 64 (Winter 1968), pp. 1–16; GS 8 ("Diskussionsbeitrag zu 'Spätkapitalismus oder Industriegesellschaft?'," 1969): 578–87; GS 8 ("Einleitung zum *Positivismusstreit in der deutschen Soziologie*," 1969, and "Zur Logik der Sozialwissenschaften," 1962): 280–353, 547–65, trans. as "Introduction" and "On the Logic of the Social Sciences" in *The Positivist Dispute in German Sociology*, pp. 1–67, 105–122.

38. GS 8 ("Gesellschaft," 1966): 9–10; trans., pp. 144–45. Cf. SE (1956, "Gesellschaft"): 22–23/16–17.

39. GS 8 ("Über Statik und Dynamik als soziologische Kategorien," 1956/1961): 228–29; trans. as " 'Static' and 'Dynamic' as Sociological Categories," *Diogenes*, no. 33 (Spring 1961), pp. 39–41.

40. Marx's laws of value and accumulation provide "models" for Adorno's conception of constituents and tendencies. See GS 8 ("Einleitung zum *Positivismusstreit*," 1969): 322–24, trans., pp. 39–40; and GS 8 ("Spätkapitalismus," 1968): 356, trans., pp. 2–3.

41. GS 8 ("Über Statik und Dynamik," 1956/1961): 234; trans., pp. 45–46. Cf. SE (1956, "Gesellschaft"): 30/26.

42. GS 8 ("Diskussionsbeitrag," 1969): 583–86.

43. See, for example, the contrasting interpretations of Herman Mörchen, *Macht und Herrschaft im Denken von Heidegger und Adorno* (Stuttgart: Klett-Cotta, 1980) and Paul Connerton, *The Tragedy of Enlightenment*.

44. ND 314/320.

45. DA 38/21.

46. GS 10.2 (S, "Fortschritt," 1964): 618–20; trans. as "Progress," *The Philosophical Forum* 15 (Fall-Winter 1983–84): 56–57.

47. GS 8 ("Diskussionsbeitrag," 1969): 586.

48. Ibid., p. 585. Cf. GS 8 ("Über Statik und Dynamik," 1956/1961): 233; trans., p. 44.

49. This is what the world would become if Marx had his way, according to Adorno's interview with Martin Jay (*Dialectical Imagination*, p. 259).

50. GS 8 ("Gesellschaft," 1966): 17–19; trans., pp. 151–53.

51. GS 8 ("Spätkapitalismus," 1968): 355; trans., p. 2.

52. GS 8 ("Gesellschaft," 1966): 14–16; trans., p. 149–50.

53. GS 8 ("Spätkapitalismus," 1968): 358–60; trans., pp. 4–7. For an earlier statement, see Adorno's "Reflexionen zur Klassentheorie," written in 1942, and published for the first time in GS 8 (1972): 373–91.

54. GS 8 ("Gesellschaft," 1966): 9–10; trans., pp. 144–45.

55. Ibid., pp. 11–12, 17–19; trans., pp. 146–47, 151–53. Cf. Marx, *Capital* 1: 78–80.

56. GS 8 ("Zur Logik der Sozialwissenschaften," 1962): 562; trans., p. 119. GS 6 (JE 1964): 454–55/62–63.

57. Cf. *Capital* 1: 166.

58. GS 8 ("Gesellschaft," 1966): 9–10; trans., pp. 144–45.

59. GS 8 ("Einleitung zum *Positivismusstreit*," 1969): 293–94; trans., pp. 13–14.

60. Ibid., pp. 290–93; trans., pp. 10–13. GS 8 ("Spätkapitalismus," 1969): 364–65; trans., pp. 10–11.

61. GS 8 ("Einleitung zum *Positivismusstreit*," 1969): 295–98; trans., pp. 15–17.

62. ND 180/178.

63. Lambert Zuidervaart, "The Artefactuality of Autonomous Art: Kant and Adorno," in *The Reasons of Art: Artworks and the Transformations of Philosophy*, ed. Peter McCormick (Ottawa: University of Ottawa Press, 1986), pp. 256–62.

64. See GS 16 (K, "Ideen zur Musiksoziologie," 1958): 9–23.

65. This tendency is clearest in Adorno's writings of the 1940s. For a humorous and biting criticism, see Karl Markus Michel, "Versuch, die 'Ästhetische Theorie' zu verstehen," in *Materialien zur ästhetischen Theorie Theodor W. Adornos*, pp. 41–107.

5 Art as Social Labor

1. Cf. GS 16 (K, "Ideen zur Musiksoziologie," 1958): 12.

2. Peter Bürger, "The Decline of the Modern Age," *Telos*, no. 62 (Winter 1984–85), pp. 117–30; the quote is from p. 120. In German, "Das Altern der Moderne," in *Adorno-Konferenz 1983*, ed. Ludwig von Friedeburg and Jürgen Habermas (Frankfurt: Suhrkamp, 1983), pp. 177–97.

3. Ibid., pp. 127, 129.

4. GS 14 (D, "Das Altern der Neuen Musik," 1955): 143–67; trans. as "The Aging of the New Music," *Telos*, no. 77 (Fall 1988), pp. 95–116. In a note on p. 95, the translators describe an earlier translation—"Modern Music Is Growing Old," *The Score*, no. 18 (December 1956), pp. 18–29—as a "peculiar, abbreviated and completely confabulated paraphrase of Adorno's essay." The essay originated as a lecture delivered at the Stuttgart Week of New Music in 1954. For an introduction that shows how Adorno's concept of musical material informs his criticisms of modern music, see Robert Hullot-Kentor, "Popular Music and Adorno's 'The Aging of the New Music'," *Telos*, no. 77 (Fall 1988), pp. 79–94.

5. See the section titled "Inherent Tendency of Musical Material" in PM 38–42/32–37.

6. Carl Dahlhaus, "Adornos Begriff des musikalischen Materials," in *Zur Terminologie der Musik des 20. Jahrhunderts*, ed. Hans Heinrich Eggebrecht (Stuttgart: Musikwissenschaftliche Verlags-Gesellschaft, 1974), pp. 9–21.

7. Peter Bürger, "Das Vermittlungsproblem in der Kunstsoziologie Adornos," in *Materialien zur ästhetischen Theorie Theodor W. Adornos*, pp. 169–84.

8. Dahlhaus, "Adornos Begriff des musikalischen Materials," pp. 13–15.

9. Tibor Kneif, *Musiksoziologie* (Cologne: Hans Gerig, 1971, 1975), pp. 96–97. Other instructive discussions of Adorno's concept of musical material include Günter Mayer, "Zur Dialektik des musikalischen Materials," (1966, 1969), and Konrad Boehmer, "Adorno, Musik, Gesellschaft" (1969), both reprinted in *Texte zur Musiksoziologie*, ed. Tibor Kneif, with an Introduction by Carl Dahlhaus (Cologne: Arno Volk, 1975), pp. 200–226 and pp. 227–38, respectively; and Wolfgang Burde, "Versuch über einen Satz Theodor W. Adornos," *Neue Zeitschrift für Musik* 132 (1971): 578–83. For a careful study that connects Adorno's developing concept of musical material with the question of artistic truth, see Lucia Sziborsky, *Adornos Musikphilosophie. Genese—Konstitution—Pädagogische Perspektive* (Munich: Wilhelm Fink, 1979).

10. PM 39–40/33–34.

11. Bürger, "Vermittlungsproblem," p. 177.

12. PM 199/220. In "Adornos Begriff des musikalischen Materials," p. 17, Carl Dahlhaus correctly notes that paying more attention to the concrete work would have altered the concept of musical material. Adorno's approach in *Philosophy of Modern Music* necessitates an emphasis on musical material rather than on the musical work of art.

13. PM 42/36.

14. PM 11/xiii.

15. The best statement of Adorno's updating of Marx on Hegel is in GS 5 (H, "Aspekte," 1957): 251–94, especially 265–77.

16. Marx, "Critique of the Hegelian Dialectic and Philosophy as a Whole," *Economic and Philosophic Manuscripts of 1844*, in Karl Marx/Frederick Engels, *Collected Works* (New

York: International Publishers, 1975), 3: 332–33. Adorno quotes the same passage at GS 5 (H, "Aspekte," 1957): 265.

17. GS 5 (H, "Aspekte," 1957): 270–74.

18. Marx, *Capital* 1: 322–68.

19. GS 14 (1962/1968 EMS, "Vermittlung"): 403/202, 408/206.

20. This is one meaning of the "precedence of the object" in *Negative Dialectics*. See ND 184–87/183–86. See also ND 198–202/198–202, which restates the view of Hegel's *Geist* presented in GS 5 (H, "Aspekte," 1957): 265–77.

21. GS 14 (1962/1968 EMS, "Vermittlung"): 398–99/198.

22. Ibid., p. 413/211.

23. GS 8 ("Spätkapitalismus," 1969): 362–64; trans., pp. 8–11. Adorno's argument seems indebted to Friedrich Pollock's book on *Automation*. See, for example, the passage quoted by Giacomo Marramao, "Political Economy and Critical Theory," *Telos*, no. 24 (Summer 1975), p. 75.

24. Rose, *Melancholy Science*, p. 119.

25. Ibid., p. 120.

26. See especially GS 14 (1962/1968 EMS, "Vermittlung"; "Nachwort: Musiksoziologie"): 394–421/194–218; 422–33/219–33.

27. Ibid., pp. 402–7/201–5.

28. Ibid., pp. 402–3/201–2.

29. Ibid., p. 418/216.

30. Ibid., p. 425/222. After pointing out Adorno's inconsistency here, Karol Sauerland mentions displaying originality and not underselling as peculiarities of artistic production in its economic aspect. See *Einführung in die Ästhetik Adornos* (Berlin: Walter de Gruyter, 1979), pp. 101–2.

31. GS 14 (1962/1968 EMS, "Nachwort: Musiksoziologie"): 422/219.

32. Ibid., pp. 422–25/219–22.

33. Ibid., p. 425/221–22.

34. Bürger, "Vermittlungsproblem," pp. 172–74.

35. Cf. AT 503–4/464–66, where Adorno raises the question about the concrete possibility of art today and connects this question with the way in which "the pure mimetic impulse" has become unbearable within a system of complete instrumental rationality.

36. ND 193–94/192–94.

37. ND 203–4/204.

38. ND 178/176.

39. ND 221–22/221–23; 226–30/226–30.

40. Susan Buck-Morss uses this apt heading for a section in her chapter "Marx Minus the Proletariat: Theory as Praxis." Buck-Morss shows that, despite their differences, Adorno, Benjamin, and Brecht shared during the 1930s a conception of the role of intellectuals differing from Lukács's view: "according to Lukács, they were the *vanguard* of the Revolution; according to Adorno, they were the revolutionary *avant-garde" (The Origin of Negative Dialectics*, p. 32). Buck-Morss voices scepticism about Adorno's conception, which strikes her as elitist.

41. Letter dated 18 March 1936, WB 132; *Aesthetics and Politics*, p. 125.

42. DA 31/15. "Verschlungenheit" has no exact English equivalent. Cumming translates it as "intricacy." "Verschlingen" can mean to twist through or around but also to devour, to wolf down. "Verschlungen" can mean intricate, complex, or tortuous. In the immediate context there is a tone of savagery which "jungliness" echoes more adequately than "intricacy." This passage projects a particular experience of Western society in the early 1940s upon the experience of "primitive" human beings.

43. DA 32/16.

44. DA 19/3.

45. DA 56–60/38–42.

46. W. Martin Lüdke, *Anmerkungen zu einer "Logik des Zerfalls": Adorno—Beckett* (Frankfurt: Suhrkamp, 1981), pp. 53–68. Lüdke criticizes several German commentators for failing to distinguish sufficiently between mimicry and mimesis when they describe Adorno's position.

47. See Adorno's excursus on theories about the origin of art in AT 480–90/447–55. For further implications of Adorno's concept of mimesis, see DA 204–234/179–208.

48. When approaching from the side of human expression, one must keep in mind Adorno's anti-subjectivistic and anti-individualistic emphases on the objective and supraindividual character of artistic expression. Cf. AT 171/163–64.

49. AT 172/164–65. Cf. ND 202/202.

50. See GS 10.2 (S, "Fortschritt," 1964), 617–38; trans. as "Progress," *The Philosophical Forum* 15 (Fall-Winter 1983–84): 55–70.

51. Cf. AT 56–62/48–55, 68–74/60–68, 248–53/237–43, 285–87/273–76, 316–26/303–13, 384–86/366–69, 421–22/396–97, and 459–60/428–29.

52. Compare ND 50–53/40–42 with AT 68–70/61–64, 384–87/366–69.

53. Compare AT 197–98/189–91 with ND 179/177 and SE (1956, "Individuum"): 46–49/44–48.

54. ND 106/99, 176/174.

55. ND 183/182.

6 Political Migration

1. See Martin Zenck, *Kunst als begriffslose Erkenntnis*, pp. 93–162. Zenck's analysis forms a backdrop for much of the present chapter.

2. AT 317/304. Cf. GS 16 (K, "Musik und Technik," 1958): 229–48; trans. as "Music and Technique," *Telos*, no. 32 (Summer 1977), pp. 79–94.

3. PM 47/42.

4. See "Musical Logic and Speech Character" in Carl Dahlhaus, *The Idea of Absolute Music*, trans. Roger Lustig (Chicago: University of Chicago Press, 1989), pp. 103–116, where the notion of music's linguistic character is discussed as an aesthetic justification of autonomous instrumental music.

5. Soren Kierkegaard, *Either/Or* (1843), vol. 1, trans. David F. Swenson and Lillian Marvin Swenson, with revisions and a Foreword by Howard A. Johnson (Garden City, N.Y.: Doubleday, Anchor Books, 1959), pp. 68–69.

6. Dahlhaus, *The Idea of Absolute Music*, p. 115.

7. Ibid. Dahlhaus quotes from passages in GS 16 (Q, "Fragment über Musik und Sprache," 1953/1956): 251–56. A slightly different and expanded version can be found in GS 16 ("Musik, Sprache und ihr Verhältnis im gegenwärtigen Komponieren," 1953/1956): 649–64.

8. "*Tönend bewegte Formen* sind einzig und allein Inhalt und Gegenstand der Musik." Eduard Hanslick, *Vom Musikalisch-Schönen. Ein Beitrag zur Revision der Ästhetik der Tonkunst*, reprint of the 1st ed., Leipzig 1854 (Darmstadt: Wissenschaftliche Buchgesellschaft, 1976), p. 32. The translation of this sentence is from *On the Musically Beautiful: A Contribution towards the Revision of the Aesthetics of Music*, trans. and ed. from the 8th German ed. of 1891 by Geoffrey Payzant (Indianapolis: Hackett, 1986), p. 29. For an explanation and defense of this translation, see Payzant's "Hanslick, Sams, Gay, and 'Tönend bewegt Formen,' " *Journal of Aesthetics and Art Criticism* 40 (Fall 1981): 40–48.

9. Ibid., pp. 35, 51–52; trans., pp. 30, 44.

10. Ibid., pp. 32–35; trans., pp. 28–32.

11. Ibid., pp. 34–40, 102–4; trans., pp. 30–34, 82–83.

12. GS 16 ("Musik, Sprache und ihr Verhältnis," 1953/1956): 653–54. Cf. GS 16 (Q, "Fragment," 1953/1956): 255–56.

13. Ibid., pp. 649–50. Cf. GS 16: 251–52.

14. Langer, *Feeling and Form*, pp. 24–41.

15. GS 16 ("Musik, Sprache und ihr Verhältnis," 1953/1956): 650–52. Cf. GS 16: 252–54.

16. Ibid., pp. 652–54. Cf. GS 16: 254–56.

17. DA 25–27/9–11.

18. GS 16 ("Musik, Sprache und ihr Verhältnis," 1953/1956): 654.

19. Ibid., pp. 663–64. Cf. GS 16 (Q, "Vers une musique informelle," 1962/1963): 493–540, especially 537–38, and Martin Zenck, "Auswirkungen einer 'musique informelle' auf die neue Musik: Zu Theodor W. Adornos Formvorstellung," *International Review of the Aesthetics and Sociology of Music* 10 (1979) 2: 137–65.

20. Kaiser, *Benjamin. Adorno*, p. 163.

21. AT 336/322. Cf. AT 16–19/7–11, 384/366–67, 461–62/429–30.

22. It is of interest that Horkheimer wrote his doctoral thesis on "Zur Antinomie der teleologischen Urteilskraft" (1922) and his *Habilitationsschrift* on *Kants Kritik der Urteilskraft als Bindeglied zwischen theoretischer und praktischer Philosophie* (Stuttgart, 1925). Adorno's unsuccessful *Habilitationsschrift* on "Der Begriff des Unbewussten in der transcendentalen Seelenlehre" (1927) also discussed Kant's philosophy. All three works were written under the direction of Hans Cornelius in Frankfurt am Main.

23. The problem of nondiscursive knowledge lies in the foundations laid for modern aesthetics by Alexander Gottlieb Baumgarten. Baumgarten's definition of aesthetics contains a remarkable mixture of subject matter and method. The problem is considerably older, however. Adorno traces it back to the early stages of civilization and a Greek dispute about whether the similar or the dissimilar knows the similar. See GS 5 (ME 1956): 147–48/142–43.

24. Immanuel Kant, *Kritik der Urteilskraft* (1790), 6th ed., ed. Karl Vorländer (Hamburg: Felix Meiner, 1924), sec. 57, p. 198; *Critique of Judgment*, trans. Werner S. Pluhar (Indianapolis: Hackett, 1987), pp. 212–13.

25. Wulff Rehfus, "Theodor W. Adorno. Die Rekonstruktion der Wahrheit aus der Ästhetik," (Cologne: Universität zu Köln, Inaugural-Dissertation, 1976), pp. 73–75.

26. Kant, *Kritik der Urteilskraft*, sec. IV, p. 15; trans., p. 18.

27. The two poles of knowledge can also be read from the dialectic of nature and freedom that motivated Kant's *Critique of Judgment*. In this connection, see GS 10.2 (S, "Fortschritt," 1964): 627–28; trans. as "Progress," *The Philosophical Forum* 15 (Fall-Winter 1983–84): 62–63.

28. The digest that follows comes from DA 24–27/8–11, 33–36/17–19.

29. Ibid. Cf. ND 29/18, 39–42/28–31, 61–63/52–53, 65–66/55–57.

30. Zenck, *Kunst als begriffslose Erkenntnis*, p. 95.

31. Kant, *Kritik der Urteilskraft*, sec. 17, p. 77; trans., p. 84.

32. *Kritik der Urteilskraft*, secs. I, II, IX, pp. 6–12, 33–34; trans., pp. 9–15, 35–37. Cf. Odo Marquard, "Kant und die Wende zur Ästhetik," *Zeitschrift für philosophische Forschung* 16 (1962): 231–43, 363–74.

33. DA 56–60/38–42.

34. ND 294/299.

35. F. W. J. Schelling, *System des transzendentalen Idealismus* (1800), ed. Ruth-Eva Schulz, with an Introduction by Walter Schulz (Hamburg: Felix Meiner, 1957), pp. 284–92.

36. Ibid., pp. 297–98. Schelling adds that, upon completion, philosophy would flow back into the ocean of *Poesie*.

37. These traces seem to·be left behind by the writings of early Benjamin and Ernst Bloch. In *Philosophical-Political Profiles*, pp. 63–79, Jürgen Habermas portrays Bloch as "a Marxist Schelling."

38. ND 228–30/229–30.

39. For a discussion of such topics, see Hershel B. Chipp, *Picasso's Guernica: History, Transformations, Meanings* (Berkeley: University of California Press, 1988).

40. Adorno's interpretation of Hegel's idea of truth is contained in GS 5 (H, "Aspekte," 1957): 280–85.

41. See Lucia Sziborsky, "Das Problem des Verstehens und der Begriff der 'Adäquanz' bei Th. W. Adorno," in *Musik und Verstehen. Aufsätze zur semiotischen Theorie, Ästhetik und Soziologie der musikalischen Rezeption*, ed. Peter Faltin and Hans-Peter Reinecke (Cologne: Arno Volk/ Hans Gerig, 1973), pp. 289–305.

42. In GS 14 (1962/1968 EMS, "Typen musikalischen Verhaltens"): 178–98/1–20, Adorno proposes a typology that includes the expert, the good listener, the culture consumer, the emotional listener, the resentment listener, jazz experts and fans, those who listen for entertainment, and the musically indifferent or anti-musical. Experts capable of "structural hearing" are rarely found outside the circle of professional musicians. Although Adorno does not expect all listeners to become *experts*, he claims that the relatively small number of *good listeners* is diminishing. J. Broeckx discusses the "Ästhetische und soziologische Implikationen in Adornos 'Typen musikalischen Verhaltens' " in the journal *Studia Philosophica Gandensia*, vol. 9 (Adorno-Heft; Meppel, 1971), pp. 73–89.

43. Cf. PM 33–34/26–27, where Adorno briefly distinguishes his philosophical method from technical analysis, apologetic commentary, and music criticism.

44. See, for example, PT 1: 13, 101, where Adorno insists that the question of truth can only be applied to judgments not to concepts. A passage on AT 189/190 suggests that the moments of truth and falsity in the nondiscursive work of art derive from discursive judgments.

45. Michael Theunissen, *Gesellschaft und Geschichte: Zur Kritik der kritischen Theorie* (Berlin: Walter de Gruyter, 1969), pp. 4–12.

46. GS 10.2 (S, "Marginalien zur Theorie und Praxis," 1969): 759–82; the quote is from p. 769.

47. See Adorno's reply to this accusation in GS 10.2 ("Resignation," 1969): 794–99; trans. as "Resignation," *Telos*, no. 35 (Spring 1978), pp. 165–68.

7 Paradoxical Modernism

1. ND 359–60/366–67.

2. GS 11 (NL II, "Versuch, das Endspiel zu verstehen," 1961): 281–321; trans. as "Trying to Understand Endgame," New German Critique, no. 26 (Spring-Summer 1982), pp. 119–50. Beckett wrote Endgame, Waiting for Godot, and the novels Molloy, Malone Dies, and The Unnamable during the five years after 1945.

3. GS 11 (NL II, "Endspiel," 1961): 316; trans., p. 146. Cf. AT 370–71/353–54.

4. See also the two essays discussed in chapter 2 above: GS 11 (NL II, "Erpresste Versöhnung," 1958; NL III, "Engagement," 1962): 251–80, 409–430; trans. as "Reconciliation under Duress," in Aesthetics and Politics, pp. 151–76, and "Commitment," in The Essential Frankfurt School Reader, pp. 300–318.

5. GS 11 (NL II, "Endspiel," 1961): 284; trans., p. 122. Adorno's essay on Kafka develops a similar dilemma and criterion for philosophical interpretation. See GS 10.1 (P, "Aufzeichnungen zu Kafka," 1953): 254–87; Prisms, pp. 254–71.

6. Hegel's Philosophy of Right, trans. with notes by T. M. Knox (London: Oxford University Press, 1952), p. 11.

7. GS 10.2 (E, "Wozu noch Philosophie," 1962/1963): 471–73.

8. See Rüdiger Bubner, " 'Philosophie ist ihre Zeit, in Gedanken erfasst' " (1970), in Hermeneutik und Ideologiekritik, pp. 210–43; "Philosophy Is Its Time Comprehended in Thought," in Bubner's Essays in Hermeneutics and Critical Theory, pp. 37–61.

9. GS 11 (NL II, "Endspiel," 1961): 284; trans., p. 122.

10. W. Martin Lüdke, "Der Kronzeuge. Einige Anmerkungen zum Verhältnis Th. W. Adornos zu S. Beckett," in the anthology Theodor W. Adorno, pp. 136–49.

11. AT 130/124–25, 272/261–62. Cf. DA 35–36/19 and PM 124–26/131–33.

12. GS 11 (NL II, "Endspiel," 1961): 281; trans., p. 119. Martin Esslin makes a similar point in The Theatre of the Absurd (1961), revised ed. (Garden City, N.Y.: Doubleday, Anchor Books, 1969), p. 6.

13. The three sections of Adorno's Endgame essay fall roughly as follows: (1) GS 11: 284–300; trans., pp. 122–34; (2) GS 11: 300–316; trans., pp. 134–46; and (3) GS 11: 316–21; trans., pp. 146–50.

14. GS 11 (NL II, "Endspiel," 1961): 282; trans., p. 120. Cf. AT 516–17/475–77.

15. Gerhard Kaiser, Benjamin. Adorno, pp. 157–64.

16. GS 5 (H, "Skoteinos," 1963): 346–49.

17. GS 11 (NL II, "Endspiel," 1961): 316–21; trans., pp. 146–50. Cf. ND 372–74/379–81.

18. Samuel Beckett, Endgame (London: Faber and Faber, 1958; French edition © Editions de Minuit 1957, 1985), pp. 23–24. Reprinted by permission of Faber and Faber Ltd. and of Rosica Colin Ltd.

19. GS 11 (NL II, "Endspiel," 1961): 316; trans., p. 146.

20. Beckett, *Endgame*, p. 47.

21. GS 11 (NL II, "Endspiel," 1961): 318–19; trans., pp. 147–49.

22. Adorno writes concerning the names in *Endgame* that "Hamm" suggests Shakespeare's Hamlet as well as Noah's son, "Clov" abbreviates "clown" and recalls Stravinsky's "Ragtime for Eleven Instruments," "Nell" was used by Dickens in the *Old Curiosity Shop*, and "Nagg" is associated with nagging, *nagen* in German (GS 11: 310–16; trans., pp. 142–46). This interpretation is ponderous compared to Beckett's own: "Hamm" is short for hammer, "Clov" in French is *clou* (nail), "Nagg" abbreviates the German *Nagel*, "Nell" comes from nail; thus a play for one hammer and three nails! See Lüdke, "Der Kronzeuge," p. 148, n. 3.

23. GS 11 (NL II, "Endspiel," 1961): 319; trans., pp. 148–49.

24. ND 22/11. Cf. ND 128/122 and GS 11 ("Offener Brief an Rolf Hochhuth," 1967): 598.

25. Beckett, *Endgame*, pp. 39, 45.

26. GS 11 (NL II, "Endspiel," 1961): 321; trans., p. 150.

27. ND 374/381.

28. ND 314/320.

29. Jay, *Marxism and Totality*, passim, especially pp. 261–75.

30. ND 314/320.

31. Lüdke, *Anmerkungen zu einer "Logik des Zerfalls,"* p. 101.

32. Ibid., p. 111.

33. Peter Dews, *Logics of Distintegration: Post-structuralist Thought and the Claims of Critical Theory* (London, New York: Verso, 1987), p. 150.

34. Hegel, *Phänomenologie des Geistes*, pp. 161–62; *Phenomenology of Spirit*, p. 129.

35. Ibid., pp. 151–71; trans., pp. 119–38, where Hegel presents stoicism, skepticism, and the unhappy consciousness as phases of the "freedom of self-consciousness."

36. ND 203/203.

37. ND 393/401.

38. ND 34/23.

39. DA 52–54/34–37; GS 11 (NL II, "Endspiel," 1961): 312–16; trans., pp. 143–46.

40. ND 394/402.

41. ND 203/203.

42. DA 24–25/8–9; ND 187/186.

43. DA 201/177. Cf. DA 28/12 and 32–33/16–17.

44. Compare DA 21/5, 27/11, and 29–30/13–14 with DA 202–3/178 and 211/186.

45. DA 40/23, 44/27, 202–4/178–79, 225/199.

46. ND 163/160. Cf. ND 148–49/145.

47. ND 160/157.

48. Ibid. Cf. GS 11 (NL III, "Parataxis. Zur späten Lyrik Hölderlins," 1964): 447–91.

49. Cf. Werner Beierwaltes, "Adornos Nicht-Identisches," in *Weltaspekte der Philosophie. Rudolf Berlinger zum 26 Oktober 1972,* ed. Werner Beierwaltes and Wiebke Schrader (Amsterdam: Rodopi, 1972), p. 13.

50. G. W. F. Hegel, *Werke in Zwanzig Bänden,* ed. Eva Moldenhauer and Karl Markus Michel, vol. 13: *Vorlesungen über die Ästhetik* (Frankfurt: Suhrkamp, Theorie Werkausgabe, 1970), p. 14; *Aesthetics: Lectures on Fine Art,* trans. T. M. Knox, vol. 1 (Oxford: Oxford University Press, 1975), p. 2.

51. Ibid., p. 167; trans., p. 123.

52. Lüdke, *Anmerkungen zu einer "Logik des Zerfalls,"* pp. 43–44.

53. Freud's theory of sublimation is close to the accounts of beauty developed by Nietzsche and Adorno. Compare DA 61–63/43–46 and ND 34/23 with Walter Kaufmann, *Nietzsche: Philosopher, Psychologist, Antichrist* (1950), 4th ed. (Princeton: Princeton University Press, 1974), pp. 211–56.

54. ND 393/400.

55. PM 24–28/16–21.

56. PM 28/20.

57. ND 389/397. Cf. AT 316/303.

58. GS 10.1 (P, "Bach gegen seine Liebhaber verteidigt," 1951): 138–51; *Prisms,* pp. 133–46.

59. ND 354/361–62.

60. ND 369/376.

61. ND 369–71/376–79.

62. ND 371/379.

63. GS 11 (NL II, "Endspiel," 1961): 300–316; trans., pp. 132–46.

64. Ibid., p. 303; trans., p. 136. The analogy between Kafka/Beckett and Schönberg/Stockhausen is made more explicit in GS 11 (NL III, "Voraussetzungen. Aus Anlass einer Lesung von Hans G. Helms," 1961): 431–46.

8 Truth and Illusion

1. AT 154–55/148–49, 162–63/155–57, 276–77/264–66. Adorno mentions that Bach's compositions united harmony and polyphony, which were fundamentally opposed to each other. Beethoven's compositions generate themselves from tonal "nothings" that become "something," namely, motives and themes.

2. ND 398/406.

3. ND 18/6.

4. Cf. ND 21/9, 63–64/53–55.

5. Compare AT 128/122–23 with AT 423/397–98.

6. AT 123/117–18, 126–27/120–22. See Sauerland's *Einführung,* pp. 45–57, for a discussion of how Adorno's "apparition" replies to Benjamin's theory of the decline of aura in modern art.

7. Compare Adorno's illustration from Beethoven's Violin Sonata op. 47 (AT 135–36/129–30) with the description of aesthetic conduct as modified mimesis on AT 489–90/454–55.

8. Kaiser, *Benjamin. Adorno,* p. 112.

9. DA 33–34/17–18. Cf. AT 132/126–27.

10. Kaiser, *Benjamin. Adorno,* p. 110.

11. AT 134/128. If one compares the descriptions of "the plus" (AT 122/116–17) with those of "spirit" (AT 134–37/128–32), several shared features emerge: the plus does not guarantee metaphysical import (*Gehalt*), spirit does not coincide with truth content (*Wahrheitsgehalt*); both the plus and spirit qualify the artwork to be an artwork; both "have their place" in the artwork's coherence but are not identical with that coherence; both speak through artworks and turn them into scripts; both are connected to the artwork's configuration but point beyond it.

12. Compare AT 129/123–24 with AT 136–37/130–32 and AT 513/473–74.

13. AT 137–39/131–34, which contains a later, more precise, and more subdued version of a passage on AT 511–12/471–73. Apart from considerations of context, the aims of Adorno's modifications might have been (1) to pose the dialectic between spirit and empirical reality as one primarily internal to specific artworks rather than as one between anonymous materials and (an artwork's) spirit, (2) to emphasize more strongly the immanence of spirit in the artwork's sensuousness, and (3) to forestall the objection that the mediation of all moments can hardly be a moment itself.

14. AT 137/131–32. For one of the musical models for Adorno's emphasis on caesurae, see his book on *Mahler,* GS 13 (M 1960): 149–319; *Mahler: A Musical Physiognomy,* trans. Edmund Jephcott (Chicago: University of Chicago Press, 1988).

15. Cf. ND 386/393.

16. GS 10.1 (P, "Zeitlose Mode. Zum Jazz," 1953): 137; *Prisms,* p. 132. Cf. AT 32–35/24–28.

17. GS 10.1 (OL, "Die Kunst und die Künste," 1967): 451–53.

18. GS 10.1 (P, "Kulturkritik und Gesellschaft," 1951): 30; *Prisms*, p. 34. Cf. GS 11 (NL III, "Engagement," 1962): 422–24; trans., pp. 312–13.

19. ND 355/362. Cf. AT 35–36/27–29.

20. Benjamin, *Ursprung des deutschen Trauerspiels*, p. 18; *The Origin of German Tragic Drama*, p. 36.

21. ND 294/299.

22. GS 10.1 (OL, "Die Kunst und die Künste," 1967): 448. Cf. AT 11–12/2–4, 271–72/260–62, 277–80/265–69.

23. "Goldmann and Adorno: To Describe, Understand and Explain" (1968), in Lucien Goldmann, *Cultural Creation in Modern Society* (1971), trans. Bart Grahl, Introduction by William Mayrl (Oxford: Basil Blackwell, 1976), p. 142.

24. See especially AT 193–97/185–90.

25. Kant, *Prolegomena zu einer jeden künftigen Metaphysik, die als Wissenschaft wird auftreten können* (1783), 6th ed., ed. Karl Vorländer (Hamburg: Felix Meiner, 1976), secs. 57–60, pp. 115–33; *Prolegomena to Any Future Metaphysics*, with an Introduction by Lewis White Beck (Indianapolis: Bobbs-Merrill, Library of Liberal Arts, 1950), pp. 99–113.

26. ND 286/291.

27. ND 164/161.

28. Cf. chapter 5 above.

29. Cf. chapter 6 above.

30. ND 385/393.

31. Cf. GS 13: 504–8, where, in a "Selbstanzeige" to *Versuch über Wagner* (1952), Adorno says the import of Wagner's compositions is thoroughly antagonistic, and therefore their truth resides in their ambivalence.

32. AT 283–84/271–72. Cf. GS 16 (K, "Ideen zur Musiksoziologie," 1958): 18–19.

33. Cf. GS 17 (Mm, "Spätstil Beethovens," 1937): 13–17. GS 17 (Mm, "Verfremdetes Hauptwerk. Zur Missa Solemnis," 1959): 145–61; trans. as "Alienated Masterpiece: The *Missa Solemnis*," *Telos*, no. 28 (Summer 1976), pp. 113–24. GS 10.1 (P, "Aufzeichnungen zu Kafka," 1953): 254–87; *Prisms*, pp. 243–71.

34. AT 137/131. Cf. AT 531/489–90 and PM 34/27.

35. The heading for AT 198–200/191–93 is misleading. The heading reads "*Wahrheit als Schein des Scheinlosen*," which Lenhardt translates as "Truth as illusion of the non-illusory." Although Adorno likes paradoxes, the notion of truth as an illusion of the non-illusory is not the paradox he intends, nor is it the notion of truth employed throughout *Aesthetic Theory* and in the rest of his writings. The passage itself says "*Wahrheit hat Kunst als Schein des Scheinlosen*" (p. 199), which Lenhardt translates as "art is true to the degree to which it is an illusion of the non-illusory" (p. 191). Adorno's

point is that art is an illusion of the non-illusory, the non-illusory being truth. A better heading for this passage would be "Art as illusion of the non-illusory." A clearer translation of the sentence quoted might be "Art possesses truth insofar as art is an illusion of the non-illusory."

36. Hegel, *Vorlesungen über die Ästhetik, Werke* 13: 82; *Aesthetics*, 1: 55.

37. ND 358/365. Cf. ND 397–400/405–8 and MM, sec. 153, p. 281/247.

38. ND 398/406.

39. ND 183–84/182. Cf. Kaiser, *Benjamin. Adorno*, p. 101.

40./ MM, sec. 61, p. 108/98.

41. See in particular Jürgen Habermas, *The Philosophical Discourse of Modernity: Twelve Lectures* (1985), trans. Frederick Lawrence (Cambridge, Mass.: MIT Press, 1987).

42. ND 24–27/13–15.

43. PT 1: 80–92.

44. PM 13/3, 28/20, 35/28.

45. ND 17/5.

46. ND 25/13–14.

47. Lenhardt's translation of this passage omits the second clause of the second sentence and, in the first clause, renders "*dafür hat sie [diskursive Erkenntnis] es [das Wahre] nicht*" as "unattainable" rather than "unattained."

48. ND 397–400/405–8.

49. ND 398/406.

50. ND 400/408.

51. ND 395/403. Cf. ND 158/155–56.

52. ND 395–96/403–4.

53. ND 396–97/404–5.

9 Models of Mediation

1. Kant, *Kritik der Urteilskraft*, sec. 44, p. 158; *Critique of Judgment*, pp. 172–73.

2. Of writings translated into English, Bürger's most sustained treatment is *Theorie der Avantgarde* (1974), 2d ed. (Frankfurt: Suhrkamp, 1980); trans. Michael Shaw, *Theory of the Avant-Garde*, Foreword by Jochen Schulte-Sasse (Minneapolis: University of Minnesota Press, 1984). The book has provoked an extensive discussion in Germany, much of it represented in W. Martin Lüdke, ed., "*Theorie der Avantgarde*": *Antworten auf Peter Bürgers Bestimmung von Kunst und bürgerlicher Gesellschaft* (Frankfurt: Suhr-

kamp, 1976). Bürger's responses to his critics can be found in his "Introduction: Theory of the Avant-Garde and Theory of Literature" and "Postscript to the Second German Edition," *Theory of the Avant-Garde*, pp. xlix–lv and 95–99, and in his *Vermittlung—Rezeption—Funktion: Ästhetische Theorie und Methodologie der Literaturwissenschaft* (Frankfurt: Suhrkamp, 1979). Also of interest here are two anthologies: Peter Bürger, ed., *Seminar: Literatur- und Kunstsoziologie* (Frankfurt: Suhrkamp, 1978), and Christa and Peter Bürger, eds., *Postmodern: Alltag, Allegorie und Avantgarde* (Frankfurt: Suhrkamp, 1987).

3. Bürger, *Theory of the Avant-Garde*, p. 16.

4. Ibid., p. 19.

5. Ibid., pp. lii, 22–23.

6. Peter Bürger, "The Institution of 'Art' as a Category in the Sociology of Literature," *Cultural Critique*, no. 2 (Winter 1986), pp. 5–33. The last half of the essay contrasts the bourgeois institution of art with the "institutionalizations" of literature in the courtly and feudal society of seventeenth-century France. This article is a translation of "Institution Kunst als Literatursoziologische Kategorie" in Bürger's *Vermittlung—Rezeption—Funktion*, pp. 173–99.

7. Bürger, *Theory of the Avant-Garde*, p. 22.

8. Ibid., pp. 13–14; "The Institution of 'Art'," p. 8.

9. Ibid., pp. 36, 46.

10. Ibid., p. 48.

11. Ibid., p. 49.

12. Ibid., pp. 57–58.

13. Ibid., pp. 50, 54.

14. Ibid., p. lii.

15. Ibid., p. 87.

16. Ibid., pp. 6–14, 20–27, 83–88.

17. Bürger, "Adorno, Bourdieu und die Literatursoziologie," *Jahrbuch für Internationale Germanistik* 17 (1985) 1: 47–56.

18. Bürger, *Theory of the Avant-Garde*, p. 87.

19. Bürger, "Adorno, Bourdieu und die Literatursoziologie," pp. 47–48, 56.

20. Göran Hermerén, "The Autonomy of Art," in *Essays on Aesthetics: Perspectives on the Work of Monroe C. Beardsley*, ed. John Fisher (Philadelphia: Temple University Press, 1983), pp. 35–49; the quote is from p. 36.

21. *Aesthetic Theory* describes this self-referential tendency as a type of "immanent critique" and considers it to be the key to continuity and tradition in art: "The truth content of works of art is part and parcel of their critical content. . . . Their continuity

consists . . . in their critical relationship. 'One work of art is the mortal enemy of another.' This unity of art history is captured by the dialectical notion of determinate negation" (59–60/52).

22. The fact that commercial films and popular music have become increasingly self-referential in recent years is one reason for thinking that the distinction between autonomous and heteronomous art is fading. In this connection see the comments on "pastiche" and "the nostalgia mode" in Fredric Jameson, "Postmodernism, or The Cultural Logic of Late Capitalism," *New Left Review*, no. 146 (July-August 1984), pp. 53–92.

23. The anti-feminist implications of a strong preference for autonomous art are discussed by Tania Modleski, "The Terror of Pleasure: The Contemporary Horror Film and Postmodern Theory," and Andreas Huyssen, "Mass Culture as Woman: Modernism's Other," in *Studies in Entertainment: Critical Approaches to Mass Culture*, ed. Tania Modleski (Bloomington: Indiana University Press, 1986), pp. 155–66 and 188–207. For specific criticisms of Adorno along these lines, see Sabine Wilke, " 'Torn Halves of an Integral Freedom': Adorno's and Benjamin's Readings of Mass Culture," in the anthology *The Aesthetics of the Critical Theorists*, pp. 124–51.

24. "Popular art" is a disputed label, as is the more pejorative-sounding "mass art." I am using it here to refer primarily to art that involves electronic media and is mass-produced and mass-distributed for a mass audience.

25. Ronald Roblin, "Collingwood and Adorno on the Popular Arts," in *The Aesthetics of The Critical Theorists*, pp. 308–336, gives an illuminating comparison in the context of the two author's more general views of art.

26. Adorno's account of standardization is explained and criticized by Bernard Gendron, "Theodor Adorno Meets the Cadillacs," in *Studies in Entertainment*, ed. Modleski, pp. 18–36.

27. Howard Becker analyzes the complex division of labor in film and other arts and explores its implications for aesthetic categories in his *Art Worlds* (Berkeley: University of California Press, 1982). See especially the first chapter, "Art Worlds and Collective Activity" (pp. 1–39).

28. See Jürgen Habermas, *The Theory of Communicative Action*, trans. Thomas McCarthy, vol. 1: *Reason and the Rationalization of Society*, vol. 2: *Lifeworld and System* (Boston: Beacon Press, 1984, 1987).

29. Bürger, *Theory of the Avant-Garde*, p. 87.

30. Ibid., p. 94.

31. Bürger acknowledges these problems but fails to address them in a satisfactory way. See *Theory of the Avant-Garde*, pp. xlix–lv, 15–20.

32. Ibid., p. 99.

33. For related criticisms of Bürger, see Peter Uwe Hohendahl, "Autonomy of Art: Looking Back at Adorno's *Ästhetische Theorie*," *German Quarterly* 54 (March 1981): 133–48; W. Martin Lüdke, "Die Aporien der materialistischen Ästhetik—Kein Ausweg?" and Burkhardt Lindner's "Aufhebung der Kunst in der Lebenspraxis? Über die Aktualität der Auseinandersetzung mit den historischen Avantgardebewegungen," both in the anthology *"Theorie der Avantgarde"*; Richard Wolin, "Modernism vs. Post-

modernism," *Telos,* no. 62 (Winter 1984–85), pp. 9–29; and Jochen Schulte-Sasse, "Foreword," in *Theory of the Avant-Garde,* pp. vii–xlvii. Hohendahl says Bürger's concept of autonomous art is too constrictive as a historiographic category. Lüdke argues that Bürger has not done justice to Adorno's concept of modernism (*Moderne*) and has not justified the application of Marxian politico-economic categories to artistic phenomena. Lindner claims that the avant-garde represents a reversal (*Umschlag*) rather than a break (*Bruch*) in the bourgeois institution of art. Wolin exempts surrealism from Bürger's claim that the historical avant-garde movements aimed to reunite art and life, and Schulte-Sasse expresses his dissatisfaction with Bürger's "refusal to reflect on future possibilities of an art integrated into social life" (p. xli).

34. See Bürger, "Adorno, Bourdieu und die Literatursoziologie," pp. 50–56.

35. I examine the notion of popularity—and suggest the notion of "social scope" as a way to correct the all-too-common equation of popularity with commercial success— in a chapter on evaluating popular art in Quentin Schultze et al., *Dancing in the Dark: Youth, Popular Culture, and the Electronic Media* (Grand Rapids, Mich.: Eerdmans, 1991).

10 Politics of Postmodernism

1. Karl Marx, *The Eighteenth Brumaire of Louis Bonaparte* (1852), in *Karl Marx: Selected Writings,* ed. David McLellan (Oxford: Oxford University Press, 1977), p. 300.

2. MM, sec. 51, pp. 94–95/86.

3. Anders Stephanson, "Regarding Postmodernism—A Conversation with Fredric Jameson," *Social Text* 17 (Fall 1987): 32. This interview is reprinted in *Postmodernism/ Jameson/Critique,* ed. Douglas Kellner (Washington, D.C.: Maisonneuve Press, 1989), pp. 43–74, an excellent anthology on the topics of this chapter.

4. Anderson, *In the Tracks of Historical Materialism;* Jay, *Marxism and Totality.*

5. Jay, *Marxism and Totality,* p. 274.

6. ND 10/xx.

7. Lukács, "Die Gegenwartsbedeutung des kritischen Realismus," *Werke* 4: 469; *Realism in Our Time,* p. 16.

8. GS 11 (NL II, "Erpresste Versöhnung," 1958): 253; "Reconciliation under Duress," p. 153.

9. Jameson's first sustained attempt to derive a methodology of "dialectical criticism" from these sources is in *Marxism and Form: Twentieth-Century Dialectical Theories of Literature* (Princeton: Princeton University Press, 1971). Jameson tries to rescue Adorno from postmodernist misreadings in *Late Marxism: Adorno, or, the Persistence of the Dialectic* (London: Verso, 1990), which I was unable to read before completing this chapter.

10. A major document of this conversation, and the main source of my discussion of Jameson, is his *The Political Unconscious: Narrative as a Socially Symbolic Act* (Ithaca: Cornell University Press, 1981).

11. See in particular Jameson's "Reification and Utopia in Mass Culture," *Social Text* 1 (Winter 1979): 130–48; "The Politics of Theory: Ideological Positions in the Post-

modernism Debate," *New German Critique,* no. 33 (Fall 1984), pp. 53–65; and "Postmodernism, or The Cultural Logic of Late Capitalism," *New Left Review,* no. 146 (July-August 1984), pp. 53–92. The latter article incorporates most of a talk given in the fall of 1982 and published as "Postmodernism and Consumer Society," in *The Anti-Aesthetic: Essays on Postmodern Culture,* ed. Hal Foster (Port Townsend, Wash.: Bay Press, 1983), pp. 111–25. See also "On Magic Realism in Film," *Critical Inquiry* 12 (Winter 1986): 301–325; and "Cognitive Mapping," in *Marxism and the Interpretation of Culture,* ed. Cary Nelson and Lawrence Grossberg (Urbana and Chicago: University of Illinois Press, 1988), pp. 347–57. For a complete list of Jameson's writings to 1989, see "Fredric Jameson—A Comprehensive Bibliography," in *Postmodernism/Jameson/Critique,* pp. 389–95.

12. Jameson, *The Political Unconscious,* p. 11.

13. Fredric Jameson, "Reflections in Conclusion," in *Aesthetics and Politics,* pp. 196–213; the quotation is from p. 209.

14. Jameson, *The Political Unconscious,* pp. 40–42, 62–63, 225–37.

15. Ibid., p. 193.

16. Ibid., pp. 226–27.

17. Ibid., pp. 63, 236–37.

18. Ibid., p. 289.

19. Ibid., p. 81.

20. William C. Dowling, *Jameson, Althusser, Marx: An Introduction to "The Political Unconscious"* (Ithaca: Cornell University Press, 1984), p. 123.

21. S. P. Mohanty, "History at the Edge of Discourse," *Diacritics* 12 (Fall 1982) 3: 45.

22. Jameson, *The Political Unconscious,* p. 68. On the same page Jameson says this need to transcend individualistic approaches is "in many ways the fundamental issue for my doctrine of the political unconscious."

23. Ibid., p. 60.

24. Cf. Jameson, "Reification and Utopia in Mass Culture," p. 140.

25. Jameson, *The Political Unconscious,* pp. 234–37.

26. Ibid., pp. 17–23.

27. Ibid., p. 17.

28. Ibid., p. 13.

29. In *New Left Review,* no. 146 (July-August 1984), pp. 53–92.

30. "The Politics of Theory," *New German Critique,* no. 33 (Fall 1984), pp. 53–65; reprinted in Fredric Jameson, *The Ideologies of Theory: Essays 1971–1986,* 2 vols., vol. 2: *The Syntax of History* (Minneapolis: University of Minnesota Press, 1988), pp. 103–113.

31. Ibid., pp. 62–63.

32. Jameson, "Cognitive Mapping," in *Marxism and the Interpretation of Culture*, pp. 347–57.

33. Stephanson, "Regarding Postmodernism," p. 42.

34. Jameson, "Postmodernism, or The Cultural Logic of Late Capitalism," p. 92.

35. In *Diacritics* 12 (Fall 1982) 3, see Terry Eagleton, "Fredric Jameson: The Politics of Style" (pp. 14–22) and Michael Sprinker, "The Part and the Whole" (pp. 57–71). See also Dominick LaCapra's review essay in *History and Theory* 21 (1982): 83–106.

36. Jameson, *The Political Unconscious*, pp. 40, 225.

37. Ibid., p. 40.

38. Ibid.

39. Ibid., pp. 20, 62–64, 160–61, 190, 220–22, 225–37, 249–53, 260–61. Cf. Jameson's "Reification and Utopia in Mass Culture," and the "Interview: Fredric Jameson" in *Diacritics* 12 (Fall 1982) 3: 72–91, especially pp. 86–89.

40. Stephanson, "Regarding Postmodernism," p. 32.

41. Jameson, *The Political Unconscious*, p. 236.

42. In *Rethinking Marxism* 1 (Spring 1988) 1: 49–72.

43. Ibid., p. 52.

44. Ibid., p. 60.

45. Ibid., p. 70.

46. Ibid., p. 65.

47. Ibid., p. 71.

48. Ibid.

49. Jameson, *The Political Unconscious*, p. 289.

50. GS 11 (NL III, "Engagement," 1962): 426; trans., pp. 314–15.

11 History, Art, and Truth

1. *Vorlesungen über die Ästhetik, Werke* 13: 82; *Aesthetics*, 1: 55.

2. This is the implied thesis of Thomas Baumeister and Jens Kulenkampff, "Geschichtsphilosophie und philosophische Ästhetik: Zu Adornos 'Ästhetischer Theorie,'" *Neue Hefte für Philosophie*, no. 5 (1973), pp. 74–104.

3. Albrecht Wellmer, "Truth, Semblance, Reconciliation: Adorno's Aesthetic Redemption of Modernity," *Telos*, no. 62 (Winter 1984–85), pp. 89–115; the quotations are from p. 115. This is a translation of "Wahrheit, Schein, Versöhnung: Adornos ästhetische Rettung der Modernität," first published in *Adorno-Konferenz 1983* (Frankfurt: Suhrkamp, 1983), pp. 138–76, and republished in Wellmer's *Zur Dialektik von Moderne und Postmoderne: Vernunftkritik nach Adorno* (Frankfurt: Suhrkamp, 1985), pp. 9–47. Other articles in this last volume, and their translations, include the following: "Zur Dialektik von Moderne und Postmoderne: Vernunftkritik nach Adorno" (pp. 48–114); trans. as "On the Dialectic of Modernism and Postmodernism," *Praxis International* 4 (January 1985): 337–62. "Kunst und industrielle Produktion: Zur Dialektik von Moderne und Postmoderne" (pp. 115–34; trans. as "Art and Industrial Production," *Telos*, no. 57 (Fall 1983), pp. 53–62. "Adorno, Anwalt des Nicht-Identischen: Eine Einführung" (pp. 135–66). Citations from these articles will give the pagination in *Zur Dialektik*, followed by the pagination of the translation, if any.

4. Wellmer, "Reason, Utopia, and the Dialectic of Enlightenment," *Praxis International* 3 (July 1983): 96.

5. For Wellmer's account of this dialectic, see "Adorno, Anwalt des Nicht-Identischen," pp. 137–52. Similar accounts occur in "Zur Dialektik von Moderne und Postmoderne," pp. 72–77, trans., pp. 347–50; and in "Wahrheit, Schein, Versöhnung," pp. 10–12, trans., pp. 90–92.

6. Wellmer, "Wahrheit, Schein, Versöhnung," p. 11; trans., p. 91.

7. Wellmer, "Zur Dialektik von Moderne und Postmoderne," p. 75; trans., p. 349.

8. Wellmer, "Adorno, Anwalt des Nicht-Identischen," pp. 152–55. Cf. "Wahrheit, Schein, Versöhnung," pp. 12–13; trans., pp. 91–92.

9. Wellmer, "Reason, Utopia, and the Dialectic of Enlightenment," pp. 93–95.

10. Wellmer, "Wahrheit, Schein, Versöhnung," pp. 26–27; trans., p. 102.

11. Wellmer, "Zur Dialektik von Moderne und Postmoderne," p. 76; trans., p. 350.

12. Wellmer, "Reason, Utopia, and the Dialectic of Enlightenment," p. 94.

13. Ibid., pp. 96–97.

14. For a summary and questioning of these correlations, see Thomas McCarthy, "Reflections on Rationalization," in Richard Bernstein, ed., *Habermas and Modernity* (Cambridge, Mass.: MIT Press, 1985), pp. 176–91.

15. Wellmer, "Reason, Utopia, and the Dialectic of Enlightenment," p. 105.

16. Ibid., p. 94.

17. Cf. "Wahrheit, Schein, Versöhnung," p. 37; trans., pp. 109–110.

18. Wellmer, "Zur Dialektik von Moderne und Postmoderne," p. 109; trans., p. 360. Cf. "Adorno, Anwalt des Nicht-Identischen," p. 164.

19. This heading deliberately recalls Axel Honneth's "Communication and Reconciliation: Habermas' Critique of Adorno," *Telos*, no. 39 (Spring 1979), pp. 45–61. For the longer original version, slightly revised, see Honneth's "Von Adorno zu Habermas:

Zum Gestaltwandel kritischer Gesellschaftstheorie," in *Sozialforschung als Kritik: Zum sozialwissenschaftlichen Potential der Kritischen Theorie*, ed. Wolfgang Bonss and Axel Honneth (Frankfurt: Suhrkamp, 1982), pp. 87–126. Although originally written in 1976, before Habermas published *The Theory of Communicative Action*, Honneth's article accurately identifies the reasons for "the change of paradigm" from Adorno to Habermas.

20. Wellmer, "Wahrheit, Schein, Versöhnung," p. 10; trans., p. 90.

21. Ibid., p. 16; trans., p. 95. The translation renders *gegenständliche Wahrheit* either as "representational" or as "cognitive truth."

22. Ibid., p. 18; trans., p. 96.

23. Ibid., p. 19; trans., p. 97.

24. Ibid., pp. 12–13; trans., p. 92. Cf. "Adorno, Anwalt des Nicht-Identischen," pp. 152–55.

25. Ibid., pp. 19–20; trans., p. 97.

26. Ibid., pp. 19–23; trans., pp. 96–100. "Zur Dialektik der Moderne und Postmoderne," pp. 103–5; trans., pp. 357–58. "Adorno, Anwalt des Nicht-Identischen," pp. 160–64.

27. Wellmer, "Wahrheit, Schein, Versöhnung," pp. 20–22; trans., pp. 98–99. Cf. "Adorno, Anwalt des Nicht-Identischen," pp. 155–59. For a more elaborate treatment, see "Zur Dialektik der Moderne und Postmoderne," pp. 85–100. The translated version of "Zur Dialektik" contains only a few paragraphs from this passage (see trans., pp. 354–55). For extended interpretations and criticisms of Habermas's universal-pragmatic theory of language and communicative action, see Wellmer's *Praktische Philosophie und Theorie der Gesellschaft: Zum Problem der normativen Grundlagen einer kritischen Sozialwissenschaft* (Konstanz: Universitätsverlag Konstanz, 1979) and *Ethik und Dialog: Element des moralischen Urteils bei Kant und in der Diskursethik* (Frankfurt: Suhrkamp, 1986).

28. Wellmer, "Wahrheit, Schein, Versöhnung," p. 38; trans., p. 110.

29. Wellmer, "Reason, Utopia, and the Dialectic of Enlightenment," pp. 94, 106–7.

30. Wellmer, "Warheit, Schein, Versöhnung," p. 43; trans., p. 114.

31. Ibid., p. 28; trans., pp. 103–4. A nearly identical passage occurs at the end of "Adorno, Anwalt des Nicht-Identischen," pp. 162–64. See also "Zur Dialektik der Moderne und Postmoderne," pp. 102–5; trans., pp. 357–58.

32. Ibid., pp. 28–30; trans., pp. 104–5.

33. Wellmer, "Zur Dialektik von Moderne und Postmoderne," pp. 49–50; trans., p. 338.

34. Wellmer, "Adorno, Anwalt des Nicht-Identischen," p. 149.

35. The pathbreaking statement of this theory is Jürgen Habermas, "Wahrheitstheorien," in *Wirklichkeit und Reflexion: Walter Schulz zum 60. Geburtstag*, ed. Helmut Fahrenbach (Pfullingen: Neske, 1973), pp. 211–65.

36. Wellmer, "Wahrheit, Schein, Versöhnung," p. 32; trans., p. 106.

37. Ibid.

38. Ibid., p. 30; trans., p. 105.

39. Ibid., pp. 30–37; trans., pp. 105–9.

40. Ibid., pp. 36–37; trans., p. 109.

41. See in this connection *Analytic Aesthetics*, ed. Richard Shusterman (Oxford: Basil Blackwell, 1989), especially Shusterman's "Introduction: Analysing Analytic Aesthetics," pp. 1–19.

42. There has been an intermittent debate in Anglo-American aesthetics about whether propositions, which need not be asserted or believed, are the locus of truth in art. Edward Casey, "Truth in Art," *Man and World* 3 (September-November 1970): 351–69, demonstrates the inadequacy of a propositional view of artistic truth's locus, as well as the shortcomings of the correspondence theory of truth to which this view is usually attached.

43. Professor Wellmer has suggested a reply along these lines in correspondence about a draft of this chapter.

44. "Perchronic" is a term suggested by Calvin Seerveld to describe traditions that "recur" in various historical periods. He distinguishes these enduring traditions from the synchronic patterns that make up a historical period and the diachronic patterns that differentiate various styles. My own suggestions are partially indebted to his approach, as presented in Calvin Seerveld, "Towards a Cartographic Methodology for Art Historiography," *Journal of Aesthetics and Art Criticism* 39 (Winter 1980–1981): 143–54; reprinted in *Opuscula Aesthetica Nostra*, ed. Cécile Cloutier and Calvin Seerveld (Edmonton: Academic Printing & Publishing, 1984), pp. 51–62.

45. GS 10.2 (E, "Wozu noch Philosophie," 1962/1963): 465.

46. Ibid., p. 462.

47. Marx, *The Eighteenth Brumaire of Louis Bonaparte*, in *Karl Marx: Selected Writings*, p. 300.

48. ND 25/13.

49. ND 18/6.

50. ND 29/17–18.

51. For a critical commentary on the relation between art and suffering in Adorno's aesthetics, see Thomas Huhn, "The Sublimation of Culture in Adorno's Aesthetics," in the anthology *The Aesthetics of the Critical Theorists*, pp. 291–307.

52. Wellmer, "Wahrheit, Schein, Versöhnung," p. 9; trans., p. 90.

53. ND 51/41.

Bibliography

The three sections below list Adorno's writings separately from secondary works on Adorno and from other primary and secondary works. For a more extensive bibliography, see René Görtzen, "Theodor W. Adorno: Vorläufige Bibliographie seiner Schriften und der Sekundärliteratur," in *Adorno-Konferenz 1983*, pp. 402–471. An earlier chronology of Adorno's writings is by Klaus Schultz, "Vorläufige Bibliographie der Schriften Theodor W. Adornos," in *Theodor W. Adorno zum Gedächtnis* (1971), pp. 177–242. Other chronological bibliographies appear in the books by Susan Buck-Morss (1977) and Gillian Rose (1978). Annotated bibliographies of the secondary literature on Adorno include Carlo Pettazzi, "Bibliographie zu Th. W. Adorno," in *Theodor W. Adorno*, 1st ed. (1977), pp. 176–91, and Peter Christian Lang, "Commentierte Auswahlbibliographie 1969–1979," in *Materialien zur ästhetischen Theorie Theodor W. Adornos* (1979), pp. 509–556. For a useful short bibliography, see Martin Jay, *Adorno* (1984), pp. 188–92.

1. Theodor W. Adorno

Section 1.1 lists Adorno's books in the order of their abbreviations, which are derived from the German titles. The list includes works coauthored by Adorno, but it does not contain all of his books. The titles of English translations are given directly after their German originals. Section 1.2 contains complete information on these translations, presenting them in the order of the abbreviations from section 1.1. Books listed without abbreviations were originally published in English. Section 1.3 contains most of Adorno's articles in English, both articles originally published in English and articles translated into English. The title of each translated article is followed by the date of the German original.

1.1 Adorno's Books in German

GS   *Gesammelte Schriften.* 23 vols. Edited by Rolf Tiedemann. Volumes 5, 7, and 13 were coedited by Gretel Adorno. Volume 9 was coedited by Susan Buck-Morss. Frankfurt: Suhrkamp, 1970–.

AKB   *Theodor W. Adorno und Ernst Krenek: Briefwechsel.* Edited by Wolfgang Rogge. Frankfurt: Suhrkamp, 1974.

AT   *Ästhetische Theorie* (1970). GS 7. 2d ed. 1972. *Aesthetic Theory* (1984).

D   *Dissonanzen. Musik in der verwalteten Welt* (1956, 1958, 1963, 1969). GS 14 (1973): 7–167.

DA   Horkheimer, Max, and Theodor W. Adorno. *Dialektik der Aufklärung. Philoso-
       phische Fragmente* (1947, 1969). GS 3. 1981. *Dialectic of Enlightenment* (1972).

E   *Eingriffe. Neun kritische Modelle* (1963). GS 10.2 (1977): 455–594.

EM   *Erziehung zur Mündigkeit. Vorträge und Gespräche mit Hellmut Becker, 1959–1969.*
       Edited by Gerd Kadelbach. Frankfurt: Suhrkamp, 1970.

EMS   *Einleitung in die Musiksoziologie. Zwölf theoretische Vorlesungen* (1962, 1968). GS
       14 (1973): 169–433. *Introduction to the Sociology of Music* (1976).

H   *Drei Studien zu Hegel* (1963). GS 5 (1970): 247–381.

I   *Impromptus. Zweite Folge neu gedruckter musikalischer Aufsätze* (1968). GS 17 (1982):
       163–344.

JE   *Jargon der Eigentlichkeit. Zur deutschen Ideologie* (1964). GS 6 (1973): 413–526.
       The Jargon of Authenticity (1973).

K   *Klangfiguren. Musikalische Schriften I* (1959). GS 16 (1978): 7–248.

KKA   *Kierkegaard. Konstruktion des Ästhetischen* (1933, 1962, 1966). GS 2. 1979. *Kier-
       kegaard: Construction of the Aesthetic* (1989).

M   *Mahler. Eine musikalische Physiognomik* (1960). GS 13 (1971): 149–319. *Mahler:
       A Musical Physiognomy* (1988).

ME   *Zur Metakritik der Erkenntnistheorie. Studien über Husserl und die phänomenologischen
       Antinomien* (1956). GS 5 (1970): 7–245. *Against Epistemology: A Metacritique* (1982,
       1983).

MM   *Minima Moralia. Reflexionen aus dem beschädigten Leben* (1951, 1962). GS 4. 1980.
       Minima Moralia: Reflections from Damaged Life (1974).

Mm   *Moments musicaux. Neu gedruckte Aufsätze 1928–1962* (1964). GS 17 (1982): 7–
       161.

ND   *Negative Dialektik* (1966, 1967). GS 6 (1973): 7–412. *Negative Dialectics* (1973).

NL   *Noten zur Literatur* I (1958), II (1961), III (1965), IV (1974). GS 11. 1974.

OL   *Ohne Leitbild. Parva Aesthetica* (1967, 1968). GS 10.1 (1977): 289–453.

P   *Prismen. Kulturkritik und Gesellschaft* (1955, 1963, 1969). GS 10.1 (1977): 9–287.
       Prisms (1967).

PM   *Philosophie der neuen Musik* (1949, 1958, 1966, 1972). GS 12. 1975. *Philosophy of
       Modern Music* (1973).

PS   Adorno, Theodor W., et al. *Der Positivismusstreit in der deutschen Soziologie.* Neuwied, Berlin: Luchterhand, 1969. (Adorno's contributions are reprinted in GS 8.) *The Positivist Dispute in German Sociology* (1976).

PT   *Philosophische Terminologie. Zur Einleitung.* Edited by Rudolf zur Lippe from lectures given in 1962–63. 2 vols. Frankfurt: Suhrkamp, 1973, 1974.

Q   *Quasi una fantasia. Musikalische Schriften II* (1963). GS 16 (1978): 249–540.

S   *Stichworte. Kritische Modelle 2* (1969). GS 10.2 (1977): 595–782.

SE   Institut für Sozialforschung. *Soziologische Exkurse. Nach Vorträgen und Diskussionen.* Frankfurt: Europäische Verlagsanstalt, 1956. *Aspects of Sociology* (1972).

SII   Horkheimer, Max, and Theodor W. Adorno. *Sociologica II. Reden und Vorträge.* Frankfurt: Europäische Verlagsanstalt, 1962. (Adorno's contributions are reprinted in GS 8.)

VA   *Vorlesungen zur Ästhetik 1967–68.* Zurich: H. Mayer Nachfolger, 1973.

VW   *Versuch über Wagner* (1952). GS 13 (1971): 7–148. *In Search of Wagner* (1981).

WB   *Über Walter Benjamin.* Edited, with notes, by Rolf Tiedemann. Frankfurt: Suhrkamp, 1970.

1.2 Adorno's Books in English

AT   *Aesthetic Theory.* Translated by C. Lenhardt. London: Routledge & Kegan Paul, 1984.

    The Authoritarian Personality. T. W. Adorno, Else Frenkel-Brunswik, Daniel J. Levinson, and R. Nevitt Sanford, in collaboration with Betty Aron, Maria Hertz Levinson, and William Morrow. *Studies in Prejudice.* Edited by Max Horkheimer and Samuel H. Flowerman. Vol. 1. New York: Harper & Brothers, 1950. Chapters 1, 7, 16, 17, 18, and 19 appear in GS 9.1 (1975): 143–509 under the title *Studies in the Authoritarian Personality.*

    Composing for the Films. With Hanns Eisler. New York: Oxford University Press, 1947. The book appeared under only Eisler's name until Adorno published a German version in 1969 titled *Komposition für den Film.* This version and an account of the manuscript's history appear in GS 15 (1976): 7–155.

DA   *Dialectic of Enlightenment.* Translated by John Cumming. New York: Seabury Press, 1972.

EMS   *Introduction to the Sociology of Music.* Translated by E. B. Ashton. New York: Seabury Press, 1976.

JE   *The Jargon of Authenticity.* Translated by Knut Tarnowski and Frederic Will. London: Routledge & Kegan Paul, 1973.

KKA   *Kierkegaard: Construction of the Aesthetic.* Translated, edited, and with a foreword by Robert Hullot-Kentor. Minneapolis: University of Minnesota Press, 1989.

M   *Mahler: A Musical Physiognomy.* Translated by Edmund Jephcott. Chicago: University of Chicago Press, 1988.

ME   *Against Epistemology: A Metacritique; Studies in Husserl and the Phenomonological Antinomies.* Translated by Willis Domingo. Oxford: Basil Blackwell, 1982; Cambridge, Mass.: MIT Press, 1983.

MM   *Minima Moralia: Reflections from Damaged Life.* Translated by E. F. N. Jephcott. London: NLB, 1974.

ND   *Negative Dialectics.* Translated by E. B. Ashton. New York: Seabury Press, 1973.

P   *Prisms.* Translated by Samuel and Shierry Weber. London: Neville Spearman, 1967; Cambridge, Mass.: MIT Press, 1981.

PM   *Philosophy of Modern Music.* Translated by Anne G. Mitchell and Wesley V. Blomster. New York: Seabury Press, 1973.

PS   *The Positivist Dispute in German Sociology.* Theodor W. Adorno et al. Translated by Glyn Adey and David Frisby. London: Heinemann, 1976.

SE   *Aspects of Sociology.* The Frankfurt Institute for Social Research. Translated by John Viertel. Boston: Beacon Press, 1972.

VW   *In Search of Wagner.* Translated by Rodney Livingstone. London: NLB, 1981.

1.3 Adorno's Articles in English

"The Actuality of Philosophy" (1931). *Telos,* no. 31 (Spring 1977), pp. 120–33.

"The Aging of the New Music" (1955). *Telos,* no. 77 (Fall 1988), pp. 95–116.

"Alienated Masterpiece: The *Missa Solemnis*" (1959). *Telos,* no. 28 (Summer 1976), pp. 113–24.

"Anti-Semitism and Fascist Propaganda." With Leo Lowenthal and Paul Massing. *Anti-Semitism: A Social Disease,* pp. 125–37. Edited by Ernst Simmel. New York: International Universities, 1946. Reprinted in GS 8: 397–407.

"Bloch's Traces: The Philosophy of Kitsch" (1960). *New Left Review,* no. 121 (May-June 1980), pp. 49–62.

"Commitment" (1962). *New Left Review,* no. 87–88 (November-December 1974), pp. 75–90. Reprinted in *Aesthetics and Politics,* pp. 177–95, and in *The Essential Frankfurt School Reader,* pp. 300–318.

"Contemporary German Sociology" (1959). *Transactions of the Fourth World Congress of Sociology,* vol. I, pp. 33–56. London: International Sociological Association, 1959.

"Culture and Administration" (1960). *Telos,* no. 37 (Fall 1978), pp. 93–111.

"Culture Industry Reconsidered" (1963). *New German Critique,* no. 6 (Fall 1975), pp. 12–19. Reprinted in *Critical Theory and Society,* pp. 128–35.

"Education for Autonomy" (–1969+1970). With Hellmut Becker. *Telos,* no. 56 (Summer 1983), pp. 103–110.

"The Essay as Form" (1958). *New German Critique,* no. 32 (Spring-Summer 1984), pp. 151–71.

"Freudian Theory and the Pattern of Fascist Propaganda." In *Psychoanalysis and the Social Sciences,* vol. 3, pp. 279–300. Edited by G. Róheim. New York: 1951. Reprinted in GS 8: 408–433.

"Functionalism Today" (1966). *Oppositions,* no. 17 (Summer 1979), pp. 31–41.

"Goldmann and Adorno: To Describe, Understand and Explain" (1968). In Lucien Goldmann. *Cultural Creation in Modern Society* (1971), pp. 129–45. Translated by Bart Grahl. Introduction by William Mayrl. Oxford: Basil Blackwell, 1976.

"How to Look at Television." *Quarterly of Film, Radio and Television* 8 (Spring 1954): 213–35. Reprinted as "Television and the Patterns of Mass Culture" in *Mass Culture: The Popular Arts in America,* pp. 474–87. Edited by Bernard Rosenberg and David Manning White. Glencoe, Ill.: Free Press, 1957.

"Husserl and the Problem of Idealism" (1940). *The Journal of Philosophy* 37 (1940): 5–18.

"The Idea of Natural History" (–1932+1973). *Telos,* no. 60 (Summer 1984), pp. 111–24.

"Introduction" (1969). In *The Positivist Dispute in German Sociology,* pp. 1–67.

"Is Marx Obsolete?" (1968). *Diogenes,* no. 64 (Winter 1968), pp. 1–16. The German title is "Spätkapitalismus oder Industriegesellschaft," now in GS 8: 354–70.

"Jazz" (1946). In *Encyclopedia of the Arts,* pp. 511–13. Edited by Dagobert D. Runes and Harry G. Schrickel. New York: Philosophical Library, 1946.

"Letters to Walter Benjamin" (1930s). *New Left Review,* no. 81 (September-October 1973), pp. 46–80. See also *Aesthetics and Politics,* pp. 110–33.

"Looking Back on Surrealism" (1956). *The Idea of the Modern in Literature and the Arts,* pp. 220–24. Edited by Irving Howe. New York: Horizon Press, 1967.

"Lyric Poetry and Society" (1951). *Telos,* no. 20 (Summer 1974), pp. 56–71. Reprinted in *Critical Theory and Society,* pp. 155–71.

"Metacritique of Epistemology" (originally published as "Einleitung" in ME, 1956). *Telos,* no. 38 (Winter 1978–79), pp. 77–103.

"Modern Music Is Growing Old" (1955). *The Score,* no. 18 (December 1956), pp. 18–29. (For a better translation, see "The Aging of the New Music," listed above.)

"Music and Technique" (1958). *Telos,* no. 32 (Summer 1977), pp. 79–94.

"Music and the New Music: In Memory of Peter Suhrkamp" (1960). *Telos,* no. 43 (Spring 1980), pp. 124–38.

"New Music and the Public: Some Problems of Interpretation" (1957). In *Twentieth-Century Music,* pp. 63–74. Edited by Rollo H. Myers. Rev. and enl. ed. London: Calder and Boyors, 1968.

"Of Barricades and Ivory Towers: An Interview with T. W. Adorno." *Encounter* 33 (September 1969) 3: 63–69.

"On Kierkegaard's Doctrine of Love." *Studies in Philosophy and Social Science* 8 (1939–1940): 413–29.

"On Popular Music." With the assistance of George Simpson. *Studies in Philosophy and Social Science* 9 (1941): 17–48.

"On the Fetish-Character in Music and the Regression of Listening" (1938/1956). *The Essential Frankfurt School Reader*, pp. 270–99.

"On the Historical Adequacy of Consciousness" (1965). With Peter von Haselberg. *Telos*, no. 56 (Summer 1983), pp. 97–103.

"On the Logic of the Social Sciences" (1962). In *The Positivist Dispute in German Sociology*, pp. 105–122.

"On the Question: 'What is German?' " (1965). *New German Critique*, no. 36 (Fall 1985), pp. 121–31.

"On the Social Situation of Music" (1932). *Telos*, no. 35 (Spring 1978), pp. 128–64. Translation of "Zur gesellschaftlichen Lage der Musik." *Zeitschrift für Sozialforschung* 1 (1932): 104–124, 356–78.

"Perennial Fashion—Jazz" (1953). In *Prisms*, pp. 119–32. Reprinted in *Critical Theory and Society*, pp. 199–209.

"Progress" (1964). *The Philosophical Forum* 15 (Fall-Winter 1983–84): 55–70.

"The Psychological Technique of Martin Luther Thomas' Radio Addresses" (–1943), in GS 9.1 (1975): 7–141.

"The Radio Symphony: An Experiment in Theory." In *Radio Research 1941*, pp. 110–39. Edited by Paul F. Lazarsfeld and Frank N. Stanton. New York: Duell, Sloan and Pearce, 1941.

"Reconciliation under Duress" (1958). In *Aesthetics and Politics*, pp. 151–76.

"Resignation" (1969). *Telos*, no. 35 (Spring 1978), pp. 165–68.

Review of Jean Wahl, *Études Kierkegaardiennes;* Walter Lowrie, *Kierkegaard;* and *The Journals of Soren Kierkegaard.* In *Studies in Philosophy and Social Science* 8 (1939): 232–35.

Review of Wilder Hobson, *American Jazz Music* and Winthrop Sargeant, *Jazz Hot and Hybrid.* With the assistance of Eunice Cooper. *Studies in Philosophy and Social Science* 9 (1941): 167–78.

"Scientific Experiences of a European Scholar in America." In *The Intellectual Migration: Europe and America, 1930–1960*, pp. 338–70. Edited by Donald Fleming and Bernard Bailyn. Cambridge, Mass.: Belknap Press, Harvard University Press, 1968, 1969).

"A Social Critique of Radio Music." *Kenyon Review* 7 (Spring 1945) 2: 208–217.

Bibliography

"Society" (1966). *Salmagundi*, no. 10–11 (Fall 1969–Winter 1970), pp. 144–53. Reprinted in *The Legacy of the German Refugee Intellectuals*, pp. 144–53. Edited by Robert Boyers. New York: Schocken Books, 1969. Also in *Critical Theory and Society*, pp. 267–75.

"Sociology and Empirical Research" (1957). In *The Positivist Dispute in German Sociology*, pp. 68–86. An excerpt under the same title is contained in *Critical Sociology: Selected Readings*, pp. 237–57. Edited by Paul Connerton. Harmondsworth, Middlesex: Penguin Books, 1976.

"Sociology and Psychology" (1955). *New Left Review*, no. 46 (November-December 1967), pp. 63–80; no. 47 (January-February 1968), pp. 79–97.

"The Sociology of Knowledge and Its Consciousness" (–1937+1953). In *The Essential Frankfurt School Reader*, pp. 452–65.

"Spengler Today." *Studies in Philosophy and Social Science* 9 (1941): 305–25.

"The Stars Down to Earth." *Jahrbuch für Amerikastudien*. Vol. 2, pp. 19–88. Heidelberg: Carl Winter, 1957. Reprinted in GS 9.2: 7–120. An abbreviated German version, published in 1962 as "Aberglaube aus zweiter Hand," is reprinted in GS 8: 147–76. See also "The Stars Down to Earth: The Los Angeles Times Astrology Column," *Telos*, no. 19 (Spring 1974), pp. 13–90.

" 'Static' and 'Dynamic' as Sociological Categories" (1956/1961). *Diogenes*, no. 33 (Spring 1961), pp. 28–49.

"Subject and Object" (1969). In *The Essential Frankfurt School Reader*, pp. 497–511.

"Theses against Occultism" (1951). *Telos*, no. 19 (Spring 1974), pp. 7–12.

"Theses on the Sociology of Art" (1967). *Working Papers in Cultural Studies*, no. 2 (Birmingham, Spring 1972), pp. 121–28.

"Theses upon Art and Religion Today." *Kenyon Review* 7 (Autumn 1945) 4: 677–82.

"Transparencies on Film" (1966). *New German Critique*, no. 24–25 (Fall-Winter, 1981–82), pp. 199–205.

"Trying to Understand *Endgame*" (1961). *New German Critique*, no. 26 (Spring-Summer 1982), pp. 119–50. Previously published as "Toward an Understanding of Endgame," in *Twentieth Century Interpretations of Endgame*, pp. 82–114. Edited by Gale Chevigny. Englewood Cliffs, N.J.: Prentice-Hall, 1969.

"Veblen's Attack on Culture: Remarks Occasioned by the Theory of the Leisure Class." *Studies in Philosophy and Social Science* 9 (1941): 389–413.

"Wagner, Nietzsche and Hitler" (review). *Kenyon Review* 9 (Winter 1947) 1: 165–72.

2. Writings on Adorno and Critical Theory

Section 2.1 lists anthologies containing articles by Adorno and articles on Adorno and critical theory. It also includes special issues of journals devoted to Adorno. Individual articles in these anthologies and special issues are not listed separately. Section 2.2 lists many of the reviews of Adorno's *Aesthetic Theory*. Additional reviews in German are cited by Görtzen in *Adorno-Konferenz 1983*, pp. 416–17. Section 2.3 contains other secondary sources on Adorno and on critical theory. Works by Benjamin, Horkheimer, Lukács, and Marcuse as well as by Bürger, Habermas, Jameson, and Wellmer are listed in section 3, along with other primary and secondary sources.

2.1 Anthologies and Special Issues of Journals

Adorno-Konferenz 1983. Edited by Ludwig von Friedeburg and Jürgen Habermas. Frankfurt: Suhrkamp, 1983.

Adorno und die Musik. Edited by Otto Kolleritsch. Studien zur Wertungsforschung, no. 12. Graz: Universal Edition, 1979.

Aesthetics and Politics: Debates between Bloch, Lukács, Brecht, Benjamin, Adorno. Edited by Ronald Taylor. Afterword by Fredric Jameson. London: NLB, 1977; Verso, 1980.

The Aesthetics of the Critical Theorists: Studies on Benjamin, Adorno, Marcuse, and Habermas. Edited by Ronald Roblin. Lewiston, N.Y.: Edwin Mellen Press, 1990.

Critical Sociology: Selected Readings. Edited by Paul Connerton. Harmondsworth, Middlesex: Penguin Books, 1976.

Critical Theory and Society: A Reader. Edited and with an Introduction by Stephen Eric Bronner and Douglas MacKay Kellner. New York: Routledge, 1989.

The Essential Frankfurt School Reader. Edited by Andrew Arato and Eike Gebhardt. Introduction by Paul Piccone. New York: Urizen Books, 1978.

Foundations of the Frankfurt School of Social Research. Edited by Judith Marcus and Zoltan Tar. New Brunswick, N.J.: Transaction Books, 1984.

Die "Frankfurter Schule" im Lichte des Marxismus. Zur Kritik der Philosophie und Soziologie von Horkheimer, Adorno, Marcuse, Habermas. Edited by Johannes Henrich von Heiseler, Robert Steigerwald, and Josef Schleifstein. Frankfurt: Verlag Marxistische Blätter, 1970.

Die Frankfurter Schule und die Folgen. Referate eines Symposiums der Alexander von Humboldt-Stiftung vom 10.–15. Dezember 1984 in Ludwigsburg. Edited by Axel Honneth and Albrecht Wellmer. Berlin: Walter de Gruyter, 1986.

Hamburger Adorno-Symposium. Edited by Michael Löbig and Gerhard Schweppenhäuser. Lüneburg: Dietrich zu Klampen, 1984.

Hermeneutik und Ideologiekritik. With contributions by Karl-Otto Apel et al. Frankfurt: Suhrkamp, 1971.

Humanities in Society 2 (Los Angeles, Fall 1979) 4. This issue contains four articles drawn from an Adorno Symposium held in May 1979 at the University of Southern California.

Journal of Comparative Literature and Aesthetics 10 (1988–89) 1. Special issue on Frankfurt School aesthetics.

Kritik und Interpretation der Kritischen Theorie. Aufsätze über Adorno, Horkheimer, Marcuse, Benjamin, Habermas. Giessen: Andreas Achenbach, 1975.

Bibliography

Materialien zur ästhetischen Theorie Theodor W. Adornos. Konstruktion der Moderne. Edited by Burkhardt Lindner and W. Martin Lüdke. Frankfurt: Suhrkamp, 1979.

Negative Dialektik und die Idee der Versöhnung. Eine Kontroverse über Theodor W. Adorno. Traugott Koch, Klaus-Michael Kodalle, and Hermann Schweppenhäuser. Stuttgart: W. Kohlhammer, 1973.

Die neue Linke nach Adorno. Edited by Wilfried F. Schoeller. Munich: Kindler, 1969.

On Critical Theory. Edited by John O'Neill. New York: Seabury Press, 1976.

Praxis International 3 (July 1983) 2. Issue on "The Critique of Critical Theory."

Revue d'Esthétique. Special issue on Adorno. Nouvelle série, no. 8 (Toulouse, 1985).

Sozialforschung als Kritik. Zum sozialwissenschaftlichen Potential der Kritischen Theorie. Edited by Wolfgang Bonss and Axel Honneth. Frankfurt: Suhrkamp, 1982.

Studia Philosophica Gandensia, vol. 9 (Adorno-Heft) (Meppel, 1971).

Theodor W. Adorno (1977). Edited by Heinz Ludwig Arnold. 2d, enl. ed. Munich: Edition Text + Kritik, 1983.

Theodor W. Adorno zum Gedächtnis. Eine Sammlung. Edited by Hermann Schweppenhäuser. Frankfurt: Suhrkamp, 1971.

Über Theodor W. Adorno. With contributions by Kurt Oppens et al. Frankfurt: Suhrkamp, 1968.

Zeitschrift für Musiktheorie 4 (Adorno-Heft, 1973) 1.

Zeugnisse. Theodor W. Adorno zum sechzigsten Geburtstag. Edited by Max Horkheimer. Frankfurt: Europäische Verlagsanstalt, 1963.

2.2 Reviews of *Aesthetic Theory*

Boyne, Roy. *British Journal of Sociology* 37 (March 1986): 154–55.

Geuss, Raymond. *Journal of Philosophy* 83 (December 1986): 732–41.

Gorsen, Peter. *Frankfurter Allgemeine Zeitung,* 8 December 1970, p. 6, under the title "Wider die Sozial Partner der Barbarei. Theodor W. Adornos 'Ästhetische Theorie'— Das Letzte Werk des Philosophen."

Günter, Joachim. *Neue Deutsche Hefte* 18 (1971) 1: 191–96, under the title "Theodor W. Adorno: Ästhetische Theorie."

Heise, Wolfgang. *Referatedienst zur Literaturwissenschaft* 4 (1972): 97–102.

Hodge, Johanna M. *British Journal of Aesthetics* 26 (Winter 1986): 79–80.

Hullot-Kentor, Bob. "Adorno's *Aesthetic Theory:* The Translation." *Telos,* no. 65 (Fall 1985), pp. 143–47. The same issue contains the translator Christian Lenhardt's "Reply to Hullot-Kentor" (pp. 147–52).

Ingram, David. *Studies in Soviet Thought* 35 (January 1988): 61–64.

Jones, Michael T. *The German Quarterly* 59 (Summer 1986): 464–66.

Knoll, Reinhold. *Literatur und Kritik* 56 (July 1971): 371.

Oppens, Kurt. *Merkur* 25 (August 1971): 802–5, under the title "Adornos Kunstphilosophie."

Redeker, Horst. *Deutsche Zeitschrift für Philosophie* 20 (1972): 928–32.

Regier, Willis. *Modern Language Notes* 101 (April 1986): 705–6.

Scheible, Hartmut. *Frankfurter Rundschau*, 1 July 1972, p. 8, under the title "Wie Adorno zu lesen sei: Die 'Ästhetische Theorie': Rezensionen und andere Missverständnisse."

Shapiro, Henry L. *Philosophical Review* 95 (April 1986): 288–89.

Swingwood, A. *Sociology* 18 (August 1984): 419–20.

Zuidervaart, Lambert. *The Journal of Aesthetics and Art Criticism* 44 (Winter 1985): 195–97. Other versions of this review appear in *Canadian Philosophical Reviews* 6 (January 1986) 1: 1–3, and *The Journal of Comparative Literature and Aesthetics* 10 (1988–89) 1.

2.3 Articles and Books on Adorno and Critical Theory

"Adorno: Love and Cognition." *The Times Literary Supplement*, 9 March 1973, pp. 253–55.

Antonio, Robert. "Immanent Critique as the Core of Critical Theory: Its Origins and Developments in Hegel, Marx and Contemporary Thought." *British Journal of Sociology* 32 (September 1981): 330–45.

Antonio, Robert. "The Origin, Development, and Contemporary Status of Critical Theory." *Sociological Quarterly* 24 (Summer 1983): 325–51.

Arato, Andrew. "Critical Theory in the United States: Reflections on Four Decades of Reception." In *America and the Germans: An Assessment of a Three-Hundred-Year History*. Vol. 2: *The Relationship in the Twentieth Century*, pp. 279–86. Edited by Frank Trommler and Joseph McVeigh. Philadelphia: University of Pennsylvania Press, 1985.

Arato, Andrew. "Introduction: The Antinomies of the Neo-Marxian Theory of Culture." *International Journal of Sociology* 7 (Spring 1977) 1: 3–24.

Baumeister, Thomas. "Theodor W. Adorno—nach zehn Jahren." *Philosophische Rundschau* 28 (1981): 1–26.

Baumeister, Thomas, and Jens Kulenkampff. "Geschichtsphilosophie und philosophische Ästhetik. Zu Adornos 'Ästhetischer Theorie.' " *Neue Hefte für Philosophie*, no. 5 (1973), pp. 74–104.

Beier, Christel. *Zum Verhältnis von Gesellschaftstheorie und Erkenntnistheorie. Untersuchungen in der kritischen Theorie Adornos*. Frankfurt: Suhrkamp, 1977.

Bibliography

Beierwaltes, Werner. "Adornos Nicht-Identisches." In *Weltaspekte der Philosophie. Rudolf Berlinger zum 26 Oktober 1972*, pp. 7–20. Edited by Werner Beierwaltes and Wiebke Schrader. Amsterdam: Rodopi, 1972. An expanded version appears in Beierwaltes, *Identität und Differenz* (Frankfurt: Vittorio Klostermann, 1980), pp. 289–314.

Benjamin, Jessica. "The End of Internalization: Adorno's Social Psychology." *Telos*, no. 32 (Summer 1977), pp. 42–64.

Berman, Russell A. "Adorno, Marxism and Art." *Telos*, no. 34 (Winter 1977–1978), pp. 157–66.

Berman, Russell A. "Adorno's Radicalism: Two Interviews from the Sixties." *Telos*, no. 56 (Summer 1983), pp. 94–97.

Blomster, W. V. "Sociology of Music: Adorno and Beyond." *Telos*, no. 28 (Summer 1976), pp. 81–112.

Böckelmann, Frank. *Über Marx und Adorno. Schwierigkeiten der spätmarxistischen Theorie.* Frankfurt: Makol, 1972.

Boehmer, Konrad. "Adorno, Musik, Gesellschaft" (1969). Reprinted in *Texte zur Musiksoziologie*, pp. 227–38. Edited by Tibor Kneif, with an Introduction by Carl Dahlhaus. Cologne: Arno Volk, 1975.

Bottomore, Tom. *The Frankfurt School.* New York: Tavistock Publications, 1984.

Bubner, Rüdiger. *Essays in Hermeneutics and Critical Theory.* Translated by Eric Matthews. New York: Columbia University Press, 1988.

Bubner, Rüdiger. "Theory and Practice in the Light of the Hermeneutic-Criticist Controversy." *Cultural Hermeneutics* 2 (1975): 337–52.

Bubner, Rüdiger. "Über einige Bedingungen gegenwärtiger Ästhetik." *Neue Hefte für Philosophie*, no. 5 (1973), pp. 38–73.

Buck-Morss, Susan. *The Origin of Negative Dialectics: Theodor W. Adorno, Walter Benjamin, and the Frankfurt Institute.* Hassocks, Sussex: Harvester Press, 1977.

Buck-Morss, Susan. "T. W. Adorno and the Dilemma of Bourgeois Philosophy." *Salmagundi*, no. 36 (Winter 1977), pp. 76–98.

Burde, Wolfgang. "Versuch über einen Satz Theodor W. Adornos." *Neue Zeitschrift für Musik* 132 (1971): 578—83.

Cahn, Michael. "Subversive Mimesis: Theodor W. Adorno and the Modern Impasse of Critique." In *Mimesis in Contemporary Theory: An Interdisciplinary Approach.* Vol. 1: *The Literary and Philosophical Debate*, pp. 27–64. Ed. Mihai Spariosu. Philadelphia: John Benjamins, 1984.

Clark, Kevin M. Review essay on Susan Buck-Morss, *The Origin of Negative Dialectics*, and Gillian Rose, *The Melancholy Science. Graduate Faculty Philosophy Journal* 8 (Spring 1982): 269–305.

Connerton, Paul. *The Tragedy of Enlightenment: An Essay on the Frankfurt School.* Cambridge: Cambridge University Press, 1980.

Dahlhaus, Carl. "Adornos Begriff des musikalischen Materials." In *Zur Terminologie der Musik des 20. Jahrhunderts*, pp. 9–21. Edited by Hans Heinrich Eggebrecht. Stuttgart: Musikwissenschaftliche Verlags-Gesellschaft, 1974.

Dahlhaus, Carl. "Soziologische Dechiffrierung von Musik. Zu Theodor W. Adornos Wagner-Kritik." *The International Review of the Aesthetics and Sociology of Music* 1 (1979): 137–47.

Dallmayr, Fred R. "On Critical Theory." *Philosophy of the Social Sciences* 10 (1980): 93–109.

Dallmayr, Fred R. "Phenomenology and Critical Theory: Adorno." *Cultural Hermeneutics* 3 (1976): 367–405.

Davidov, Iu. N. "The Problem of Art in the Social Philosophy of the Frankfurt School." *Soviet Studies in Philosophy* 24 (Fall 1985): 62–85.

Dawydov, Juri. *Die sich selbst negierende Dialektik. Kritik der Musiktheorie Theodor Adornos.* Frankfurt: Verlag Marxistische Blätter, 1971.

Degenaar, Johannes. "Critical Notice: Thought Thinking Against Itself." *Philosophical Papers* 5 (October 1976): 162–65.

Dews, Peter. *Logics of Disintegration: Post-structuralist Thought and the Claims of Critical Theory.* London, New York: Verso, 1987.

Dubiel, Helmut. *Theory and Politics: Studies in the Development of Critical Theory.* Translated by Benjamin Gregg. Cambridge, Mass.: MIT Press, 1985.

Fehér, Ferenc. "Negative Philosophy of Music—Positive Results." *New German Critique,* no. 4 (Winter 1975), pp. 99–111.

Fehér, Ferenc. "Rationalized Music and Its Vicissitudes (Adorno's Philosophy of Music)." *Philosophy and Social Criticism* 9 (Spring 1982) 1: 41–65.

Figal, Günter. *Theodor W. Adorno. Das Naturschöne als spekulative Gedankenfigur. Zur Interpretation der "Ästhetischen Theorie" im Kontext philosophischer Ästhetik.* Bonn: Bouvier Verlag Herbert Grundmann, 1977.

Focht, Ivan. "Adornos gnoseologistische Einstellung zur Musik." *International Review of the Aesthetics and Sociology of Music* 5 (1974): 265–76.

Friedman, George. *The Political Philosophy of the Frankfurt School.* Ithaca: Cornell University Press, 1981.

Frow, John. "Mediation and Metaphor: Adorno and the Sociology of Art." *Clio* 12 (Fall 1982) 1: 57–65.

Geuss, Raymond. *The Idea of a Critical Theory: Habermas and the Frankfurt School.* Cambridge: Cambridge University Press, 1981.

Geyer, Carl-Friedrich. *Kritische Theorie: Max Horkheimer und Theodor W. Adorno.* Freiburg: Karl Alber, 1982.

Grenz, Friedemann. *Adornos Philosophie in Grundbegriffen. Auflösung einiger Deutungsprobleme.* Frankfurt: Suhrkamp, 1974.

Grenz, Friedemann. " 'Die Idee der Naturgeschichte.' Zu eine frühen, unbekannten Text Adornos." In *Natur und Geschichte*, pp. 344–50. Deutscher Kongress für Philosophie, Kiel 8.–12. Oktober 1972. Edited by Kurt Hübner and Albert Menne. Hamburg: Felix Meiner, 1973.

Held, David. *Introduction to Critical Theory: Horkheimer to Habermas*. Berkeley: University of California Press, 1980.

Heller, Agnes. "The Positivism Dispute as a Turning Point in German Post-War Theory." *New German Critique*, no. 15 (Fall 1978), pp. 49–56.

Hohendahl, Peter U. "Autonomy of Art: Looking Back at Adorno's *Ästhetische Theorie*." *German Quarterly* 54 (March 1981): 133–48.

Hohendahl, Peter U. "The Dialectic of Enlightenment Revisited: Habermas' Critique of the Frankfurt School," *New German Critique*, no. 35 (Spring-Summer 1985), pp. 3–26.

Honneth, Axel. "Communication and Reconciliation: Habermas' Critique of Adorno." *Telos*, no. 39 (Spring 1979), pp. 45–61.

Hrachovec, Herbert. "Was lässt sich von Erlösung Denken? Gedanken von und über Th. W. Adornos Philosophie." *Philosophisches Jahrbuch* 83 (1976): 357–70.

Huhn, Thomas. "Adorno's Aesthetics of Illusion." *Journal of Aesthetics and Art Criticism* 44 (Winter 1985): 181–89.

Hullot-Kentor, Robert. "Back to Adorno." *Telos*, no. 81 (Fall 1989), pp. 5–29.

Hullot-Kentor, Robert. "Popular Music and Adorno's 'The Aging of the New Music.' " *Telos*, no. 77 (Fall 1988), pp. 79–94.

Huyssen, Andreas. "Adorno in Reverse: From Hollywood to Richard Wagner." *New German Critique*, no. 29 (Spring-Summer 1983), pp. 8–38.

Jacoby, Russell. "Marxism and the Critical School." *Theory and Society* 1 (Summer 1974): 231–38.

Jay, Martin. *Adorno*. Cambridge, Mass.: Harvard University Press, 1984.

Jay, Martin. "Adorno in America." *New German Critique*, no. 31 (Winter 1984), pp. 157–82.

Jay, Martin. "The Concept of Totality in Lukács and Adorno." *Telos*, no. 32 (Summer 1977), pp. 117–37.

Jay, Martin. "Critical Theory Criticized: Zoltán Tar and the Frankfurt School." *Central European History* 12 (March 1979): 91–98.

Jay, Martin. *The Dialectical Imagination: A History of the Frankfurt School and the Institute of Social Research 1923–1950*. Boston: Little, Brown, 1973.

Jay, Martin. "The Frankfurt School's Critique of Marxist Humanism." *Social Research* 39 (Summer 1972): 285–305.

Bibliography

Jay, Martin. *Permanent Exiles: Essays on the Intellectual Migration from Germany to America.* New York: Columbia University Press, 1985.

Kaiser, Gerhard. *Benjamin. Adorno. Zwei Studien.* Frankfurt: Athenäum Fischer Taschenbuch, 1974.

Kellner, Douglas. *Critical Theory, Marxism, and Modernity.* Baltimore: Johns Hopkins Press, 1989.

Kellner, Douglas. "The Frankfurt School Revisited: A Critique of Martin Jay's *The Dialectical Imagination.*" *New German Critique,* no. 4 (Winter 1975), pp. 131–52.

Kellner, Douglas, and Rick Roderick. "Recent Literature on Critical Theory." *New German Critique,* no. 23 (Spring-Summer 1981), pp. 141–70.

Kerkhoff, Manfred. "Die Rettung des Nichtidentischen. Zur Philosophie Th. W. Adornos." *Philosophische Rundschau* 20 (1974): 150–78 and 21 (1975): 56–74.

Klapwijk, Jacob. *Dialektiek der verlichting. Een verkenning in het neomarxisme van de Frankfurter Schule.* 2d ed. Amsterdam: Van Gorcum, 1977.

Knapp, Gerhard. *Theodor W. Adorno.* Berlin: Colloquium, 1980.

Kofler, Leo. "Weder 'Wiederspiegelung' noch Abstraktion: Lukács oder Adorno?" In *Zur Theorie der modernen Literatur: Der Avantgardismus in soziologischer Sicht,* pp. 160–87. 2d ed. Düsseldorf: Bertelsmann Universitätsverlag, 1974.

Krahl, Hans-Jürgen. "The Political Contradictions in Adorno's Critical Theory." *Telos,* no. 21 (Fall 1974), pp. 164–67.

Künzli, Arnold. *Aufklärung und Dialektik. Politische Philosophie von Hobbes bis Adorno.* Freiburg: Rombach, 1971.

Kuspit, Donald B. "Critical Notes on Adorno's Sociology of Music and Art." *Journal of Aesthetics and Art Criticism* 33 (Spring 1975): 321–27.

Lang, Peter Christian. *Hermeneutik, Ideologiekritik, Ästhetik: Über Gadamer und Adorno sowie Fragen einer aktuellen Ästhetik.* Königstein/Ts.: Forum Academicum, 1981.

Leiss, William. "Critical Theory and Its Future." *Political Theory* 2 (August 1974): 330–49.

Lohmann, Hans-Martin. "Adornos Ästhetik." In *Adorno zur Einführung,* pp. 71–82. Willem van Reijen. Hannover: SOAK, 1980.

Löwenthal, Leo. "Recollections of Theodor W. Adorno." *Telos,* no. 61 (Fall 1984), pp. 158–65.

Lüdke, W. Martin. *Anmerkungen zu einer "Logik des Zerfalls": Adorno—Beckett.* Frankfurt: Suhrkamp, 1981.

Lunn, Eugene. *Marxism and Modernism: An Historical Study of Lukács, Brecht, Benjamin, and Adorno.* Berkeley: University of California Press, 1982.

Lyotard, Jean-François. "Adorno as the Devil." *Telos,* no. 19 (Spring 1974), pp. 127–37.

Bibliography

Marramao, Giacomo. "Political Economy and Critical Theory" (1973). *Telos*, no. 24 (Summer 1975), pp. 56–80.

"Marxism and Critical Theory: Martin Jay and Russell Jacoby." *Theory and Society* 2 (Summer 1975): 257–63.

Mayer, Günter. "Zur Dialektik des musikalischen Materials" (1966, 1969). Reprinted in *Texte zur Musiksoziologie*, pp. 200–226. Edited by Tibor Kneif, with an Introduction by Carl Dahlhaus. Cologne: Arno Volk, 1975.

Mörchen, Hermann. *Macht und Herrschaft im Denken von Heidegger und Adorno*. Stuttgart: Klett-Cotta, 1980.

Müller, Harro. "Gesellschaftliche Funktion und ästhetische Autonomie: Benjamin, Adorno, Habermas." *Literaturwissenschaft: Grundkurs 2*, pp. 329–40. Edited by Helmut Brackert and Jörn Stückrath. Reinbeck bei Hamburg: Rowohlt, 1981.

Müller-Strömsdörfer, Ilse. "Die 'helfende Kraft bestimmter Negation.' Zum Werke Th. W. Adornos." *Philosophische Rundschau* 8 (1960): 81–105.

Narskii, I. S. "Adorno's Negative Philosophy." *Soviet Studies in Philosophy* 24 (Summer 1985): 3–45.

Neumaier, John J. "The Frankfurt School in Soviet Eyes." *Philosophical Forum* 17 (Summer 1986): 322–34.

Paetzhold, Heinz. *Neomarxistische Ästhetik*. 2 parts. Part 2: *Adorno, Marcuse*. Düsseldorf: Pädagogischer Verlag Schwann, 1974.

Plessner, Helmuth. "Adornos Negative Dialektik. Ihr Thema mit Variationen." *Kant-Studien* 61 (1970): 507–519.

Plessner, Helmuth. "Zum Verständnis der ästhetischen Theorie Adornos." *Philosophische Perspektiven*, no. 4 (1972), pp. 126–36.

Puder, Martin. "Adornos Philosophie und die gegenwärtige Erfahrung." *Neue Deutsche Hefte* 23 (1976): 3–21.

Puder, Martin. "Die Frankfurter Schule und die Neue Linke." *Neue Deutsche Hefte* 18 (1971) 1: 113–22.

Puder, Martin. "Zur 'Ästhetischen Theorie' Adornos." *Neue Rundschau* 82 (1971): 465–77.

Pütze, Peter. "Nietzsche and Critical Theory" (1974). *Telos*, no. 50 (Winter 1981–82), pp. 103–114.

Raddatz, Fritz J. "Der hölzerne Eisenring. Die moderne Literatur zwischen zweierlei Ästhetik: Lukács und Adorno." *Merkur* 31 (1977): 28–44.

Rehfus, Wulff. "Theodor W. Adorno. Die Rekonstruktion der Wahrheit aus der Ästhetik." Cologne: Universität zu Köln, Inaugural-Dissertation, 1976.

Reijen, Willem van. *Adorno zur Einführung*. Hannover: SOAK, 1980.

Bibliography

Reijen, Willem van. *Filosofie als Kritiek: Inleiding in de Kritische Theorie.* Alphen aan den Rijn/Brussel: Samson Uitgeverij, 1981.

Ries, Wiebrecht. " 'Die Rettung des Hoffnungslosen.' Zur 'theologia occulta' in der Spätphilosophie Horkheimers und Adornos." *Zeitschrift für philosophische Forschung* 30 (1976): 69–81.

Rohrmoser, Günter. *Das Elend der kritischen Theorie. Theodor W. Adorno, Herbert Marcuse, Jürgen Habermas.* Freiburg: Rombach, 1970.

Rose, Gillian. *The Melancholy Science: An Introduction to the Thought of Theodor W. Adorno.* London: Macmillan Press, 1978.

Sauerland, Karol. *Einführung in die Ästhetik Adornos.* Berlin: Walter de Gruyter, 1979.

Savile, Anthony. "Beauty and Truth: The Apotheosis of an Idea." In *Analytic Aesthetics,* pp. 23–46. Edited by Richard Shusterman. Oxford: Basil Blackwell, 1989.

Scheible, Hartmut. "Von der bestimmten zur abstrakten Negation. Max Horkheimer und die Antinomien der Kritischen Theorie." *Neue Rundschau* 87 (1976): 86–111.

Schmidt, Alfred. *Die Kritische Theorie als Geschichtsphilosophie.* Munich: Carl Hanser, 1976.

Schmidt, Alfred. "Nachwort des Herausgebers: Zur Idee der kritischen Theorie." In *Max Horkheimer, Kritische Theorie: Eine Dokumentation,* 2: 333–58. Edited by Alfred Schmidt. Frankfurt: S. Fischer, 1968; reprinted as a single-volume study edition, 1977.

Schmidt, James. "Offensive Critical Theory? Reply to Honneth." *Telos,* no. 39 (Spring 1979), pp. 62–70.

Schmucker, Joseph F. *Adorno—Logik des Zerfalls.* Stuttgart: Frommann-Holzboog, 1977.

Siebert, Rudolf J. "Adorno's Theory of Religion." *Telos,* no. 58 (Winter 1983–84), pp. 108–114.

Slater, Phil. *Origin and Significance of the Frankfurt School: A Marxist Perspective.* London: Routledge & Kegan Paul, 1977.

Söllner, Alfons. "Geschichte und Herrschaft—Eine kritische Studie zum Verhältnis von Philosophie und Sozialwissenschaft in der Kritischen Theorie." *Philosophisches Jahrbuch* 83 (1976): 333–56.

Specht, Silvia. *Erinnerung als Veränderung. Über den Zusammenhang von Kunst und Politik bei Theodor W. Adorno.* Mittenwald: Mäander Kunstverlag, 1981.

Spülbeck, Volker. *Neomarxismus und Theologie. Gesellschaftskritik in Kritischer Theorie und Politischer Theologie.* Freiburg: Herder, 1977.

Subotnik, Rose Rosengard. "Adorno's Diagnosis of Beethoven's Late Style: Early Symptom of a Fatal Condition." *Journal of the American Musicological Society* 29 (1976): 242–75.

Subotnik, Rose Rosengard. "Why Is Adorno's Music Criticism the Way It Is? Some Reflections on Twentieth-Century Criticism of Nineteenth-Century Music." *Musical Newsletter* 7 (Fall 1977) 4: 3–12.

Bibliography

Sziborsky, Lucia. *Adornos Musikphilosophie. Genese—Konstitution—Pädagogische Perspektiven.* Munich: Wilhelm Fink, 1979.

Sziborsky, Lucia. "Das Problem des Verstehens und der Begriff der 'Adäquanz' bei Th. W. Adorno." In *Musik und Verstehen. Aufsätze zur semiotischen Theorie, Ästhetik und Soziologie der musikalischen Rezeption,* pp. 289–305. Edited by Peter Faltin and Hans-Peter Reinecke. Cologne: Arno Volk/Hans Gerig, 1973.

Tar, Zoltán. *The Frankfurt School: The Critical Theories of Max Horkheimer and Theodor W. Adorno.* Foreword by Michael Landmann. New York: John Wiley, 1977.

Therborn, Göran. "The Frankfurt School." *New Left Review,* no. 63 (September-October 1970), pp. 65–96.

Theunissen, Michael. *Gesellschaft und Geschichte. Zur Kritik der kritischen Theorie.* Berlin: Walter de Gruyter, 1969.

Tichy, Matthias. *Theodor W. Adorno. Das Verhältnis von Allgemeinem und Besonderem in seiner Philosophie.* Bonn: Bouvier Verlag Herbert Grundmann, 1977.

Tomberg, Friedrich. "Utopie und Negation. Zum ontologischen Hintergrund der Kunsttheorie Theodor W. Adornos." *Das Argument,* no. 26 (July 1963), pp. 36–48.

Ulle, Dieter. "Bürgerliche Kulturkritik und Ästhetik. Bemerkungen zu Theodor Adornos Schrift 'Ästhetische Theorie.'" *Weimarer Beiträge* 18 (1972) 6: 133–54.

van den Burg, Axel. "Critical Theory: Is There Still Hope?" *American Journal of Sociology* 86 (November 1980): 449–78.

Waldman, Diane. "Critical Theory and Film: Adorno and 'The Culture Industry' Revisited." *New German Critique,* no. 12 (Fall 1977), pp. 39–60.

Weitzman, R. "An Introduction to Adorno's Music and Social Criticsm." *Music and Letters* 52 (1971): 287–98.

Werkmeister, O. K. "Das Kunstwerk als Negation. Zur geschichtlichen Bestimmung der Kunsttheorie Theodor W. Adornos." In his *Ende der Ästhetik,* pp. 7–32. Frankfurt: S. Fischer, 1971.

Wiggershaus, Rolf. *Die Frankfurter Schule.* Munich: Carl Hanser, 1986.

Wilson, H. T. "Critical Theory's Critique of Social Science: Episodes in a Changing Problematic from Adorno to Habermas." *History of European Ideas* 7 (1986): 127–47, 287–302.

Wohlfart, Günter. "Anmerkungen zur ästhetischen Theorie Adornos." *Philosophisches Jahrbuch* 83 (1976): 370–91. A revised version appears in *Zeitschrift für Ästhetik und allgemeine Kunstwissenschaft* 22 (1977): 110–34.

Wohlfarth, Irving. "Hibernation: On the Tenth Anniversary of Adorno's Death." *Modern Language Notes* 94 (December 1979): 956–87.

Wolin, Richard. "The De-Aestheticization of Art: On Adorno's *Aesthetische Theorie.*" *Telos,* no. 41 (Fall 1979), pp. 105–127.

Bibliography

Wolin, Richard. *Walter Benjamin: An Aesthetic of Redemption.* New York: Columbia University Press, 1982.

Zenck, Martin. "Auswirkungen einer 'musique informelle' auf die neue Musik: Zu Theodor W. Adornos Formvorstellung." *International Review of the Aesthetics and Sociology of Music* 10 (1979) 2: 137–65.

Zenck, Martin. *Kunst als begriffslose Erkenntnis. Zum Kunstbegriff der ästhetischen Theorie Theodor W. Adornos.* Munich: Wilhelm Fink, 1977.

Zima, Peter V. "Dialektik zwischen Totalität und Fragment." In *Der Streit mit Georg Lukács,* pp. 124–72. Edited by Hans-Jürgen Schmitt. Frankfurt: Suhrkamp, 1978.

Zuidervaart, Lambert. "The Artefactuality of Autonomous Art: Kant and Adorno." In *The Reasons of Art: Artworks and the Transformations of Philosophy,* pp. 256–62. Edited by Peter McCormick. Ottawa: University of Ottawa Press, 1986.

Zuidervaart, Lambert. "Contra-Diction: Adorno's Philosophy of Discourse." In *Philosophy of Discourse.* Edited by George H. Jensen and Chip Sills. Heinemann Educational Books, forthcoming.

Zuidervaart, Lambert. "Methodological Shadowboxing in Marxist Aesthetics: Lukács and Adorno." *Journal of Comparative Literature and Aesthetics* 10 (1988–89) 1. Reprinted in *The Aesthetics of the Critical Theorists,* pp. 244–90.

Zuidervaart, Lambert. "The Social Significance of Autonomous Art: Adorno and Bürger." *Journal of Aesthetics and Art Criticism* 48 (Winter 1990): 61–77.

3. Other Primary and Secondary Works

Anderson, Perry. *Considerations on Western Marxism.* London: NLB, 1976; Verso, 1979.

Anderson, Perry. *In the Tracks of Historical Materialism.* Chicago: University of Chicago Press, 1984.

Arato, Andrew. "Lukács' Theory of Reification." *Telos,* no. 11 (Spring 1972), pp. 25–66.

Arato, Andrew, and Paul Breines. *The Young Lukács and the Origins of Western Marxism.* New York: Seabury Press, 1979.

Aronowitz, Stanley. "Culture and Politics." *Politics and Society* 6 (1976): 347–96.

Arvon, Henri. *Marxist Esthetics* (1970). Translated by Helen R. Lane. Introduction by Fredric Jameson. Ithaca: Cornell University Press, 1973.

Baynes, Kenneth, James Bohman, and Thomas McCarthy, eds. *After Philosophy: End or Transformation?* Cambridge, Mass.: MIT Press, 1987.

Beardsley, Monroe C. *Aesthetics from Classical Greece to the Present: A Short History.* New York: Macmillan, 1966; paperback reprint by University of Alabama Press, 1975.

Becker, Howard. *Art Worlds.* Berkeley: University of California Press, 1982.

Beckett, Samuel. *Endgame*. London: Faber and Faber, 1958.

Benhabib, Seyla. *Critique, Norm, and Utopia: A Study of the Foundations of Critical Theory*. New York: Columbia University Press, 1986.

Benhabib, Seyla. "Modernity and the Aporias of Critical Theory." *Telos*, no. 49 (Fall 1981), pp. 39–59.

Benjamin, Walter. "Doctrine of the Similar (1933)." *New German Critique*, no. 17 (Spring 1979), pp. 65–69.

Benjamin, Walter. *Illuminationen. Ausgewählte Schriften*. Frankfurt: Suhrkamp, 1977.

Benjamin, Walter. *Illuminations*. Edited and with an Introduction by Hannah Arendt. Translated by Harry Zohn. New York: Schocken Books, 1969. (The contents and arrangement of this English edition differ from the German edition of 1977. The English edition is based on the 1955 edition of Benjamin's *Schriften*. The German edition of 1977 presents the critically revised text of Benjamin's *Gesammelte Schriften*, 1972–.)

Benjamin, Walter. *The Origin of German Tragic Drama*. Translated by John Osborne. London: NLB, 1977.

Benjamin, Walter. *Reflections: Essays, Aphorisms, Autobiographical Writings*. Edited with an Introduction by Peter Demetz. Translated by Edmund Jephcott. New York: Harcourt, Brace, Jovanovitch, 1978.

Benjamin, Walter. "Über das Programm der kommenden Philosophie." In *Zeugnisse. Theodor W. Adorno zum sechzigsten Geburtstag*, pp. 33–44.

Benjamin, Walter. *Understanding Brecht*. Translated by Anna Bostock. Introduction by Stanley Mitchell. London: NLB, 1973; Verso, 1983.

Benjamin, Walter. *Ursprung des deutschen Trauerspiels* (–1925+1928). Edited by Rolf Tiedemann. Frankfurt: Suhrkamp, 1955, 1963, 1974.

Berman, Russell A. "Modern Art and Desublimation." *Telos*, no. 62 (Winter 1984–85), pp. 31–57.

Bernstein, Richard J., ed. *Habermas and Modernity*. Cambridge, Mass.: MIT Press, 1985.

Bourdieu, Pierre. *Distinction: A Social Critique of the Judgement of Taste* (1979). Translated by Richard Nice. Cambridge, Mass.: Harvard University Press, 1984.

Breines, Paul. Review of *Dialectic of Defeat: Contours of Western Marxism*, by Russell Jacoby. *Telos*, no. 52 (Summer 1982), pp. 203–9.

Breines, Paul. "*The Two Marxisms:* Vintage Gouldner." *Theory and Society* 10 (March 1981): 249–64.

Bubner, Rüdiger. "Hegel's Aesthetics—Yesterday and Today." In *Art and Logic in Hegel's Philosophy*, pp. 15–33. Edited by Warren E. Steinkraus and Kenneth Schmitz. Atlantic Highlands, N.J.: Humanities Press, 1980.

Bubner, Rüdiger. *Modern German Philosophy*. Translated by Eric Matthews. Cambridge: Cambridge University Press, 1981.

Bürger, Christa, and Peter Bürger, eds. *Postmodern: Alltag, Allegorie und Avantgarde.* Frankfurt: Suhrkamp, 1981.

Bürger, Peter. "Adorno, Bourdieu und die Literatursoziologie." *Jahrbuch für Internationale Germanistik* 17 (1985) 1: 47–56.

Bürger, Peter. "The Decline of the Modern Age." *Telos,* no. 62 (Winter 1984–85), pp. 117–30.

Bürger, Peter. "The Institution of 'Art' as a Category in the Sociology of Literature." *Cultural Critique,* no. 2 (Winter 1986), pp. 5–33.

Bürger, Peter. "Literary Criticism in Germany Today." In *Observations on the Spiritual Situation of the Age,* pp. 207–220. Edited by Jürgen Habermas. Translated by Andrew Buchwalter. Cambridge, Mass.: MIT Press, 1984.

Bürger, Peter, ed. *Seminar: Literatur- und Kunstsoziologie.* Frankfurt: Suhrkamp, 1978.

Bürger, Peter. "The Significance of the Avant-Garde for Contemporary Aesthetics: A Reply to Jürgen Habermas." *New German Critique,* no. 22 (Winter 1981), pp. 19–22.

Bürger, Peter. *Theorie der Avantgarde.* 2d ed. Frankfurt: Suhrkamp, 1980.

Bürger, Peter. *Theory of the Avant-Garde.* Translated by Michael Shaw. Foreword by Jochen Schulte-Sass. Minneapolis: University of Minnesota Press, 1984.

Bürger, Peter. *Vermittlung—Rezeption—Funktion: Ästhetische Theorie und Methodologie der Literaturwissenschaft.* Frankfurt: Suhrkamp, 1979.

Callinicos, Alex. *Marxism and Philosophy.* Oxford: Clarendon Press, 1983.

Casey, Edward S. "Truth in Art." *Man and World* 3 (September-November 1970): 351–69.

Cassirer, Ernst. *The Logic of the Humanities.* Translated by Clarence Smith Howe. New Haven: Yale University Press, 1960, 1961.

Colletti, Lucio. *Marxism and Hegel* (1969). Translated by Lawrence Garner. London: NLB, 1973; Verso, 1979.

Dahlhaus, Carl. *Esthetics of Music* (1967). Translated by William W. Austin. Cambridge: Cambridge University Press, 1982.

Dahlhaus, Carl. *Foundations of Music History* (1977). Translated by J. B. Robinson. Cambridge: Cambridge University Press, 1983.

Dahlhaus, Carl. *The Idea of Absolute Music* (1978). Translated by Roger Lustig. Chicago: University of Chicago Press, 1989.

Diacritics 12 (Fall 1982) 3. Special Issue on Fredric Jameson.

Dooyeweerd, Herman. *A New Critique of Theoretical Thought* (1953–1958). Translated by David H. Freeman, William S. Young, and H. De Jongste. Reprint ed. 4 vols. Philadelphia: Presbyterian and Reformed Publishing, 1969.

Bibliography

Dowling, William C. *Jameson, Althusser, Marx: An Introduction to "The Political Unconscious."* Ithaca: Cornell University Press, 1984.

Dufrenne, Mikel. "The Truth of the Aesthetic Object." In *The Phenomenology of Aesthetic Experience* (1953), pp. 501–538. Translated by Edward S. Casey et al. Evanston: Northwestern University Press, 1973.

Eagleton, Terry. " 'Aesthetics and Politics.' " *New Left Review*, no. 107 (January-February 1978), pp. 21–34.

Eagleton, Terry. *Literary Theory: An Introduction.* Minneapolis: University of Minnesota Press, 1983.

Eagleton, Terry. *Marxism and Literary Criticism.* London: Methuen, 1976.

Eaton, Marcia Muelder. *Basic Issues in Aesthetics.* Belmont, Calif.: Wadsworth, 1988.

Echeverria, Edward J. *Criticism and Commitment: Major Themes in Contemporary 'Post-Critical' Philosophy.* Amsterdam: Rodopi, 1981.

Esslin, Martin. *The Theatre of the Absurd* (1961). Revised ed. Garden City, N.Y.: Doubleday, Anchor Books, 1969.

Feenberg, Andrew. *Lukács, Marx and the Sources of Critical Theory.* Totowa, N.J.: Rowman and Littlefield, 1981.

Fehér, Ferenc. "Grandeur and Decline of a Holistic Philosophy." *Theory and Society* 14 (July 1985): 863–76.

Foster, Hal, ed. *The Anti-Aesthetic: Essays on Postmodern Culture.* Port Townsend, Wash.: Bay Press, 1983.

Gadamer, Hans-Georg. *Truth and Method* (1960). Rev. ed. Edited by Donald G. Marshall and Joel C. Weinsheimer. New York: Continuum, 1988.

Gadamer, Hans-Georg. *Wahrheit und Methode. Grundzüge einer philosophischen Hermeneutik.* Unchanged reprint of the 3rd, enl. ed. Tübingen: J. C. B. Mohr (Paul Siebeck), 1975.

Goodman, Nelson. *Languages of Art: An Approach to a Theory of Symbols.* Indianapolis: Bobbs-Merrill, 1968.

Goudzwaard, Bob. *Capitalism and Progress. A Diagnosis of Western Society.* Translated and edited by Josina Van Nuis Zylstra. Grand Rapids, Mich.: William B. Eerdmans, 1979.

Gouldner, Alvin W. *The Two Marxisms: Contradictions and Anomalies in the Development of Theory.* New York: Seabury Press, 1980.

Gregg, Benjamin. "Modernity in Frankfurt: Must a History of Philosophy Be a Philosophy of History?" *Theory and Society* 16 (January 1987): 139–51.

Habermas, Jürgen. "The Dialectics of Rationalization: An Interview with Jürgen Habermas." By Axel Honneth, Eberhard Knödler-Bunte, and Arno Wildman. *Telos*, no. 49 (Fall 1981), pp. 5–31.

Habermas, Jürgen. "The Entwinement of Myth and Enlightenment: Re-reading *Dialectic of Enlightenment.*" *New German Critique*, no. 26 (Spring-Summer 1982), pp. 13–30.

Habermas, Jürgen. "The Inimitable Zeitschrift für Sozialforschung: How Horkheimer Took Advantage of a Historically Oppressive Hour." *Telos*, no. 45 (Fall 1980), pp. 114–21.

Habermas, Jürgen. "Modern and Postmodern Architecture." In *Critical Theory and Public Life*, pp. 317–29. Edited by John Forster. Cambridge, Mass.: MIT Press, 1985.

Habermas, Jürgen. "Modernity versus Postmodernity." *New German Critique*, no. 22 (Winter 1981), pp. 3–14. Reprinted as "Modernity—An Incomplete Project" in *The Anti-Aesthetic: Essays on Postmodern Culture*, pp. 3–15. Edited by Hal Foster. Port Townsend, Wash.: Bay Press, 1983.

Habermas, Jürgen. "Neoconservative Culture Criticism in the United States and West Germany: An Intellectual Movement in Two Political Cultures." *Telos*, no. 56 (Summer 1983), pp. 75–89. Reprinted in *Habermas and Modernity*, pp. 78–94. Edited by Richard J. Bernstein. Cambridge, Mass.: MIT Press, 1985.

Habermas, Jürgen. *The Philosophical Discourse of Modernity: Twelve Lectures* (1985). Translated by Frederick Lawrence. Cambridge, Mass.: MIT Press, 1987.

Habermas, Jürgen. *Philosophical-Political Profiles.* Translated by Frederick G. Lawrence. Cambridge, Mass.: MIT Press, 1983.

Habermas, Jürgen. *Philosophisch-politische Profile.* Frankfurt: Suhrkamp, 1971.

Habermas, Jürgen. *The Theory of Communicative Action.* Translated by Thomas McCarthy. Vol. 1: *Reason and the Rationalization of Society.* Vol. 2: *Lifeworld and System.* Boston: Beacon Press, 1984, 1987.

Habermas, Jürgen. "Wahrheitstheorien." In *Wirklichkeit und Reflexion. Walter Schulz zum 60. Geburtstag*, pp. 211–65. Edited by Helmut Fahrenbach. Pfullingen: Neske, 1973.

Hamburger, Käte. *Wahrheit und ästhetische Wahrkeit.* Stuttgart: Klett-Cotta, 1979.

Hanslick, Eduard. *On the Musically Beautiful: A Contribution towards the Revision of the Aesthetics of Music.* Translated and edited from the 8th German ed. of 1891 by Geoffrey Payzant. Indianapolis: Hackett, 1986.

Hanslick, Eduard. *Vom Musikalisch-Schönen. Ein Beitrag zur Revision der Ästhetik der Tonkunst.* Reprint of the 1st ed., Leipzig 1854. Darmstadt: Wissenschaftliche Buchgesellschaft, 1976.

Hart, Hendrik. *Understanding Our World: An Integral Ontology.* Lanham, Md.: University Press of America, 1984.

Hegel, Georg Wilhelm Friedrich. *Aesthetics: Lectures on Fine Art.* Translated by T. M. Knox. 2 vols. Oxford: Oxford University Press, 1974, 1975.

Hegel, Georg Wilhelm Friedrich. *On Art, Religion, Philosophy. Introductory Lectures to the Realm of Absolute Spirit.* Edited, with an Introduction, by J. Glenn Gray. New York: Harper Torchbooks, 1970.

Bibliography

Hegel, Georg Wilhelm Friedrich. *Phänomenologie des Geistes* (1807). 6th ed. Edited by Johannes Hoffmeister. Hamburg: Felix Meiner, 1952.

Hegel, Georg Wilhelm Friedrich. *Phenomenology of Spirit*. Translated by A. V. Miller. Oxford: Oxford University Press, 1977.

Hegel, Georg Wilhelm Friedrich. *Vorlesungen über die Ästhetik*. Vols. 13–15 of *Hegel's Werke in Zwanzig Bänden*. Edited by Eva Moldenhauer and Karl Markus Michel on the basis of the *Werke* of 1832–45. Theorie-Werkausgabe. Frankfurt: Suhrkamp, 1970.

Heidegger, Martin. "The Origin of the Work of Art" (1935). In *Poetry, Language, Thought*, pp. 17–87. Translated by Albert Hofstadter. New York: Harper & Row, 1971.

Heller, Agnes. "Lukács and the Holy Family." *Telos*, no. 62 (Winter 1984–85), pp. 145–53.

Henrich, Dieter. "Art and Philosophy of Art Today: Reflections with Reference to Hegel." In *New Perspectives in German Literary Criticism: A Collection of Essays*, pp. 107–133. Edited by Richard E. Amacher and Victor Lange. Translated by David Henry Wilson et al. Princeton: Princeton University Press, 1979.

Hermerén, Göran. "The Autonomy of Art." In *Essays on Aesthetics: Perspectives on the Work of Monroe C. Beardsley*, pp. 35–49. Edited by John Fisher. Philadelphia: Temple University Press, 1983.

Hofstadter, Albert. *Truth and Art*. New York: Columbia University Press, 1965.

Honneth, Axel. "Work and Instrumental Action." *New German Critique*, no. 26 (Spring-Summer 1982), pp. 31–54.

Horkheimer, Max. "Art and Mass Culture." *Studies in Philosophy and Social Science* 9 (1941): 290–304.

Horkheimer, Max. *Critical Theory: Selected Essays*. Translated by Matthew J. O'Connell et al. New York: Continuum, 1972.

Horkheimer, Max. *Critique of Instrumental Reason*. Translated by Matthew J. O'Connell et al. New York: Continuum, 1974.

Horkheimer, Max. *Eclipse of Reason*. New York: Oxford University Press, 1947; Seabury Press, 1974.

Horkheimer, Max. "Notes on Institute Activities." *Studies in Philosophy and Social Science* 9 (1941): 121–23. Reprinted in *Critical Theory and Society*, pp. 264–66.

Horkheimer, Max. "On the Problem of Truth" (1935). In *The Essential Frankfurt School Reader*, pp. 407–43.

Horkheimer, Max. *Die Sehnsucht nach dem ganz Anderen. Ein Interview mit Kommentar von Helmut Gumnior*. Hamburg: Furche, 1970.

Horkheimer, Max. "Traditionelle und kritische Theorie." *Zeitschrift für Sozialforschung* 6 (1937): 245–94.

Horkheimer, Max. "Zum Problem der Wahrheit." *Zeitschrift für Sozialforschung* 4 (1935): 321–64.

Hospers, John. *Meaning and Truth in the Arts*. Chapel Hill: University of North Carolina Press, 1946, 1974.

Howard, Dick. *The Marxian Legacy* (1977). 2d ed. Minneapolis: University of Minnesota Press, 1987.

Huyssen, A. "Mapping the Postmodern." *New German Critique*, no. 33 (Fall 1984), pp. 5–52.

Jacoby, Russell. *Dialectic of Defeat: Contours of Western Marxism*. Cambridge: Cambridge University Press, 1981.

Jameson, Fredric. "Cognitive Mapping." In *Marxism and the Interpretation of Culture*, pp. 347–57. Edited by Cary Nelson and Lawrence Grossberg. Urbana and Chicago: University of Illinois Press, 1988.

Jameson, Fredric. Foreword to Jean-François Lyotard, *The Postmodern Condition: A Report on Knowledge*, pp. vii–xxi. Translated by Geoff Bennington and Brian Massumi. Minneapolis: University of Minnesota Press, 1984.

Jameson, Fredric. "History and Class Consciousness as an Unfinished Project." *Rethinking Marxism* 1 (Spring 1988): 49–72.

Jameson, Fredric. Interview with Fredric Jameson. By Leonard Green, Jonathan Culler, and Richard Klein. *Diacritics* 12 (Fall 1982) 3: 72–91.

Jameson, Fredric. "Introduction to Adorno." *Salmagundi*, no. 10–11 (Fall 1969–Winter 1970), pp. 140–43.

Jameson, Fredric. *Marxism and Form: Twentieth-Century Dialectical Theories of Literature*. Princeton: Princeton University Press, 1971.

Jameson, Fredric. "On Magic Realism in Film." *Critical Inquiry* 12 (Winter 1986): 301–25.

Jameson, Fredric. *The Political Unconscious: Narrative as a Socially Symbolic Act*. Ithaca: Cornell University Press, 1981.

Jameson, Fredric. "The Politics of Theory: Ideological Positions in the Postmodernism Debate." *New German Critique*, no. 33 (Fall 1984), pp. 53–65.

Jameson, Fredric. "Postmodernism and Consumer Society." In *The Anti-Aesthetic: Essays on Postmodern Culture*, pp. 111–25. Edited by Hal Foster. Port Townsend, Wash.: Bay Press, 1983.

Jameson, Fredric. "Postmodernism, or the Cultural Logic of Late Capitalism." *New Left Review*, no. 146 (July-August 1984), pp. 53–92.

Jameson, Fredric. "Reflections in Conclusion." In *Aesthetics and Politics*, pp. 196–213. Edited by Ronald Taylor. London: NLB, 1977; Verso, 1980.

Jameson, Fredric. "Regarding Postmodernism—A Conversation with Fredric Jameson." With Anders Stephanson. *Social Text*, no. 17 (Fall 1987), pp. 29–54. Reprinted in Douglas Kellner, ed., *Postmodernism/Jameson/Critique* (Washington, D.C.: Maisonneuve Press, 1989), pp. 43–74.

Bibliography

Jameson, Fredric. "Reification and Utopia in Mass Culture." *Social Text*, no. 1 (Winter 1979), pp. 130–48.

Jauss, Hans Robert. "The Idealist Embarrassment: Observations on Marxist Aesthetics." *New Literary History* (Autumn 1975): 191–208.

Jay, Martin. "For Gouldner: Reflections on an Outlaw Marxist." *Theory and Society* 11 (November 1982): 759–78.

Jay, Martin. "Habermas and Modernism." *Praxis International* 4 (April 1984): 1–14. Reprinted in Richard Bernstein, ed., *Habermas and Modernity* (Cambridge, Mass.: MIT Press, 1985), pp. 125–39.

Jay, Martin. *Marxism and Totality: The Adventures of a Concept from Lukács to Habermas.* Berkeley: University of California Press, 1984.

Johnson, Pauline. *Marxist Aesthetics: The Foundations within Everyday Life for an Emancipated Consciousness.* London: Routledge & Kegan Paul, 1984.

Kaiser, Volker. Review of Albrecht Wellmer, *Zur Dialektik von Moderne und Postmoderne.* *German Quarterly* 60 (Summer 1987): 463–65.

Kant, Immanuel. *Critique of Judgment.* Translated, with an Introduction, by Werner S. Pluhar. With a Foreword by Mary J. Gregor. Indianapolis: Hackett, 1987.

Kant, Immanuel. *Kritik der Urteilskraft* (1790). 6th ed. Edited by Karl Vorländer. Hamburg: Felix Meiner, 1924.

Kant, Immanuel. *Prolegomena to Any Future Metaphysics.* With an Introduction by Lewis White Beck. Indianapolis: Bobbs-Merrill, Library of Liberal Arts, 1950.

Kant, Immanuel. *Prolegomena zu einer jeden künftigen Metaphysik, die als Wissenschaft wird auftreten können* (1783). 6th ed. Edited by Karl Vorländer. Hamburg: Felix Meiner, 1976.

Kaufmann, Walter. *Nietzsche: Philosopher, Psychologist, Antichrist* (1950). 4th ed. Princeton: Princeton University Press, 1974.

Kellner, Douglas, ed. *Postmodernism/Jameson/Critique.* Washington, D.C.: Maisonneuve Press, 1989.

Kellner, Douglas. "Remarks on Alvin Gouldner's *The Two Marxisms.*" *Theory and Society* 10 (May 1981): 265–77.

Kierkegaard, Søren. *The Concept of Irony, with Constant Reference to Socrates.* Translated with an Introduction and Notes by Lee M. Chapel. Bloomington: Indiana University Press, Midland Books, 1965.

Kierkegaard, Søren. *Either/Or* (1843). 2 Vols. Vol. 1. Translated by David F. Swenson and Lillian Marvin Swenson, with revisions and a Foreword by Howard A. Johnson. Garden City, N.Y.: Doubleday, Anchor Books, 1959.

Kneif, Tibor. *Musiksoziologie.* Cologne: Hans Gerig, 1971, 1975.

Kneif, Tibor, ed. *Texte zur Musiksoziologie.* With an Introduction by Carl Dahlhaus. Cologne: Arno Volk, 1975.

Kolakowski, Leszek. *Main Currents of Marxism*. Vol. 3: *The Breakdown*. Translated by P. S. Falla. Oxford: Oxford University Press, 1978.

Korsch, Karl. *Marxism and Philosophy*. Translated with an Introduction by Fred Halliday. New York and London: NLB, 1970.

Korsch, Karl. *Marxismus und Philosophie* (1923). Edited and introduced by Erich Gerlach. Frankfurt: Europäische Verlagsanstalt, 1966.

Kortian, Garbis. *Metacritique. The Philosophical Argument of Jürgen Habermas*. Translated by John Raffan, with an Introductory Essay by Charles Taylor and Alan Montefiore. Cambridge: Cambridge University Press, 1980.

LaCapra, Dominick. Review essay on Fredric Jameson, *The Political Unconscious. History and Theory* 21 (1982): 83–106.

Laing, Dave. *The Marxist Theory of Art*. Atlantic Highalnds, N.J.: Humanities Press, 1978.

Langer, Susanne K. *Feeling and Form. A Theory of Art Developed from "Philosophy in a New Key."* New York: Charles Scribner's Sons, 1953.

Leiss, William. *The Domination of Nature*. New York: George Braziller, 1972; Boston: Beacon Press, 1974.

Lichtheim, George. *From Marx to Hegel*. New York: Herder & Herder, 1971; Seabury Press, 1974.

Lindner, Burkhardt. "Der Begriff der Verdinglichung und der Spielraum der Realismus Kontroverse. Ausgehend von der frühen Differenz zwischen Lukács und Bloch." In *Der Streit mit Georg Lukács*, pp. 91–123. Edited by Hans-Jürgen Schmitt. Frankfurt: Suhrkamp, 1978.

Lüdke, W. Martin, ed. *"Theorie der Avantgarde": Antworten auf Peter Bürgers Bestimmung von Kunst und bürgerlicher Gesellschaft*. Frankfurt: Suhrkamp, 1976.

Lukács, Georg. *Essays on Realism*. Edited and introduced by Rodney Livingstone. Translated by David Fernbach. Cambridge, Mass.: MIT Press, 1980.

Lukács, Georg. *Essays über Realismus. Probleme des Realismus I*. Georg Lukács Werke, Vol. 4. Neuwied: Luchterhand, 1971.

Lukács, Georg. *Geschichte und Klassenbewusstsein. Studien über marxistische Dialektik* (1923). Darmstadt/Neuwied: Sammlung Luchterhand, 1968.

Lukács, Georg. *History and Class Consciousness. Studies in Marxist Dialectics*. Translated by Rodney Livingstone. London: Merlin Press, 1971.

Lukács, Georg. *Realism in Our Time: Literature and the Class Struggle*. Translated by John and Necke Mander. Preface by Georg Steiner. New York: Harper & Row, 1964.

Lukács, Georg. *Die Theorie des Romans. Ein geschichtsphilosophischer Versuch über die Formen der grossen Epik* (1916/1920). Darmstadt/Neuwied: Sammlung Luchterhand, 1971, 1977.

Lukács, Georg. *The Theory of the Novel. A Historical-Philosophical Essay on the Forms of Great Epic Literature.* Translated by Anna Bostock. Cambridge, Mass.: MIT Press, 1971.

Lukács, Georg. *Writer and Critic, and Other Essays.* Edited and translated by Arthur Kahn. London: Merlin Press, 1970.

McLellan, David. *Karl Marx: His Life and Thought.* London: Macmillan, 1973.

McLellan, David. *Marxism After Marx: An Introduction.* Boston: Houghton Mifflin, 1979.

Marcuse, Herbert. *The Aesthetic Dimension. Toward a Critique of Marxist Aesthetics* (1977). Translated and revised with Erica Sherover. Boston: Beacon Press, 1978.

Marcuse, Herbert. "The Affirmative Character of Culture." In *Negations: Essays in Critical Theory,* pp. 88–133.

Marcuse, Herbert. *One Dimensional Man: Studies in the Ideology of Advanced Industrial Society.* Boston: Beacon Press, 1964.

Marcuse, Herbert. "Über den affirmativen Charakter der Kultur." *Zeitschrift für Sozialforschung* 6 (1937): 54–94.

Marquard, Odo. "Kant und die Wende zur Ästhetik." *Zeitschrift für philosophische Forschung* 16 (1962): 231–43, 363–74.

Marx, Karl. *Capital. A Critique of Political Economy.* Vol. 1: *The Process of Capitalist Production.* Translated from the 3rd German ed. by Samuel Moore and Edward Aveling. Edited by Frederick Engels. New York: International Publishers, 1967.

Marx, Karl. *A Contribution to the Critique of Political Economy* (1859). Translated by S. W. Ryazanskaya. Edited with an Introduction by Maurice Dobb. New York: International Publishers, 1970.

Marx, Karl. *Das Kapital. Kritik der politischen Ökonomie.* 4 vols. Vol. 1: *Der Produktionsprozess des Kapitals* (1867). *Karl Marx/Friedrich Engels Werke.* Vol. 23. Berlin: Dietz, 1962, 1977.

Marx, Karl. *Karl Marx: Selected Writings.* Edited by David McLellan. Oxford: Oxford University Press, 1977.

Marx, Karl, and Friedrich Engels. *Collected Works.* Vol. 3: *Marx and Engels: 1843–44.* New York: International Publishers, 1975.

Marx, Karl, and Friedrich Engels. *Karl Marx/Frederick Engels on Literature and Art.* Edited by Lee Baxandall and Stefan Morawski, with an Introduction by Stefan Morawski. New York: International General, 1973.

Marx, Werner. *Hegel's Phenomenology of Spirit: Its Point and Purpose—A Commentary on the Preface and Introduction.* Translated by Peter Heath. New York: Harper & Row, 1975.

Merleau-Ponty, Maurice. *Adventures of the Dialectic* (1955). Translated by Joseph Bien. Evanston: Northwestern University Press, 1973.

Miller, James. "Some Implications of Nietzsche's Thought for Marxism." *Telos,* no. 37 (Fall 1978), pp. 22–41.

Mittenzwei, Werner. "The Brecht-Lukács Debate." In *Preserve and Create: Essays in Marxist Literary Criticism*, pp. 199–230. Edited by Gaylord C. LeRoy and Ursula Beitz. New York: Humanities Press, 1973.

Modleski, Tania, ed. *Studies in Entertainment: Critical Approaches to Mass Culture*. Bloomington: Indiana University Press, 1986.

Negt, Oskar, ed. *Aktualität und Folgen der Philosophie Hegels*. 2d ed. Frankfurt: Suhrkamp, 1970.

Nietzsche, Friedrich. *Beyond Good and Evil: Prelude to a Philosophy of the Future* (1886). Translated, with an Introduction and Commentary, by R. J. Hollingdale. London: Penguin Books, 1973.

Nietzsche, Friedrich. *The Birth of Tragedy* (1872) and *The Case of Wagner* (1888). Translated, with Commentary, by Walter Kaufmann. New York: Vintage Books, 1967.

Payzant, Geoffrey. "Hanslick, Sams, Gay, and 'Tönend Bewegte Formen.' " *Journal of Aesthetics and Art Criticism* 40 (Fall 1981): 40–48.

Pollock, Friedrich. "State Capitalism: Its Possibilities and Limitations." *Studies in Philosophy and Social Science* 9 (1941): 200–25.

Rader, Melvin. "Marx's Interpretation of Art and Aesthetic Value." *British Journal of Aesthetics* 7 (July 1967): 237–49.

Radnoti, Sandor. "The Effective Power of Art: On Benjamin's Aesthetics." *Telos*, no. 49 (Fall 1981), pp. 61–82.

Rose, Margaret A. *Marx's Lost Aesthetic: Karl Marx and the Visual Arts*. Cambridge: Cambridge University Press, 1984.

Ryan, Michael. *Marxism and Deconstruction: A Critical Articulation*. Baltimore: Johns Hopkins University Press, 1982.

Schelling, F. W. J. *System des transzendentalen Idealismus* (1800). Edited by Ruth-Eva Schulz, with an Introduction by Walter Schulz. Hamburg: Felix Meiner, 1957.

Schmidt, Alfred. *Der Begriff der Natur in der Lehre von Marx* (1962). Rev., enl. ed., with a Postscript. Frankfurt: Europäische Verlagsanstalt, Basis, 1971.

Schmidt, Alfred. *Geschichte und Struktur. Fragen einer marxistischen Historik*. Munich: Carl Hanser, 1971.

Schmitt, Hans-Jürgen, ed. *Der Streit mit Georg Lukács*. Frankfurt: Suhrkamp, 1978.

Seerveld, Calvin G. *Rainbows for the Fallen World: Aesthetic Life and Artistic Task*. Toronto: Tuppence Press, 1980.

Seerveld, Calvin G. "Towards a Cartographic Methodology for Art Historiography." *Journal of Aesthetics and Art Criticism* 39 (Winter 1980–1981): 143–54. Reprinted in *Opuscula Aesthetica Nostra*, pp. 51–62. Edited by Cécile Cloutier and Calvin Seerveld. Edmonton: Academic Printing & Publishing, 1984.

Shusterman, Richard, ed. *Analytic Aesthetics*. Oxford: Basil Blackwell, 1989.

Sparshott, Francis. *The Theory of the Arts.* Princeton: Princeton University Press, 1982.

Stephanson, Anders. "Regarding Postmodernism—A Conversation with Fredric Jameson." *Social Text* 17 (Fall 1987): 29–54.

Taylor, Charles. *Hegel and Modern Society.* Cambridge: Cambridge University Press, 1979.

Tertullian, Nicolae. "Lukács' Aesthetics and Its Critics." *Telos,* no. 52 (Summer 1982), pp. 159–67.

Trotsky, Leon. *Literature and Revolution.* Ann Arbor: University of Michigan Press, 1960.

Van der Hoeven, Johan. *Karl Marx: The Roots of His Thought.* Toronto: Wedge, 1976.

Wellmer, Albrecht. "Art and Industrial Production." *Telos,* no. 57 (Fall 1983), pp. 53–62.

Wellmer, Albrecht. "Communications and Emancipation: Reflections on the Linguistic Turn in Critical Theory." In *On Critical Theory,* pp. 231–63. Edited by John O'Neill. New York: Seabury Press, 1976.

Wellmer, Albrecht. *Critical Theory of Society.* Translated by John Cumming. New York: Herder and Herder, 1971.

Wellmer, Albrecht. *Ethik und Dialog: Elemente des moralischen Urteils bei Kant und in der Diskursethik.* Frankfurt: Suhrkamp, 1986.

Wellmer, Albrecht. *Kritische Gesellschaftstheorie und Positivismus.* Frankfurt: Suhrkamp, 1969.

Wellmer, Albrecht. "On the Dialectic of Modernism and Postmodernism." *Praxis International* 4 (January 1985): 337–62.

Wellmer, Albrecht. *Praktische Philosophie und Theorie der Gesellschaft. Zum Problem der normativen Grundlagen einer Kritischen Sozialwissenschaft.* Konstanz: Universitätsverlag Konstanz, 1979.

Wellmer, Albrecht. "Reason, Utopia, and the Dialectic of Enlightenment." *Praxis International* 3 (July 1983): 83–107. Reprinted in Richard J. Bernstein, ed., *Habermas and Modernity,* pp. 35–66.

Wellmer, Albrecht. Review of Richard Bernstein, *Restructuring of Social and Political Theory. History and Theory* 18 (1979): 84–103.

Wellmer, Albrecht. "Truth, Semblance, and Reconciliation: Adorno's Aesthetic Redemption of Modernity." *Telos,* no. 62 (Winter 1984–85), pp. 89–115.

Wellmer, Albrecht. *Zur Dialektik von Moderne und Postmoderne. Vernunftkritik nach Adorno.* Frankfurt: Suhrkamp, 1985.

Whitebook, Joel. "The Problem of Nature in Habermas." *Telos,* no. 40 (Summer 1979), pp. 41–69.

Williams, Raymond. "Base and Superstructure in Marxist Cultural Theory." *New Left Review*, no. 82 (November-December 1973), pp. 3–16.

Williams, Raymond. *Keywords: A Vocabulary of Culture and Society.* London: Fontana Paperbacks, 1976; Flamingo edition, 1983.

Williams, Raymond. *Marxism and Literature.* Oxford: Oxford University Press, 1977.

Wolin, Richard. "Modernism vs. Postmodernism." *Telos*, no. 62 (Winter 1984–85), pp. 9–29.

Wolterstorff, Nicholas. *Works and Worlds of Art.* Oxford: Clarendon Press, 1980.

Wood, Allen. *Karl Marx.* London: Routledge & Kegan Paul, 1981.

Zipes, Jack. "Beckett in Germany—Germany in Beckett." *New German Critique*, no. 26 (Spring-Summer 1982), pp. 151–58.

Zuidervaart, Lambert. "Realism, Modernism, and the Empty Chair." In *Postmodernism/Jameson/Critique*, pp. 203–227. Edited by Douglas Kellner. New York: Maisonneuve Press, 1989.

Index

Studies in Contemporary German Social Thought
Thomas McCarthy, General Editor

Theodor W. Adorno, *Against Epistemology: A Metacritique*

Theodor W. Adorno, *Prisms*

Karl-Otto Apel, *Understanding and Explanation: A Transcendental-Pragmatic Perspective*

Seyla Benhabib and Fred Dallmayr, editors, *The Communicative Ethics Debate*

Richard J. Bernstein, editor, *Habermas and Modernity*

Ernst Bloch, *Natural Law and Human Dignity*

Ernst Bloch, *The Principle of Hope*

Ernst Bloch, *The Utopian Function of Art and Literature: Selected Essays*

Hans Blumenberg, *The Genesis of the Copernican World*

Hans Blumenberg, *The Legitimacy of the Modern Age*

Hans Blumenberg, *Work on Myth*

Susan Buck-Morss, *The Dialectics of Seeing: Walter Benjamin and the Arcades Project*

Jean Cohen and Andrew Arato, *Civil Society and Political Theory*

Helmut Dubiel, *Theory and Politics: Studies in the Development of Critical Theory*

John Forester, editor, *Critical Theory and Public Life*

David Frisby, *Fragments of Modernity: Theories of Modernity in the Work of Simmel, Kracauer and Benjamin*

Hans-Georg Gadamer, *Philosophical Apprenticeships*

Hans-Georg Gadamer, *Reason in the Age of Science*

Jürgen Habermas, *On the Logic of the Social Sciences*

Jürgen Habermas, *Moral Consciousness and Communicative Action*

Jürgen Habermas, *The New Conservatism: Cultural Criticism and the Historians' Debate*

Jürgen Habermas, *The Philosophical Discourse of Modernity: Twelve Lectures*

Jürgen Habermas, *Philosophical-Political Profiles*

Jürgen Habermas, editor, *Observations on "The Spiritual Situation of the Age"*

Jürgen Habermas, *The Structural Transformation of the Public Sphere: An Inquiry into a Category of Bourgeois Society*

Axel Honneth and Hans Joas, editors, *Communicative Action: Essays on Jürgen Habermas's* Theory of Communicative Action

Hans Joas, *G. H. Mead: A Contemporary Re-examination of His Thought*

Reinhart Koselleck, *Critique and Crisis: Enlightenment and the Pathogenesis of Modern Society*

Reinhart Koselleck, *Futures Past: On the Semantics of Historical Time*

Harry Liebersohn, *Fate and Utopia in German Sociology, 1887–1923*

Herbert Marcuse, *Hegel's Ontology and the Theory of Historicity*

Guy Oakes, *Weber and Rickert: Concept Formation in the Cultural Sciences*